Mexico's Human Rights Crisis

PENNSYLVANIA STUDIES IN HUMAN RIGHTS

Bert B. Lockwood, Series Editor

A complete list of books in the series
is available from the publisher.

Mexico's Human Rights Crisis

Edited by

Alejandro Anaya-Muñoz and Barbara Frey

PENN

UNIVERSITY OF PENNSYLVANIA PRESS

PHILADELPHIA

Published by
University of Pennsylvania Press
Philadelphia, Pennsylvania 19104-4112
www.upenn.edu/pennpress

Printed in the United States of America on acid-free paper
10 9 8 7 6 5 4 3 2 1

Library of Congress Cataloging-in-Publication Data
ISBN 978-0-8122-5107-4

To the victims of human rights violations in Mexico

CONTENTS

List of Abbreviations   ix

Introduction   1
    Alejandro Anaya-Muñoz and Barbara Frey

PART I. THE CRISIS UNFOLDS

Chapter 1. Deadly Forces: Use of Lethal Force by Mexican Security
Forces 2007–2015   23
    Catalina Pérez Correa, Carlos Silva Forné,
    and Rodrigo Gutiérrez Rivas

Chapter 2. Violence-Induced Internal Displacement in Mexico,
the Inter-American Commission on Human Rights, and
Official State Responses   43
    Laura Rubio Díaz-Leal

Chapter 3. Women's Human Rights in the Armed Conflict in
Mexico: Organized Crime, Collective Action, and State Responses   63
    Sandra Hincapié

Chapter 4. The Invisible Violence Against Women in Mexico   86
    Regina Tamés

PART II. THE CRISIS FOR MIGRANTS

Chapter 5. Superfluous Lives: Undocumented Migrants
Traveling in Mexico   107
    Javier Treviño-Rangel

Chapter 6. Emigration, Violence, and Human Rights Violations
in Central Mexico   124
Benjamin James Waddell

Chapter 7. Bridging Legal Geographies: Contextual Adjudication
in Mexican Asylum Claims   147
Ariadna Estévez

Chapter 8. Mexican Asylum Seekers and the Convention
Against Torture   167
Susan Gzesh

PART III. THE INSTITUTIONAL CRISIS

Chapter 9. *Democracia a la Mexicana*: A Framework Conducive
to Human Rights Violations   187
Daniel Vázquez

Chapter 10. Factors Blocking the Compliance with International
Human Rights Norms in Mexico   207
Alejandro Anaya-Muñoz and Natalia Saltalamacchia

Chapter 11. Human Rights and Justice in Mexico: An Analysis
of Judicial Functions   227
Karina Ansolabehere

Chapter 12. The Judicial Breakthrough Model: Transnational
Advocacy Networks and Lethal Violence   250
Janice Gallagher

Notes   273

Bibliography   285

List of Contributors   315

Index   319

Acknowledgments   327

ABBREVIATIONS

ACHR	American Convention on Human Rights
ASF	Auditoría Superior de la Federación (National Audit Office of Mexico)
BIA	Board of Immigration Appeals
CADHAC	Ciudadanos en Apoyo a los Derechos Humanos (Citizens in Support of Human Rights)
CAT	Convention Against Torture and Other Cruel, Inhuman or Degrading Treatment
CEAV	Comisión Ejecutiva de Atención a Víctimas (Executive Commission of Assistance to Victims)
CEDAW	Convention on the Elimination of All Forms of Discrimination Against Women
CED Committee	UN Committee on Enforced Disappearances
CEDEHM	Centro de Derechos Humanos de las Mujeres (Center for Women's Human Rights)
CIESAS	Centro de Investigaciones y Estudios Superiores en Antropología Social (Center for the Investigation and Study of Social Anthropology)
CMDPDH	Comisión Mexicana de Defensa y Promoción de los Derechos Humanos (National Commission for the Defense and Promotion of Human Rights)
CNDH	Comisión Nacional de los Derechos Humanos (National Human Rights Commission)
CONAPO	Consejo Nacional de Población (National Population Council)
CONEVAL	Consejo Nacional de Evaluación de la Política de Desarrollo Social (National Council for the Evaluation of Social Development)
DHS	Department of Homeland Security
DTO	drug trafficking organization

EOIR	Executive Office for Immigration Review
FEMOSPP	Fiscalía Especial para Movimientos Sociales y Políticos del Pasado (Special Prosecutor's Office for Political and Social Movements from the Past)
GATE	Grupo de Armas y Tácticas Especiales (Special Weapons and Tactics Team)
GIRE	Information Group on Reproductive Choice
IACHR	Inter-American Commission on Human Rights
IACtHR	Inter-American Court on Human Rights
ICE	Immigration and Customs Enforcement
ICHRP	International Council on Human Rights Policy
ICRC	International Committee of the Red Cross
ICTJ	International Center for Transitional Justice
IDMC	Internal Displacement Monitoring Centre
IDP	internally displaced person
IMDHD	Instituto Mexicano de Derechos Humanos y Democracia (Mexican Institute of Human Rights and Democracy)
IMSS	Instituto Mexicano del Seguro Social (Mexican Institute of Social Security)
INA	Immigration and Nationality Act
INEGI	Instituto Nacional de Estadística y Geografía (National Institute of Statistics and Geography)
INFONAVIT	Instituto del Fondo Nacional de la Vivienda para los Trabajadores (National Fund for Workers' Housing Institute)
INM	Instituto Nacional de Migración (National Institute of Migration)
INMUJERES	Instituto Nacional de las Mujeres (National Institute for Women)
JDMS	judicial decision-making sites
MDG	Millennium Development Goals
MPJD	Movimiento por la Paz con Justicia y Dignidad (Movement for Peace with Justice and Dignity)
NGO	nongovernmental organization
OAS	Organization of American States
OCIJ	Office of the Chief Immigration Judge
OECD	Organization for Economic Cooperation and Development

OHCHR	Office of the United Nations High Commissioner for Human Rights
PAN	Partido Acción Nacional (National Action Party)
PGR	Procuraduría General de la República (Federal Attorney General's Office)
PND	Plan Nacional de Desarrollo (National Development Plan)
PRD	Partido de la Revolución Democrática (Party of the Democratic Revolution)
PRI	Partido Revolucionario Institucional (Institutional Revolutionary Party)
RENAVI	Registro Nacional de Víctimas (National Registry of Victims of Crime)
SAMI	Southwest Asylum and Migration Institute
SCJN	Suprema Corte de Justicia de la Nación (National Supreme Court of Justice)
SEDENA	Secretaría de la Defensa Nacional (Ministry of National Defense)
SEDESOL	Secretaría de Desarrollo Social (Ministry of Social Development)
SEGOB	Secretaría de Gobernación (Ministry of the Interior)
SEIDO	Subprocuraduría Especializada en Investigación de Delincuencia Organizada (Specialized Assistant Attorney General for the Investigation of Organized Crime)
SEMAR	Secretaría de la Marina (Ministry of the Navy)
SESNSP	Secretariado Ejecutivo del Sistema Nacional de Seguridad Pública (Executive Secretariat of the National System of Public Security)
SRE	Secretaría de Relaciones Exteriores (Ministry of Foreign Affairs)
TAN	transnational advocacy network
TPP	Permanent People's Tribunal
UNAM	National Autonomous University of Mexico
UNHCR	United Nations High Commissioner for Refugees
UNODC	United Nations Office on Drugs and Crime
UNSRED	United Nations Special Rapporteur on Enforced Disappearances
USCIS	United States Citizenship and Immigration Services

INTRODUCTION

Alejandro Anaya-Muñoz and Barbara Frey

In the spring of 2016, a disturbing video circulated on social media, showing two Mexican military officers and a Federal Police agent brutally torturing a young detainee, Elvira Santibañez Margarito, in Guerrero, a Mexican state torn apart by drug violence. The public outcry from the video elicited an unprecedented public apology from Gen. Salvador Cienfuegos, Mexico's Secretary of National Defense (Martinez Ahrens 2016), who nonetheless took the occasion to assert that the torture of Santibañez Margarito was an isolated case (Castillo Garcia 2016). Far from being isolated, however, the systematic practice of torture has been thoroughly documented in Mexico over the past decade, along with many other serious human rights violations (Human Rights Council 2014; Amnesty International 2015; IACHR 2015a). Indeed, what was unusual about the Santibañez Margarito case was that, because the government was caught red-handed, it publicly acknowledged the violation. Despite the government's apology, however, it is not clear that any of the three state agents have been successfully prosecuted for committing torture.

The case of Elvira Santibañez Margarito typifies Mexico's human rights crisis over the past decade. Behind the smokescreen of criminal violence, state actors are engaging or acquiescing in human rights violations with almost total impunity. The disappearance of forty-three students from the Ayotzinapa teachers' training college in Iguala, Guerrero, was the most high profile case of this pattern. Though outrageous, the case of the forty-three was sadly not unique: other massive atrocities have been well documented in Allende, State of Coahuila; Tlatlaya, State of México; and Apatzingan and Tanhuato, State of Michoacán (IACHR 2015a: 13). This is not to mention the "pandemic of femicides" (Rama and Diaz 2014) taking place in the states of Mexico and Chihuahua. Once known as a welcome refuge for those fleeing from repression and still recognized as a vocal advocate for human rights globally, Mexico is now in the midst of its own human rights crisis.

This book describes the violation of the human rights of hundreds of thousands at the hands of state and nonstate actors in Mexico. The volume offers a broad account of those violations, identifies key explicative factors, and proposes interpretative frameworks for understanding the dire situation facing Mexico today. In this introduction, we offer the framework of the book's central argument, followed by a brief overview of three categories of violence that demonstrate why we have chosen to identify the past decade in Mexico as a human rights crisis: extrajudicial killings, disappearances, and torture. We then set forth the theoretical and policy contributions of the book as a whole and summarize each chapter's contributions to explaining the human rights crisis and the opportunities for ending it.

This volume clearly illustrates that Mexico's grave human rights situation is unfolding in the midst of a context of violence unparalleled in the country's recent history. Starting in 2005, a tide of brutal drug-related killings captured media attention, causing growing concern among government officials and the public. The federal government, led by President Vicente Fox (2000–2006), reacted with "shows of force," sending joint forces—the Army, the Navy, and the Federal Police—to battle organized crime in several violence-prone states. The bloody response by powerful drug cartels to the government's security actions dominated the political agenda as never before. In 2006, incoming President Felipe Calderón (2006–2012) launched his now infamous "war on drugs," empowering the Mexican Armed Forces to carry out domestic law enforcement. In his first public speech as president, Calderón asserted, "Today, delinquency aims to frighten and paralyze society and the government; public insecurity threatens everybody and has turned into the main problem of states, cities and entire regions. One of the three priorities that [my government will pursue] is, precisely, the fight to recover public security and legality" (cited in Anaya Muñoz 2012b: 123, 122–129). On the ground, the government's "war" against criminal organizations added to the mix of armed violence carried out by the criminal organizations themselves. As the literature shows, human rights violations are magnified in the context of armed conflict (Cardenas 2007). Because of this, we argue that a key explicative factor behind Mexico's human rights crisis—though by no means a justification for the pattern of atrocities that has resulted—is the ongoing "drug war."

In addition to the "drug war," this book demonstrates that the other key factor underlying the current crisis is the state of impunity in Mexico. As different observers (Human Rights Watch 2009; Acosta 2012) and most of this volume's chapters stress, an almost total lack of accountability for crimes in Mexico provides the poisonous cauldron in which systemic human rights violations have been allowed to fester. The numbers are stark. Scholars estimate that 4.5 percent of crimes are fully investigated; 1.6 percent of cases go to trial (often aided by coerced confessions); and only 1.1 percent result in convictions (Zepeda Lecuona 2003, 2005; see also Magaloni Kerpel 2007; Ingram and Shirk 2012: 121–123). In other words, no justice is seen in 99 percent of the crimes committed in Mexico (Le Clerk and Rodriguez 2016). In its assessment of impunity, the Inter-American Commission on Human Rights (IACHR) highlighted that, in modern history, Mexico's federal courts have rendered only six convictions for enforced disappearances and fifteen for torture. A comparison of this handful of convictions with the tens of thousands of denounced cases reveals the appalling toll of impunity (IACHR 2015a: 12–13).

A question we have struggled with is whether impunity is a constant or a variable in driving the current crisis. We conclude that even if impunity has not triggered the current crisis, it has facilitated its emergence and nurtured its catastrophic violence. While the "drug war"—with its corruptive impacts upon public institutions—is the key explanatory variable of Mexico's human rights crisis, impunity is, at the very least, the central enabling condition in which that crisis has flourished. These two factors, of course, are not unique to Mexico. So our argument might resonate in other contexts, beyond Mexico.

Extrajudicial Killings

Between 2007 and 2016, at least 209,401 people were murdered in Mexico (see Table I.1); on average, nearly 21,000 per year. The increase in homicides became a source of concern starting in 2008, when officials acknowledged more than 14,000 homicides, climbing to a peak of 27,213 in 2011. The number of homicides declined after 2012 but rose again in 2016 (see Table I.1). 2017 became the most violent year in Mexico's recent history, with more than twenty-nine thousand homicides, according to the Executive Secretariat of the National System of Public Security (SESNSP for its acronym in Spanish) (Aristegui Noticias 2018).

The recent trend in homicides contrasted with a steady decline from the early 1990s. Homicides hit their lowest point in decades in Mexico in 2007: a rate of 7.8 per 100,000. The positive trend reversed dramatically in the early

Table I.1. Homicides in Mexico, 2007–2015

	2007	2008	2009	2010	2011	2012	2013	2014	2015	2016
Absolute number of homicides	8,867	14,006	19,803	25,757	27,213	25,967	23,063	20,010	20,762	23,953
Homicides per 100,000 inhabitants	7.8	12.2	17	21.7	22.6	21.3	18.6	15.7	NA	NA

Sources: INEGI, Mortality Statistics http://www.inegi.org.mx/est/contenidos/Proyectos/registros/vitales/mortalidad/default.aspx) (last consulted: August 31, 2017); World Bank 2017.

Calderón period, increasing to 12.2 in 2008 and 22.6 in 2011. The global homicide average is 5.3 per 100,000. Mexico's recent homicide numbers are similar to Brazil's (23.8 in 2012) but remain far below those of Honduras (92.7 in 2012). The picture in Mexico is bleaker, however, if we look at the homicide levels for particularly violent states or municipalities—for example, the State of Chihuahua, which had a rate of 120 in 2009 (Heinle, Molzahan, and Shirk 2015).

Available statistics do not allow us to determine how many of these homicides can be attributed to state actors. So we cannot demonstrate how these numbers correlate with extrajudicial or arbitrary executions. In this sense, from a broader human rights perspective, between 2007 and 2016, nearly 210,000 people were denied their right to life in Mexico. The government is blatantly failing to fulfil its obligation to protect that right and to uphold the right to justice for victims and their families by investigating the deaths and prosecuting the responsible parties. The sheer size of the figure amounts to a major crisis, by any international comparative standard.

Disappearances

Disappearances are another brute manifestation of the crisis. Table I.2 shows the data from the SESNSP on the number of disappearances registered annually by the state-level attorney generals' offices and by the Federal Attorney General's Office (PGR) between 2007 and 2016. As in the case of executions, disappearances increased sharply starting in 2008, with the explosion of narco-violence and the government's "war on drugs." 2011 was a particularly violent year, but 2016 registered an even higher number of disappearances. According to the government's own numbers, there were at least 30,124 disappearances registered from 2007 to 2016, an average of 3,012 per year. Even these startling figures on disappearances might be misleadingly low because the family members of the victims, fearing for their own security, often do not report crimes to the authorities (Open Society Justice Initiative 2016: 14).

The Mexican government holds firmly to a public narrative that fails to distinguish the "disappeared" from the "missing," thus leaving the impression that they are not necessarily human rights violations. The term preferred by the government, in its public accounting, is "persons not accounted for" *(personas no localizadas)* (IACHR 2015a: 12, 31).

Table I.2. Disappearances in Mexico, 2007–2016

Year	Prior to 2007	2007	2008	2009	2010	2011	2012	2013	2014	2015	2016
State jurisdiction	243	622	800	1,363	3,155	4,028	3,264	3,673	3,921	3,538	4,670
Federal jurisdiction	57	26	28	39	150	92	114	183	248	106	64
Total	300	648	828	1,402	3,305	4,120	3,378	3,856	4,186	3,664	4,734

Sources: Executive Secretariat of the National System of Public Security (SESNSP) http://secretariadoejecutivo.gob.mx/rnped/estadisticas-fueroco-mun.php and http://secretariadoejecutivo.gob.mx/rnped/estadisticas-fuerofederal.php (last consulted: August 21, 2017).

Time-series data by the Mexican government (SESNSP and PGR) do not disaggregate by disappearances perpetrated by state actors (or with their support or acquiescence) and those committed by nonstate actors. As a result, we do not know with certainty how many of these thirty thousand disappearances meet the narrow legal definition of "enforced disappearances." International organizations have been frustrated by these gaps in information. In a 2016 special report on human rights in Mexico, IACHR, for instance, confirmed "the existence of a practice of forced disappearances at the hands of agents of the State, or with their participation, acquiescence, or tolerance" but acknowledged that existing data did not allow it to estimate the number with any accuracy (IACHR 2015a: 12, 63–67). Similarly, the UN Committee on Enforced Disappearances (CED Committee) observed a "situation of widespread disappearances in much of the State party's territory, *many of which may be classified as enforced disappearances*" (Committee on Enforced Disappearances 2015: 2, emphasis added). But again, the committee could not give a more specific estimation.

The Mexican government effectively benefits from disregarding its responsibility to investigate or to categorize these cases. In its appearance before the UN Human Rights Council in 2015, for instance, the Mexican government emphasized that it was working to prevent "disappearances carried out by organized crime," omitting mention of any efforts made to prevent enforced disappearances involving state actors. Gaps and incoherence in federal and state laws that are supposed to criminalize enforced disappearance further compound the lack of accountability in the cases.

Civil society is left to try to fill the gap in the government's information. One recent study, by the Observatory on Disappearances and Impunity in Mexico, shed light on the extent of state "acquiescence" in disappearances. Based on an analysis of 548 NGO cases in the State of Nuevo Leon, researchers found that, from 2005 to 2015, 46.76 percent of reported disappearances were carried out by state agents, 46.04 percent by criminal organizations, and 7.19 percent by individual or private actors. Of the cases in which the state was responsible, 49.25 percent were from the municipal level, 24.63 percent from the state level, and 26.12 percent from the federal level (Ansolabehere 2017).

Another way to approximate the number of enforced disappearances in Mexico is to use the government's own categorization. SESNSP made available a database containing information on cases occurring between January 2014 and June 2015, in which it disaggregated enforced disappearances from those perpetrated by nonstate actors. The database reports 820 "ordinary" disappearances and 106 enforced disappearances (Procuduría General de la República n/d). The government thus classified about 11 percent of the total number of cases as enforced disappearances, which would suggest that at least 3,314 of the 30,124 disappearances registered from 2007 to 2016 meet the legal definition of enforced disappearance.

In the end, of course, these estimates risk becoming heartless exercises in the context of more than thirty thousand missing persons, whose grieving and distressed families receive no support from the state in the search for their disappeared loved ones, nor in the pursuit of justice in relation to the crime.

The culture of impunity in Mexico can be seen vividly with regard to disappearances. Families of the disappeared testify that state- or federal-level investigations of reported disappearances run the gamut from nonexistent to incompetent. The government has admitted as much, reporting 99 preliminary inquiries at the federal level into cases of enforced disappearance between 2006 and 2013, and 192 preliminary inquiries at the state level during the same period (Committee on Enforced Disappearances 2015, paras. 73–74).

Torture

Another manifestation of the human rights crisis in Mexico is the widespread use of torture, as suggested by the case of Elvira Santibañez Margarito. In his 2014 report on Mexico, the UN Special Rapporteur on torture, Juan Mendez, concluded that "torture and ill-treatment are generalized in Mexico" and stressed that "[m]ost victims are detained for alleged links with organized crime" (Human Rights Council 2014: 7). As in the case of disappearances and extrajudicial executions, "[it] is difficult to know the real number of cases of torture. At present, there is no national register of cases and each state has its own data. Moreover, many cases are not reported out of fear of reprisals or distrust of the authorities and there is a tendency to classify acts of torture and ill-treatment as less serious offences" (Human Rights Council 2014: 7).

International human rights monitors echo Mendez's findings. In a report published in 2014, Amnesty International concluded that torture and other cruel, inhuman, or degrading treatment or punishment is a widespread practice in Mexico and that it "play[s] a central role in policing and public security operations by military and police forces across Mexico" (Amnesty International 2014: 5). The notion of "generalized" perpetration of torture, explicitly used by the UN Special Rapporteur on torture, Amnesty International, and

Table I.3. Torture and cruel, inhuman, or degrading
treatment: Complaints received by the CNDH, 2007–2016

Year	Number of complaints
2007	399
2008	1,008
2009	1,138
2010	1,180
2011	1,668
2012	1,662
2013	1,083
2014	744
2015	677
2016	744

Source: Comisión Nacional de los Derechos Humanos, Annual
Reports 2007 to 2016. http://www.cndh.org.mx/Informes_Anuales
_Actividades (last consulted: September 21, 2017).

IACHR, not only provides evidence of a human rights crisis in Mexico but
also suggests the possible perpetration of crimes against humanity.

Human rights monitors correlate the rise in torture to the "war on
drugs" and the related increase in violence. Complaints received by the
National Human Rights Commission (CNDH) offer evidence of this connection. Table I.3 shows that, between 2007 and 2016, CNDH received 10,303
complaints regarding torture and cruel, inhuman, or degrading treatment.
Throughout this period, torture complaints were the third or fourth most
frequently received by CNDH. Again, we can observe a clear peak in 2008,
and particularly in 2011.

The sheer numbers of victims of homicides, disappearances, and torture
and their sharp increase in the past decade in Mexico supports the designa-
tion of a human rights crisis. Mexico's feeble apparatus for the administration of justice to respond to these violations further deepens this crisis. The
contributors to this volume present ample evidence and nuanced analysis of
the dramatic situation that is unfolding. Even as they consider distinct manifestations of this crisis, the authors underline that the line between state and
nonstate actors is extremely blurred in Mexico (Hincapié, Treviño-Rangel,
Waddell, Estévez, Gzesh, and Gallagher, this volume). For example, following
Auyuero (2007), Ariadna Estévez (this volume) talks of "gray areas of power."
One could also recall the metaphor of "the mud"—el lodo, the mixture of
water and dirt in which it is impossible to differentiate one from the other.

From an interpretivist perspective, the case of Mexico challenges us to consider a different, more complex understanding of what constitutes a human rights violation and to problematize the role of the state as *the* perpetrator (Brysk 2005; Hessbruegge 2005; Cornet, Haschke, and Gibney 2016). As stressed by Alison Brysk, "the human rights tradition [is] a necessary and continuing struggle to limit state repression," but "abuse does not always wear a uniform" (Brysk 2005: 1). This volume shows that in some contexts abuses are perpetrated through a complex distribution of labor in which those in uniform participate in different ways, but not always by pulling the trigger or dissolving bodies in acid. States, furthermore, are not the sole locus of public power in such contexts and are not always clearly distinguishable from other key, dominant actors—that is, organized-crime groups. Seen clearly in the case of disappearances, the government's disavowal of responsibility for the disappearances of individuals when there is no explicit proof of the "authorization, support or acquiescence" of state actors does not diminish the gravity of the violence being done to those victims and their families. The line between a classic state-sponsored human rights violation and a crime that is never investigated is blurred, at best; at worst, the blurred line is a justification for doing nothing. By explaining a situation of generalized violence that is either carried out, condoned, or ignored by the state, this volume furthers a conceptual and theoretical challenge to the human rights literature. Addressing this challenge in future research is fundamental for understanding the situation not only in Mexico but also in other countries of Latin America and beyond.

From a policy perspective, on the other hand, the book's chapters make different recommendations. Some of them are very concrete (like the need to develop reliable data and indicators on the violation of human rights) or situation-specific (like the call to guarantee access to social and economic rights by the victims of internal displacement [see Rubio Díaz-Leal, this volume]). But more broadly speaking, all the chapters suggest the urgent need to curb the violence and to tackle impunity. The "war" has to stop, and militarization has to be replaced by the diligent investigation, prosecution, and punishment of crime. In order to achieve this solution, and therefore to address impunity, Mexico needs to develop the capacities of its police forces, prosecutors, and courts. Impunity and corruption define the cesspool in which violations flourish, so the acknowledged human rights fix requires strong, independent, and transparent institutions that can clearly differentiate and shield themselves from the power of organized crime. Mexico needs to reclaim its democratic institutions and its authority and legitimacy as a state. Only with strong, efficient, and "clean" institutions can the government and society aspire to tackle human rights violations and escape the current crisis. This "stateness" problem is not unique to Mexico and clearly is a key factor to achieving meaningful human rights change (Risse and Ropp 2013).

Ten years have passed since President Calderón launched his "war on drugs," and the strengthening of the armed forces sharply contrasts with the complete lack of advancements in democratic institution building. This has been Mexico's "lost decade" for human rights. Paradoxically, therein lies the opportunity. The toll in human suffering and the utter failure of the government's response support the demands by domestic civil society groups and transnational human rights advocates for a different approach to security and the development of strong institutions for the administration of justice. These actors have to push their agenda harder than ever. In this way, this book seeks to contribute to building momentum for a human rights–based response to the challenges posed by insecurity and organized crime in Mexico. As argued by some authors in this volume, even if the ultimate solution to Mexico's human rights challenges will not come "from above," international actors play a key role, empowering domestic advocates and promoting important legal and institutional reforms that improve the chances for domestic mobilization and litigation efforts (Rubio Díaz-Leal, Ansolabehere, and Gallagher, this volume).

Structure of the Book

Following this Introduction, a series of chapters deepen our understanding of the human rights crisis in Mexico. Three of these chapters focus on the human rights consequences that flow directly from the ongoing "war on drugs" in the country and the impunity that characterizes the government's response to those violations. In Chapter 1, Catalina Pérez-Correa, Carlos Silva Forné, and Rodrigo Gutiérrez Rivas explore how lethal Mexican security forces are in their efforts to combat organized crime. They show that even if President Enrique Peña Nieto (2012–2018) abandoned the inflammatory "war on drugs" rhetoric favored by his predecessor Felipe Calderón—and despite the decline in the number of clashes between security forces and members of organized crime—the "lethality index" of Mexico's security forces remains alarmingly high. The Army, Navy, and Federal Police continue to kill a disproportionate number of alleged criminals, compared to those they wound during clashes. The authors explain that for the 2008–2015 period, the Federal Police killed 6.8 persons for each person wounded; the Army killed 7 from 2007 to April 2014, and the Navy 19.4 from 2012 to 2013. The authors stress that these figures have no international precedent. The lethality index is even more worrisome for some states, notably the states of Guerrero, México, and Zacatecas. Using this data, the authors demonstrate how Mexico's human rights crisis has extended across presidential administrations and state institutions and is characterized by the diffusion of "worst practices" in the struggle against organized crime. Although they do not argue explicitly that these killings by state actors prove a pattern of extrajudicial executions, the authors conclude that these killings constitute a "strong indicator that there is a deliberate policy or normalized practice of the illegal use of lethal force" in the country. This, they argue, takes place with blatant impunity and is a direct consequence of the "logic of war" that has captured Mexico's security agenda. The authors point out a growing opacity by the government in general and security forces in particular to release information regarding the use of force. This, they suggest, is yet another worrisome sign of the lack of willingness to prevent or address violations at the hands of state actors.

In Chapter 2, Laura Rubio Díaz-Leal focuses on the largely understudied drama of internal displacement. Drawing upon fieldwork to compensate for the lack of official data, the author concludes that nearly three hundred thousand people in Mexico have fled their homes in the past decade, escaping from criminal violence and persecution. In a context of fear and insecurity, internal displacement is both a reactive strategy, in the case of already victimized families, and a preventive one, in the case of those seeking to avoid victimization. Rubio Díaz-Leal stresses that, in spite of the overwhelming size of the phenomenon, the government continues to deny its existence. The government is thus failing to protect the right to security and the right not to be subjected to forced displacement. The author further argues that the government is denying the economic and social rights of internally displaced persons (IDPs), thus increasing the vulnerability of victims, particularly women, children, and the elderly. This situation underscores the interdependence and indivisibility of human rights, not as an abstract notion but as a crude empirical reality. The chapter also offers the reader the volume's first view of the role of transnational advocacy, and of international human rights bodies as a locus for advocacy by victims and civil society organizations, a subject addressed by several other contributors.

In Chapter 3, Sandra Hincapié focuses on violence against women in the context of the current crisis. Hincapié builds her case upon the claim that the situation in Mexico constitutes an internal "armed conflict," and she shows the many ways in which women's rights are being violated by state and non-state actors within that context. Against the backdrop of a broad and diverse framework of international norms regarding women's human rights, peace, and security, Hincapié emphasizes how women have become commodities for organized criminal groups and thus direct victims of violence. Trafficking in persons, pornography, and prostitution, and forced involvement in drug trafficking are crimes that directly affect a large but undetermined number of women in Mexico. In addition, the author documents a sharp increase in gender-based homicides (femicides), an increase that correlates with the rise in overall organized crime–related violence in the country. Distressingly, the author describes how, before being murdered, women suffer serious violations of their liberty and physical integrity, including disappearance and torture. But women are the victims not only of brutal criminals, they (particularly those who are allegedly involved in organized crime) also suffer from torture and sexual violence at the hands of security forces. The chapter, nevertheless, also underscores a different side of this story of gender-related violence—how mothers, wives, daughters, and other direct victims of violence against women are becoming human rights defenders. To complete the picture, the chapter offers an analysis of the state's responses to violence against women. The author's conclusion, in this respect, is not surprising: Authorities, despite having a legal and institutional mandate to address violence against women, are not only neglectful but often work to obstruct the proper functioning of the extant procedural framework to respond to victims.

In Chapter 4, Regina Tamés changes the focus from the human rights violations directly related to Mexico's current security crisis to an issue largely ignored by mainstream human rights discussions, particularly in the academic field—the systematic violation of women's reproductive rights. The chapter reminds us that, in addition to the current crisis, Mexico continues to face other silent, longstanding, structural human rights problems. Describing in detail patterns of neglect and abuse that constitute obstetric violence (that is, violence during pregnancy and childbirth and postpartum), as well as maternal mortality and sexual violence against women (including against girls), the author explicitly argues that violations to reproductive rights are human rights violations. Stressing this claim might seem unnecessary to those familiar with the human rights discourse and reproductive rights, but making this problem visible remains paramount in a society marked by stereotypes and discriminatory views about women. The chapter is rich in data, references to the normative framework, and, particularly, insights from specific cases, litigated and advocated by domestic civil society organizations in Mexico. Tamés makes clear that, unlike those working in relation to the "mainstream human rights agenda" addressed in other chapters of this volume, domestic advocates for reproductive rights have not yet relied extensively on the involvement of international human rights bodies; the struggle for reproductive human rights remains largely a local one in Mexico. Empirically, the chapter's analysis reveals the daunting shortcomings of Mexico's health system, together with inadequate legislation, systemic inequalities, and discriminatory practices based on stereotypes, which all have perverse effects on the human rights of women and girls. This emerging human rights agenda is consistent with the others addressed in this volume in highlighting a pattern of violations that are not taken seriously by those who have the power to prevent them.

A second group of chapters focuses on the violation of the human rights of migrants, in both Mexico and the United States. In Chapter 5, Javier Treviño-Rangel describes and interprets the atrocities suffered by undocumented migrants in transit through Mexico. With original empirical evidence gathered through extensive fieldwork, the author challenges the common account on the matter—that is, that the severe violation of human rights (including disappearances, executions, torture, and sexual violence) faced by migrants is the outcome of securitization policies adopted by the Mexican government at the behest of its U.S. counterparts. In other words, Treviño-Rangel is not convinced that the systematic and extremely brutal abuses of migrants in transit result from public policies devised on the assumption that migrants are a threat to security. Contrary to this popular account, Treviño-Rangel offers a simpler but more distressing interpretation. He argues that petty material gains lead authorities and ordinary Mexicans to directly extort and abuse migrants or to deliver them to organized crime. Underlying this reason is a deeper and more complex sociological process. Progressively, migrants in transit (most of them from Central America) have come to be seen "as a [disposable] commodity that could, potentially, generate some income," not only for organized crime but, as already stressed, for local authorities and common Mexican citizens. As do other chapters in this volume, Chapter 5 shows a disturbing pattern of complicity between authorities at all levels of government and organized crime. Migrants are often detained by agents of the National Institute of Migration (INM) or police forces and handed over to criminal groups, which in turn extort them (demanding ransom from their relatives and friends in the United States) and torture or kill those who are not able to pay. Some of them, furthermore, are forced to work for their captors. These inhumane "transactions" between government officials and criminals tend to be superfluous or banal. Through his field research, the author found that they can involve no more than a bottle of whiskey.

In Chapter 6, Benjamin Waddell explores the violence of emigration from Mexico and its relationship to the violation of human rights on Mexican soil. Waddell does not focus on migrants and the abuses they suffer but on the local communities they leave behind; he details the possible consequences of mass migration on social conditions in rural communities in Mexico. Waddell's argument is that migration deprives rural communities in Mexico of the human and social capital required for local (social and economic) development. The direct outcome, he argues, is a deprived, almost toxic social context in which crime and state-sponsored violence are prone to flourish. Waddell asserts that massive migration is related, at least indirectly, to the violence perpetrated by nonstate as well as state actors. His underlying theoretical argument suggests that migrants tend to be the more entrepreneurial members of their home communities, so when they travel to "the other side" of the border *(el otro lado),* they deprive their hometowns of the human and social capital required to promote prosperity and well-being. The picture is further complicated by the rising social, political, and economic power of criminal groups in the regions left behind. Combining descriptive statistics with qualitative evidence gathered through fieldwork in the State of Michoacán, Waddell develops a complex, empirically based sociological and economic argument about the probable links between emigration, violence, and the violation of human rights. Within this broader story, once more, the links between authorities and organized crime clearly come to the surface. The author stresses the blurring that occurs between the local governments and criminal organizations: "If you work for the police, you work for the local *capo* because *el capitán* [the local police chief] is on the take and you need the extra cash," Waddell was told by one of his informants.

Chapters 7 and 8 shift the human rights focus northward, considering the U.S. asylum system as a site of violations and missed opportunities. In Chapter 7, Ariadna Estévez examines the issue of asylum-seeking in the United States by Mexicans fleeing drug-related and gender-based violence and persecution. The author describes the scope of the phenomenon, the characteristics of asylum seekers, and the reasons that lead them to cross the border in search of protection. The gendered face of this manifestation of Mexico's human rights crisis is explicitly underlined by the author, complementing Sandra Hincapié's account in Chapter 4. Estévez finds that U.S. judges are basing their decisions to deny asylum requests on a narrow interpretation of asylum law and on the basis of a limited understanding of the complexities of Mexican politics, such as a naive belief that the Mexican state is actually willing and/or able to protect its citizens. Additionally, the U.S. asylum system places a heavy burden on petitioners to prove that they have suffered persecution and are at risk because of their membership in a "social group" or because of their political opinions. Estévez argues that judges are failing to fully grasp the complexities of the situation of violence in Mexico; in particular, they do not acknowledge the "grey areas of power" (Auyero 2007) that characterize the Mexican social and political landscape within which persecution, executions, torture, and disappearances are taking place. As do many other chapters in this volume, Chapter 7 notes not only the government's complicity with drug cartels, but the complex mixture of state and nonstate bases of authority, power, and violence in contemporary Mexico. Ultimately, the author argues in favor of an approach to asylum that fully grasps the complexities of the Mexican context and in this way "effectively [bridges] Mexican and American legal geographies."

From a prescriptive point of view, Estévez recommends that advocates chart the U.S. immigration law system and identify those judges with lower "denial rates" and with professional, ethnic, and political backgrounds that might render them more likely to sympathize with this "bridging" approach. In Chapter 8, Susan Gzesh does precisely that—focusing on petitions for protection under the "non-refoulement" clause of the Convention Against Torture and Other Cruel, Inhumane or Degrading Treatment (CAT). Gzesh identifies U.S. Circuit Courts of Appeals and specific judges who base their decisions on a more nuanced understanding of the complex conditions in Mexico. Complementing Estévez's account, Gzesh begins by offering a straightforward description of the judicial route for petitions of protection by foreigners who fear persecution or torture in their countries of origin. Gzesh then underlines the possible advantages of requesting protection in the U.S. immigration system under CAT, as opposed to asking for political asylum. The author suggests that protection under CAT might be more "promising" because it does not require petitioners to prove that they will face persecution if sent back to Mexico because of their membership in a particular social group or because of their political opinions. Instead, applicants are required to show that there are "substantial grounds" to expect that they will be tortured if they are sent back to Mexico. The author recognizes the legal and, notably, the diplomatic obstacles to arguing for relief under CAT. However, examining the jurisprudence of federal courts of appeals in cases of petitions of protection under CAT by Mexican nationals, Gzesh finds "interesting decisions and trends," particularly related to the interpretation of the clause that requires "consent and acquiescence" by government authorities of acts of torture perpetrated by nonstate actors (that is, criminal organizations). In this way, Gzesh emphasizes the legal and theoretical tensions that invite reexamination of the definition of international human rights crimes, such as torture.

The promising CAT decisions highlighted by Gzesh underscore the importance of Estévez's call for a more nuanced understanding of the complexities of Mexican law enforcement and the complicities between police forces and organized crime. Chapter 8 offers some more space for optimism, identifying arguments already made by influential judicial decision-makers in the United States that could affect immigration judges nationwide and that, therefore, might offer better chances of protection for Mexicans escaping violence, persecution, and extreme abuse in their country, regardless of whether the perpetrator is a state agent, a cartel operative, or both.

A final group of chapters focuses on domestic and transnational elements and processes that shape the current human rights crisis in Mexico. In Chapter 9, Daniel Vázquez calls our attention to "the elephant in the room"—the extremely low quality of Mexico's "democracy." The chapter begins with a troubling observation: "We were wrong to believe that human rights violations in Mexico would end with the transition to democracy. Violations did not end with democracy, but instead merely shifted their patterns." This situation, argues Vázquez, is due to particular features of Mexico's political system, characterized by authoritarian legacies (particularly at the subnational level), the lack of authentic freedom of expression (because of the absence of a plural media environment), and a failed neoliberal economic model of development. Beyond that, however, Vázquez stresses five key features of "Mexican style democracy": (a) clientelism, not elections, as the central mode of political intermediation in the country; (b) the government's systematic denial of the country's shortcomings and challenges (for example, the denial of poverty, of the influence of organized crime at all levels of government, of corruption, and of the magnitude of the violations of human rights); (c) simulation, that is, the implementation of actions that appear to address the country's problems but are actually only fake or cosmetic; (d) corruption; and (e) impunity, a theme that, as already stressed, emerges as a key explanatory variable throughout the book. This *democracia a la Mexicana,* concludes Vázquez, provides a framework in which human rights violations are only prone to spread further. In his own words, "If what one is looking for is a fuller enjoyment and exercise of human rights, the first thing that should be dismantled is the logic of Mexican-style democracy." .

In Chapter 10, Alejandro Anaya-Muñoz and Natalia Saltalamacchia inquire why, after more than two decades of transnational and domestic activism and pressure from human rights advocates, the human rights situation in Mexico has not advanced toward "rule consistent behavior," as would be predicted by the spiral model of human rights change (Risse, Ropp, and Sikkink 1999) and in general by the literature on the transnational advocacy of human rights. They stress that human rights pressure has indeed elicited positive reactions from the Mexican government, particularly commitments related to international human rights norms and domestic legal and institutional reforms. The authors question why these commitments have not led to improvements in compliance. Anaya-Muñoz and Saltalamacchia explore which domestic conditions may have blocked the transition from commitment to compliance or, in other words, the *socialization process.* These conditions include limited state capacities (or limited statehood), decentralization, and securitization. An empirical analysis of Mexico's state-level police forces as well as of the system of prosecutors and courts leads the authors to identify weak institutional capacities (and therefore limited statehood), which has in turn resulted in almost complete impunity, conditions ripe for human rights violations. The authors conclude that limited statehood, conflict, and securitization are factors that account for the blockage of the commitment-compliance gap in Mexico. Despite these factors, they find that the federal apparatus for policing and for the administration of justice protects human rights no better than its subnational counterparts. Decentralization, therefore, does not appear to be a blocking factor. Anaya-Muñoz and Saltalamacchia's findings beg for a more nuanced understanding of the relationship and the distinction between "voluntary" and "involuntary" sources of noncompliance, stressing that the notion of "involuntary" sources of noncompliance, though analytically relevant, can have perverse policy consequences. Furthermore, the authors question whether lack of capacities is not ultimately based on lack of willingness by state actors. Anaya-Muñoz and Saltalamacchia conclude with a critique of capacity-based arguments for eschewing explanations based on willingness.

In Chapter 11, Karina Ansolabehere highlights the effects of international norms and decisions on local legal processes. She assesses, in particular, the influence of the rulings of the Inter-American Court on Human Rights (IACtHR) on the decisions by Mexico's National Supreme Court of Justice (SCJN). The author finds a troubling—though not surprising—decoupling between the outcomes of two of the key roles or functions of the Mexican Federal Judiciary: diffusion and application of norms. While SCJN has been active in the diffusion of human rights norms, it has not been diligent about applying those norms in its own rulings. Through its emphasis on decoupling, the chapter thus questions the dominant emphasis in the literature on "activist judiciaries" and on international influences that enquire whether domestic courts are "pro-rights" or not. As Ansolabehere shows, the matter is more complicated. Judiciaries play different roles or exercise different functions in relation to international human rights norms, and they do so in differentiated ways. The author notes that while international human rights norms and the decisions of international organs had become influential in Mexico's foreign and domestic policymaking since the early 2000s (Saltalamacchia Ziccardi and Covarrubias Velasco 2011; Anaya Muñoz 2009), only very recently, after the *Radilla Pacheco* ruling by IACtHR and the 2011 constitutional reform, did Mexico's judiciary became explicitly mindful of them. This new approach to human rights by SCJN, however, did not play out in the same way in the two concrete functions or roles it plays, namely, norm diffusion and norm application, especially in achieving accountability for human rights violations. Examining the judicial precedents adopted by Mexico's SCJN between 1995 and 2015, the author finds that, as of 2012, SCJN has become a "sounding board" for international norms, convening discussions and adopting decisions regarding "the status of international human rights law, the ways to align domestic law with external sources, the specific interpretative techniques for achieving these ends, and the authority held by lower-level judges not to enforce domestic legal norms if they are found contrary" to the American Convention on Human Rights (ACHR). Although tensions remain and some issues are still being "rearranged," this diffusion process is generally favorable to international human rights protection. On the other hand, as Ansolabehere shows, "the path toward accountability for human rights violations is not one that Mexico has chosen to travel." She highlights the lack of accountability in the courts in disappearance cases to explain how impunity is operationalized institutionally. Like Anaya-Muñoz and Saltalamacchia in the previous chapter, Ansolabehere illustrates that "talking the talk," as opposed to "walking the walk," is the dominant strategy of Mexican authorities in responding to international pressures and influences.

In the final chapter of this volume, Janice Gallagher uses a different lens to explore impunity, examining the impact of civil society activism in state-level court cases regarding "lethal violence," such as homicides and disappearances. Gallagher digs into local justice processes to understand why only a few cases are investigated and prosecuted while the majority languish in impunity. Drawing on extensive original empirical research on homicides and disappearances in the northern border states of Chihuahua and Nuevo León, Gallagher demonstrates that the involvement of human rights actors, including local, national, and international NGOs, is the key to making progress in the judicial process. The author introduces a key conceptual and empirical difference, not emphasized by the literature before, between organizations and groups that focus on *activism* (defined as the exertion of critical pressure) and those that focus on *advocacy* (the construction of channels of interaction between victims and authorities). Theoretically, Gallagher seeks to further recommend the influential boomerang model by (a) insisting that advocates and activists should focus more on the authorities at the local level, favoring, in this case, a focus on the local "judicial decision-making site," and (b) identifying a different kind of tactic used by transnational advocacy networks (TANs) to influence governments—relationship politics. She defines relationship politics as "the ability to locate strategically positioned judicial decision-makers and influence their actions through repeated interactions with TAN members." The author finds that the results of activists are different from those of advocates. While the critical and confrontational pressure by the former weakens the "blockage" that shields authorities, the latter's direct and more positive interactions with judicial decision-makers puts advocates in a better position to break that blockage and thus to achieve better results within the judicial process. Comparing the cases of Chihuahua and Nuevo León, Gallagher explains how the intervention by national and international NGOs and groups in local human rights processes can have opposite results at the local level. Building collaborative relations with public officials, under certain circumstances, is likely to be more productive than sheer pressure or shaming.

PART I

The Crisis Unfolds

CHAPTER 1

Deadly Forces

Use of Lethal Force by Mexican Security Forces 2007–2015

Catalina Pérez Correa, Carlos Silva Forné,
and Rodrigo Gutiérrez Rivas

Introduction

On June 30, 2014, the media reported on clashes between members of the Ministry of National Defense (SEDENA) and presumed members of an organized-crime ring in the community of San Pedro Limón, in Tlatlaya municipality, the State of México. This incident resulted in the deaths of twenty-two civilians (among them a fifteen-year-old teenager) and left one soldier wounded. After carrying out the standard procedures, the prosecutor's office in the State of México declared in a public statement (Ferri 2014) that a shoot-out had occurred and that the number of shots exchanged had been similar on both sides. On July 9, after an eyewitness appeared, *Esquire* magazine reported that the deaths in Tlatlaya could have been arbitrary executions on the part of the Mexican Army. The publication gave rise to numerous inquiries, including the opening of an investigation by the National Human Rights Commission (CNDH). On October 21, through recommendation 51/2014, CNDH indicated that on the basis of the investigations carried out, it was able to affirm that Army members engaged in extrajudicial executions and in illegal alterations of the crime scene, "with the intention, very probably, of simulating that the deaths had occurred in the context of a shoot-out" (CNDH 2014). On September 26, in response to national and international pressure, the Ministry of the Interior stated that if illegal deprivations of life were involved, they constituted an exception and not common Army practice (Reforma 2014).

In 2011, the authors of this chapter made a study to evaluate the use of lethal force by federal security forces (Silva, Pérez Correa, and Gutiérrez 2012). Our interest and concern then, as it is now, grew out of daily press reports that indicated that members of the Army (or the Federal Police or the Navy) had been attacked and that a shoot-out had resulted between the Army and the aggressors. The outcome was usually many aggressors dead, only a few wounded, and few soldier casualties. These attacks occurred in the context of the increasing use of federal forces, especially the Army, to carry out public security tasks and to fight the war on drugs.

In our previous study, we examined the proportion of civilians killed in comparison to civilians wounded during clashes, as well as the total number of people killed, including both civilians and security forces. We called the first indicator the "lethality index," utilizing the terminology of Ignacio Cano (1997, 2003, 2010) in studies on Brazil. Five years have passed since our initial study was carried out, and a new presidential administration has since taken power. Enrique Peña Nieto began his government with a less bellicose discourse than the one that characterized Felipe Calderón's government. That discursive change seemed to augur the gradual withdrawal of Mexican Army members from public-security tasks. However, the cases of Tlatlaya, Apatzingán, Ecuandureo/Tanhuato, and Nochixtlan have sparked renewed concern in the public debate over the excessive use of lethal force by the Army and other federal armed forces, as these cases opened doubts regarding the possibly systematic and normalized nature of the use of lethal force.

In this context, we set out to compile new information on the dead and wounded in shoot-outs in which members of Mexico's federal security forces (the Federal Police, the Army, and the Navy) participated. To do that, in line with the previous study, we built a database from press reports and requested information from the federal security forces. The findings, although encouraging in some ways, depict a general situation that is of concern. We found that the current administration, compared with its immediate predecessor, registers a smaller number of clashes and deaths during clashes; however, the same cannot be said of their lethal nature, which remains at high and worrisome levels. This is especially true in some states, such as Guerrero and Zacatecas, where the lethality index is extremely high. Particularly worrisome are the indexes for the Federal Police, based both on official figures and press reports, and these indexes force academics and decision-makers to question this institution's performance under the current administration. Finally, we found a growing opacity, or lack of transparency, on the part of the Army—an alarming institutional stance in light of the Army's recent clashes that have left many civilians dead and few wounded, such as those in Tlatlaya, the State of México, and Rio Bravo, the State of Tamaulipas.

This chapter is divided into five parts. The first part outlines the context and methodology of this research; the second presents the study's main results; the third discusses the difficulties of obtaining information that allows for at least a minimal analysis of the use of lethal force by the state; the fourth presents the legal framework that currently governs the use of lethal force., We conclude with some final reflections.

Context and Methodology

The use of lethal force by the state can be measured by different indicators. The most widely used indicators internationally (Loche 2010: 45) are (a) the percentage of (intentional) homicides in which the police or a member of other security forces was responsible; (b) the number of civilian deaths over the number of police (or members of other security forces) deaths during clashes; and (c) the number of civilians killed for every civilian wounded during clashes (referred to as the lethality index). As Cano (2003) has pointed out, the more indicators analyzed, the greater the certainty regarding the excessive use of lethal force by the police. In this chapter, we study the second and third of the just-listed indicators. We do not analyze the first indicator because we do not have that information.

The indicators used in this chapter have been used in other countries to evaluate the legitimacy of the use of lethal force. In Brazil (particularly in São Paolo and Rio de Janeiro) the relation of dead and wounded has been used to assess the use of force by the police (Chevigny 1987, 1993; Cano 1997, 2010). The lethality index has also been used in Argentina (Centro de Estudios Legales y Sociales 2002; Sozzo 2002; Aimar et al. 2005) and Venezuela (Birkbeck and Gabaldón 2002). Ignacio Cano (2010: 37) showed that for the military police of Rio de Janeiro, between 1993 and 1996, the lethality index was 3.9. However, when in the *favelas*[1] and in clashes in which the opponents were black or mixed race, the index reached 8 or 9 civilians killed for every wounded (Cano 2010), pointing to biases in the use of lethal force by the Rio police. According to the author, such high indexes point to the existence of extrajudicial killings.

In our previous study to evaluate the use of lethal force by federal security forces in Mexico (Silva, Pérez Correa, and Gutiérrez 2012), two lethality indexes were calculated. A first indicator was calculated on the basis of press information from January 2008 to May 2011.[2] Due to limitations in coverage and possible biases in the source used,[3] a second indicator was calculated using data provided by SEDENA and obtained via access-to-information requests.[4]

Based on the press information, the study found that from 2008 to 2011, the Mexican Army had a lethality index of 9.1 (civilians dead/civilians wounded), the Federal Police had an index of 2.6, and the Navy had an index of 17.3 (although the number of incidents involving the Navy were few). It also found evidence that the Navy and the Army used lethal force more often than police forces (whether federal, state, or municipal police). According to the figures provided by the Army, its lethality index was lower (6.3) than what was calculated on the basis of press information. Data provided by the Army, however, gave evidence of a rise over time in the Army's lethality index—in 2008 the index was 2.8, but in 2010 it rose to 6.8, and in 2011 to 6.5.[5] In other words, not only was the lethality index of the Mexican Army well above the worrisome index of the Brazilian police, but the institution became more lethal as it increased its participation in combating drug trafficking. Finally, in some states, during 2011 the lethality index reached levels as high as 10.2 (in Tamaulipas) and 9.4 (in Guerrero), even higher levels than those reached by the Rio de Janeiro police (Silva, Pérez Correa, and Gutiérrez 2012: 59–60).

As stated before, there are no unique indicators that can determine whether extrajudicial executions were carried out in a given situation, or if a security force as a whole is using lethal force in an excessive and disproportionate fashion. To prove in a specific case the existence, or nonexistence, of extrajudicial executions, detailed information on the incident must be evaluated (Human Rights Committee 2007, 2010). Every time that the state uses lethal force, it is essential that the institutions of prosecution and judicial administration carry out the appropriate investigations. However, in a context of generalized impunity, and given a lack of effective judicial institutions, it is necessary to build indicators to evaluate the legitimate and proportional use of lethal force utilized by the various security bodies. These are not indicators that, by themselves, can prove arbitrary deprivations of life, but high values, when analyzed together, serve to bring public attention to the situation and highlight the need to carry out serious and specific investigations in each case.

As in our previous study, in this chapter, we build our analysis around two sources: official data and press reports. The official data was provided via INFOMEX[6] by the Federal Police, SEDENA, and the Navy. The period encompasses the beginning of the war on drugs to the time when the information requests were made. In December 2016, former president Felipe Calderón declared the war on drugs and deployed thousands of Army and Air Force elements to different parts of the country. By the end of January 2017, at least 23,200 soldiers had been deployed across the country to combat organized crime (Pérez Correa 2012: 2). Requests were made in 2014 and again in 2016, petitioning for information about shoot-outs, civilians killed and wounded by the institution during clashes, and police officers (or soldiers) killed and wounded during clashes, by state and date, from 2007 to the moment when the information was released.[7]

A database with the same variables was built on the basis of press information[8] during the same period. In this case, it is important to take into account that due to its selection criteria, press information tends to have an upward bias in the indicators that we analyze. For that reason, this information must be used cautiously and must be compared with official data. In contrast to our previous study, on this occasion we had significant difficulty obtaining information regarding the Army, which points to growing opacity in that institution.

Results

The main results of this study are divided into the following parts: (1) the evolution in the number of clashes from 2007 to 2015; (2) the number of civilians killed versus the number of security-force members killed in clashes; (3) the lethality index by security force and its evolution during the 2008–2015 period; and (4) the lethality index in state jurisdictions.

Number of Clashes from 2007 to 2015

There are significant variations in the number of clashes over the course of the period. The total number of clashes involving the federal forces, especially

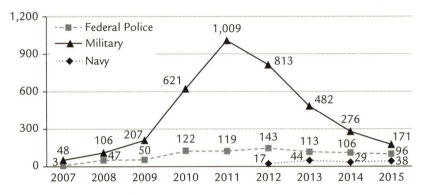

Figure 1.1. Total clashes with presumed members of organized crime networks according to type of security force (2007–2015). As stated earlier in the chapter, information from the different information requests show inconsistencies. In the first request (number 0413100088114), the Federal Police reported 143 clashes in 2012, 113 in 2013, and 79 in 2014 (with information until November 5). In the second request (number 0413100158815), the institution reported 15 clashes in 2012, 132 in 2013, and 106 for 2014. For the Navy, in the first request (number 0001300092314), the institution reported 44 clashes in 2013 and 43 in 2014. However, in the second request (number 0001300105915, the institution reported 41 clashes in 2013 and 29 in 2014. Sources: Information for 2015 in the case of the military is only to November; for the years 2007 and 2013, information requests number 0413100088114 (Federal Police) and 0001300092314 (Navy); for the years 2014 and 2015, information requests number 0413100158815 (Federal Police) and 0001300105915 (Navy); for the Army, years 2007–2011, information request number 0000700211714, and for 2012–2015, information request number 0000700213015.

the Army, grew sharply between 2007 and 2011 and later declined in 2012, with that downward trend continuing after 2013. It is important to remember that the Peña Nieto administration began in December 2012. Figure 1.1 shows the variations for each of the federal security forces.

As the figure shows, SEDENA reached a maximum number of clashes in 2011 and later reduced that figure steadily over the course of the following years. The information for 2015 is incomplete, so the percentage of reduction cannot be calculated with precision. The Federal Police, with lower and more stable numbers, showed an increasing number of clashes from 2008 to 2012 and a 33-percent decline in the subsequent three years. Finally, although the information provided by the Navy is limited and its participation is lower, the number of clashes involving naval personnel increased after 2012.

Table 1.1. Deployed soldiers and operations against drug trafficking and organized crime, SEDENA (2006–2014).

Year	Deployed soldiers (average)	Period	No. of operations
2006	37,253	—	—
2007	45,000	2007	28
2008	45,106	2008	56
2009	48,650	2009	98
2010	49,650	2010	89
2011	52,690	2011	87
2012	49,650	(Jan–Nov) 2012	92
2013	34,529	Dec 2012–Dec 2014	14
2014	35,615	—	—

Source: Deployed soldiers: SEDENA response to information request number 0000700211414; Operations 2007–2012: SEDENA response to information request number 0000700008513; Operations 2012–2014: SEDENA response to information request number 0000700211414.

The increase in clashes leading up to 2011, until nearly the end of Calderón's administration, was just as sharp as the decrease that followed (starting in 2012) in the first two years of Peña Nieto's government.[9] The significant decline in clashes in the last few years could be explained by a number of factors, such as a smaller deployment of members of the federal forces; variations in the number and characteristics of the operations carried out (such as highway military checkpoints); and the reconfiguration and/or displacement of criminal groups to regions or activities that foster less contact with federal security forces.

Looking at the deployment of Army forces in Table 1.1, it is possible to see that from 2006 to 2011 there was a constant increase in the number of soldiers deployed in operations against drug trafficking and organized crime, reaching 52,690 soldiers in 2011. In contrast, 2012 and 2013 showed a significant decline, whereas the figure increased again slightly in 2014 (information for 2015 was not available). The number of operations rose from 2007 to 2009 and then remained constant (albeit slightly lower) until 2012.

From December 2012 to December 2014, the official information was provided in aggregate form, reporting just fourteen operations, a figure that is strikingly lower than that of previous years. Questions remain regarding a possible change in the definition of the term "operations" with the Peña

Nieto administration, or there could be other reasons that explain such a marked decline.

The decrease in the number of deployed soldiers ran parallel to the decline in the number of clashes involving the Army. However, pinpointing these relationships would require more information to take into account other possible variables, which is beyond the scope of this text.

The decline in the number of clashes brought with it, not unexpectedly, lower totals throughout the country for the number of dead and wounded as a result of these incidents. The total number of presumed criminals killed by the Army in clashes (according to figures provided by SEDENA) fell from 1,297 in 2011 to 459 in 2013.[10] This significant decline is an outcome that moves in the desired direction. However, it does not imply a change in other indicators, as we will show.

Civilians Killed versus Members
of Federal Forces Killed in Clashes

The ratio of civilians killed to security agents killed in clashes cannot, as other indicators, prove by itself the existence of extrajudicial killings. However, high values of this indicator may suggest an excessive use of force. According to Paul Chevigny (1990), the deaths of more than ten or fifteen civilians for every security official killed in clashes suggest that lethal force is being used more than necessary. The results in Mexico in the period under analysis are shown in Table 1.2.

With regard to the Federal Police, this indicator rose in 2012 (10.4); it later fell during the first two years of the current administration but then reached its highest value in 2015. Press data show an increase in 2014, in contrast to the decline seen in the official figures. The press figures follow a similar upward trend from 2008 (2.4) to 2012 (16.2); in 2013 the number fell to 7.2, but in 2014 it rose again to reach 17.[11]

With regard to the Army, according to official data, the indicator hit its highest mark in 2011 (32.4). However, since 2009 the figure surpassed the threshold of concern set forth by Chevigny. The decline in the relationship between the numbers of dead civilians and dead soldiers in clashes in 2014 (5.4) should be viewed with caution since the Army provided information from *only* the first quarter of the year (as we will explain); this means that the case of Tlatlaya, mentioned at the beginning of this chapter, was not included.

Table 1.2. Number of civilians killed per number of police or soldiers killed in clashes (2007–2015)

Year	Federal Police	Army	Navy
2007	—	1.6	—
2008	1.1	5.1	—
2009	2.6	17.6	—
2010	3.5	15.6	—
2011	9.4	32.4	—
2012	10.4	23.5	—
2013	6.7	20.0	23.3
2014	6.8	5.4*	40.0
2015	12.4	—	10.0

Source: Based on information as follows: For the years 2007 and 2013, information requests 0413100088114 (Federal Police) and 0001300092314 (Navy). For the years 2014 and 2015, information requests 0413100158815 (Federal Police) and 0001300105915 (Navy). For the Army (SEDENA), information request 0000700211714.[1] In 2014, the Military reported figures on the dead and wounded in clashes from January to April 5, 2014.

* Again in this case, information gained through requests from security forces showed inconsistencies. In the first request (0413100088114), the Federal Police reported 167 civilians and 16 police officers killed in clashes for 2012, 101 civilians and 15 police officers killed in 2013, and 41 civilians and 8 police officers killed in 2014 (up to November). However, in the second information request (0413100158815), the same authority reported 179 civilians and 16 officers killed in 2012, 112 civilians and 16 officers killed in 2013, and 68 civilians and 10 police officers killed in 2014.

In the case of the Navy, the first information request (0001300092314) reported 31 civilians and 4 officers killed in clashes in 2012, 70 civilians and 3 officers killed in 2013, and 67 civilians and no officers killed in 2014. In the second information request (0001300105915), the institution reported 8 civilians and no officers killed in 2012, 63 civilians and 3 officers killed in 2013, and 80 civilians and 2 officers killed in 2014.

If we turn to the press database regarding the Army, the information shows a significant increase in the indicator from 2008 (5.5) to 2012 (42.1). In 2013 the figure declined to 18.8, but in 2014 it reached 53 civilians killed for every soldier killed in clashes (159 civilians and 3 soldiers died in total). As we have mentioned, press information tends to overestimate the indicators. However, in light of the lack of official information starting in 2014, these figures are practically the only available data.

The official information provided by the Ministry of the Navy (SEMAR) presents problems that make it impossible for us to build the indicators we are analyzing, as no naval personnel died in 2011 or 2012, according to SEMAR's data. For 2013–2014, the data are worrisome. In 2013, the Navy reported twenty-three civilians killed for every Navy member killed; forty in 2014; and then a reduction to ten in 2015. If we consider the press information, the figure calculated from the press information is always very high.[12] Even more, in 2010 and 2013 the relationship cannot be calculated at all because no naval personnel died (fifty civilian deaths were reported in clashes in 2010 and thirty-three in 2013). The ratios for the rest of the years are 24 in 2009, 34.3 in 2011, 36 in 2012, and 74 in 2014. These are very high levels that have held steady in the first two years of the Peña Nieto administration. In fact, they reached their maximum value in 2014 according to both the press database and official information.

Lethality Index of the Federal Forces 2007–2015

The lethality index, as we have mentioned, is the number of civilians killed for every civilian wounded in clashes. The expectation is that in shoot-outs between civilians and security forces, the number of deaths would not exceed the number of wounded by much and, therefore, the value of the index would not be much greater than one. In fact, when analyzing the use of conventional weapons in armed conflicts, medical studies invert the index to report the wounded over the dead, since the first group is bigger than the second in the context of war (Kimmerle and Baraybar 2008). So, for example, according to Coupland and Meddings (1999), the Vietnam War had a ratio of 4 wounded for every person killed in the period from 1964 to 1973, and the conflict between Israel and Lebanon had an index of 4.5 wounded for every person killed in 1982. In contrast, when war crimes or shootings against civilians are involved, more people die than those wounded. The authors note cases such as the Wah Mee massacre in Seattle, which left thirteen people dead and none wounded, or the shooting in a McDonald's in San Ysidro, California, in 1984 that caused the death of twenty-one people and wounded eleven, yielding an index of 1.9. Other data indicate that, in the context of war, the number of dead does not surpass the number of wounded. According to the U.S. Defense Intelligence Agency (DIA), during the Gulf War 300,000 Iraqi military personnel were wounded and 100,000 were killed. This means there was an index of 3 wounded for every person killed (Crawford 2013).

In its manual for war surgery, the International Committee for the Red Cross (ICRC) (ICRC 2010) also noted that "the ratio of dead to survivors in modern conflict tends to be about 1:4" but observes that protective equipment, and different weapons systems, affect lethality. ICRC notes that military rifle bullets have a 30–40 percent lethality, or 1 death in every 3–4 wounded; randomly formed fragments have a 20 percent lethality for shells and 10 percent for grenades; preformed fragments have a 15 percent lethality for shells and 5 percent for grenades; and a blast injury has a fatality of about 22 percent. The manual also notes, "A well-laid ambush with small arms can easily result in more than 40 percent of a small patrol being killed" (ICRC 2010: 113).

The data analyzed regarding Mexico's federal forces show extremely high lethality indexes.[13] Using official data, we calculate that for the period of 2008–2015, the Federal Police had an average of 6.8 civilians killed per civilians wounded in clashes, while the Army's figure reached 7 from 2007 to April 2014. The information from the Navy allowed only the calculations for 2012 and 2013 as no wounded were reported in 2014 and 2015. Given this lack of data, we omit this information in the analysis that follows. The values of the index for the other institutions varied significantly during the period, as can be seen in Figure 1.2.

ARMY

In the case of the Army, from 2007 to 2015, the institution reported 3,907 civilians shot and killed and 494 civilians wounded during clashes. The lethality index rose each year from 2007 (1.6) to 2012 (14.7). The Army's lethality index declined to 7.7 in 2013 but rose again in 2014 to reach 11.6 people killed for every person wounded. Once again, it is important to note that in 2014 the information provided covered only the first quarter of the year.

If we compare the final two years of the Calderón administration (2011–2012) with the data available from the first two years of the Peña Nieto administration (2013–April 5, 2014), we find that the Army's lethality index fell from 11.2 to 8.1. Although this could be seen as an improvement in the use of lethal force, it is still a very high figure, similar to the average for the Calderón administration, which was 7.9.

If we analyze the press database, we see that the Army's lethality index rose from 2008 (3.4) to 2011 (19.5) and then began to fall, although it remained at high levels: 16.1 in 2012, 11.8 in 2013, and 7.3 in 2014 (see Table 1.3). Although the calculations based on press information do not follow the trend seen in official data for each year, in general terms they seem to move in similar ways.

The outcome in both cases—official information and press reports—is that the lethal nature of clashes involving the Army reached its highest levels in 2011

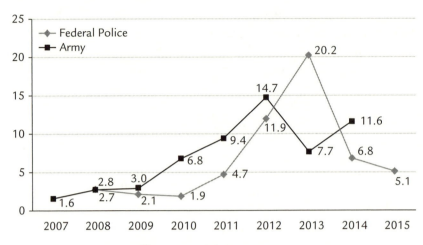

Figure 1.2. Lethality index of Federal Police and Army (2007–2015). In 2014, the Army reported figures on the dead and wounded in clashes from January to April 5, 2014. Again in this case, information given through information requests shows inconsistencies. In the first request (0413100088114), the Federal Police reported 167 civilians killed and 14 wounded in 2012, 101 civilians killed and 5 wounded in 2013, and 41 civilians killed and 9 civilians wounded in 2014. In the second information request (0413100158815), the Federal Police reported 172 civilians dead and 4 wounded in 2012, 112 civilians dead and 6 wounded in 2013, and 68 civilians dead and 10 wounded in 2014. For the Navy, the first request (0001300092314) reported 31 civilians killed and 2 wounded in 2012, 70 killed and 3 wounded in 2013, and 67 killed and 3 wounded up to November 2014. In response to the second request, however, (0001300105915), the institution reported 8 civilians killed in 2012, 63 killed in 2013, and 80 killed in 2014. In these years, there were no civilians reported wounded. Sources: For the years 2007 and 2013, information request number 0413100088114 (Federal Police). For the years 2014 and 2015, information request number 0413100158815 (Federal Police). For the Army (SEDENA), information request number 0000700211714.

and 2012, but despite the subsequent decline, the index was still very high in a context in which official information was not subject to public scrutiny.

FEDERAL POLICE

In the case of the Federal Police, from 2007 to 2015, according to official data, 725 civilians were shot and killed and 144 were wounded. The lethality index in clashes remained at low levels until 2010, when it rose dramatically, not only until the end of the Calderón administration but through the first year of the Peña Nieto administration (2013), reaching a figure of 20.2 civilians killed for

Table 1.3. Civilians killed and wounded and lethality index in clashes, organized by federal security force, Press articles 2008–2014.

Year	Army			Federal Police			Navy*		
	Civilians killed	Civilians wounded	Lethality index	Civilians killed	Civilians wounded	Lethality index	Civilians killed	Civilians wounded	Lethality index
2008	44	13	3.4	44	19	2.3	—	—	—
2009	95	24	4.0	74	17	4.4	24	6	4.0
2010	327	40	8.2	35	9	3.9	50	2	25.0
2011	526	27	19.5	92	3	30.7	103	7	14.7
2012	370	23	16.1	162	13	12.5	36	1	36.0
2013	225	19	11.8	65	16	4.1	33	2	16.5
2014	168	23	7.3	51	2	25.5	74	1	74.0
Total	1755	169	10.4	523	79	6.6	320	19	16.8

Source: Based on press articles 2008–2014.

*In 2008 no clashes involving the Navy's participation were identified in the press analyzed.

every person wounded, which was higher than the lethality index for the Army in 2012. In 2012 alone, the Federal Police reported 167 civilians shot and killed. However, in 2014, the figures showed a sharp decline in the index to 6.8 civilians killed for every civilian wounded, and then dropped again to 5.1 in 2015.

If we compare the last two years of the Calderón administration (2011–2012) with the available data from the first two years of the Peña Nieto government (2013–2014), we find that the lethality index rose significantly from 6.9 to 11.2. The difference is even more striking if we compare the Federal Police's average lethality index for the Peña Nieto administration (7.6) to the value for the Federal Police during the entire previous six years (4.1).

The calculation of the Federal Police's lethality index on the basis of press figures also shows low values until 2010 and a rise in 2011, when it shoots up to 30.7. It later shows sharp fluctuations: 12.5 in 2012, 4.1 in 2013, and 25.5 in 2014. It must be taken into account that few people are wounded in the clashes reported upon by the press, which means that small changes in the denominator from one year to the next cause significant variations in the value of the index. For that reason, we remain wary of the use of press data as the sole basis for calculating the use of lethal force by the different institutions.

NAVY

With regard to the Navy, as we have mentioned, the official information does not allow us to calculate the lethality index for several years since the column corresponding to "wounded civilians" was marked "not available" or "nonexistent" in 85 percent of the clashes reported. However, if we consider press information, the lethality index has always remained very high: 25 in 2010, 14.7 in 2011, 36 in 2012, 16.5 in 2013, and 74 in 2014. The official data are needed due to possible biases in the press figures; however, based on the latter, the Navy's lethality index reaches values that point to the urgent necessity to investigate possible cases of extrajudicial executions.

As one can see, there was a clear increase in the lethality index of the Army and the Federal Police during the years of Calderón's administration. In the first years of the Peña Nieto government (2013–2015), and in the context of a significant decrease in the number of clashes involving presumed members of organized-crime networks, the lethality of the federal security forces throughout the country shows (a) a possible downward trend for the Army, but the values are still very high in a context of greater opacity that makes it impossible to evaluate them accurately; (b) greater lethality on the part of the Federal Police; (c) values for the Navy that are always worrisomely high based on press data, and official information that is nonexistent in practical terms.

The Lethality Index in State Jurisdictions

Information from states that have had the greatest presence of federal forces reveals the persistence of focal points of concern under the Peña Nieto administration. From January 2013 to March 2014, the Army killed 540 civilians in clashes and wounded 67—which yields a lethality index of 8.1. In Table 1.4 we present the number of clashes, the number of killed and wounded, and the lethality index for some states where a significant number of deaths in clashes were registered during the same period.

The State of Tamaulipas had the highest number of people killed in clashes, with a lethality index of 5.9. This is not a "low" value for an indicator whose standard should be close to 1, nor does this mean that an undue or disproportionate use of force was not employed. The number seems low compared with that of other states where there were practically no civilians wounded during clashes.

The lethality index in the states of Guerrero (26.3) and Zacatecas (58) stand out. In the State of México, according to the Army's data, from January 2013 to April 5, 2014, there were seventeen clashes in which the institution participated. During those clashes, thirty civilians died while just one was wounded. Three months later the events of Tlatlaya, mentioned at the beginning of this chapter, took place. If the Army had continued to report its data, twenty-two deaths and no wounded would be added to these statistics.

In the case of the Federal Police, the number of dead and wounded in clashes was lower than that of the Army, but from 2013 to 2015 its lethality index was higher: 7.6 (281 dead and 37 wounded), a worrisome figure for

Table 1.4. Clashes, civilians killed and wounded, and the lethality index of the Army in select states, January 2013–April 5, 2014

State jurisdiction	Number of clashes	Opponents killed in clashes	Opponents wounded in clashes	Lethality index
Tamaulipas	309	190	32	5.9
Guerrero	67	79	3	26.3
Zacatecas	24	58	1	58.0
Veracruz	18	49	3	16.3
Coahuila	25	45	2	22.5
Estado de México	17	30	1	30.0

Source: Based on information from request 0000700211714.

Table 1.5. Civilians killed and wounded and the lethality index of the Federal Police in select state jurisdictions, January 2013–November 2014

State jurisdiction	Number of clashes	Civilians killed in clashes	Civilians wounded in clashes	Lethality index
Tamaulipas	88	55	7	7.9
Michoacán	42	32	4	8.0
Zacatecas	9	14	0	—
Guerrero	17	17	0	—

Source: Based on information from request 0413100088114.

a civil police force that did not have such a high lethality index previously. In Table 1.5 we select some states in the country and present the number of clashes, civilians killed, civilians wounded, and the lethality index of the Federal Police.

In the states of Tamaulipas and Michoacán, the largest number of civilians died in clashes with the Federal Police, and these states also had high lethality indexes (7.9 and 8.0, respectively). In Zacatecas and Guerrero, although these states had a lower number of civilians killed, the lethality index cannot be calculated because there were no civilians wounded in clashes.

Evaluating the Use of Force and the Importance of Transparency

As we have mentioned, there are no single values that allow analysts to determine if lethal force was used, or not, in a proportional and reasonable way in a given situation, or to evaluate a security corps' actions in general. For this reason, it is necessary that all the information required to evaluate the use of force in a more accurate way be made available. In this chapter, we use two indicators as a proxy: the number of civilians killed per police officer or other security-force member killed in clashes, and the number of civilians killed for every civilian wounded in clashes. To build these indicators, as mentioned, we solicited information from the various entities: the Army, the Navy, and the Federal Police.

The first response from SEDENA indicated that the ministry did not have information regarding civilian deaths and recommended we ask the Federal

Attorney General's Office (PGR). Therefore, we made an information request to the PGR (number 0001700326814), soliciting the same information. The PGR responded that it had zero records of clashes in 2006, 2007, 2008, or 2009. It reported one clash in 2010 and another in 2012 but none in 2011 or 2013. In 2014, the PGR reported three clashes with thirty-four civilians killed.[14] In other words, while in 2012 SEDENA reported 814 clashes and the Federal Police reported 142, the PGR recorded 1. In 2013, while SEDENA reported 482 clashes and the Federal Police 113, the PGR had no record of any clashes.

This is worrisome because it shows that civilian authorities either do not accurately report information or, worse, do not know of or investigate the results of clashes with alleged members of organized crime. This lack of investigation contributes to impunity when lethal force is used unlawfully as well as to the disposition to more readily use lethal force.

The characterization of clashes as "aggressions" to security forces seems to have resulted in the construction of a framework that legitimizes the use of public force, specifically lethal force, precluding the need for any investigation. This mind-set makes the evaluation of proportionality and legality impossible, as scholars have been noted in contexts such as Venezuela (Del Olmo 1990; Gabaldóon and Birkbeck 2002), Argentina (Chevigny 1995; CELS 2002), Brazil (Cano 1997, 2003, 2010), Guyana (Mars 2002), the United States (Skolnick and Fyfe 1993), and India (Belur 2010).

An appeal was filed to challenge the Army's claim that it did not have the information requested. In response, the Army provided information about "presumed aggressors dead and wounded as a consequence of aggressions against military personnel" from 2007 to April 5, 2014, indicating that since April 2014, the Army had stopped gathering such data because its task after a clash is only to preserve the scene, not to investigate.

One of the main concerns that arises from this study is the decision by the Mexican Army to stop gathering information about its actions during clashes. This decision violates the principle of transparency and the right to life.[15] As the Special Rapporteur on Extrajudicial Executions of the UN Human Rights Council has expressed, countries' lack of information on this matter "reflects a lack of accountability and thus a general violation of the right to life" (United Nations General Assembly 2014). And without any oversight, there will be greater incentives for members of the security corps to use force, including lethal force, in an illegal, disproportionate, and unnecessary way.[16]

Legal Framework in Mexico Regarding
the Use of Lethal Force by Security Forces

The use of lethal force by officials in charge of security, in the framework of a constitutional state, must be of an exceptional nature and must always be commensurate with due respect for human rights. This requirement has been established in two of the most relevant international documents on this matter—the *Code of Conduct for Law Enforcement Officials* (the Code)[17] and the *Basic Principles on the Use of Force and Firearms by Law Enforcement Officials* (the Principles).[18] Article 3 of the Code establishes that "law enforcement officials may use force only when strictly necessary." The Principles stress the principle of exceptionality in the use of force (Article 4), which states that officials "may use force and firearms only if other means remain ineffective." In reference to the protection of human rights, the Code indicates in its Article 2 that "in the performance of their duty, law enforcement officials shall respect and protect human dignity and maintain and uphold the human rights of all persons." The preamble to the Principles uses similar wording, establishing that "the use of force . . . should be commensurate with due respect for human rights." Additionally, Principle 8 establishes that "exceptional circumstances such as internal political instability or any other public emergency may not be invoked to justify any departure from these basic principles."

In this section we analyze the efforts that the Mexican government has made, mainly through the Army, in terms of issuing rules to regulate the use of lethal force. We center our attention on two recently created sets of rules addressing this matter. The first, issued by SEDENA, is the *Directive That Regulates the Legitimate Use of Force by Personnel from the Mexican Military and Air Force* (the Directive).[19] The second is the *Manual on the Use of Force to Be Applied to the Three Armed Forces* (the Manual).[20] It is useful to analyze some of the most important elements of both instruments to understand the legal framework in which the lethal use of force is being employed in the country.

The Directive, still valid today, was the first of the documents that was produced within Mexican domestic law. Article 6 states the four principles that guide Army personnel in the use of force: opportuneness, proportionality, rationality, and legality. In this same article, each of these principles is defined in a very general way, indicating that the use of force is opportune when it is used at the required time; proportional when force is used in the magnitude, intensity, and duration necessary to achieve control of the situation, in light of the level of resistance faced by the security forces; rational when the use of force is the product of a decision that assesses the objectives pursued, the circumstances, and the capacities both of the security forces and of the individuals to be controlled; and legal when the use of force is employed in adherence with rules and regulations and with respect for human rights. Although these definitions seek to embody the mandates established in the international Principles and Code, they are very general and ambiguous and, unfortunately, leave much room for discretion. Nevertheless, the Directive states that the use of force should always privilege dissuasive or persuasive strategies, and only when the lives or physical integrity of Army personnel or third parties is at risk may lethal force be used (Art. 9, point IV).

The *Manual on the Use of Force* was drafted with the explicit objective of fulfilling the Directive.[21] It is important to highlight that because its purpose is to make operational an obligatory Directive, this (obligatory) nature also extends to the Manual. Chapter 1, section 3 states that the use of force by members of the armed forces is appropriate only when it is strictly inevitable or indispensable. The Manual also reiterates that the use of force will be carried out in strict observance of human rights, regardless of the type of aggression faced by the forces. In defining the principles, the Manual is a little more specific than the Directive. With regard to the principle of opportuneness, the Manual establishes that "any kind of unnecessary action must be avoided when there is a clear danger or risk to the lives of people who are uninvolved in the incidents." Proportionality is defined as the relationship between the threat and the level of force used to neutralize it.[22] Progress has been made in the efforts to harmonize domestic regulations on the use of force with international rules, yet the challenge lies in their implementation. Without reports or information on clashes, the legality and rationality with which lethal force is used cannot be evaluated. Another evident challenge is the investigation of each of these events by the civil authorities, regardless of whether the dead and wounded were members of organized criminal groups. If force is used without subsequent oversight, the incentives are for a more tolerant and even disproportionate use of lethal force, as seems to have happened in Mexico since the 2006 onset of the war on drugs.

Conclusions

The indexes presented here highlight the ongoing concern about the excessive and disproportionate use of lethal force by Mexican federal forces. Although the total number of clashes and deaths in clashes has declined significantly since 2012, the relationship between civilians killed and members of security forces killed in clashes, as well as the lethality index, has remained high. These outcomes suggest possible institutional inertia in the excessive and disproportionate use of lethal force set in motion by the war on drugs.

The Army's inclusion in public-security tasks seems to bring with it the inevitable use of force, based on the logic of war, the goal of which is the elimination of an enemy. Recent events such as those in Tlatlaya, Apatzingán, and Ecuandureo/Tanhuato have grabbed the attention of news media and society due to their high death counts and the confirmation of—or doubts about—the excessive and illegitimate use of force by the federal security forces. Although these cases call for further investigation, our interest is to make more visible each and every one of the clashes in which force has been used with lethal outcomes. These events, when analyzed in an aggregated way, show a pattern of behavior on the part of the federal forces that is far below national and international standards, which demand that force be used respecting the principles of exceptionality, necessity, and proportionality. Although the lethality index—and other indicators we have taken into account—are not proof in and of themselves of the existence, or absence, of extrajudicial executions, when these indexes are systematically high, it indicates there may be a deliberate policy or normalized practice of the illegal and disproportionate use of lethal force.

There is a pressing need to design and implement mechanisms of effective oversight regarding the use of force that enable the evaluation of the legality of the actions of security forces. It is vital to have the best information possible, to investigate each instance of lethal force used by the state in depth, and to probe the related circumstances and characteristics. However, a growing opacity, especially on the part of the Army, goes in the opposite direction. Along with the absence of a legal framework that correctly regulates the use of force, that opacity puts both state agents and society as a whole in a position of uncertainty and risk. The scant controls that we have today create incentives favoring the excessive use of force. Information and mechanisms of control are key elements for safeguarding the rule of law, starting with the fundamental rights of all persons and, more specifically, with the right to life.

CHAPTER 2

Violence-Induced Internal Displacement in Mexico, the Inter-American Commission on Human Rights, and Official State Responses

Laura Rubio Díaz-Leal

Introduction

As described in the Introduction to this volume, the dramatic surge in insecurity and criminal violence in Mexico since 2007 has resulted in an unprecedented humanitarian crisis that accounts for a massive number of intentional homicides, disappearances, and cases of torture (see also CMDPDH 2015: 12; SESNSP 2014). Additional violations include 8,595 arbitrary detentions (Observatorio Ciudadano del Sistema de Justicia 2015: 40); 89 aggressions against human rights defenders (HRW 2014: 7); the assassinations of more than 80 journalists, and the disappearances of 17 journalists (Sánchez and De la Rosa 2015); and the finding of clandestine graveyards in at least 14 states of the country. Self-defense forces and volunteer police proliferated in 2013, as did the government's efforts to demobilize them. As stressed in different chapters of this volume, impunity and corruption reign, compounding fear among ordinary Mexicans, fomenting their frustration and mistrust of the government. This is the context in which forced displacement takes place (Rubio and Albuja 2014).

Direct victimization and fear of being victimized have prompted significant internal displacement, transnational mobility, and a significant increase in asylum applications in the United States and Canada in the past ten years (see Chapters 7 and 8). The evidence suggests that at least 311,000 people have been displaced by violence in 16 of the 32 states of Mexico (IDMC 2017: 115). Nevertheless, there has been very little research on the link between political and insecurity crises and forced displacement in Mexico (Rubio 2015). The Mexican government systematically denies that forced displacement exists, thus depriving internally displaced persons (IDPs) of the possibility of exercising their basic human rights and leaving thousands of families vulnerable, without any assistance or protection. It is argued that at present the incipient responses are inadequate, ad hoc in character, and limited in scope, and that at times they have even prompted new forced displacements or the revictimization of IDPs. As a result, civil society's advocacy efforts on behalf of the victims of forced displacement have focused both on articulating the needs and on pushing for a more adequate and integrated response within the country, and regional instruments such as the Inter-American Commission on Human Rights (IACHR) have had to press for emergency responses in specific cases of displaced persons or communities at risk.

This chapter draws upon quantitative and qualitative research and fieldwork conducted in seven states of the country from 2012 to 2015. My premise is that violence and the threat of violence lead to forced displacement, both internal and external, as a preemptive and/or reactive strategy of survival.

The first part of the chapter establishes the background of insecurity, criminal violence, and human rights violations in the country, which has led to forced displacement, and discusses the evidence of internal displacement. The second part focuses on the government's responses in the aftermath of an IACHR hearing that evaluated three main areas: (1) official recognition of the problem; (2) diagnosis and conceptual stalemate; and (3) humanitarian assistance and protection in specific cases. The concluding section of the chapter assesses such responses and offers policy recommendations.

Criminal Violence and Forced
Internal Displacement in Mexico

In Mexico, religious intolerance, communal disputes over land tenure, and control of natural resources were precursors of forced internal displacement in the 1970s and 1980s in states such as Nayarit, Hidalgo, Oaxaca, Guerrero, and Chiapas. In the 1990s, these problems combined with increasing insecurity and conflicts in which the Army and local police intervened, causing forced internal displacement; the resulting violence displaced Triqui families from Copala, Oaxaca (De Marinis 2011; Paris Pombo 2012). In 1994, the Zapatista uprising in Chiapas caused unprecedented massive internal displacement, leading more than twenty-five thousand people to flee violence (Arana and Del Riego 2012: 22–23). Although the Zapatista conflict ended officially with the San Andrés Accords in February 1996, violence and paramilitary activity continued well after the agreement was signed, including the Acteal massacre in December 1997, in which forty-five indigenous people died, including women and children. Twenty years later, IDPs from Chiapas are still living in a protracted displacement situation without any government support or assistance, and with no durable solutions in sight. Furthermore, in 2015 and 2016, religious intolerance continued to cause new waves of forced displacement in Chiapas (IDMC 2016, 2017).

According to the latest report by IACHR on Mexico's human rights situation after an *in loco* visit in September–October 2015, the country was experiencing its worst human rights crisis, due in great measure to political structural problems, which result in high rates of forced and involuntary disappearances, extrajudicial killings, homicides, torture, extortions, forced displacement, corruption, and impunity (OAS 2015). Other international actors such as Zeid Ra'ad Al Hussein, the UN High Commissioner for Human Rights, have voiced the same concern (UN 2015). This observed rise in criminal violence and human rights violations in Mexico has created new patterns of displacement.

The first flows of forced internal displacement related to criminal violence took place in the states of Chihuahua and Baja California as insecurity worsened in the period 1993–1998, particularly in the Valley of Juárez, Chihuahua. Here "femicides," drug-related crimes, and corruption among government officials became commonplace. Femicides are thought to be the result of "a combination of increasing male economic insecurity, growing drug gang activity, as well as high levels of impunity associated with the corruption of the municipal police, and connections between the state's political elite and the big drug-lords" (González 2002, cited in Rubio and Albuja 2014: 75–76). Displacement during these years was sporadic and seldom documented. At the turn of the century, and particularly from 2007 onward, gang and cartel rivalries were responsible for the bloodiest and most vicious crimes in Mexico. Gang violence terrorized *ejidatarios* (members of a land collective), peasants, farmers, cattle breeders, micro-, small, medium, and large businesspersons alike, and most of society in the Golden Triangle—the area of the Sierra Madre Occidental where the states of Sinaloa, Durango, and Chihuahua converge—in Tierra Caliente (Michoacán and Guerrero); in the northeast (Nuevo León, Tamaulipas, and Coahuila); and in the Gulf of Mexico (Veracruz). In these regions, federal authorities implemented joint military operations to bring down crime, deactivate the cartels, arrest kingpins, and confiscate drugs, arms, and other assets. The first of these operations was carried out in December 2006 in Michoacán as part of President Felipe Calderón's security strategy. The resulting fragmentation of the big cartels, the emergence of new and smaller criminal groups all over the country, and high levels of corruption and impunity created the conditions for forced displacement to increase (Rubio and Pérez 2016).

The human rights crisis that began during Calderón's tenure (2006–2012) has continued and worsened in Enrique Peña Nieto's administration (2012–2018). An environment of fear and insecurity, violence, corruption, and impunity is part of the context in which internal and transnational displacement takes place, as both a reactive and a preemptive strategy by victimized families to safeguard their lives or by terrorized families to avoid victimization. Reactive and preemptive strategies are thus considered legitimate causes of displacement, a fact that is often obscured and overlooked in analyses of internal mobility.

General assumptions about the underlying causes of both inward and outward migration revolve around economics: that is, a domestic circular northbound mobility from the southern provinces, which responds to natural economic (mainly agricultural) cycles; and a transnational, also northbound mobility, which responds to economic deprivation and marginalization. Studies of these different migration flows are plentiful; however, there has been very little research on the link between political and insecurity crises and forced displacement in Mexico (Rubio 2015). Hence, different actors have underestimated the role violence has been playing in forced displacement. From the perspective of humanitarian protection, indigenous communities, peasants, and inhabitants of low-income suburban areas are the most numerous victims of and the most vulnerable to forced displacement. They experience the most difficulties in finding refuge, resettling, and starting a new life elsewhere (Albuja and Rubio 2011). Fieldwork carried out between 2011 and 2016 in Sinaloa, Veracruz, Aguascalientes, Durango, the State of México, Mexico City, and Baja California reveals that well-to-do families who are victimized and are forced to flee their homes experience a loss of their livelihoods and, as a consequence, a significant deterioration of their lifestyles, leading them to poverty, and in some cases to extreme poverty.[1] This research contradicts official arguments that poverty and unemployment are still the main causes of forced displacement in Mexico (Rubio 2015).

Although there is still no national census of the displaced population, empirical evidence suggests that wherever there have been serious outbursts of violence, there has been a breakdown of the traditional social order followed by forced internal displacement (Rubio and Albuja 2014). Comparing homicide rates with population census data, we can establish a clear and direct relationship between violence and population movement. States and localities hit by intense violence in recent years have experienced markedly increased levels of out-migration (both internal and external). The four states losing the most population in the country—Guerrero, Sinaloa, Chihuahua, and Durango—are among the most violent states, but not the poorest. According to Gutiérrez and Rivera (2012), from 2005 to 2010 in the "104 municipalities with the highest levels of violence—i.e., those with proportions of homicides that account for 75 per cent of all homicides and other crimes in the 12 states—the rate of outmigration was 15 times higher than in municipalities without such high levels of violence. Controlling for the effects of other drivers of migration, including economic and demographic conditions and urbanization, the number of people leaving violent municipalities such as Ciudad Juárez, Acapulco, Chihuahua and Culiacán, was 4.5 times higher than those leaving non-violent municipalities" (cited in Rubio and Albuja 2014: 83). Approximately six of every thousand inhabitants from the municipalities with out-migration could have fled because of violence; but it could have been more since many people flee within the same state, and these population movements are not recorded in any survey (Rubio and Albuja 2014).

Different surveys by the National Institute of Statistics and Geography (INEGI) confirm the relationship between violence and forced displacement. The National Survey on Occupation and Employment tells us that at least one of every thousand inhabitants changed residence in 2010 because of insecurity (INEGI 2011). The National Survey on Victimization and Perception of Public Security indicates that from 2011 to 2014, between 1.3 and 1.5 percent of Mexican households had members who changed residence as a consequence of insecurity. With this survey we cannot know who fled, where they fled to, and if their relocation was permanent or temporary (INEGI 2013a, 2014a, 2015). Finally, the National Survey of Demographic Dynamics indicates that in 2014, 6.4 percent of the total of internal migration was caused by violence—that is 185,936 persons, of which 22.5 percent fled from the state of Veracruz and 9.2 percent from the State of México (INEGI 2014a).

As we can see, existing national statistics can give us indications only that forced internal displacement exists and can provide only some suggestion of its intensity and spatial characteristics. It should be clear, however, that none of these surveys is designed to diagnose or measure forced displacement as such, and that they shed only some light onto a reality that thousands of Mexicans are experiencing today. Hence, quantitative methods and disaggregated census data are required, not only to understand the direct causes of displacement but also to know the age and sex of this displaced population, the place of origin and destination of the displaced, and most important, the assistance and protection needs of IDPs.

Based on a systematic monitoring of forced internal displacement registered in the national and local press from 2011 to date, on fieldwork carried out in seven states from 2012 to 2016, on more than three hundred interviews, and on focalized studies on internal displacement in Chiapas, Ciudad Juárez, and Sinaloa, we can affirm that at least 311,000 people have been internally displaced in Mexico.[2] Since 2008 there have been at least 150 episodes of massive displacements (of more than ten families) in sixteen states: Baja California, Chiapas, Chihuahua, Coahuila, Durango, the State of México, Guerrero, Michoacán, Morelos, Nuevo León, Oaxaca, Sonora, Tamaulipas, Sinaloa, Veracruz, and Jalisco. These displacements were caused by cartel and gang rivalries, clashes between the police and the national security forces with these groups, high levels of crime affecting Mexicans all over the country, and religious intolerance against minorities (author's data).

The exodus of IDPs was particularly intense during Felipe Calderón's last three years (2010–2012). The relative decline in crime at the beginning of Enrique Peña Nieto's presidency seemed to be the harbinger of a decline in forced internal displacement and of the return of IDPs to their homes, but it was not to be. The conditions of insecurity and impunity that caused displacement continued in 2014–2016 in Durango, Chihuahua, Sonora, Guerrero, Veracruz, Michoacán, and Tamaulipas; in other parts of the country such as the State of México, Puebla, Veracruz, Sinaloa, Colima, and Guanajuato, they intensified.

Assessing the Vulnerabilities of the Displaced

In June 2014 and February 2015 I and the CMDPDH interviewed two hundred IDPs from six hundred Sinaloan families living now in Choix, Ahome, Salvador Alvarado, Guasave, Los Mochis, Mazatlán, and Culiacán, in the State of Sinaloa (following a preliminary census conducted by K. and E., two defenders of the rights of the Sinaloan internally displaced).[3] Our findings show that those most affected by displacement are women, children, and the elderly, and that the most vulnerable are IDPs living in poverty and extreme poverty in Choix, the northernmost municipality bordering Sonora and Chihuahua, where they even lack access to drinking water. Although we cannot make generalizations about these families, or about IDPs living in other parts of the country, there are a number of experiences that are common to most of the families we interviewed there and elsewhere: they are living in crammed houses with relatives, or sharing the rent of a house with two other families; invading abandoned or empty houses; or living in shanty homes without running water, electricity, and firm floors. IDPs with mortgages from government housing institutions such as the National Fund for Workers' Housing Institute (INFONAVIT) had stopped payments altogether. This has had three very negative consequences for IDPs: their houses have been vandalized or occupied by criminals; they are in the process of losing their rights to their homes; and if they try to find formal employment in their places of refuge, once they are registered at the Mexican Institute of Social Security (IMSS)—which is a required legal step—the employer discounts a significant sum of their debt every month, leaving them very little money to live on. None of the IDPs interviewed had been able to renegotiate their debt with INFONAVIT based on their extraordinary circumstances and vulnerability.

Furthermore, cramped living arrangements have resulted in sexual abuses against girls and young women. Most families have lost a relative, their homes, and other property to crime but seldom denounce it. It is common to have at least one family member with unattended health issues, and more than one with post-traumatic stress disorders, depression, and anxiety, including many children and older people. Young widowers with small children face extreme difficulties in making ends meet. In Sinaloa, Chiapas, Veracruz, and Oaxaca, male heads of families typically commute three or four hours to work as day laborers for a meager pay of 40 to 70 pesos a day (US$2.30–3.40). One of every four families has had trouble registering their children in school, and for two of every four families, displacement meant losing access to the social support they used to receive from government programs such as Prospera.[4] Of all the mayors of the municipalities hosting IDPs in Sinaloa, for instance, only one (that is, the mayor of Choix) has responded to the pleas of displaced families and provided some assistance.[5]

In some cases, the state governments, such as those of Sinaloa and Veracruz, promised to assist IDPs in returning safely to their homes with the support of the Army. However, IDPs claim that state authorities relegated their safety to municipal authorities, and as a result, federal security forces collaborating with the local criminal organizations had stopped IDPs from entering their communities (Radio Fórmula 2012; González 2014).

In this way, the governments in Sinaloa and other states where IDPs have organized themselves (for example, Chiapas, Oaxaca, and Guerrero) have denied the internally displaced the ability to exercise their basic human rights: their rights to freedom of movement and residence; personal security; judicial protection; property rights; access to food, health care, education, and means of livelihood; and the right to live a family life, among others.

IACHR, Internal Displacement in Mexico, and the Mexican Government's Responses

Since 2011, different civil society initiatives, mainly from scholars and local human rights organizations, have aimed at making the phenomenon of internal displacement and the plight of the internally displaced visible and have advocated on their behalf. These efforts have brought unwelcome pressure on the Mexican government to officially recognize the problem of displacement, diagnose it, legislate in favor of victims, and design and implement policies to protect and assist them. Results to date have been meager. One of the most important public manifestations of the Mexican government's lack of political will to acknowledge the problem was shown in the November 1, 2013, hearing (149 period of sessions) of IACHR. In the hearing, the petitioners presented the evidence of violence-induced internal displacement in Mexico from 2009 to 2013: 57 episodes of massive internal displacements mainly in 7 states, affecting 170,000 people.[6]

They also highlighted the need for official recognition of the phenomenon; a national diagnosis; legislation for the protection and assistance of IDPs; a national policy to prevent, protect, and assist victims of displacement; and the creation of a national registry of IDPs and of a specialized committee within the recently established National System for the Assistance of Victims of Crime. The Mexican government's responses to the petitioners at the hearing were evasive: it presented its legal and institutional advances in the protection of asylum seekers and refugees, as well as the National Program for the Social Prevention of Violence and Crime, none of which refer to internally displaced persons either directly or indirectly. In spite of IACHR commissioners' urging to address the issue, government representatives were unwilling to recognize that Mexico is experiencing a forced-displacement crisis.

The lack of will to accept the phenomenon contradicts the general spirit of Mexico's human rights foreign policy since 2000 and constitutes a serious rift between Mexican foreign and domestic policies. Mexico's diplomats have been champions of the rights of both refugees and the internally displaced in multilateral fora, particularly in the United Nations and in the Organization of American States (OAS) (Rubio and Bachi 2015). In the OAS, as late as May 2014, Mexico presented a project for the protection and assistance of internally displaced persons, which was integrated fully in a resolution at the OAS General Assembly (Permanent Council of the Organization of American States, Committee on Juridical and Political Affairs OAS 2014). That resolution summarized Mexico's recommendations for addressing the humanitarian consequences of forced internal displacement. Mexico's resolution emphasized the need (1) to develop policies and programs to respond to the needs of vulnerable IDPs, particularly when they have lost all access to protection and means of livelihood and are at risk; (2) to consider the benefits of incorporating within national legislations the Guiding Principles on Internal Displacement and apply them in the design and implementation of programs to protect IDPs; (3) to assist particularly vulnerable groups; (4) to adopt a human rights and gender-based perspective; (5) to implement preemptive measures to avoid forced displacement in the future; (6) to comply with one's international commitments as party-states to international human rights law; (7) to commit to protect IDPs before and during displacement, and to search for durable solutions to their displacement; (8) to take into account the differentiated needs of populations affected by displacement; (9) to strengthen the international exchange of good practices; (10) to promote national and international initiatives to collect data, diagnose, and disseminate quantitative and qualitative information on IDPs; and (11) to call on UN organizations, the inter-American system, and humanitarian agencies to support states that request assistance to deal with the causes of displacement and protect IDPs in all stages of displacement (Permanent Council of the Organization of American States, Committee on Juridical and Political Affairs OAS 2014).

Mexican diplomats have frequently taken a stand for global human rights and social, humanitarian, and environmental causes such as this. However, Mexico's actions have not always translated into a domestic policy consistent with its foreign-policy positions. Politicians and diplomats seem to have distanced themselves from the realities of Mexican society, particularly when it comes to the effects of violence, corruption, and impunity.

In the aftermath of the IACHR hearing, Mexican government officials expressed two concerns that reflected official thinking about victims of crime in general, and IDPs in particular: First, if the government acknowledged forced internal displacement as a victimization category, it would be "recognizing criminals," since "most IDPs are criminals fleeing persecution" (Fazio 2014; Animal Político 2012). The tendency to criminalize victims of crime was common during Felipe Calderón's tenure, and it still is in Peña Nieto's administration; by criminalizing victims, the government evades taking responsibility for them; escapes claims of reparation; avoids justice; and allows the perpetuation of the official thinking that unemployment and poverty are still the main causes of internal and external displacement (Rubio 2015; CNN 2015).

Second, the category of internal displacement contained in the UN Guiding Principles on Internal Displacement, presented in 1998 and accepted by most countries, including Mexico, presents serious problems for Mexican authorities who argue that the key drivers, including armed conflict and generalized violence, contained in the definition do not exist in Mexico. For the government, the label evokes imagery related to bloody conflicts nonexistent in Mexico.[7] The presence of human rights violations is a sufficient condition for the application to Mexico of the Guiding Principles' definition, established in introductory paragraph 2. Nonetheless, the government's primary misapprehension regarding the definition is related to the legitimacy of displacement as *both* preemptive *and* reactive strategies for survival; that is, the definition recognizes as an IDP any person fleeing the effects of violence (once they have been directly victimized) *and* any person who flees due to the fear of being victimized. Direct victimization is, according to Mexican authorities, a precondition for the recognition of victims of displacement, if at all. Accordingly, rather than building the required conceptual, political, legal, and institutional framework to give an appropriate response, the government has championed an ad hoc case-by-case approach to granting IDP status.

The pernicious consequences of the unwillingness to apply the internationally recognized legal definition do not end there. This interpretation causes confusion within the Federal Public Administration, damaging the possibility that IDPs may receive any assistance. For instance, in the 2013 General Law for Victims of Crime, IDPs are included among the victims who should be considered for reparation and assistance. However, internal displacement was not defined therein; and because it has not been well defined and no complementary law has been passed to fill this conceptual gap, it has resulted in delays in assistance as well as in registration in the National Registry of Victims of Crime (RENAVI). Since 2013, when the Executive Commission of Assistance to Victims (CEAV) was created, only two cases of internal displacement have been officially recognized and included in the registry. These cases have received meager psychosocial assistance with inexperienced psychologists, inadequate legal counsel, and insufficient support to cover travel expenses to go to Mexico City for proceedings related to their cases. Because there is no committee within CEAV to deal with forced internal displacement, there are no officials within the commission who have a sound knowledge of forced internal displacement, international norms, and the rights of the displaced, and thus no one to advocate on their behalf.[8]

Disagreements over the legality of assisting IDPs and the proper way to implement the UN Guiding Principles of Internal Displacement have caused serious rifts within CEAV. The commission (by majority 5 out of 7 votes) reached a decision on July 29, 2014, to consider forced internal displacement as an autonomous victimizing crime that needs to be addressed with a differentiated, specialized, and integrated approach (CEAV 2014). But it has not been generally categorized as a crime, leaving victims of forced displacement without the possibility of registering for and receiving assistance.[9] Although some other ministries have shown a willingness to assist IDPs, they have not been able to do so because their rules of operation state as a prerequisite that for persons to receive assistance they must be registered at RENAVI.[10]

Furthermore, according to the Victims' Law (Article 79), all states should develop their legal and institutional frameworks. But to date, the majority of states have not done so, among them Chiapas, Chihuahua, Sinaloa, and Guerrero, the states with the more numerous displacement flows. Some states argue that they do not have the financial capacity to respond to victims within their jurisdictions (CEAV 2016a). If local authorities do not respond to victims' requests for assistance within thirty days, it is the federal government's obligation to respond, but it seldom does.

The lack of official recognition has also had a negative impact on the political will to diagnose the phenomenon. At the IACHR hearing, the petitioners highlighted the need for a national quantitative and qualitative study of forced internal displacement. The General Secretary of the National Population Council (CONAPO) claimed the council was conducting a study on internal displacement and that it would soon be made public. At the time of writing (September 2017), no official national study has been published. Furthermore, in the aftermath of the IACHR hearing, in interviews with Mexican officials and in writing to INEGI, the petitioners and the NGO Mexican Commission for the Defense and Promotion of Human Rights (CMDPDH) requested IACHR and the Mexican government introduce questions in the 2015 midcensus survey and in the 2020 population census (which INEGI carries out) that would allow researchers to gather information on internal displacement. Precise questions are needed to identify and differentiate specific causes of migration and to trace places of origin and destination at the municipal level. This information is paramount to identifying the areas that have lost or gained population because of violence, as well as the age/gender composition of IDP communities, information particularly significant to design a national policy to protect and assist IDPs and prevent future displacements.[11]

In January 2015, INEGI responded to the written request, saying that the midcensus survey conducted in 2015 would not include the suggested questions. According to INEGI, a pilot survey carried out to gauge the need for such questions was not "satisfactory" (Cervera 2015). In the pilot survey applied in seven cities (San Miguel de Allende, Guanajuato; Zihuatanejo, Guerrero; Manzanillo, Colima; Nogales, Sonora; Hidalgotitlán, Veracruz; Zinacantán, Chiapas; and León, Guanajuato), INEGI asked if any members of the family had changed residence because of violence, natural disasters, or perceived threats due to religious preferences. The preliminary findings did not identify religious intolerance, violence, or natural disasters as drivers of displacement and continued to show economic causes as the most salient. As a result, INEGI decided that displacement is not a phenomenon that could be detected through a survey of homes, and it omitted the suggested questions in the midcensus survey (Cervera 2015). Analyzing the demographic and economic characteristics of the chosen cities for the pilot survey, as well as their criminal tendencies, we were not surprised that economic considerations for migration were paramount. The first three cities are touristic centers of great national and international affluence; and León is a manufacturing hub of relative importance to the country; they are safer, and the living costs are much higher than elsewhere. Although the relative security could be a pull factor for families fleeing violence from other municipalities, high living costs would make it impossible for vulnerable and impoverished displaced families to settle there.

It is surprising, however, that displacement caused by religious intolerance or remnants of violence from the Zapatista conflict was not detected in Zinacantán, Chiapas. Among the indigenous groups supporting the Zapatista army in the 1990s were Tzotziles from the area, who were displaced after repeated outbursts of violence and intimidation by the security forces and later by paramilitary and political groups. When efforts to return to the displaced communities were carried out in 2004 and later in 2009, the residents of Zinacantán achieved only partial success due to ongoing violence (Arana and Del Riego 2012). It also surprises us that no displacement was detected in Nogales, Sonora, which is both an expelling and receiving area of migrants (from El Fuerte, one of the most violent areas of Sinaloa, and other more violent municipalities in Sonora such as Cajeme). Similarly, fieldwork in Veracruz reveals that Hidalgotitlán figures among the localities where IDPs from Chihuahua have settled.

The choice of cities for the pilot survey does not reflect a review of existing census data (2010) related to the states and municipalities that lost and gained population in the previous five years, nor of existing crime rates and victimization information. Although INEGI did consultations with civil society, that is, academics and NGOs, before the implementation of the midcensus survey, forced-displacement specialists and human rights NGOs working with displaced families were not included, in spite of formal requests.[12] If a home survey cannot detect forced internal displacement flows, as INEGI argues, a nationwide study that combines sound quantitative and qualitative methods is of the utmost importance here since, as noted earlier, other surveys have revealed a direct relationship between violence and forced displacement and offer indications of the phenomenon affecting thousands of families around the country.

Legislative efforts in Congress to reform existing laws or to create a national law on forced internal displacement have stagnated since 1998, when the first initiative was presented. After the IACHR hearing in November 2013, discussions took place to reform the General Population Law to include a definition of forced internal displacement from the Guiding Principles on Internal Displacement, to designate a public institution as the focal institution with an adequate budget to deal with forced displacement, and to ensure a sound national policy to protect, assist, and prevent forced displacement. These proposed reforms did not prosper in the Senate. The most recent attempt to legislate in favor of IDPs took place in 2015 when attempts to reform Article 73 of the Mexican Constitution to grant the Senate faculties to legislate in favor of IDPs did not succeed. Finally, at the local level, only Chiapas (2012) and Guerrero (2014) have passed legislation on IDPs, which has not been implemented to date; and thus there are still no policies or programs to protect and assist IDPs in Chiapas and Guerrero, two states that have suffered among the highest flows of forced internal displacement.

Since forced displacement requires responses from various sectors, after a series of visits from UN human rights rapporteurs, a high-level Inter-ministerial Working Group on Internal Displacement was established in 2004 with the leadership of the Ministry of the Interior (SEGOB) to address the problem of forced internal displacement in Chiapas.[13] Representatives of ministries and offices concerned with education, housing, health care, social development, security, foreign affairs, agriculture, and the environment would allegedly participate. Its aims were to guarantee the physical protection of IDPs; to help them recover their means of livelihood; to find durable solutions to their displacement; to elaborate a legal framework for IDPs; to consult IDPs on official actions affecting their lives; and to develop a community development program for IDPs and a national program to document and register displaced persons. There is no evidence that this group ever met beyond a seminar on forced internal displacement in Tlaxcala, which took place the same year (IDMC 2012). In the current context, a high-level working group of this sort is needed to develop a coordinated response, and one that contemplates durable solutions for the full rehabilitation of the displaced communities in their places of origin or elsewhere. In 2015, after a series of requests from human rights organizations, under the auspices of the Human Rights Public Policy Department within SEGOB, this group was reinstated and has convened three times.[14] The attendance of low-level officials with very little decision-making capacity, the political distractions generated by the disappearance of the forty-three students in Ayotzinapa, Guerrero, and other political issues have made this group and the development of a joint and integrated response to IDPs a low priority for the government.

In August 2014, IACHR published its report *Human Rights of Migrants and Other Persons in the Context of Human Mobility in Mexico*, in which it acknowledged that in the present context of violence, Mexico is not only a country of origin, transit, and destination, as well as of mixed migration flows and the return of migrants, but also a country that experiences internal-displacement flows that are not recognized by Mexican authorities. The report established that the fact that there is no official information as to the extent of IDPs shows how invisible the problem is and concluded that IDPs can no longer be masked as economic migrants (OAS 2014).

A third important intervention of IACHR regarding IDPs took place in April 2015 when it ordered the Mexican government to adopt precautionary measures for two defenders of the human rights of internally displaced communities in Sinaloa, E. and K. (IACHR 2015b). Since 2008, the control of territory and drug distribution routes became the main source of rivalry between criminal organizations in Sinaloa. Violence reached its peak in 2010 when armed groups stormed into the Sierra, forcibly recruiting youngsters, imposing forced labor on families, terrorizing them with death threats, and so on (Durin 2013: 178; Valdez 2013). As a result, homicide rates escalated in Sinaloa to 78.91 homicides per 100,000 inhabitants, four times the national rate, with a total of 2,250 reported deaths in 2010 (SESNSP 2014), and Sinaloa experienced one of the major and more numerous flows of internal displacement in the country. According to a local human rights NGO, violence has displaced between twenty-five thousand and thirty thousand people, affecting eleven of the eighteen municipalities of the state (Valdez 2012). Most families from the Sierra and the *ejidos* find refuge in the main suburban or urban areas, where they try to get some kind of assistance from the local government.

During 2013 and 2014, IDPs organized themselves with the leadership of human rights defenders K. and E. (the former in Guasave, Los Mochis and Choix; and the latter in Guamuchil and Culiacán) and have consistently made demands to the municipal, state, and federal governments for support and assistance, to no avail. The intervention of K. and E. on behalf of IDPs has put their lives, and those of their families, at risk, particularly since February 2015 when criminals have made consistent threats against them and their families. In March 2015, four international and local NGOs sent a request for precautionary measures to IACHR, not only for K. and E., deemed to be in great danger, but also for 421 IDPs living in Choix where violence was mounting. Local authorities stopped assisting them after there was an attempted murder against the mayor on March 6, 2015; four members of the communities represented by K. had either disappeared or been killed, and they had no access to food and running water.[15] After a review of the evidence, IACHR imposed precautionary measures on Mexican authorities to protect K. and E.,

but not the Choix IDP community, on the grounds that there was not sufficient evidence that the community was at risk (IACHR 2015b).

On June 4, 2015, the Human Rights Under-Secretary of SEGOB announced
in a private meeting with the representatives of the IDP defenders and personnel of the Federal Attorney General's Office (PGR) and security forces that
in response to the IACHR decision, the Mexican government would immediately incorporate K. and E. into the Mechanism for the Protection of Human
Rights Defenders and Journalists. The mechanism would oversee the implementation of the precautionary measures available and accepted by the beneficiaries. Although this was an important step forward, the inclusion of K.
and E. in such a mechanism only recognized them as human rights defenders
at risk and not as victims of forced internal displacement. The immediate
effect of this decision was that the precautionary measures adopted were ad
hoc in character and short-term, intended only to avoid the immediate threat
and to safeguard their lives, but not to give them any access to other sustain-
able measures to cope with their uprootedness.

Furthermore, some of the actions taken actually increased their risk and
forced them to flee again. For instance, the precautionary measures included
accompaniment by police officers to return to Sinaloa; once reestablished
there, local and federal police made periodic rounds to ensure that they were
alright, and they were given a panic button to alert local and federal authorities of any danger. On various occasions, K. and E. perceived danger, but no
one responded to their alerts. Similarly, the police made their rounds at odd
times, scaring not only the defenders but their neighbors, raising suspicions
among them as to the intention of the police rounds and the connection of the
defenders with the police. After various similar incidents, the families started
to receive death threats, this time not from criminals but from their neighbors,
forcing them to flee. For a fourth time in less than eighteen months, K. was
internally displaced. Assistance from the government has included only temporary housing and a small stipend for food and transportation. K., as many
other IDPs, is a single mother of three, with a pending debt to a subsidized-
housing agency and no possibility of formal employment. K.'s children, stig-
matized by their situation, struggle to adjust to life in another state where they
know no one and to get an education in extremely adverse circumstances.

During a meeting of the Internal Displacement Working Group at
SEGOB (March 2015), CMDPDH used the case of K. to convey the need for
both emergency assistance and protective measures, as well as an integrated
long-term assistance program for IDPs. Not one of the recommendations

presented by CMDPDH has been analyzed or implemented by the government. Rather than building the required conceptual, political, legal, and institutional framework to give an appropriate response, the government has continued championing an ad hoc, case-by-case approach, with little long-term support. In early February 2016, CEAV notified K. and E. that as of February 14, 2016, they would be registered in RENAVI as victims of human rights violations, a decision that might allow them to be beneficiaries of some reparations. This decision formally ended their inclusion in the Mechanism for the Protection of Human Rights Defenders and Journalists, without any alternative assistance and protection measures in place. The prospects for proper reparation are still very grim in a political environment tainted by the unwillingness to recognize forced internal displacement.

Building Integrated Responses to Forced Displacement: Policy Recommendations and Final Considerations

Internally displaced populations are extremely vulnerable since they live in conditions of insecurity and have lost their patrimony and their livelihoods, employment, education, and family and social networks. Involuntary uprootedness, characterized by violence and significant material loss, have left thousands of IDPs all over the country terrorized, traumatized, and without any access to assistance and protection. Mexico's inescapable responsibility to protect such vulnerable groups is a constitutional mandate derived from two fundamental sources: its constitutional commitment to protect its population from external and internal threats (Articles 1–6, 24, 25, 27, 89 of the Constitution), and its international commitments as a party to international human rights instruments.

International organizations helping IDPs around the world focus on developing and implementing both short-term relief programs and durable solutions. These durable solutions include the restitution of the rights of the displaced and their full rehabilitation in their places of origin (if conditions are appropriate for a safe return), in their first place of refuge, or in a third location. Emergency and relief measures include assistance in all stages of displacement: at the place of origin once the conditions of violence explode, during displacement, and upon arriving at a refuge site (Long 2010). These measures should include the provision of their basic needs: physical protection, housing, food, and health care.

As for durable solutions, Mexico's set of recommendations for the attention, protection, and assistance of IDPs, presented in 2014 at the OAS's General Assembly, continue to serve as relevant measures of the state's responsibility (Permanent Council of the Organization of American States, Committee on Juridical and Political Affairs 2014):

- "To consider the benefits of incorporating within national legislation the Guiding Principles on Internal Displacement and apply them in the design and implementation of programs to protect IDPs." This action is long overdue in Mexico. A generally applicable legal framework would bridge the conceptual and legal stalemate that has paralyzed authorities in recent years.
- "To promote national and international initiatives to collect data, diagnose, and disseminate quantitative and qualitative information on IDPs." This represents the most important starting point for designing public policy on forced displacement and implementing programs according to the specific needs of vulnerable IDPs. Official recognition is the first step. Without it, no public funds will be invested in developing appropriate research methods to diagnose forced internal displacement and to profile the displaced population. Once official recognition takes place, internal organizations such as the Joint IDP Profiling Service could be called on to assist public agencies in developing the adequate techniques to collect data on IDPs. The resulting study should serve as the basis of all policies and programs. Once a legal definition of forced internal displacement and a diagnosis have been disseminated within the Federal Public Administration, a registry of IDPs should be created, or CEAV's RENAVI should include victims of forced internal displacement.
- The official recognition should be followed by a public "commitment to protect IDPs before and during displacement" (Permanent Council of the Organization of American States, Committee on Juridical and Political Affairs OEA 2014). This implies a public commitment to provide both emergency relief and long-term assistance, particularly the implementation of durable solutions. The durable solution preferred by most governments and international human rights organs is the return of displaced communities to their places of origin. In the Mexican context, this might not be possible to achieve in the foreseeable future, particularly in states such as Sinaloa, Veracruz, Guerrero, Tamaulipas,

México, and Michoacán, where violence is still rampant. Impunity, corruption, and persistent insecurity and violence will make it impossible for IDPs to feel safe to return. Testimonies of displaced persons reveal that in some cases when they have attempted to return, they were prevented from doing so by Army officials in collaboration with criminal groups. For those who were able to return, what they found was distressing: their houses had been burned, sacked, and vandalized or were occupied by criminals; whole towns were deserted; churches had been destroyed; and businesses had been looted.[16] Therefore, the implementation of durable solutions should include assistance to exercise their rights to dignified housing arrangements in secure environments; access to education for their children; employment opportunities for adult IDPs; health care, including access to counseling for post-traumatic stress disorders; legal counseling; and accompaniment. These actions might include a relocation or resettlement program that should include a community, rights-based, and differentiated approach so that the special needs of children, the elderly, and women are met. By following these recommendations, Mexico would be "complying with one's international commitments as party-states to international human rights law" (Permanent Council of the OAS, Committee on Juridical and Political Affairs 2014).

Housing institutions such as INFONAVIT should develop an extraordinary action plan to enable IDPs with mortgages to avoid judicial action against them. The aim should be to help IDPs not to lose their homes and, if conditions are not ripe for them to return, to assist them in transferring their mortgages elsewhere in the country.

If conditions for the safe return of IDPs are achieved, state authorities should lead a voluntary return program that includes the reconstruction and rehabilitation of homes, schools, medical clinics, and churches, as well as community development and productive, entrepreneurial projects that allow families to rebuild their means of livelihood and social networks. In all cases, IDPs should participate in the decision-making processes that will affect their lives.

Most countries struggling with forced internal displacement require assistance in the implementation of durable solutions. In order for international organs such as the UN High Commissioner for Refugees (UNHCR) or other humanitarian agencies to intervene, they need the state to officially recognize the problem and formally request assistance. Mexican authorities would benefit from working with these international organs as well as with other states that already have experience with forced internal displacement.

Mexico needs to "implement preemptive measures to avoid forced displacement in the future" (Permanent Council of the OAS, Committee on Juridical and Political Affairs 2014). These measures require an early-warning system to ensure adequate security for the most vulnerable populations or targeted groups. If displacement is unavoidable, local authorities should assist IDPs before and during their displacement.

The fact that IACHR has been involved and has made consistent calls to the Mexican government represents a unique opportunity for an official review of the existing circumstances causing forced internal displacement in Mexico, as well as for a reassessment of the government's responses. Without this review, civil society alone will not have be able to put the topic in the government's agenda.

CHAPTER 3

Women's Human Rights
in the Armed Conflict in Mexico

Organized Crime, Collective Action,
and State Responses

Sandra Hincapié

Introduction

Armed conflict caused by criminal organizations has exacerbated violence against women as well as increased the targeting of women and children for human trafficking and sex slavery. To address these violations, thousands of women in Mexico's various regions are adopting the discourse of human rights, both to mobilize collective action and to demand justice. Women are defending their own human rights: providing accompaniment and security for victims, promoting accountability by state and federal government actors, and creating networks to search for disappeared persons. Through collective action, women are exposing how the Mexican state, despite formally accepting international norms on violence against women, has not recognized the gravity of the violence.

This chapter analyzes the effects of Mexico's human rights crisis on women. The study builds upon extensive literature on gender violence in Mexico, which explains the objectification of women resulting in multiple and varied gender-based subjugations and humiliations (Cobo 2011; Álvarez and Pérez 2010; Castañeda, Ravelo, and Pérez 2013). The chapter will contribute to this literature by considering the situation of women in the specific context of armed conflict brought about by criminal violence in collusion with state authorities.

The chapter first presents international agreements regarding violence against women as a potential tool for collective action; second, it analyzes violence against women in the context of organized crime; third, it examines the collective action of mothers, wives, daughters, and direct victims, who are transforming the rhetoric of human rights into a tool for self-advocacy; fourth, it considers the state's responses.

Women, Armed Conflict, and Peacebuilding on the International Stage: Tools for Collective Action in Human Rights

Research on human rights spans diverse disciplines, such as law, political science, philosophy, international relations, and sociology, using diverse interpretative frames (Sen 2010; Vásquez and Estévez 2010; Stammers 2009; Risse, Ropp, and Sikkink 2013; Risse, Ropp, and Sikkink 1999; Simmons 2009; Landman 2006). Recognizing this diversity of perspectives, I understand human rights as a set of normative principles and ethical propositions that serve as a framework for state action. This normative framework is translated into mechanisms that generate expectations for, and the possibility of, the enforceability of national and international laws. Human rights are also a resource for the mobilization of collective social action (Hincapié 2015). These three defining aspects of human rights correspond with three distinct categories of advocacy, as presented in Table 3.1.

Based on this table, the Convention on the Elimination of All Forms of Discrimination Against Women (CEDAW) (1979) is both a normative goal and a mobilization resource for global civil society. A key precedent for the Americas was the Inter-American Convention on the Prevention, Punishment, and Eradication of Violence Against Women ("Convention Belém do Pará") (1994), adopted in Brazil by thirty-one of the thirty-four states of the Organization of American States (OAS). Ratified by Mexico in 1998, the Belém Convention recognized violence against women as both a crime and a violation of women's human rights, and it established measures to prevent, punish, and eradicate such violence within both the public and private spheres. Subsequently, Beijing's Fourth World Conference on Women (1995) agreed upon a platform and program of action for the prevention of all forms of violence against women and girls, concretizing specific demands raised collectively in defense of the human rights of women.

Table 3.1. Human rights: Defining aspects and corresponding advocacy categories

Defining aspects	Advocacy categories
Repertoires or discourses that defend a group of principles or ethical propositions (that are not immutable nor incontrovertible)	IDEAS
Concrete *mechanisms* that are legally binding in nature within states and international institutions	INSTITUTIONS
Mobilization resources to fulfill diverse objectives (empowerment, efficacy and compliance, the inclusion of other groups and/or new demands, transformation)	COLLECTIVE ACTION

Despite these normative precedents, the international community has only recently begun to call attention to how armed conflicts exacerbate women's experiences of exclusion and discrimination due in large part to the patriarchal social standards that structure women's lives. International attention to the situation of women in armed conflicts has come about only recently because of the collective efforts of civil society in response to the armed conflicts of the 1990s, especially in Rwanda and Bosnia (Hill, Aboitiz, and Poelhman-Doumbouya 2003; Nowrojee 2003; Amnesty International 2009b).

Preventing grave human rights violations against women in armed-conflict situations has become a subject of increasing concern for the United Nations. Resolution 1325 (2000) explicitly recognizes that armed conflicts affect women and girls in a unique manner, as these groups are particularly vulnerable. In addition, the resolution underlines the role of women in building and maintaining peace and urges states to take action to prevent and resolve conflicts, while promoting the active participation of women and gender-based perspectives in all security policies (Tryggestad 2009; Bell and O'Rourke 2010).

As we observe in Table 3.2, since the enactment of Resolution 1325 in 2000, the UN Security Council has developed a series of resolutions on women, peace, and security, elaborating on specific aspects of this primary resolution. The Security Council's resolutions 1820 (2008), 1888 (2009), 2106 (2010), and 2122 (2013) are dedicated to addressing sexual violence against women in armed conflicts, clarifying that when used as a tactic, violence against women constitutes a war crime. These resolutions strengthened the protections of women and girls from sexual violence in the contexts of armed conflicts. The resolutions called for implementing concrete measures for the

Table 3.2. International instruments on women, peacebuilding, and security

Year	Initiative
1974	Declaration on the Protection of Women and Children in Emergency and Armed Conflict
1979	Convention on the Elimination of All Forms of Discrimination Against Women
1982	Declaration 3763 of the UN General Assembly on the Participation of Women in Promoting International Peace and Cooperation
1985	Nairobi Forward-looking Strategies for the Advancement of Women
1990	Guidelines on the Protection of Refugee Women from the Office of the United Nations High Commissioner for Refugees
1993	Vienna Declaration and Programme of Action
1993	UN Declaration on the Elimination of Violence Against Women
1994	Inter-American Convention on the Prevention, Punishment and Eradication of Violence Against Women "Convention of Bélem do Pará"
1995	Beijing Declaration and Platform for Action, Fourth World Conference on Women
1999	Optional Protocol to the Convention on the Elimination of All Forms of Discrimination Against Women
2000	Windhoek Declaration: Namibia Action Plan for Mainstreaming a Gender Perspective in Multidimensional Peace Support Operations
2000	UN Convention Against Transnational Organized Crime
2000	Resolution 1325 of the United Nations Security Council on Women, Peace and Security
2000	European Parliament Resolution on Gender Aspects of Conflict Resolutions and Peacebuilding
2008	Resolution 1820 of the United Nations Security Council on Women, Peace and Security
2009	Resolution 1888 of the United Nations Security Council on Women, Peace and Security
2009	Resolution 1889 of the United Nations Security Council on Women, Peace and Security
2010	Resolution 1960 of the United Nations Security Council on Women, Peace and Security
2013	Resolution 2106 of the United Nations Security Council on Women, Peace and Security
2013	Resolution 2122 of the United Nations Security Council on Women, Peace and Security

protection of women and girls (1820); training military personnel (1888 and 1960); combating the impunity associated with crimes of sexual violence, and promoting the political, economic, and social empowerment of women in the interest of preventing sexual violence (2106); and demanding reports on Resolution 1325's implementation and the promotion of the active participation of women in conflict prevention, resolution, and eventual recovery (2122).

Critiques directed at specific aspects of Resolution 1325 include its legal weakness, which prevents it from operating effectively; the absence of preemptory mechanisms; and the fragmentation of its actions and lack of funding (Barrow 2009; Swaine 2009; Puerchguirbal 2010; Haeri and Puerchguirbal 2010). Despite these critiques, Resolution 1325 and its subsequent developments act together as a series of recommendations for the states regarding women, peace, and security and are key reference points for the guarantee of women's rights, especially in combating sexual violence in situations of armed conflict. These recommendations are as much legal in character—by guaranteeing access to justice and legal protection for women—as they are commitments to provide social assistance, promotion of women's human rights, and education on gender issues (Carter 2010; Bell and O'Rourke 2010).

In the case of Mexico, whose armed conflict is a result of the organized criminal activity in its territory, it is important also to take note of the UN Convention Against Transnational Organized Crime (2000), which Mexico ratified in 2003. Appendix II of this Convention contains the Protocol to Prevent, Suppress, and Punish Trafficking in Persons, Especially Women and Children, adding to the list of international efforts to prevent violence against women.

The challenges facing our societies require that international measures adopted to prevent violence against women by armed actors explicitly confront the irregular actions of criminal organizations and address the great danger that these actions represent to the enjoyment of women's rights and the related obligations of states. Nevertheless, as the Inter-American Commission on Human Rights (IACHR) noted in its *Report on Citizen Security and Human Rights* (2009), the American Convention on Human Rights (ACHR) is clear in establishing the state's responsibility to protect the fundamental rights of all persons under its jurisdiction and to prevent any type of infringement of these rights, whether such a violation be perpetrated by government forces, by third parties, or by individuals involved in criminal behavior. In this way, IACHR quotes the Inter-American Court on Human Rights (IACtHR), stating:

Said international responsibility may also be generated by acts of private individuals not attributable in principle to the State. The States Party to the Convention have *erga omnes* obligations to respect protective provisions and to ensure the effectiveness of the rights set forth therein under any circumstances and regarding all persons. The effect of these obligations of the State goes beyond the relationship between its agents and the persons under its jurisdiction, as it is also reflected in the positive obligation of the State to take such steps as may be necessary to ensure effective protection of human rights in relations amongst individuals. The State may be found responsible for acts by private individuals in cases in which, through actions or omissions by its agents when they are in the position of guarantors, the State does not fulfill these *erga omnes* obligations embodied in Articles 1(1) and 2 of the Convention. (IACHR 2009: 15)

In this same report, IACHR specifically underlined that, in agreement with the Convention Belém do Pará, states have the increased obligations to prevent, punish, and eradicate any type of violence against women.

Violence Against Women in the Context of Organized Crime in Mexico

Since the 1990s, the fields of political science and international relations have been researching wars and internal armed conflicts, calling into question the theoretical and legal bases of conventional wartime dynamics. The study of these "new wars" illuminates diverse aspects of violent conflicts by offering typologies drawn from the analysis of different conflict dimensions, including the motivations, objectives, microdynamics, and intensity of the given conflict that might differ from and question the classic definitions of civil wars (Van Creveld 1991; David 1997; Shaw 1999; Waldmann and Reinares 1999; Kaldor 2001; Kalyvas 2003, 2006; Fearon and Laitin 2003; Sambanis 2004; Eriksson and Wallensteen 2004; Collier and Hoeffler 2004; Dorff 2005; Hegre and Sambanis 2006).

Drawing from this research, I would characterize the current Mexican situation as an internal armed conflict, and some authors have even come to consider it a case of civil war (Waldmann 2012; Schelder 2016). Beyond the polemic about the appropriate category for the armed conflicts led by criminal organizations in Mexico, it is undeniable that during the last ten years those organizations have radically transformed themselves, through processes of fragmentation, competitiveness, organizational expansion, and diversification of activities, all of which have allowed them to possess greater territorial control, increasing levels of violence and diminishing public security (Beittel 2015; Guerrero 2011; Finklea et al. 2010).

This transformation of criminal organizations, as well as the diversification of their activities, has brought about unprecedented human degradation in their quest for financial profit (Grayson and Logan 2012). Women, in particular, have become a target and source of funding for criminal organizations by means of human trafficking, prostitution, child trafficking, pornography, and drug trafficking, among other activities. Similarly, the expansion of these organizations' territorial control and their collusion with state agents have contributed to the exacerbation of gender violence as a widespread social pattern, facilitating the perpetrators' impunity (ONU Mujeres 2012).

Thus far, the focus of debates on gender violence in Mexico has been on femicide, as the most lethal manifestation of violence against women (Lagarde 2011; Segato 2006; Sagot and Carcedo 2011). In Mexico's General Law on Women's Access to a Life Free of Violence, femicide is defined as "the most extreme form of gender violence against women, produced by the violation of their human rights in public and private spheres and formed by the set of misogynist actions that can lead to the impunity of society and the State and culminate in homicide and other forms of violent death of women" (Presidencia de la República 2007: 6).

As observed in Figure 3.1, drawing from the official data presented in the report *La violencia feminicida en México, aproximaciones y tendencias 1984–2014* (Feminicidal Violence in Mexico, Approximations and Tendencies), there has been a significant and constant increase in the murder of women in Mexico since 2007; between the year 2008 (1,087 homicides) and the year 2012 (2,761 homicides), there was a growth of 250 percent in the number of female homicides in Mexico.

The dramatic increase in the killing of women correlates with the escalation of armed conflict, especially when one takes into account the increase of those murders that occurred in public. As shown in Figure 3.2, historically, greater numbers of homicides against women were committed in the private sphere, such as in the home. Since 2007, there has been an increase

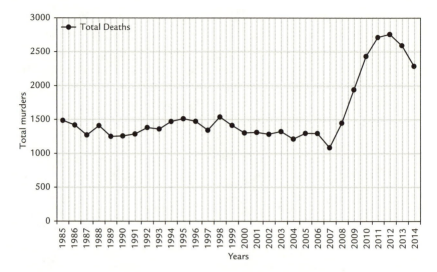

Figure 3.1. National rate of female deaths and presumed murder in Mexico (1985–2014). Source: Based on data from SEGOB, INMUJERES, UN Women, 2016.

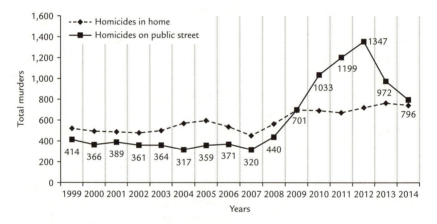

Figure 3.2. Total female deaths by murder and the crime scene in Mexico (1999–2014). Source: Based on data from SEGOB, INMUJERES, UN Women, 2016.

in homicides carried out in public places. Public violence against women became the prevailing trend as of 2009, though this did not translate into a decrease in private-sphere violence, arriving at its highest point in 2012. These figures correspond with the escalation of armed clashes involving organized crime and state security forces; the increase in public violence

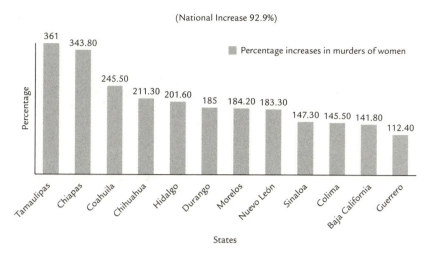

Figure 3.3. States with major percentage increases in murders of women (2007–2014). Source: Based on data from SEGOB, INMUJERES, UN Women, 2016.

against women has also been documented in diverse reports (Berber 2016; Escalante 2011).

This correlation is even clearer if we assess Figure 3.3. In the border states of Tamaulipas and Chiapas, female murder rates increased by more than 340 percent from 2007 to 2014. Almost all the border states saw the greatest increases in the country, including Coahuila, Chihuahua, Sinaloa, and Baja California, reflecting the active presence of organized crime. We also find substantial increases in interior states, such as Hidalgo and Morelos; for the same reason, in all these states, there is an active presence of organized crime.

Although the number of femicides alone demonstrates the gravity of the human rights situation of women in Mexico, I am interested in highlighting the connection between this increase in femicides and gender violence in the context of the expansion and consolidation of criminal organizations. Investigations of femicides in Ciudad Juárez, undertaken by Patricia Ravelo for the Center for the Investigation and Study of Social Anthropology (CIE-SAS), have identified a systematic pattern of wounds present on the bodies of murdered women and girls, which coincides with the patterns of cuts and mutilations often associated with "sadistic pornography." According to the investigator, the marks found on the bodies correspond to injuries associated with the torture and violent sex employed in the "transnational criminal industry" within which the organized-crime groups that operate in Mexico have inserted themselves (Excelsior 2015).

In accordance with this information, femicides are the last link in a chain of indignities that in many cases begins with kidnapping and forced disappearance, human trafficking, subjugation to torture, and sexual slavery, only to end with on-camera murders in which every detail of death is recorded. This is all part of the exploitative machinery in Mexico run by armed organizations, which relies on subjugating women and girls to gender violence.

Disappearance, Human Trafficking, Sexual Slavery: Women and Girls as Criminal Targets

Mexico is a country of origin, transit, and receipt for female victims of human trafficking, an industry that is approaching $150 billion globally every year according to U.S. Secretary of State John Kerry's cover letter to the annual *Trafficking in Persons Report 2016* (2016).

In the supplementary Protocol to the United Nations Convention Against Transnational Organized Crime, human trafficking is defined as follows:

> "Trafficking in persons" shall mean the recruitment, transportation, transfer, harbouring or receipt of persons, by means of the threat or use of force or other forms of coercion, of abduction, of fraud, of deception, of the abuse of power or of a position of vulnerability or of the giving or receiving of payments or benefits to achieve the consent of a person having control over another person, for the purpose of exploitation. Exploitation shall include, at a minimum, the exploitation of the prostitution of others or other forms of sexual exploitation, forced labour or services, slavery or practices similar to slavery, servitude or the removal of organs; (b) The consent of a victim of trafficking in persons to the intended exploitation set forth in subparagraph (a) of this article shall be irrelevant where any of the means set forth in subparagraph (a) have been used (art. 3).

With the spread of organized crime in Mexico and the diversification of its activities, human trafficking for the purposes of sexual exploitation has become one of organized crime's principal funding sources. In this context, women and girls are targets of criminal activities in every state of the country. In the last few years, particular attention has been directed to the situation of female migrants in transit to the United States who are frequently trafficked. This population largely includes migrants coming from Central and South America, although women from Eastern Europe, Asia, and Africa have also been identified as victims of trafficking in Mexico (U.S. Department of State 2016: 267).

The country's tourist areas, as well as cities on the northern border, have been specifically identified as final destinations for female victims of trafficking for the purposes of exploitation and sexual slavery (U.S. Department of State 2016: 267–270). In 2014, the Specialized Assistant Attorney General for the Investigation of Organized Crime (SEIDO), a department of the Federal Attorney General's Office (PGR), managed to ascertain how a network of small family-operated organizations dedicated to human trafficking in the State of Tlaxcala organized itself in conjunction with larger criminal organizations such as Los Zetas, Guerreros Unidos, and the Gulf Cartel, which control corridors used for different criminal purposes (Flores 2014).

Drawing from diverse sources and testimonies, Evangelina Hernández documented how in Tenancingo, municipality of Tlaxcala, human trafficking represents one of the most important sources of revenue for criminal organizations (2015). She identified changes in human trafficking dynamics, showing that it is now marked by coordination between (1) family clans, those traditionally dedicated to the recruitment and abduction of women for their sexual exploitation, and (2) larger criminal organizations. In this manner, female trafficking has undergone both an expansion and sophistication that overlaps with the drug trade and the movement of illegal migrants through the use of routes controlled by large criminal organizations (Gurney 2014).

This evolution of female trafficking's diverse objectives corresponds with the diversification of organized crime's economic activities in Mexico. These violations of women's human rights are interconnected—enforced disappearance is associated with human trafficking and sexual slavery, which itself includes sadistic pornography and often culminates in femicide—as activities that are lucrative for criminal organizations prevalent throughout Mexico's national territory.

Sexual Violence by State Security Forces

In the framework of the fight against organized crime, civil society and international organizations have denounced the Mexican state for employing torture as a systematic practice in obtaining detainee confessions (Open Society 2016; Human Rights Council 2014; IACHR 2015a). Women have not been exempt from these torture practices, many of which have even been made public through videos published on social-media sites (Martínez 2016; Flórez 2016).

In addition to torture, women arrested for suspected links to criminal organizations are being subjected to sexual violence by the police and by diverse members of the armed forces. After interviewing one hundred female prisoners in Mexican jails, all accused of belonging to criminal organizations, Amnesty International established sexual violence as a "standard practice" of state authorities, police, marines, and/or soldiers during arrest and inter-rogation in an attempt to obtain confessions from these women (Amnesty International 2016: 5).

According to Amnesty International's report, Mexico's security forces use a variety of forms of sexual violence against women accused of connections with organized crime, ranging from sexual harassment to groping, genital electric shocks, and multiple rape. According to the testimonies collected from these imprisoned women, 72 percent have suffered some form of sexual violence and 97 percent some form of physical violence, and 100 percent of those interviewed suffered psychological violence.

The illustrative testimony of one detainee, Mónica Esparza Castro, was documented by the National Human Rights Commission (CNDH) in its Rec-ommendation 15/2016 (CNDH 2016). According to Mónica, the policy officer said to her, "Welcome to the party" when she entered the cell and saw her brother and husband sitting naked with blood streaming down their bodies. The police officers grabbed Mónica and began to simulate drowning her by plunging her head into a bucket of water on repeated occasions. They then suffocated her with plastic bags, beat her buttocks with a wooden board, and dragged her along the floor by her hair. They continued to ask her questions that Mónica could not answer. Mónica witnessed her husband being beaten with metal-studded whips and the skin on his leg being peeled off with a knife.

> The municipal police applied electric shocks to Mónica's genitals and legs. Following this, a representative of the Torreón security depart-ment grabbed Mónica and started brusquely kissing her and biting her face and neck and then raped her in front of her husband and brother. Six police officers then raped her one after the other, then mastur-bated in her face and forced her to give them oral sex and swallow

the sperm. While Mónica was being brutally raped, uniformed Army officers looked on. (Amnesty International 2016: 21)

Despite the evidence submitted in the CNDH's recommendation, Mónica remains in prison, awaiting her sentence on charges of participation in organized crime, and none of those responsible for the sexual violence and torture committed against her has been prosecuted.

The previous information demonstrates that, in situations of armed conflict, and as a result of the spread of criminal organizations throughout the Mexican territory and the pursuit of state authorities, women are being subjected to a high degree of sexual violence by all warring parties.

Women in Movement: From Victims to Activists

Collective action by women to denounce gender violence in Mexico has been fundamental to bringing international visibility to the situation and pushing for improved state practices. The movement in Ciudad Juárez was a paradigmatic case of women's mobilization and collective action, serving as a direct precursor to the actual human rights crises.

In this northern-border city, women began to organize themselves locally in the mid-1990s to denounce the systematic murders of women in the absence of an effective response from the official authorities.[1] Starting in 2001, especially after the tragic incident of Cotton Field,[2] the women of Ciudad Juárez worked to garner international attention. The creation of transnational advocacy networks, and the reporting about Ciudad Juárez by various international organizations such as the Inter-American Commission on Human Rights (IACHR) (2003) and Amnesty International (2003), led to a gradual governmental acknowledgment of the situation (Anaya Muñoz 2011 and 2012; Martín Fernández and Villarreal 2008; Aikin 2011 and 2012). Despite this transnational collective action, human rights violations against women escalated, starting in 2007, because of the increase in organized criminal activities (Hincapié and López 2016). In this new setting, marked by massive violations of women's human rights, the collective action of women in the local and regional arena has been decisive. Mothers, wives, and victims themselves, ripped from their everyday lives by violent events, have carried out collective action, including denouncing violations and demanding justice for the victims. They have also created organizations, working to weave together key

networks for peacebuilding and women's empowerment, transitioning personally from victims to human rights activists.

Table 3.3 offers relevant examples of the collective action of women in
Mexican cities and states as a response to the human rights crises. Without
exception, these initiatives emerged as a response by ordinary women to
violent events. Despite her lack of experience as an activist, when a woman
exposed her pain and desperation, she could find dozens of others who recognized themselves in her pain. They also found in the rhetoric of human
rights a way to translate a private emotion into a public act.

Alma Trinidad Camacho's son, a sixteen-year-old high school student,
was killed in a 2008 massacre in Culiacán, Sinaloa, when an armed com-
mando indiscriminately fired a gun in front of an auto shop where he had
brought his car to be repaired. Trinidad Camacho demanded justice for
her son's case. She made signs and organized sit-ins and marches. She met
with other mothers in the same situation, and together, they created the
organization Voces Unidas por la Vida (Voices United for Life). She said, "I
wanted to head to the street to protest, to tell our authorities that it wasn't
working and everyone turned a deaf ear. . . . With all of this, I became aware
of the country in which we live. I did not want to continue, I was afraid, you
know how things are handled in Sinaloa when you interfere with interests,
the authorities do not protect you" (Manjarrés 2013). Despite threats, the
women's collective actions did not stop in Culiacán—one of the cradles of
Mexican drug trafficking, characterized by some as a "narco-dictatorship"
(Tercero 2010: 56). They continued their marches, complaints, and documentation of cases, exposing their grievances not only in Culiacán but also
in the nation's capital (Carrasco 2010). Since its foundation, Voces Unidas
por la Vida's members have worked with state authorities to investigate and
search for disappeared persons, collecting information on the cases and
even carrying out excavations in places pointed out by some anonymous
informants (Zavaleta 2017).

In Tijuana, also in 2008, Cristina Palacios—the mother of Alejandro
Hodoyán, who disappeared at the hands of the Army—created the Asociación Ciudadana Contra la Impunidad (Citizen's Association Against Impunity), mobilizing dozens of mothers and family members of the victims of
criminal violence in the municipalities of Tijuana, Rosarito, Ensenada, and
Mexicali. Subsequently, the Asociación Unidos por los Desaparecidos de Baja
California (Association United for the Disappeared of Baja California Association) also emerged (Robledo 2015; Villareal 2014).

Table 3.3. Relevant local initiatives of female collective action facing a context of violence

Year	Name	City	Founders
2001	Nuestras Hijas de Regreso a Casa, A. C. (Our Daughters Coming Home)	Ciudad Juárez	Marisela Ortiz and Norma Andrade
2002	Justicia para Nuestras Hijas, A. C. (Jusice for our Daughters)	Chihuahua	Norma Ledezma
2008	Voces Unidas por la Vida (Voices United for Life)	Culiacán	Alma Trinidad Camacho
2008	Asociación Ciudadana contra la Impunidad (Citizen's Association Against Impunity)	Tijuana	Cristina Palacios Roji
2011	Amores DNL. Agrupación de Mujeres Organizadas por los Ejecutados, Secuestrados y Desaparecidos de Nuevo León ("Amores"—Group of Women for Those Executed, Kidnapped and Disappeared, Nuevo León)	Nuevo León	
2011	Buscamos a Nuestras Hijas (Searching for Our Daughters)	Xalapa	Bárbara Ibarra
2011	Comité de Madres y Familiares con Hijas Desaparecidas en Ciudad Juárez (Committee of Mothers and Families with Disappeared Daughters in Ciudad Juárez)	Ciudad Juárez	Olga Esparza and Norma Laguna
2013	Colectivo de Familiares de Desaparecidos Orizaba-Córdoba (Collective of Families of the Disappeared Orizaba-Córdoba)	Orizaba-Córdoba	Aracely Salcedo
2013	Familias Unidas en la Búsqueda y Localización de Personas Desaparecidas, Piedras Negras–Coahuila (Families United in the Search and Tracking of Disappeared Persons, Piedras Negras–Coahuila)	Piedras Negras–Coahuila	María Hortencia Rivas and Yolanda Vargas González
2014	Colectivo Solecito (Solecito Collective)	Veracruz	Lucía Díaz Genao

On the other side of the country, in Xalapa, Veracruz, in June 2011, Bár-bara Ibarra's daughter was disappeared, and her body was found by accident three months later. During her search, Ibarra convened marches and sit-ins, including a June 20, 2011, march involving almost two hundred people, many of whom were mothers of other disappeared individuals. In the days follow-ing the march, Redes Universitarias Xalapeñas (Xalapeñas University Net-work) joined the demonstrations, demanding a statement by the authorities (Villareal 2014: 15–16).

The year 2011 marked a turning point in Veracruz as continuous shoot-ings, disappearances, and massacres evidenced the spread of organized crime. In September 2011, for instance, thirty-five murder victims were found aban-doned in two trucks in Boca del Río. The disappearance of females was made more visible thanks to the collective action of mobilized mothers. In the search for her daughter, Bárbara Ibarra initiated a mobilization effort that gave rise to the association Busquemos a Nuestras Hijas (Searching for Our Daugh-ters), a leader in filing complaints on femicides and the disappearances of females in Veracruz. Through the collective action of these organized moth-ers, state institutions are pressured to end impunity for the outrages against women. "In Veracuz [sic] women are killed with cruelty; they die after this humiliation. They kill them with a clean shot. They hang their cadavers on trees. The government only sees the frosting on the shit. Always, when inves-tigating, the government focuses its attention on the victim, in all that they did wrong to justify these deaths. Then comes the impunity" (León 2016).

In the municipality of Orizaba, Veracruz, Fernanda Rubi Salcedo Jiménez disappeared on September 7, 2012. Her mother, Aracely Salcedo, launched a search, and in the process of this search, other mothers of disappeared girls united, giving rise to the Colectivo de Familias de Desaparecidos Orizaba-Córdoba (Collective of Families of Disappeared Persons Orizaba-Córdoba) in 2013. From then on, the collective has documented cases, carried out investigations, and organized independent searches, marches, sit-ins, and public complaints, and members have accompanied other relatives through-out all these activities. In this journey, the members of the collective have suffered all types of harassment and threats; Aracely Salcedo, who has led the complaints procedure and has received injunctive relief, affirms this fact: "Since I began searching for my daughter, the threats and harassments by telephone or via private Facebook messages have continued. Truthfully, we now do not know from where they are attacking us, if it is from the side of the Government or that of the criminal organizations. . . . At least 25 times they have stopped me on the highway, but I am not a criminal, I am only looking for my disappeared child" (Sinembargo 2016).

In the face of government inaction and the collusion of government officials with criminal organizations, these organized women have pursued on their own account the work of searching for and identifying bodies. In August 2016, after the training they received from the National Search Brigade for Disappeared People, twelve female members of the Colectivo de Familias de Desaparecidos Orizaba-Córdoba found charred skeletal remains in a community building in Moyoapan, Veracruz, thanks to anonymous reports about the clandestine grave. Search parties discovered at least fifteen graves in 2016 (León 2016b; Mejía 2016).

In August 2016, Colectivo Solecito (Solecito Collective), an association of mothers and sisters of disappeared persons, found seventy-five clandestine graves in Veracruz on a tip by anonymous informants (Ureste 2016). The Colectivo Solecito, led by Lucia de los Angeles Diaz Ganeo, supports the search for disappeared persons; it documents cases, and together with state authorities, it is carrying out a campaign for the free collection of DNA samples from relatives for identification purposes.

In another area of the country, María Hortencia Rivas Rodríguez, receiving no help from state authorities, searched for her son Victor Manuel Guajardo Rivas, who disappeared in July 2013, allegedly at the hands of the Special Weapons and Tactics Team (GATE), an elite police group in the state of Coahuila. Her incessant search led her to meet hundreds of other mothers of the disappeared. In 2013, after years of public demonstrations, the women in Coahuila organized Familias Unidas en la Búsqueda y Localización de Personas Desaparecidas (Families United in the Search for Disappeared Persons). The organization, headed by María Hortencia Rivas and Yolanda Vargas González, provides legal advice and psychological support. It maintains an immediate-response system through which it has freed more than seventy persons using early alerts and mobilization efforts (Tavera 2015: 115–117).

In Ciudad Juárez, Chihuahua, the city where the collective action to denounce femicides in Mexico began, a new surge in collective action arose in response to the intensification of organized crime and armed conflict. A particularly key event was the 2010 assassination of Marisela Escobedo in the Government Plaza in Chihuahua, where she had traveled to demand justice for the femicide of her daughter in Ciudad Juárez in 2008. The growing number of disappearances of women and girls in the city led to the formation of the Comité de Madres y Familiares con Hijas Desaparecidas (Committee of

Mothers and Relatives with Disappeared Daughters) in March 2011. These collectives have been the driving force behind rallies such as the 2013 "Caminata por la Justica" ("Walk for Justice") that toured the region to denounce impunity, to demand the identification of human remains, and to assist victims (Barrios 2013; Coria 2013).

A similar women's organization was established in 2013 in Nuevo León, the Agrupación de Mujeres Organizadas por los Ejecutados Secuestrados y Desaparecidos de Nuevo León—AMORES DNL (Group of Women Organized for Those Executed, Kidnapped, and Disappeared in Nuevo León). A predecessor, Lucha por Amor, Verdad y Justicia (LUPA: Fight for Love, Truth, and Justice), had been created in 2001, and it split into two groups: Fuerzas Unidas por Nuestros Desaparecidos in Nuevo León and AMORES DNL. This group and other NGOs in the state have created a search model that works hand in hand with the state authorities and have successfully influenced the classification of the crime of forced disappearances in the state penal code so that it meets international standards (Cervantes 2015; Villareal 2014).

All of these local initiatives led by women add to the multiple networks and collectives that exist, such as the Red de madres buscando a sus hijos (Network of Mothers Searching for Their Children) and many others, which every year since 2012 have celebrated the March of National Dignity: mothers looking for their children and seeking truth and justice. Each May, women march through Mexico's main cities, demanding justice. In May 2016, the fifth March of National Dignity included hundreds of Mexican women gathered in the capital, accompanied by mothers from Guatemala, El Salvador, and Honduras, while simultaneous marches proceeded in Veracruz, Morelos in Michoacán, Guerrero, and Guanajuato (Olvera 2016).

The most important factor to emphasize is that the women who have been direct and indirect victims of grave human rights violations within the armed-conflict situation affecting the country, have risen above their own pain to empathize with other families similarly affected. Faced with these deeply painful events and the impunity and inaction of state authorities, women have identified the rhetoric of human rights as a framework and mobilization resource for collective action.

As a result, the collectives of relatives created in response to Mexico's human rights crises, composed in large part by women, have become the motivating forces for the denunciation and documentation of cases, the construction of support networks,[3] and the demand for justice and accountability.

The Institutional Response to Collective Action:
Measures and Efficacy

The collective action of the women in Ciudad Juárez between 1995 and 2005 transformed that situation, in particular, into a paradigmatic one around which organizations both inside and outside of the country mobilized to denounce femicide violence.

The state response to the collective action by women in Ciudad Juárez led to diverse measures. In 2003, the government created the National Institute for Women (INMUJERES). In 2004, it established the Federal Commission for the Prevention and Eradication of Violence Against Women in Ciudad Juárez as part of the Ministry of the Interior (SEGOB), operating until 2007. Also in 2004, the government named a Special Prosecutor for Investigating Offenses Related to the Homicides of Women in the Municipality of Ciudad Juárez. But of all of the institutional responses, the most important result of the collective action was the 2007 adoption of the General Law on Women's Access to a Life Free of Violence and the reform of the Federal Code of Criminal Procedure to include the crime of femicide.

Despite these legal gains, in a landscape of intensifying sexual violence against women due to the expansion of organized crime, there are no reliable official data about violence against women. This lack of data is in part due to the state's institutional and governmental resistance to effectively implement the General Law on Women's Access to a Life Free of Violence. As Anaya-Muñoz and Saltalmacchia emphasize in Chapter 10 with respect to human rights, these legal and institutional reactions have not diminished the femicides and violence toward women.

The 2016 *Quantitative Diagnostic of Sexual Violence Care in Mexico,* written by the Committee on Sexual Violence of the Executive Commission for Victims' Assistance, demonstrated that the state does not keep reliable data on sexual violence (a finding that correlates with other findings in this book, including extrajudicial executions [Chapter 1], disappearances, and torture):

> All of this brings to light, once again, at least two serious deficiencies as relating to information: the resistance or inability of some agencies to send information to the CEAV and/or problems for the capture and systematization of information about the people assisted. Overcoming these two major obstacles is imperative to achieving a registry and systematization of information on the victims of sexual violence that

in turn would allow the establishment with certainty, of the volume and characteristics of people who are assisted. (CEAV 2016: 408–409)

In this same way, the investigation of the efficacy of the fight against human trafficking in Mexico, implemented by the Security, Justice, and Legality National Citizen Observatory in 2014, noted unequivocally,

> Without any doubt, we can affirm based on the information available that México has a serious problem not only in fighting, preventing and eradicating human trafficking, but also in generating the necessary statistics for a reliable assessment. . . . This landscape is extremely troubling for human trafficking which, only behind drug and arms trafficking, is the most lucrative enterprise of organized crime. And we only are partially aware of the intricate reality surrounding its prevalence and impact in our country. (Rivas 2014: 83)

The lack of reliable statistics and effective actions to combat human trafficking on the part of state authorities has already been noted by the *Diagnostic on the Situation of Human Trafficking in Mexico,* produced by CNDH (2013), and reaffirmed in the *Quantitative Diagnostic of Sexual Violence Care in Mexico,* developed by the Sexual Violence Committee of the Executive Commission of Assistance to Victims (CEAV) (CEAV 2016). All of the reports and diagnostics explain that official statistics that would quantify the size of the problem are absent because human trafficking in Mexico is a clandestine activity, invisible, in many cases socially accepted, and only recently categorized as a crime, and thus its prosecution, similar to its statistical recording, is practically nonexistent (UNODC 2014: 61–62).[4]

Even without verifiable information, the increase in trafficking of women is highlighted in the federal government's reports. The Inter-Ministerial Commission[5] in its 2013 Annual Report indicated that human trafficking "had increased exponentially" in the country "as a result of organized crime" (SEGOB 2014: aa). In the same way, the National Program for the Prevention, Sanction, and Eradication of Crimes, on the topic "Human Trafficking for Victim's Protection and Care 2014–2018," highlights in its diagnostic of human trafficking that

> organized crime and the past models for combating crime increased the levels of violence and multiplied the forms in which crime has extended its effects on the most vulnerable strata of the population.

The crime modalities have constantly grown and changed, resulting in an expansion in their areas of operation and in the diversification of criminal activities, positioning human trafficking in the
top spots for negative social impact and for the illegal earnings that it
generates, transforming it, thus, into a serious threat for the majority
of the population. (SEGOB 2016)

While the analyses carried out by Mexico's own state authorities clearly note
the seriousness of the women's human rights situation, the authorities continue to balk at issuing emergency measures to protect females in the national
territory. One of the few provisions and measures taken has been the Gender
Alert System, which could be an important tool for intervening in serious situations of violence against women. This system is designed to allow the intervention of federal authorities when state governments do not act in grave
situations of violence against women.

But the Gender Alert System has been difficult to implement. Since
2008, civil society organizations have presented declaratory requests for the
Gender Alert System in seventeen states, based on the substantial increase
in femicides. Until 2013, no Alert had been approved. Because of this lack
of response, the National Citizen Observatory for Femicide requested the
reform of the General Law on Women's Access, given its ineffectiveness and
the procedural difficulties to accessing its benefits.

The fact that not a single Gender Violence Alert was declared between
2008 and 2013, despite the substantial increase in femicides, demonstrates
the federal government's failure to guarantee women and girls the right to
life and integrity within the violent situation created by organized criminal
activity.

Thanks to the mobilization of civil society organizations, the General Law
regulations regarding the Gender Violence Alert were reformed in 2013. The
revised law requires the development of special reports, including indicators
that measure violence against women, as well as the allocation of necessary
budgetary resources. Finally, the law includes a public notice requirement.
The revised law does not allow civil society to call for Gender Violence Alerts;
it is a complex process explained in the law, causing unnecessary delays, such
as in Guanajuato where the alert was requested three times between 2013 and
2015 (Zamora 2015). Still, thanks to the persistent actions of family collectives, the Alert was declared for the first time in July 2015 in eleven municipalities of the State of México (Ixtapaluca, Nezahualcóyotl, Valle de Chalco,

Toluca, Tlalnepantla, Naucalpan, Tultitlán, Chimalhuacán, Chalco, Cuauti-
tlán Izcalli, and Ecatepec), followed two weeks later in eight municipalities in
the State of Morelos (Cuautla, Cuernavaca, Emiliano Zapata, Jiutepec, Puente
de Ixtla, Temixco, Xochitepec, and Yautepec) (Rosagel 2016).

In both states, the Alert's enactment was possible only after lengthy procedures. The Mexican Commission for the Defense and Promotion of Human
Rights (CMDPDH), an important national NGO, had to lodge various complaints starting in 2010, which exposed the negligence of state authorities
toward violence against women in the State of México (Martínez 2016). In
October 2015, the Second Administrative Judge for the State of México, Paula
María García Villegas, ordered the state government to apologize for the femicides and repair the damage caused by the Gender Violence Alert's unjusti-
fiable delay. Additionally, on June 27, 2016, the Gender Violence Alert was
activated for fourteen municipalities of the State of Michoacán: Apatzingán,
Hidalgo, Huetamo, La Piedad, Lázaro Cárdenas, Los Reyes, Maravatío, Morelia, Pátzcuaro, Sahuayo, Tacámbaro, Uruapan, Zamora, and Zitácuaro.

Results from the Gender Violence Alerts are discouraging. In Morelos,
for instance, an NGO that closely monitors the Alert's implementation noted
that one year after its implementation there, cases of femicide have not been
resolved, nor have the aggressors been punished. Once again, the Mexican
government has fallen short of its obligation to protect the human rights of
women.

Various requests to enact the Gender Violence Alert in states such as
Sinaloa and Guanajuato have been denied. According to the academic and
feminist ex-legislator Marcela Lagarde, the authorities "hinder the Gender
Violence Alert, as if it were an assault on their governments" (Villela 2016).

Conclusions

In this chapter, I have analyzed the human rights situation of women in Mexico in the context of the armed conflict caused by the activity of both criminal organizations and security forces throughout the national territory. I
have demonstrated the need to advance the characterization of grave human
rights violations directed toward women within the structural framework of
armed conflict.

In the context of armed conflict, the patterns of gender violence in society have worsened. Further, women in Mexico are becoming the targets of

direct violence by criminal organizations, being kidnapped and utilized as a funding source via human trafficking and sexual slavery, among other forms of violence. The invisibility of this phenomenon in its entirety—from the escalation of crimes to the lack of state response—impedes its prevention, documentation, transformation, and resolution. Instead, it favors impunity. The state is not meeting its international obligations to prevent gender-based violence, nor to protect women and girls who face such violence in armed conflicts, nor to encourage the participation of women in the processes of conflict resolution and peacebuilding.

Despite this, women in Mexico are leading sustained collective efforts to make visible the various expressions of gender violence and the general human rights crisis. Women around the country are spearheading collective action campaigns that are adopting human rights as mobilization resources, expanding rights rhetoric in broad social collectives, creating support and advocacy networks, condemning the violence of criminal organizations and their collusion with state authorities, as well as looking to dialogue with governments to design public policies that guarantee respect for human rights.

CHAPTER 4

The Invisible Violence Against Women in Mexico

Regina Tamés

Introduction

Mexico is immersed in a crisis of human rights violations related to murders, trafficking, torture, disappearances, femicide, censorship, and corruption, causing challenges that prevent advances in the country. However, in addition to the more publicly recognized issues mentioned above, there is a silent and invisible wave of ongoing human rights violations perpetrated specifically against women. The violation of women's right to health, particularly reproductive health, coupled with the government's lack of recognition or response to the same, constitutes a serious violation of women's human rights across the country. Women are over half of the Mexican population, and a large percentage face violations of their right to health, related to reproduction, every day. Violence and discrimination against women related to reproduction is not a minor occurrence in Mexico, although many see it as such. This violence and discrimination is exacerbated by the impunity and corruption within the Mexican state.

According to official data, in 2015, there were almost 62 million Mexican women, 32.2 million of whom were of reproductive age (51.9 percent). The Mexican state, therefore, has a big task in ensuring that all women can exercise their reproductive rights without violence or coercion. The women and girls most affected by these human rights violations are those in a situation of vulnerability because they either are minors, belong to an indigenous group, or have limited economic resources.

Violations of women's right to health include discrimination in accessing services, outright denial of maternal health services, and the provision of substandard health care due to structural problems within the health sector, including insufficient infrastructure and capacity to provide adequate prenatal and delivery care and attend to obstetric emergencies in federal and state public hospitals and clinics. As a consequence, many women suffer violence during pregnancy or labor or even die during or after childbirth. Another example is rampant sexual violence, and often the resulting unwanted pregnancies, faced by girls and women. The vast majority of survivors of sexual violence who request legal abortion are denied services by the state. According to UN Women, each year in Mexico, fifteen thousand rapes are reported (and many more go unreported), and only 20 percent of them result in a conviction (Secretaría de Gobernación, Instituto Nacional de las Mujeres, and ONU Mujeres 2016). To make matters worse, access to justice for women or families who face human rights violations is limited, and even when women do manage to exercise their legal rights to redress, they do not receive comprehensive reparations—remedial damages—for thoseviolations.

In this chapter I argue that reproductive rights violations are human rights violations and that, therefore, Mexico is in dire need of improved public policy and legislation related to women's reproductive rights in order to comply with its international human rights obligations as well as international standards. To illustrate this need, the chapter analyzes three topics in depth: obstetric violence, maternal mortality, and sexual violence against women. I also address the need for stronger mechanisms to redress the violations of women's reproductive rights that occur in the health sector, through the analysis of real cases of such violations and of the responses of the states of Chiapas, México, and Oaxaca when women and/or their families decided to seek justice.

Context: Violence, Reproductive Rights, and Grievance Mechanisms

In the past ten years, the Mexican government has been urged to respond to the undeniable violence against women in the country, primarily due to an alarming number of killings and disappearances of women in Ciudad Juárez. The Inter-American Court of Human Rights (IACtHR) ruled against Mexico in the "Cotton Fields" case in 2009 *(González et al. v. Mexico),* which resulted in the adoption of a federal law as well as state laws regarding violence against women. The federal and some state-level penal codes now include the crime of femicide, which, succinctly, refers to the murder of a woman for reasons based solely on her gender.

Regardless of the visibility of violence against women and attempts by the Mexican state to prevent, eradicate, and sanction it, these efforts have not translated into laws and public policies that address the issue properly, much less in a comprehensive manner. Policies have fallen short, even though the General Law on Women's Access to a Life Free from Violence, adopted in 2007, recognizes many forms of violence in addition to femicide that the state is responsible for preventing, such as institutional, economic, and psychological violence. Many violations against women are still not identified as such—including violence in institutional health-care settings. This type of violence has been normalized within Mexican society, and the state has made little effort to address it from a human rights perspective. Indeed, it could be argued that abusive practices against women occurring in institutional health-care settings constitute cruel and inhumane treatment or even torture. As stated by the UN Special Rapporteur on torture and other cruel, inhuman, or degrading treatment or punishment in his report on said practices in reproductive health settings, "While the prohibition of torture may have originally applied primarily in the context of interrogation, punishment or intimidation of a detainee, the international community has begun to recognize that torture may also occur in other contexts" (Human Rights Council 2013a: paragraph 15). This conceptualization of abuse in health-care settings as torture is a relatively recent phenomenon, noted by the rapporteur. Practices amounting to torture are actually quite common, despite being invisible. The Special Rapporteur's report on this subject is crucial since it "sheds light on often undetected forms of abusive practices that occur under the auspices of healthcare policies, and emphasizes how certain treatments run afoul of the prohibition on torture and ill-treatment" (15).

In order for women to exercise their reproductive rights, they must be able to exercise them without any type of violence; however, freedom from violence and reproductive rights have not been clearly linked in Mexican public policy. On the one hand, the state adopts legislation and policy regarding violence against women, while on the other, it adopts separate policies for reproductive health. The challenge is to bridge the state's policymaking by integrating both issues in order to address violence against women in the exercise of their reproductive rights.

Reproductive rights are protected in Article 4 of the Mexican Constitution, which recognizes individual autonomy to decide the number and spacing of children, as well as the right to health protection for every person. These rights are also recognized in the international agreements signed and ratified by Mexico, which, in accordance with Article 1 of the Mexican Constitution, constitute domestic law. Human rights standards can help limit the state's power but also require the state to formulate and implement public policies, interpret and apply legal norms, and develop laws and regulations in accordance with the state's human rights commitments. The state's obligations to promote, respect, protect, and guarantee human rights include the assurance that all individuals can make free decisions concerning reproduction.

The state has also developed regulations in the sphere of reproductive rights. Every six years, for example, the state publishes a National Health Program including policies on maternal health, contraception for adolescents, and violence against women. The Federal Health Ministry in 2014 belatedly published the Maternal and Prenatal Health Program for the 2013–2018 period. This program established women's reproductive rights, specifically those related to maternal and prenatal health, as its principal objective.

The Ministry of Health also develops technical norms to interpret policies regarding medical matters. Relevant to this chapter are two of these norms, the first on the treatment of maternal health (NOM 007) and the second on the prevention of violence against women (NOM 046), both of which were recently updated, in 2016.

When reproductive rights are violated, women and/or their families can seek redress through the justice system. The various grievance mechanisms that exist in the country—including penal, administrative, and civil—lack a human rights perspective, are not accessible, and do not allow for comprehensive reparations for the victims (GIRE 2015a). Therefore, the mechanisms that have been used most often to redress human rights violations are complaint procedures before the national or state-level human rights commissions. These autonomous bodies receive complaints concerning acts or omissions committed by public servants that violate human rights, as well as issue public, autonomous, and nonbinding recommendations. Given the nonbinding nature of the recommendations, compliance ultimately depends on the political will of the public institution in question.

Nevertheless, diligent investigation and clear recommendations by human rights commissions, stressing the unequivocal obligations of public institutions, contribute to public servants' daily actions and to the reduction of human rights violations. In cases of reproductive rights violations, the federal and state human rights commissions can offer an effective route to access justice, though not without limitations, by including recommendations from a human rights perspective and contributing to demanding and implementing measures of nonrepetition. It is also essential that the National Human Rights Commission (CNDH) and state-level human rights commissions systematically establish comprehensive reparations for damages in their recommendations, which should meet international human rights standards, including (a) the obligation to investigate the evidence and identify, judge, and, where appropriate, sanction those responsible; (b) restitution measures; (c) satisfaction measures; (d) rehabilitation measures; (e) indemnity; and (f) measures of nonrepetition.

Obstetric Violence in Mexico

Obstetric violence is a specific form of violence against women that violates their human rights through any omission or act committed by health personnel that results in physical or psychological harm to a woman during pregnancy or birth or postpartum. Obstetric violence is manifested by a lack of access to reproductive health services; by cruel, inhumane, or degrading treatment; or by overmedication—all of which undermine a woman's ability to make free and informed decisions over her reproductive processes.

Over the course of many years, groups of midwives, civil society organizations, and public health experts, among others, have denounced the abuses committed in Mexico by health-care workers in clinics, health centers, and hospitals, both public and private, against pregnant women during childbirth. These abuses are not new. What is novel are recent attempts by various actors to make this type of conduct visible: to name it and frame it as a human rights violation and, more specifically, to conceptualize it as obstetric violence.

The Information Group on Reproductive Choice (GIRE), in *Omission and Indifference: Reproductive Rights in Mexico* (2013), reported that the magnitude of obstetric violence in the country was still unknown. According to the 2010 Population and Housing Census, 7 out of 10 Mexican women over the age of 15 have had at least one live birth, which indicates that 71.6 percent of the female population in Mexico is reproductively active and, therefore, has required medical care during pregnancy, labor, or the postpartum period. Hence the population susceptible to suffering obstetric violence is enormous. The 2016 National Census for Household Dynamics, published in 2017, included data regarding obstetric violence for the first time. The data demonstrate that in the last five years, 33.4 percent of women between 15 and 49 years old who had a child had suffered some sort of mistreatment by the person that attended the birth (INEGI 2017).

In Mexico, the manifestations of obstetric violence include

> scolding, taunts, irony, insults, threats, humiliation, manipulation of information and denial of treatment, not providing referrals to other services in order to receive timely assistance, delaying urgent medical care, indifference to women's requests or complaints, failure to inform or ask women about decisions made during the various stages of labor, use of women for didactic purposes without any respect for their dignity, pain management during childbirth used as punishment, and coercion to obtain "consent," and even acts of deliberate harm to a woman's health, among even more serious and obvious violations of their human rights. (Villanueva 2010: 148)

The CNDH, in its 2014 activity report, stated that the most frequently reported violations perpetrated by state actors are those related to the right to health. These include medical negligence, disregard for the patient, hospital seclusion, irregular clinical records, inadequate medical procedures, and various omissions related to the provision of medication, hospital services, information about health status, and the necessary infrastructure for the adequate provision of health services, to name just a few. These reveal the seriousness of the structural problems within the Mexican health system, which need to be addressed urgently (CNDH 2015a: page 9).

When a pregnant woman faces obstetric violence, several human rights are subject to violation, such as the right to health, the right to information, the right for women to live free from violence, the right to privacy, the right to personal integrity, and the right to not be submitted to torture or cruel, inhuman, or degrading treatment or punishment.

Regional efforts to develop a definition of obstetric violence have been made in legislation in Argentina, Mexico, and Venezuela, but there is still an immense gap when it comes to the interpretation and implementation of the law. In Mexico, the federal legislation referring to violence against women provides definitions of institutional, physical, and psychological violence but does not explicitly include or define obstetric violence. At the state level,

Chiapas (2009), Durango (2007), Guanajuato (2010), and Veracruz (2008) have included definitions of obstetric violence in their legal frameworks (Tamés 2014: 23–28). These laws focus, in general, on the fact that women should have all available information to make decisions during pregnancy and childbirth and postpartum, that they should be treated with dignity, that cultural values should be taken into consideration throughout their treatment, that medicalization should be avoided when not justified, and that women must participate in the decisions affecting their health at all times.

Sanctions against behavior that constitutes obstetric violence vary from one state to another. In general, they range from fines or disciplinary measures, such as suspending the medical licenses of those responsible, to administrative measures to enforce the law. Exceptions to this trend have occurred in cases in Chiapas, Guerrero, and Veracruz, which consider obstetric violence a criminal offense that could lead to possible penal sanctions against those responsible, and the punishments are more severe for public servants.

Criminal sanctions should not always be the immediate answer to address obstetric violence, except in specific behaviors such as forced sterilization. Criminal law should be used as a last resort since it threatens doctors and ultimately would not encourage them to use safer, nonviolent forms of obstetric practice. Neither does the use of criminal law promote a change of mentality or public policies to prevent and eliminate disrespect and abuse during childbirth.

GIRE has documented and/or litigated twenty-four cases of obstetric violence throughout Mexico since 2013. A case that exemplifies the litigation strategies employed by GIRE is that of Irma López. In October 2013, a photograph of an indigenous woman giving birth in the courtyard of a hospital in Oaxaca was published and went "viral" on social media. It did not take long for the public to express their indignation. Irma López, although in labor, was not admitted to the hospital but instead was told to wait, and as a result her infant was born in the hospital's courtyard. Cases such as Irma's are common in Mexico, as demonstrated a few days later by a similar case in Puebla and another in Chiapas, where a woman died as the result of a badly performed cesarean.

Irma's case was brought to the CNDH, which in 2014 adopted Recommendation 01/2014, finding the State of Oaxaca responsible for the human rights violations committed against her, including her right to health and personal integrity, as well as violations of the rights of her newborn (CNDH 2014b).

The government of Oaxaca showed the political will to comply with the CNDH recommendation. On March 20, 2014, the government of Oaxaca, Irma, and GIRE, as her legal representative, signed an agreement establishing obligations for the state. Pursuant to the agreement, the State of Oaxaca will provide the following:

1. Monitoring of the criminal and administrative procedures derived from the denial of health services;
2. Courses and workshops to train facilitators in the skills required to provide pregnancy and prenatal care;
3. Timely, quality, and accessible health services for Irma and her son, and accompaniment when they seek care at their community health center and at the general hospital in San Juan Bautista Tuxtepec, Oaxaca;
4. Financial compensation;
5. A scholarship for Irma's son;
6. A statement recognizing its responsibility, including a public apology in Mazateco, which was made in Irma's community and through official media;
7. Guarantees of nonrepetition consisting of (a) completing the construction of a primary-care hospital in Jalapa de Díaz, including the medical and hospital infrastructure within eight months; (b) building, modifying, and properly equipping fifty labor and delivery wards in six jurisdictions in Oaxaca; and (c) disseminating the criteria and procedures established in the Official Mexican Norm 007;
8. Food support for Irma and her son.

At present, more than three years later, there are no delivery rooms, nor has the construction of the Jalapa de Díaz General Hospital been completed.

Cases of obstetric violence such as Irma's help to demonstrate why certain forms of obstetric violence can constitute cruel and inhumane treatment or even torture. As already suggested, the Special Rapporteur on torture, Juan E. Méndez, identified "certain forms of abuses in health-care settings that may cross a threshold of mistreatment that is tantamount to torture or cruel, inhuman or degrading treatment or punishment" (Human Rights Council 2013a: summary). Unfortunately, the World Health Organization (WHO) does not use concepts of international law to designate conduct that can constitute cruel, inhuman, or degrading treatment during labor and delivery; rather, it refers to these as acts in which there is a "lack of respect" or "ill-treatment" (WHO 2014a).

Irma's case was the first to be studied by CNDH, which concluded that it was indeed a case of obstetric violence, as argued by GIRE. Before this case, situations like hers were customarily classified as medical malpractice. In classifying Irma's case as obstetric violence, CNDH set a landmark precedent by recognizing the difference between medical malpractice and obstetric violence, thus identifying and naming structural problems in the health system as violence against women. Since that conclusion and recommendation from 2014, thirty-one more recommendations recognizing obstetric violence as a human rights violation have been adopted by CNDH against different Mexican states.[1] So far, however, no cases from Mexico or from any other country, dealing directly with obstetric violence, have been submitted to international human rights mechanisms.

One important achievement is that CNDH published, in June 2017, a general recommendation that includes a definition of obstetric violence as well as the Mexican state's obligations to prevent it, strengthening the recognition of this topic as a human rights issue.

Maternal Mortality in Mexico

A fatal consequence of obstetric violence is maternal mortality. Many of the cases that result in the death of a pregnant woman have included previous violations related to obstetric violence. WHO estimates that every day, approximately 830 women die from preventable causes related to pregnancy and childbirth, from which 99 percent of all maternal deaths occur in developing countries; and maternal mortality is higher in women living in rural areas and among poorer communities (WHO 2016). Therefore, there should be no doubt that maternal mortality is a human rights issue.

Maternal mortality is a reflection of the multiple human rights violations that women face in accessing obstetric-care services. It is defined as the death of a woman during pregnancy or childbirth or within forty-two days after childbirth, from any cause related to or aggravated by the pregnancy, childbirth, or postpartum recovery, or its management, but not from accidental causes. Since most maternal deaths are preventable, maternal mortality has been recognized as a human rights issue by various international mechanisms. UN Human Rights Council resolution 11/8 "Preventable maternal mortality and morbidity and human rights" expressed its concern for the high maternal mortality rate (MMR) worldwide—maternal deaths per 100,000. The council also requested that states renew their commitment to eliminate preventable maternal mortality and morbidity in compliance with their human rights obligations (Human Rights Council 2009).

Despite certain advances made in preventing maternal mortality, Mexico did not reach the goal set in 1990 in the framework of the Millennium Development Goals (MDGs), to achieve a 75 percent reduction of the MMR by 2015. The MMR was 57.2 in 2008, 51.5 in 2010, and 42.3 in 2012; and in 2013, the last year of official data released as of May 2015, there were 38.2 maternal deaths for every 100,000 births. In order to reach the objective established by the MDGs, the MMR in 2015 should have been 22.25. This commitment, taken on by Mexico fifteen years ago, was far from being accomplished.

In absolute terms, in 2014 there were 872 maternal deaths in Mexico compared to 1,119 in 2008 (Freyermuth, Luna, and Muños 2016). But the reduction of maternal mortality in the country has not been uniform, and some states have shown more advances than others. From 1990 to 2014 only one state, Morelos, achieved a reduction of more than 75 percent in the MMR. Of particular concern are the states of Sinaloa and Coahuila, where the MMR has increased in this period to 17.1 and 197.7 percent, respectively (Freyermuth, Luna, and Muños 2016). The states that continue to lead the country with the highest MMR (over 46 in 2014) are Chiapas, Chihuahua, Durango, Guerrero, Hidalgo, Michoacán, Oaxaca, and Tlaxcala.

The Inter-American Commission on Human Rights (IACHR) has reiterated that the lack of access to adequate maternal health services is a violation of women's human rights, specifically the rights to personal integrity, health, and nondiscrimination. It has furthermore indicated that it is essential that states fulfill their international obligations in this regard and that immediate priority measures are needed to decrease maternal mortality (IACHR 2010: 1 and 6).

Preventable maternal mortality is linked to structural flaws in health systems, which represent a violation of women's rights to life, health, and nondiscrimination. The deaths of many women have been the result of a series of actions and omissions on the part of the health-service providers who treated the women, as well as shortcomings such as quality of care, lack of personnel, lack of infrastructure, and budget shortfalls in the public health system. This means that the deaths are preventable, but in Mexico there are no mechanisms in place to actually prevent them or guarantee access to justice to victims of maternal mortality.

Maternal mortality, moreover, should be analyzed from a human rights approach, since it violates not only the right to life but also the right to non-discrimination, as it particularly affects women in vulnerable situations. The multiple layers of discrimination faced by women in Mexico is reflected in the differentiated effects that maternal mortality has on certain groups: 12.7 percent of the maternal deaths in the country in 2014 occurred among women with no social security or health protection, and 10.4 percent were women with no schooling. These percentages, however, increase in certain states: in Morelos, 33.3 percent of deaths registered were of women with no schooling, and 39.3 percent of the maternal deaths in Mexico City were women with no health coverage (Freyermuth, Luna, and Munos 2016: 12, 21, and 29).

Among these women with no health protection, 15.3 percent were indigenous women (CNDH and CIESAS 2017: 210). Indeed, this could also indicate that indigenous women suffer a disproportionate burden in accessing maternal health services for health problems that do not put their lives at risk, which brings to light a serious problem of discrimination in the right to health in Mexico.

Adolescents are also at risk. In 2014, 127 girls and women under 19 years of age died of causes related to maternity across the country, 5 of them between the ages of 10 and 14. That same year, girls and adolescents represented 14.5 percent of all maternal deaths (Freyermuth, Luna, and Muños 2016: 52). The MMR specifically increases in younger adolescents (between 10 and 14 years of age), being almost twice as high as that of women between the ages of 20 and 24 (Secretaría de Salud, Dirección General de Epidemiología 2014: 1). According to WHO, pregnant girls under the age of sixteen run a risk of maternal death four times higher than that of women between the ages of twenty and thirty, and the mortality rate for their infants is approximately 50 percent higher as well (WHO 2014b).

In 2013, Mexico received and accepted two recommendations related to maternal mortality from Uruguay and Bosnia-Herzegovina during its evaluation before the UN Human Rights Council's Universal Periodic Review, urging the country to "increase efforts to reduce the maternal mortality rate, in particular by adopting a broad strategy on safe maternity, in which priority is given to access to prenatal, postnatal and obstetric quality health services" (Human Rights Council 2013b: para. 148.155) and to "implement the CERD and the CEDAW recommendations on adequate and accessible health services in order to lower the high maternal and infant mortality among the indigenous population"(para. 148.157). The international human rights framework to which Mexico has subscribed, and to which it is committed, exposes and recognizes that maternal mortality is the product of a series of human rights violations—in particular, the right to life, to access to health without discrimination, and to information.

A case that exemplifies these violations and the arguments used by GIRE to litigate maternal mortality is that of Susana. Susana was a twenty-six-year-old indigenous Tzotzil woman married to Romeo. On October 4, 2013, she went to the Women's Hospital of San Cristóbal de las Casas, in Chiapas, with symptoms indicating the need for a caesarean. Susana was a victim of mistreatment by hospital personnel from the moment she arrived. There was no translator from Tzotzil (Susana's language) to Spanish. Personnel from the hospital threw her mother-in-law out, so Susana had to face the whole procedure alone, and she was left naked because there were not enough robes. A few hours later, the family was informed that the caesarean had been carried out as well as the extraction of her gallbladder, of which they had no prior knowledge, nor had Susana or a relative given informed consent for that procedure. The medical report subsequent to the surgery reported Susana's condition as stable. However, two days later, still in the hospital, Susana experienced respiratory failure and died.

Susana's family members were notified of her death without any additional information as to the reasons why. At the same time, her newborn daughter was handed to them, naked, without any documentation and covered in blood. They were not given any indication of what to feed her despite her mother's death. The hospital personnel were unjustifiably hasty in discharging the baby, thereby exposing her to unnecessary risks, which would later result in a diagnosis of hypothermia for which she had to be treated at a private clinic.

CNDH learned of the case after the Chiapas Human Rights Commission began its investigation. CNDH recognized that Susana's death was the result of a series of human rights violations and, therefore, identified her, her children, and Romeo, her husband, as victims.

In order to defend Susana's case, the first step was to determine that it was related to a preventable maternal death and not attributable to accidental or unavoidable factors.

Health personnel of the Women's Hospital in San Cristobal de Las Casas violated Susana's family's right to information. Romeo, her husband, had to wait for two days for information about Susana's condition subsequent to her being admitted to the hospital. At that point, he was told that she was in recovery, with the surgical procedures to which she had been submitted being concealed from him, as well as the seriousness of her condition. The absence of a timely notification about Susana's and her daughter's conditions represents a violation of human rights on the part of the state, occurring as it did in the context of structural discrimination against indigenous people by the health services.

CNDH's investigation resulted in the publication of Recommendation 29/2014 on Susana's case, which determined that there were enough elements to prove that the human rights violations against Susana, her husband, Romeo, and her children were attributable to the Chiapas government through the public Women's Hospital. The recommendation included compensation to the victims and their registration in the National Victims Registry, as well as an investigation of the criminal and administrative complaints for the case. Additionally, the recommendation included measures to guarantee nonrepetition in clinics, hospitals, and health centers that are dependent on the state Ministry of Health, including the proper integration of medical files and the review of health personnel's credentials and training (CNDH 2014c).

These measures were important but insufficient in preventing and responding to maternal mortality in Chiapas and to the additional information and requests presented by GIRE, in representation of the family. Nonetheless, on November 19, the Chiapas government issued a public apology, a measure that was not included in the recommendation, for Susana's death, representing the first public apology offered in Mexico by an authority in a maternal mortality case. Furthermore, compensation for Susana's children was incorporated into a trust fund operated by the Ministry of the Interior (SEGOB). This was accomplished through a convention of acknowledgment of human rights violations by the Mexican state on March 4, 2015, signed by SEGOB, the Chiapas government, and Romeo in his own name and on behalf of his children, as well as Susana's father.

Unfortunately, Susana's case is only one of the fourteen maternal mortality cases GIRE has documented and litigated since 2013. Even though, in these particular cases, access to justice seems to be closer for the families, the structural problems in the health system continue, allowing these situations to occur over and over again. Adoption of nonrepetition measures is still a challenge for local governments.

In several cases analyzed by international human rights mechanisms, both through the Inter-American and UN systems, the resolutions have included obligations for the state to pay reparations to the women who have been harmed and their families. One clear example is the case of *Alyne da Silva vs. Brazil,* addressed by the Committee on the Elimination of Discrimination Against Women (CEDAW 2011), which condemned Brazil for the death of a twenty-eight-year-old woman of African descent, who died because of a succession of acts constituting obstetric violence. The committee ordered Brazil to pay compensation to her family and to take measures of nonrepetition and prevention, such as guaranteeing the right to safe motherhood and facilitating access to obstetric care, giving professional training to health-sector workers, allowing access to effective legal remedies, and ensuring that health services comply with both international and national standards. But no Mexican cases have yet been brought to the international arena.

Sexual Violence Against Girls and Teenagers

In Mexico, according to official government figures, two out of ten teenagers between fifteen and nineteen years old have been pregnant more than once, and it is estimated that 17.4 percent of total births are by women under twenty years old. Among OECD countries, Mexico has the highest birth rate among women aged fifteen to nineteen years (United Nations Population Fund 2013). Many of these pregnancies are a result of rape as recognized by the government in the National Strategy to Reduce Adolescent Pregnancy (2015–2018), even though there are no official figures about the number of pregnancies resulting from rape. Additionally, as I mentioned when addressing maternal mortality rates, pregnant girls less than sixteen years old face four times the risk of maternal death than women in their twenties (WHO 2009: 410).

According to a recent report of the Executive Commission of Assistance to Victims (CEAV) in Mexico, "The Other Invisible Victims," one out of every four girls suffers from sexual abuse before turning eighteen; six out of ten of the incidents of sexual abuse are committed at home by family members or people close to the family. This same report points out that, from 2010 to 2015, 60 percent of the cases of sexual violence against children were committed by a person close to the victim; nine out of ten victims were women; nine out of ten aggressions were committed by men between ages sixteen and forty-five; and from those aggressions registered in a five-year period (more than 2.6 million), there were only eighty-three thousand investigations and only ten out of every thousand aggressors were placed on criminal trial (CEAV 2016b).

Comprehensive care for the victims of sexual violence—which in Mexico includes access to legal abortion in cases of rape—is an essential component to guaranteeing the right to a life free of violence. Mexico is one out of ten countries in Latin America in which abortion is legal on the grounds of rape; the others are Argentina, Brazil, Bolivia, Chile, Colombia, Costa Rica, Guyana, Panama, and Uruguay. Despite the fact that abortion after rape is legal in all Mexican states, in practice it is difficult to access. Only in Mexico City does legislation allow women to access elective abortion services up to twelve weeks of gestation.

The CEDAW Committee's concluding observations to Mexico in 2012 called for the state to ensure that the right to abortion existed in law, but also to eliminate unjustified obstacles so that women could in fact access abortion services. These obstacles and the forcing of (especially) young girls to carry a pregnancy to term arguably constitute cruel, inhumane, and degrading treatment (CEDAW 2012). The Committee on the Rights of the Child also made observations to Mexico in 2015, including the obligation of the government to eliminate the requirement for rape survivors to report the crime to the public prosecutor's office in order to obtain authorization for legal abortion services (Committee on the Rights of the Child 2015: para. 50(c)).

Despite the right to an abortion in the case of rape under state and federal laws, there are many hidden legal obstacles, such as the twelve-week gestational limit, the requirement to report the crime, and the need for authorization from a public prosecutor or a judge, depending on the state. These obstacles revictimize girls and women and, on many occasions, force them to continue an unwanted pregnancy. Establishing a period of twelve weeks does not take into consideration the age of the victim, the risks to her life and health that a pregnancy entails, her physical or psychological condition, or the circumstances under which she may have finally reported her aggressor. Additionally, in cases involving girls and adolescents, authorities have the obligation to apply the principle of the superior interest of the child to guarantee access to health services for those who have the right. Furthermore, the obligation to report the rape and the need for a judge's authorization in order to access a legal abortion is a breach of the right to health, since these girls and women face a major barrier in accessing an emergency medical service. There are fourteen states in Mexico that require authorization to access legal abortion in cases of rape[2] and seventeen states that require a prior report to authorities to guarantee access to abortion.[3] The requirement that a prior report be made emanates from the presumption that women would lie in order to access this service. This supposition is based on a gender stereotype that is perpetuated through norms such as those that are being challenged.

The problem becomes worse when the lack of authorization due to the absence of a prior report of the rape results in the imposition of an unwanted pregnancy or the criminalization of a woman who decides to terminate her pregnancy. In any of these scenarios, women's rights are seriously transgressed because the state is unjustifiably predetermining the access to a right.

In reality, authorities constantly deny legal abortion after rape, and a particularly worrisome trend is that legal abortions are being denied to young girls, some as young as ten years of age, who are pregnant as a result of sexual assault (GIRE 2015b). Public data show that between April 2007 and December 2012, public prosecutors' offices reported that they authorized only thirty-nine[4] legal abortions for rape survivors, and between August 2012 and December 2013, they reported twelve authorizations.[5] However, these numbers contrast with the authorizations the ministries of health reported in the same periods. From April 2007 to December 2012, ministries of health said that they received fifty-nine authorizations of legal abortions for rape survivors,[6] while from August 2012 to December 2013, public information shows that state health ministries reported receiving fourteen authorizations.[7]

As the data show, not all authorizations reported by the public prosecutors' offices coincide with those received by the state health ministries, and this inconsistency indicates a serious problem regarding public information. Moreover, the extremely low number of cases authorized, as shown by the obtained data, demonstrates that women have little or no access to terminate pregnancies resulting from rape, even though rape is the only legal grounds for accessing abortion in all states and should be part of the comprehensive care provided to rape survivors. This lack of access also violates the General Law for Victims, which stipulates that rape survivors can request legal abortion services directly in the health sector and do not require previous reporting or authorization from police.

In 2016, there were two important policy changes for survivors of sexual assault. The first one was the revision of the National Code of Penal Procedures, effective June 18, 2016, which eliminated the requirements for accessing legal abortion services. This revision means that the states—such as the State of México—with penal codes requiring authorization or a prior report of rape to guarantee access to abortion services must modify their codes. Despite this revision, no state penal codes requiring gestational time limits, previous reporting, or authorizations have yet been changed.

The second policy change was the modification of the Mexican Official Norm 046 (NOM 046). This norm is obligatory for all health institutions, public and private, within the Mexican health system. NOM 046 outlines, among other things, how rape survivors can access abortion care. In the previous version of the norm, women were required to report a rape to law-enforcement authorities who then authorized—although more often than not, denied—access to abortion services. Now, women can request abortion care directly from the health sector. Another landmark revision to the norm is that adolescents aged twelve and above can request and access abortion services in cases of rape without the permission of their parents or guardians.

From January 2013 to date, GIRE has documented and litigated thirty-six cases of girls and women who were denied legal abortions. Rosa's case illustrates the reality of young girls and women in Mexico who try to get access to a legal abortion as a rape victim.

Rosa is the second of four children. She is fourteen years old and lives in Tlalnepantla, State of México. Her father raped her for almost a year and threatened to harm her mother if Rosa said anything. Dealing with a violent man, Rosa chose not to report what was happening to her. She started her third year of middle school, but she had no desire to attend school or even to leave the house. On October 6, 2014, her mother, realizing that something was amiss with Rosa because of her behavior, tried to find out if anything was wrong and asked Rosa's godmother to take her to the doctor. At the clinic, the doctor sent her for an ultrasound, which revealed that she was approximately sixteen weeks pregnant.

Rosa told her mother what had happened, and the next day they both went to the public prosecutor's office to file a report of rape against her father. They were told that since the pregnancy was so advanced, she could not have an abortion, and they gave her the addresses of various places that could assist her in continuing with the pregnancy. Article 151 of the Code of Penal Procedures of the State of México states that a judge can authorize an abortion in cases of rape provided that the pregnancy does not exceed twelve weeks. The period imposed in the Code of Penal Procedures made the termination of her pregnancy inaccessible and violated, among other rights, her right to health and to a life free of violence.

Rosa traveled to Mexico City to get an abortion and has fortunately continued her education. GIRE contended that the Code of Penal Procedures' time restraint for abortion after rape is discriminatory and presented a legal stay, citing violations of the right to health, equality, personal integrity, and privacy, as well as the principles of nondiscrimination and the best interest of the child. GIRE argued that the superior legal hierarchy of the General Law for Victims annuls the State of México's legal abortion time limit in Rosa's case. Sadly, the legal stay was rejected, as well as a second appeal filed by GIRE to the Appellate Court.

Conclusions

Mexico lacks effective public policies addressing violence against women in the context of reproductive rights. I have illustrated three specific cases: girls who are raped and forced to give birth; girls and women for whom the delivery room is their grave; and women who are treated inhumanely during childbirth. All of these cases constitute serious human rights violations for which the Mexican state should be accountable. The state has the duty to adopt preventive measures as well as to provide reparations, including access to justice and nonrepetition measures. What happened in these cases also violated the right to life and/or the right to be free of cruel, inhuman, or degrading treatment, for which the Mexican state should be accountable.

Making the situation even more unbelievable is the idolization of women in Mexico with regard to reproduction, which might lead one to presume that their rights would be respected. Pregnant women are considered fortunate soon-to-be mothers, and, therefore, society seems to applaud them for having fulfilled their natural mission as women. And yet, it is at this very time, during pregnancy and childbirth, when many women experience violence—violence that is invisible or normalized. These women suffer violence at the hands of health personnel, public and private; the worst part is that they are accustomed to it and would never think of reporting or denouncing it.

PART II

The Crisis for Migrants

CHAPTER 5

Superfluous Lives

Undocumented Migrants Traveling in Mexico

Javier Treviño-Rangel

Introduction

In September 2008, members of the Beta Group (Grupo Beta) illegally detained five Nicaraguan citizens (Amnesty International 2010a: 15). The Grupo Beta is the body created by Mexican authorities to provide humanitarian assistance to migrants in Mexico regardless of their nationality or legal status. This humanitarian branch of the government handed the five foreigners over to the local police of a small town in the State of Chiapas, where they were illegally detained for at least three days. They were later driven in a municipal police van to an isolated ranch and forced to surrender the telephone numbers and details of their relatives in the United States. One of them resisted this extortion and was raped as punishment. When they were released, the police threatened to shoot them in the back. The youths ran and dispersed. One of them managed to reach Home of Mercy (Hogar de la Misericordia), a shelter for undocumented migrants run by a Roman Catholic priest. The shelter staff persuaded the Nicaraguan to file a complaint with the Special Prosecutor for Crimes Against Migrants in Chiapas. In order to wait for the process and outcome of the criminal investigation, he had to request a special humanitarian visa to remain legally in Mexico. However, he disappeared from the shelter without a trace. The shelter team feared that this young migrant was either threatened, and therefore decided to run away, or murdered (Amnesty International 2010a: 15).

The story of this undocumented migrant seems to be a tale from Kafka-land, where nothing is what it seems: humanitarian groups created to pro-tect migrants in a country with a punitive immigration policy; humanitarian groups that illegally detain foreign nationals; special prosecutors designated to exclusively investigate abuses committed against migrants in a country whose government systematically denies that such abuses occur; humani-tarian visas emitted by the government as a protection against abuses com-mitted by government humanitarian groups; and so on. However, the story of this Nicaraguan youth is a reality lived by tens of thousands of foreign-ers, mainly from Central America, who cross Mexico each year to reach the United States. It is for this reason that the investigations of various local and international human rights organizations, including UN bodies, assert that the situation of undocumented foreign citizens in Mexico is a "major human crisis" (Amnesty International 2010a: 37).

To date, scholars have largely avoided the issue of undocumented migra-tion in transit through Mexico. The few existent studies on this issue argue that this human rights crisis resulted from a process of securitization of Mex-ican migration policy (Armijo 2011; Castillo and Toussaint 2010; Isacson and Meyer 2012; Venet Rebiffé and Palma Calderón 2011). This literature maintains that the Mexican government perceives undocumented migrants in transit as a security threat and, consequently, has tightened its immigration laws and increased the number of agents, financial resources, and bureau-cratic mechanisms in order to detain these migrants and get them to leave the country. However, as I show in this chapter, there is insufficient evidence to support these claims. The story of the Nicaraguan youth just described sheds light on a much more complex and disturbing problem. The young migrant was not detained illegally, held incommunicado, and treated in a cruel and degrading manner by different agents of the Mexican state because he was considered a serious threat to national security. He suffered all kinds of abuse simply because he was perceived as a commodity that could, potentially, gen-erate some income.

The chapter reflects on the following questions. Can the concept of secu-ritization help us to understand the human rights crisis of transit migrants in Mexico? If not, what does? What structural elements contribute to the current crisis? The securitization of migration would entail a process in which state officials show great concern about immigrants who are deemed a security threat. However, I claim, undocumented migration faces exactly the opposite process. The human rights crisis of transmigrants may be explained not as resulting from increased attention to, or concerns about, them by the state or society, but rather because the lives of migrants simply do not matter. To use Hannah Arendt's concept, their lives have become "superfluous" (Arendt 1978). This is what we are currently witnessing in Mexico, not a process of the securitization of migration, but rather a process that has completely dehumanized transmigrants, stripped them of all dignity, and denied that they are anything more than what I call disposable commodities.

This chapter is based on in-depth semistructured interviews with undocumented migrants, experts, academics, human rights activists, members of migrant-rights organizations, and agents of the Mexican state who have some link with the creation or implementation of migration policy in Mexico, Guatemala, and El Salvador.[1] It also draws on a large number of reports published by migrant-rights organizations.

Context and Background: Serious Human Rights Abuses Against Foreign Citizens

In August 2010, the international press reported that Mexico's state authorities discovered at a ranch the bodies of seventy-two foreign citizens (Aranda 2010; Tuckman 2010). One man was still alive to tell the story. The dead were mostly Central American migrants who were in transit in Mexico. Approached for comment, Mexican President Felipe Calderón claimed that this massacre was clear evidence of the success of his "war on drugs" (*La Jornada* 2010).[2] He argued that drug kingpins were losing the battle against the administration. The kidnapping, torture, and killing of migrants proved that criminal organizations were desperately exploring new illegal markets. "These guys are completely crazy," the president said about drug kingpins, hence the need for them to be "eradicated" (*La Jornada* 2010).

Investigations into the case demonstrated that the massacre was not perpetrated only by "crazy" criminals who "lost their minds." The killings would not have been possible without the diligent participation of a large number of state officials (Evans 2014). For months, these foreigners had been illegally detained in ordinary passenger buses by members of the traffic police and municipal security forces, as well as by members of the National Institute of Migration, who then handed them over to the criminal organization "Los Zetas" (an organization created and trained by former members of the Mexican military) (Evans 2014; Turati 2013).

Since 2008, migrant shelters have reported on the increasing number of atrocities committed against migrants. They have also reported an increase in the intensity of the abuses (Fray Matías de Córdova 2008; Belén, Posada del Migrante, et al. 2009). The reports published by these shelters received little attention in the media; international human rights organizations largely ignored them, and the Calderón administration denied the allegations. It was not until 2009, a few months before the massacre, that the National Human Rights Commission (CNDH), Mexico's official human rights organ, published a disturbing report on the kidnapping of migrants (CNDH 2009). This report officially confirmed what the shelters had reported previously: every year more than eighteen thousand undocumented migrants are abducted in Mexico. In other words, a foreign citizen is kidnapped every half hour.[3]

According to CNDH, undocumented foreign nationals are kidnapped "frequently" and "everyday" somewhere in the country (CNDH 2009: 11). Once captured, they are transferred in overcrowded trucks, on journeys that can last for days, from the place of capture to what criminal organizations call "safe houses," or to hotels or isolated ranches. At these sites they are starved, ill-treated, tortured, and extorted. In 80 percent of cases reported by CNDH, detained migrants received no food "or ate once a day; in many cases the food was in bad state or consisted only of bread." Many witnesses narrated how the kidnapped migrants are "forced to strip naked and to remain so throughout their captivity." Some detained migrants are "forced to use drugs," or parts of their bodies are burned (17). Women and men suffer rape.

The kidnappers demand sums of money that range "from 5,000 dollars up" from the kidnapped transmigrants or their families. The payments are made through well-known international businesses that manage money transfers, such as Western Union (IACHR 2013: 51). The ransom payments, however, do not guarantee the release of the migrants. Some migrants are selected for forced labor. Men in particular are forced to work for criminal organizations "as gunmen, to murder other migrants, or to move drugs" to the United States. Organized-crime groups coerce boys to work as lookouts (64). Some migrants are selected for death. The Inter-American Commission on Human Rights (IACHR) has testimonies given by migrants who declared they "witnessed mass killings in which several dozen people were murdered and that they had been held in captivity with upwards of 400 people" (67). It is no surprise that, as noted by the former UN Special Rapporteur on Migrants, Mexico is the country with the highest rate of dead international migrants—in only two years, between 2010 and 2012, he counted 1,500 dead migrants reported by the national press alone (Bustamante 2012). The Mesoamerican Migrant Movement estimates that approximately twenty thousand Central American citizens disappear in Mexico every year (Movimiento Migrante Centroamericano 2016).

The situation for migrant women is even more precarious. Amnesty International has demonstrated that "sexual violence, or the threat of sexual violence, is often used as a means of terrorizing women and their relatives" (Amnesty International 2010a: 15). Many criminal gangs use sexual violence as part of the "price" migrant women have to pay for their release. Amnesty International (2010a: 15) has reported that "as many as six in 10 migrant women and girls are raped" while in detention or during their journey through Mexico. Migrant women are also victims of human trafficking for purposes of prostitution (IACHR 2013: 64).

The marked increase in the amount and intensity of these abuses took place during the administration of Felipe Calderón, between 2006 and 2012. The migrant human rights crisis emerged in the context of the "war on drugs," which was the central policy of his presidency (IACHR 2013: 42). Furthermore, it is important to note that, along with these "new" abominable acts—extortion; abduction; physical, psychological, and sexual violence; human trafficking; murders; and forced disappearances—we need to consider also the list of human rights violations that migrant-rights organizations have historically reported. These include arbitrary arrest and a lack of due process; discrimination in access to the public and social services to which foreign-born nationals of other states are entitled by law; inhumane detention conditions; obstacles in accessing and getting justice for crimes committed against them; and an inability to defend themselves when exploited by unscrupulous employers (41).

Whether dealing with "old" or "new" types of human rights violations, President Calderón denied or downplayed the Mexican government's responsibility. For him, "unscrupulous" criminals perpetrating abuses were being exterminated by his administration (Presidencia de la República 2011). However, as many nongovernmental human-rights organizations and shelters have shown, mass kidnapping and its aftermath are possible because local and federal authorities collaborate willingly in the process (CNDH 2009; Amnesty International 2010a; Mastrogiovanni 2013).

The Purported Securitization of Migration in Mexico

There are surprisingly very few scholarly studies about the gross violations of human rights perpetrated against undocumented migrants traveling through Mexico (Aikin and Anaya Muñoz 2013). The existing literature on this subject, mainly published by nongovernmental organizations, contends that the "securitization" of Mexican migration policy is the cause of the terrible abuses against migrants. The authors who make up this cluster of literature commonly explain the human rights crisis of transmigrants as follows: after the 9/11 terrorist attacks in the United States, international migration in Mexico went through a process of securitization, which resulted in the current human rights crisis. They assert that (a) since 2001, the U.S. government has seen immigration as a threat to the United States's national security and has imposed this vision on the Mexican government; (b) consequently, the Mexican government now perceives undocumented migration to be a national security threat; and (c) Mexico has, therefore, introduced new and more restrictive immigration laws, invested more money, and deployed more staff to cope with this threat (for example, Armijo 2011; Castillo and Toussaint 2010; Isacson and Meyer 2012; Venet Rebiffé and Palma Calderón 2011).

As I have argued elsewhere, studies on the alleged securitization of migration in Mexico are not entirely convincing (Treviño-Rangel 2016). There are three key reasons why ideas about securitization are of little help in understanding the plight of transmigrants. First, according to the literature on this topic, the securitization of migration has substantively affected multiple laws and regulations on migration issues in Mexico. That is, according to some experts and activists, there is a clear and growing link between migration and security reflected in various legal provisions in the country (Isacson and Meyer 2012: 15; Venet Rebiffé and Palma Calderón 2011: 21). However, neither the Constitution nor the new Law on National Security says anything about immigration as a potential risk to the security of the country (Guevara 2014: 94).

According to existing literature, the new immigration law of 2011 is part of the securitization process, given that it links immigration to security. However, the authors of this literature overlook the fact that the linking of ideas about security and immigration in Mexican immigration laws is nothing new, nor was it imposed by the United States after 9/11. The association between immigration and diverse ideas about security appears in Mexico's legal frameworks from the beginning of the nineteenth century (Guevara 2014: 95). Authors who believe in the securitization of migration in Mexico also overlook the facts that Mexican immigration laws have historically been restrictive and, above all, that the relationship between immigration and security has been inspired by racial prejudice, more so than by fears about threats to the national security (Treviño-Rangel 2005, 2008).

Second, the existent literature states that immigration policy is securitized because immigration authorities, with the help of the Federal Police, implement practices such as migration "filters" in Mexico. Certainly, Mexican authorities are implementing dubious and possibly unconstitutional practices to police undocumented migration throughout the country—practices that, actually, make possible the perpetration of human rights abuses (Guevara 2014: 107). Yet the United States did not impose such practices after 9/11; rather, Mexico has been implementing them for at least forty years. Moreover, neither the budget of the National Institute of Migration (INM) nor the number of its employees increased substantially during the Calderón government (Treviño-Rangel 2016: 279).

Finally, according to securitization theories, issues are securitized through discourse—a discourse that makes aspects of reality thinkable as a security peril and thus amenable to intervention by security experts through exceptional measures. This is how in countries like the United States, Canada, or Great Britain, different actors have promoted the securitization of migration (Bourbeau 2011). In these countries, government authorities, along with political party leaders, members of the legislatures, conservative groups, and some media have sponsored speeches that portray immigration as a threat to national security, political stability, and culture. However, in Mexico, state officials have never suggested that immigration is a security menace (Treviño-Rangel 2016). There is no public evidence to that effect. On the contrary, the deployment of new and old controversial laws and practices that clearly harm undocumented migrants are justified and promoted in the name of human rights. The Calderón administration was well versed in Orwellian Newspeak.

Migrants as Disposable Commodities

The concept of securitization is very popular among activists and experts working in the field of international migration in Mexico; consequently, it has dominated discussions on the subject for at least the past five years. However, it seems to be of little help in describing what happens to undocumented foreign nationals. So, if securitization does not explain the serious human rights crisis experienced by transit migrants, what does?

In this chapter I argue that one potential explanatory factor is that migrants in transit have gradually turned into what I term disposable commodities. The kidnapping of more than eighteen thousand transmigrants every year is a business that generates at least $50 million (IACHR 2013: 54). However, mass kidnappings must be seen as a branch of a larger industry. Whether they are kidnapped or not, undocumented migrants have to pay tariffs that range from $2,000 to $9,000 each to cover all costs related to their journeys from Central America to the United States.[4] The money is used not only to pay smugglers but also to bribe the security forces—for example, immigration officers, traffic police, municipal police, Federal Police—that migrants encounter, for instance, on the streets, at bus terminals, and at road-blocks. Money is also used to pay for basic services, which are deliberately overpriced: a night in a hostel, a ride in a taxi, salt on the table. These ser-vices, provided by ordinary Mexicans, are more expensive for undocumented migrants than for Mexicans and come with a warning: either you accept the unreasonable rate, or you might be delivered to a criminal gang or a security officer—an officer who may, in turn, hand you over to a criminal gang or send you to a prisonlike detention center where you could be held indefinitely.

The migration industry clearly facilitates the commission of unimag-inable abuses against migrants. "Migration industry" is simply a metaphor that seeks to communicate the idea that transit migration through Mexico is a lucrative and growing business, from which multiple actors directly or indirectly profit. In this successful business, made possible by the active par-ticipation, collusion, or acquiescence of multiple state actors, migrants are not considered as risks to national security or as potential terrorists. They are not even seen as a risk to public safety. Within this growing industry, I argue, transmigrants are merely disposable commodities. In Mexico, undoc-umented migrants play a role as commodities who have been stripped of all dignity, who have been excluded from the social world, and who have been completely dehumanized. Transmigrants are not only de facto banned from the political community, they are no longer regarded as humans. And they are disposable because their elimination is regarded as irrelevant.

From this perspective, what occurs to undocumented migrants in Mexico does not seem to be a process of securitization but, rather, a variant of what Arendt referred to as "superfluity"—a process through which the life of some parts of the population become "superfluous," a process of complete dehu-manization. The kidnapping of transmigrants and what comes with it—extor-tion, torture, murder, disappearance (IACHR 2013: 48)—can be undertaken on a gigantic scale because transmigrants' lives are deemed to be dispensable. The municipal police do not chase undocumented migrants because they have high ideals of national security but because they are tempted by dull and petty rewards: a six-pack of beer is what some police officers receive in return for delivering migrants to criminal organizations (CNDH 2009: 15).

This criminal industry is managed by a large number of individuals who willingly allow the human rights abuses to take place. It is important to emphasize this because, on the one hand, the Calderón administration tried to make us believe that abuses committed against transmigrants are the actions of furious criminals and crazy drug traffickers (*La Jornada* 2010; Presidencia de la República 2011); and on the other hand, activists and experts are convinced that the inconceivable abuse suffered by transmigrants is caused by state agents hunting them, motivated by an ideology of securitization. However, the migration industry is not driven by exceptionally wicked individuals with pathological motives, but rather by ordinary people who do not seem to realize the immorality of what they are doing, and who gradually accept as normal actions that are repugnant. It is not only members of organized crime or state agents who participate in these horrifying activities, but many ordinary Mexicans: taxi drivers, hotel managers, Western Union employees, and passenger-bus owners.

In what follows, I briefly describe how multiple actors are involved to different degrees in the migration industry and how they engage undocumented migrants as if they were disposable commodities. I show how organized crime, state security forces, and ordinary Mexicans diligently accept the process of dehumanization of transmigrants.

Criminal Organizations

Multiple criminal organizations, with networks spanning from Central America (Honduras, El Salvador, Guatemala) to the United States, participate in the migration industry in Mexico. This sanguinary industry, as we know it today, emerged during the Calderón administration. The war on drugs that President Calderón devised in the first two weeks of his administration, as Andreas Schedler rightly put it, "destabilized the entire system of criminal actors." That is, Calderón's strategy of "leader decapitation . . . fractured all relationships: within cartels, among cartels, and between cartels and the state" (Schedler 2014: 9). It is in this context of confusion that some cartels came to see undocumented migrants as an extraordinarily lucrative business and opted to become involved in it. Of all the criminal groups that presently take part in this industry, the "Zetas" organization is the most important. This cartel turned migration in transit into a large-scale business through two activities: first, by perpetrating mass kidnappings, up to sixty kidnappings per day; and, second, by using diverse techniques for exploiting migrants, including, for example, forced labor, prostitution, and the transportation of drugs (Mastrogiovanni 2013: 87).

According to a member of the Migrant Program at the Human Rights Institute of the Central American University in El Salvador, it is in the context of the war on drugs in Mexico that the institute started to receive cases of "missing migrants," "injured migrants," and "disappeared migrants": "We started to see requests for the repatriation of the bodies of migrants." It was during the Calderón administration "that transit through Mexico became difficult and several things happened, . . ." and there was enough "evidence [to show] that there is a problem that transit to the United States is no longer as easy as it was before."[5] Similarly, a human rights official in southeastern Mexico asserted, "The change goes hand in hand with organized crime, to the extent that it starts to diversify its activities, it sees the migrant as a gold mine." For him, "in 2006 there were sporadic complaints about some abusive police that found it easy to stop them and take something from them. Now, [however,] we see the systematic presence of organized crime gangs that are very familiar with the logistics and operation of the trains."[6]

These criminal groups operate beyond the logic of securitization. Trying to imagine an ideal world, I asked a Guatemalan migrant what would happen if he had a transit visa that permitted him to cross freely through Mexico. He replied, "I think everything would be the same, considering my experience . . . I think even (with a visa) . . . in one way or another the Zetas would find a way to capture people and always get their money, they would have their methods I imagine."[7]

Journalist Federico Mastrogiovanni (2013: 53) explains the logic of the cartels in relation to transmigrants in the following way: in the context of the war on drugs in Mexico, Central American migrants "went from being consumers of goods and services" to being "commodities themselves." Drawing on in-depth ethnographic research, Mastrogiovanni (167) persuasively concludes that Mexico is "a country that has lost its ethics and takes advantage of migrants as if they were not human." A migrant from Guatemala proves him right:

> If you have money . . . you definitely go, because this is a big organization. Now, if you don't have money . . . you have two [options]: calls [to extort family members] . . . or the other alternative is that they will

want to use you to work for the Zetas, for them, to go do things. If you do not [accept], you can lose your life there. It doesn't hurt them, you know how they do it there? They kill some 10 [people], and they'll never reappear, they throw gasoline on them, and there it remains, and no one will see anything for those people. Those are the disappearances there are. "Ay, I never knew anything about my son"—says a lady. Well, you won't see him anymore, because over there [in Mexico] there is such high crime that so many interests are involved that killing someone is like killing an animal.[8]

State Officials

As human rights organizations have documented extensively in recent years, the ruthless migration industry is possible because of the participation of many agents of the Mexican government, mainly the security forces.

State agents are involved in the migration industry in at least four ways. First, there are the state officials of the different police forces or the Ministry of Defense that know that abuses are being committed against migrants but act as if they do not know. Most of the stories about the mass kidnappings of migrants reported by human rights activists and journalists mention dozens of people captured and then held captive in "safe houses." CNDH has evidence, for example, of how a migrant from El Salvador was kidnapped along with sixty-two other people. The young Salvadoran was transferred to a house where a criminal group held another 133 kidnapped migrants (CNDH 2009: 49). Can sixty people disappear without the authorities' registering the crime? Can 133 people be held captive without the security forces' awareness? In addition, many of these kidnappings occur only a few meters distance from one of the many locations where security forces are located, such as police offices, military checkpoints, mixed security forces units, immigration screening points, and police roadblocks. Can these events really happen without the security forces' knowledge? State agents do not seem to follow the logic of securitization. Rather than trying to impede undocumented migration, state officials seem to prefer to look the other way.

A second group of state agents actively collaborates with organized crime. CNDH reported the story of a young Nicaraguan kidnapped along with thirty people. The migrants were loaded onto a bus and taken to the house where they would remain captive. According to the testimony of the migrant, "we passed several police checkpoints, but they never stopped us, rather they let us pass" (CNDH 2009: 42). These state actors cannot argue that they do not know what is going on. They know the fate that awaits these Central American citizens, know that they are being transferred to be extorted, tortured, and perhaps killed. Still these state actors prefer to do nothing. By not acting, whatever the reason behind their inaction, some state officials diligently collaborate with organized crime.

Other state actors collaborate with organized crime as guardians of the migration industry. Journalist Alejandro Almazan (2013) recounts the story of eight kidnapped migrants who managed to escape from the criminal group that detained them. The migrants sought help from the police. However, the police arrested them and returned them to the criminal group that had held them captive. "These got out of your henhouse," said the police to the kidnapper. As a reward, the criminal gang paid the police 500 pesos ($28) for each returned migrant. In the testimonies collected by CNDH, previously kidnapped migrants confirmed that "the police were colluding with the kidnappers": "individuals from various units came" to the safe houses in which captives were held; in return, "the kidnappers gave them money or alcoholic beverages" (CNDH 2009: 15).

A third group of state agents collaborates with the members of organized crime by abducting migrants on passenger buses, on trains, in airports, in bus stations, at police roadblocks, or on the streets. The war on drugs has facilitated this activity simply by leading to the presence of more security forces on the streets to supposedly combat drug trafficking. One of the journalists I interviewed told me about how he accompanied dozens of migrants on board a train between two cities in southern Mexico in April 2010.[9] At some point in the State of Oaxaca, members of the Federal Police stopped the train. In the distance, a group of soldiers watched what was happening but did not intervene. Some migrants managed to escape the raid. Other migrants were arrested by the police, who stole from them and beat them. The police then proceeded to divide the migrants into two groups. The first group, surprisingly, was released. The second group was handed over to agents of the INM, who arrived at the scene an hour later. The released group was subsequently recaptured by the police themselves, who then handed them over to Los Zetas.[10] The journalist concluded that Mexican security forces are serving as "recruitment agencies" for organized crime.

A fourth group of state agents actively participates in the migration industry without even entering into contact with organized crime. There are state officials who illegally detain migrants in order to extort money from them later. There are state agents who not only do not demonstrate any intention of halting irregular migration flows, they actually contribute to it. Mastrogiovanni (2013: 90) has shown that the minimum passage fee paid by a migrant arrested by corrupt officials of the National Institute of Migration is 1,000 pesos ($56): this fee guarantees the migrant freedom of movement until they reach another police checkpoint or until they come across another migration official. Similarly, the Federal Police also take part in this industry. A Guatemalan migrant along with her two ten- and sixteen-year-old children successfully crossed Mexico in seventeen days because each paid $6,000. Some of that money was to pay members of the Federal Police. The young woman and her two children left Tecun Uman, Guatemala, via motorboat. After sixteen hours at sea, they arrived in Puerto Escondido, Mexico, where members of the Federal Police awaited them in a van, in which they would be transported to the city of Oaxaca. From there, the migrants continued on their way with a smuggler.[11]

These testimonies show that if undocumented migrants have enough money, they may transit through Mexico without being detained or deported by the authorities.[12] The multiple security forces that have mushroomed in Mexico in the last decade are not stopping migrants inspired by securitized policies, but for the money or benefits they receive in return, such as a bottle of whiskey. Migrants are not seen as a security threat but as a disposable commodity.

Ordinary Mexicans and Bystanders

The migration industry is also possible due to the participation of a large number of individuals who are neither members of organized crime nor agents of the security forces. Unfortunately, the transmigrant human rights crisis involves many ordinary Mexicans. Here I briefly outline at least three ways in which "ordinary" Mexican citizens, who are beyond securitization theories, facilitate the commission of atrocities.[13]

First, there are the citizens who are well aware of the precarious situation of transmigrants—citizens who exploit the vulnerability of undocumented migrants to earn some money. As CNDH (2009: 5) reported, migrants "are highly identifiable to those who want to abuse them." Whether they are traveling alone, accompanied by a smuggler or a Federal Police agent, or kidnapped by members of organized crime or the municipal police, migrants use taxis, restaurants, and hotels. These services are available for both Mexicans and foreigners. However, migrants are forced to pay much higher prices. A Guatemalan consul in Mexico describes it as follows: "The taxi driver charges them three times the price, the water bottle worth 7 pesos is sold to them for 25, the phone card is sold to them at double the price . . . and that is how it is with everything, everything, everything."[14]

In the context of the human rights crisis faced by migrants, a second group of Mexican citizens left their position as bystanders and decided to act. However, instead of helping transmigrants, this group of Mexicans became actively involved in committing atrocities. Of the many journalistic investigations that Alejandro Almazan has conducted on migrants, the interview he carried out with a priest in the State of Sonora, in northern Mexico, stands out. This is how the priest responded when asked about the situation of transmigrants: "They say the Zetas were the initiators, but here they already kidnapped migrants even before . . . I arrived in Altar [Sonora] in 2005 and this was already a mess. You should have seen: everyone, even children, extorting migrants" (Almazan 2013).

A final group of ordinary Mexicans to consider is that of the bystanders of these atrocities. Having caused no suffering by their own actions, bystanders know that wrongful acts are committed but refrain from preventing or opposing them. Bystanders are neither victims nor perpetrators, yet they are central to any atrocity because their disinterest and lack of action facilitates the evildoing (Bauman 2003). Mexicans can hardly argue that they do not know what is happening to transmigrants in the country. This is particularly true for those Mexicans who live in the migrant transit areas. When the bodies of seventy-two migrants who had been kidnapped from ordinary passenger buses were discovered, Joy Olson (2012: 10) asked the following pertinent questions: "How could 72 people be kidnapped and no one notice? Bus drivers must have known something. The bus company must have noticed. Other travelers?"

Within the category of bystanders, we must also include the large number of public servants in the federal government in Mexico City, who do not deal directly with migrants but have the power "to do something," and yet do not. According to Mastrogiovanni, the inaction and apparent indifference of senior officials in the federal government are related, again, to economic motives: the authorities tolerate the corruption of local police and migration agents because the earnings serve to supplement the low wages of these local agents.[15] This may be true for state agents of the INM or the governors of the states in the country, but what about other political actors, such as members of Congress, who could radically transform immigration laws? If Mexico is the country with the highest registered number of migrant deaths in the world, what is the role of Congress? How do the legislators respond to the humanitarian crisis? A distinguished member of Congress and member of the Committee on Migration Affairs of the House of Representatives explained, "Rhetorically it is important, but in actions, in practice, it is not considered a priority." [16] Migrants in transit are thus mere disposable commodities, whose transient lives have become, to use Judith Butler's (2009) term, "ungrievable."

Before reaching the end of this chapter, a final clarification is necessary. The situation of migrants in transit would be even worse if it were not for the brave and invaluable help of some Mexicans. They are a minority, and analysis of them is beyond the scope of this chapter, but their extraordinary work must be acknowledged. In interviews of dozens of migrants, among many disturbing stories, there is always some anecdote about a Mexican who witnessed an injustice, who was aware of the abuse committed, and who then did something to prevent it, such as, for example, the Mexicans that hide migrants in their homes before a police raid. The story of these extraordinary Mexicans is yet to be written. Another group of Mexicans who "do something" to alleviate the suffering of migrants in transit are the human rights activists and migrant-rights defenders. This group is more visible and better known. With very limited resources, they are striving relentlessly so that agents of the Mexican state—particularly the growing number of security agents—respect the human rights of transmigrants. Their task is particularly invaluable because, as shown by IACHR, "those who defend migrants' rights in Mexico have to work in a hostile environment, which on numerous occasions has a direct impact on the defenders' lives, person, liberty, security and honor." IACHR has warned that "the work that individuals and civil society organizations do to defend human rights increasingly exposes them to threats, abuse, harassment, intimidation, attacks on their fundamental rights and freedoms, perpetrated by state and non-state agents" (IACHR 2013: 105).

Conclusions

The situation of transmigrants in Mexico continues to deteriorate. Unfortunately, our knowledge of the many factors that contribute to the human rights crisis experienced by migrants in transit is still limited. So far, some activists and experts have tried to explain this crisis through securitization theory. For them, the United States has imposed the securitization of Mexican immigration policy since the terrorist attacks of September 11, 2001. This is the reason why, they argue, the Mexican government seeks to detain undocumented migrants, whom it perceives as a security threat. However, as I have tried to show in this chapter, securitization is not an entirely convincing argument. In the context of the war on drugs, what we are witnessing in Mexico is not a process of the securitization of migration but a process of dehumanization, in which migrants are disposable commodities. "The characters in these pages," to use the description of Primo Levi (2013: 135) about life during the Holocaust, "are not men. Their humanity is buried, or they themselves have buried it, under an offence received or inflicted on someone else."

In other words, in Mexico it is difficult to say that we are seeing the implementation of a rational policy—securitization—created by the state for stopping undocumented migrants who suddenly came to be seen as a threat to national security. Securitization cannot explain, for example, acts of "extreme cruelty" perpetrated both by "organized crime or by authorities" (CNDH 2009: 18).

This chapter addresses the human rights crisis faced by undocumented migrants in Mexico with a focus on the presidency of Felipe Calderón (2006–2012). Unfortunately, the situation facing transmigrants does not seem to be improving with the current administration of Enrique Peña Nieto.[17] As indicated by the latest report by Amnesty International (2016: 252), migrants "passing through Mexico continued to be subjected to mass kidnapping, extortion, disappearances and other abuses committed by organized crime groups, often working in collusion with state agents."

Clearly, the future of the human rights of transit migrants in Mexico does not seem very promising. So what is to be done? As I said before, migrant-rights advocates and shelter workers are carrying out a titanic effort.

Compared to what they do, my contribution is very modest. First, I hope that this chapter invites critical reflection on the nature of the Mexican political system. Can a holocaust take place in a democracy? This chapter, like others in this book, shows that the current human rights crisis is possible because many practices, laws, institutions, and values of the authoritarian era have barely shifted during the so-called Mexican democracy (see Chapter 9). Second, I am an academic interested in human rights, so the role of my research "may be just that of 'bearing witness,' a simple issue of 'rehumanising' victims or generating association between victims and bystanders" (Stanley

2009: 13). This is relevant in Mexico where society seems to have "normal-ized" the atrocities suffered by undocumented foreign nationals transiting through the country. As noted by a former UN advisor on the human rights of migrants, "You couldn't name one public demonstration, one collective manifestation in the streets of a large city of Mexico to protest the violations of migrants' human rights. Not even one!"[18] By breaking the silence and nam-ing human rights violations for what they are, this chapter may at least con-tribute to dismantling the culture of denial that surrounds the commission of state crimes in Mexico. Herein lies, at least in part, some sort of opportunity to turn the tides.

CHAPTER 6

Emigration, Violence, and Human Rights Violations in Central Mexico

Benjamin James Waddell

Introduction

In this chapter I focus on the social context in which violence and human rights violations have unfolded in modern Mexico. I analyze the relationship between mass emigration and violence in the state of Michoacán. Based on qualitative evidence from the field, I argue that rising crime—including state-sponsored violence—is likely conditioned by the social, economic, and cultural deficits forged by decades of mass emigration. My results have important implications for policy makers interested in reducing human rights violations within regions experiencing high emigration.

Economic Development, Democratization, and Migration

In theory, economic development should plant the seeds of democratic values and norms, and in time, the spread of democracy should foster a more stable world in which human rights violations are less likely to occur. Still, despite improved development levels and reductions in overall violence in recent decades (Pinker 2011), the world has also witnessed blatant crimes against humanity including genocides in Cambodia, Rwanda, Sudan, and, most recently, Syria and Iraq. These events bring up an important question. What leads to increases in state-led violence during the initial phases of development?

In *Political Order in Changing Societies,* Thomas Huntington (1968) argued that during the early stages of development, state-led violence tends to increase. Huntington's analysis suggested a parabolic relationship between development and human rights violations, a notion that has since been corroborated (Mitchell and McCormick 1988). Subsequent research finds a similar inverted-U relationship between internal violence and the type of political regime, such that societies experience more crime during the initial stages of democratization but eventually stabilize as democratic norms and values take hold (Fein 1995; Regan and Henderson 2002). This nonlinear pattern is related to the fact that as economic growth and democratic norms expand, governments are unable to keep up with the expectations of citizens, and this gap has a destabilizing effect on society. This is in part due to *economic* enabling structures, such as poverty and inequality, which may encourage people to participate in criminal activity as a form of accessing social mobility. This has been particularly evident in Latin America during the era of neoliberal reform. *Political* enabling structures, such as corruption, clientelism, and authoritarian vestiges from the past, also contribute to criminal activity as countries transition toward democracy. During such transition periods it is often difficult to distinguish between state-sponsored violence and nonstate violence due to the fact that the government cloaks its extrajudicial activities beneath the guise of paramilitary groups, vigilantes, partisan gangs, and death squads (Zinecker 2007: 8). Such activities fall under what Guillermo O'Donnell (2004) has referred to as "brown areas" of rule.

Economic and political enabling structures contribute to nonlinear patterns of violence during periods of economic development and democratization. However, they do not fully explain why some countries experience extreme levels of violence during periods of transition while others do not. To date, researchers have focused on three main factors in explaining nonlinear patterns of violence: (1) regime type, (2) institutional structures, and (3) rule implementation. A fourth factor—the social context from which human rights violations emerge—has received far less attention. In particular, existing research has failed to examine the degree to which major demographic shifts affect levels of internal state- and nonstate-sponsored violence during periods of economic and political transition.

The Lasting Effects of Mass Emigration

We know relatively little about the degree to which mass emigration contributes to increases in state-sponsored violence. However, we know a great deal about the lasting effects of immigrants on levels of violence within migrant-receiving societies, which is a useful point of departure for this discussion. In the United States, criminologists find that immigrants revitalize local neighborhoods (Lee, Martinez, and Rosenfeld 2001; Martinez 2002; Martinez et al. 2004; Reid et al. 2005) by strengthening social organizations such as churches, schools, and NGOs (Ousey and Kubrin 2009), rejuvenating local economies (Vélez 2009), attracting investment in areas previously lacking business capital (Reid et al. 2005), and, ultimately, making crime less profitable (Martinez 2002). As Lyons and colleagues point out, "Contrary to much public opinion and political rhetoric, our research joins a chorus of others in suggesting that immigration generally makes neighborhoods safer" (2014: 624).

If the influx of immigrants into urban cities in the Global North contributes to a decrease in violence, then it seems at least plausible that the outflow of emigrants in migrant-sending regions in the Global South may contribute to social, economic, and political disintegration by undermining communal stability and draining regions of the exact same forms of capital that contribute to urban renewal in immigrant neighborhoods in the Global North.

While the effects of emigration in the Global South are not entirely pernicious, existing research finds that it fosters social disintegration within migrant-sending regions by abetting conspicuous consumption and exacerbating local inequalities (Mines and de Janvry 1982; Reichert 1981; Wiest 1973). This is particularly evident at the beginning of the migrant cycle (Adams 1989; Adams, Cuecuecha, and Page 2008; Barham and Boucher 1998; Milanovic 1987; Mckenzie and Rapoport 2006).

Ultimately, emigration and remittances (money sent home by migrants living abroad) can deter community members from participating in the labor market altogether (Azam and Gubert 2005). Research in this vein finds that if remittance flows are large enough to provide for the welfare of the entire household, they can have the perverse effect of discouraging individuals from participating in productive sectors (Gubert 2000; Germenji and Swinnend 2004). Azam and Gubert (2005: 1334) find that the more money migrants send home, the less incentive their families have to work.

The communal hazards related to emigration are particularly pernicious for those individuals who receive little or no help from families abroad. In developing regions around the world, and in rural communities in particular, emigration is often seen as the best means through which to achieve material success. This is especially true in rural townships where local economies expand and contract in accordance with the ebb and flow of migrant remittances (Massey and Basem 1992). In these areas, cash flows from abroad allow some individuals, mainly the relatives of migrants, to participate in a market economy that was traditionally closed off to rural peasants. However, only a relatively small percentage of society benefits from remittances, and those who do are not prone to making the types of investments that would contribute to long-term community development. Instead, remittance recipients typically spend their money on material goods like televisions, electronics, durable goods, and new homes (Massey et al. 1994). While such activities can generate employment in the short run, they are not the types of activities that underpin long-term community well-being. Thus, while emigration introduces conspicuous consumption to marginalized communities in the Global South, it does not appear to stimulate the type of economic development that would permit individuals not directly tied to diaspora communities to participate in mass consumption and economically active sectors.

While diaspora communities contribute directly to the improved welfare of some individuals, and even stimulate employment within communities of origin as migrants build second homes and purchase goods in local markets, in time emigrants inhibit the policy environments that would improve the welfare of those they leave behind. Extant research documents the mechanisms driving this process well. Based on research conducted in Mexico, Goodman and Hiskey (2008) demonstrate that while remittances provide communities with much needed resources in the short run, in the long run they reduce community pressure on the state to solve development problems, and this process, in time, facilitates government desertion (185). Related to this phenomenon, Adida and Girod (2011: 19) find that access to clean water and drainage improves in Mexican municipalities that receive relatively higher levels of remittances. However, these researchers also reveal that local governments reduce their support for communities as financial transfers from abroad increase. Finally, in a panel study of eighteen countries in Latin America, Doyle (2013) finds that over time, remittances "translate into reduced support for political parties who advocate redistribution" (24).

The adverse effects of emigration extend beyond the economic and political spheres. For example, while existing research demonstrates that in Mexico migrant fathers remain ostensibly involved in the lives of their offspring (Nobles 2011), fathers also report a decreased sense of obligation to their children (D'Auberterre 2000). In addition, the absence of fathers in migrant households is associated with a number of social issues. Children growing up in households with a migrant father have lower rates of immunization, are less likely to be breastfed, have increased odds of illness (Schmeer 2009), report lower educational aspirations (Nobles 2011), and are more likely to drop out of school (McKenzie and Rapoport 2006). In a field survey conducted in Mexico, UNICEF researchers found that children of migrants were more likely to be associated with teen pregnancies, alcohol abuse, drug use, robberies, and imprisonment (Cortes 2008: 22–23). Finally, in the case of El Salvador, Heidrun Zinecker (2007) finds that emigration and remittances have contributed to high levels of violence by reducing pressure on local government, increasing relative deprivation by driving up inequality, and undermining the types of social capital that would typically discourage violence (Zinecker 2007: 22).

Available evidence demonstrates that emigration and remittances aggravate social inequalities while restricting access to the types of productive sectors that would allow those left behind to enjoy the material luxuries that remittances afford select members of the community. In these situations, and in the absence of other sources of employment, it would not be particularly surprising if some residents turned to criminal activity as a means of acquiring material success.

A Theoretical Model for Understanding
Migration and Violence in Modern Mexico

According to Émile Durkheim's anomie theory, large social change—such as mass emigration to the city or another country—disrupts the values and norms that moderate human interaction and, in consequence, incites criminal behavior (Durkheim [1897] 1951, [1883] 1951). Robert Merton (1938) built on Durkheim's work, contending that relative deprivation best explained criminal activity. In doing so, Merton shifted from anomie's focus on the breakdown of cultural norms toward a theory that emphasized structural strain to explain why some people resort to criminal activity while others do not (Lanier et al. 2015: 219). He argued when criminal behavior is most likely to emerge: "When a system of cultural values extols, virtually above all else, certain common symbols of success for the population at large while its social structure rigorously restricts or completely eliminates access to approved modes of acquiring these symbols for a considerable part of the same population, that anti-social behavior ensues on a considerable scale" (1938: 680). Building on anomie and strain theory, social disorganization theorists have argued that ecological factors influence criminal behavior

(Sampson, Morenoff, and Earls 2005). They contend that one should expect crime to be higher in neighborhoods with elevated unemployment, lack of access to education, poor infrastructure, dilapidated housing, and weak institutions. As Shaw and McKay (1972) point out, in these situations transient populations further diminish the quality of relationships among residents, and this diminishment promotes social isolation. Finally, as Thomas (2011:385) argues, "If residents are unable to sustain routine contacts and relationships and if organizations are nonexistent or have weak foundations of economic and social support, the more social decay and disorganization a neighborhood experiences, and we should observe higher crime rates there." In other words, if focusing on individuals as perpetrators of crime sheds light on who breaks the law, by analyzing the environment in which crime takes place we may very well gain a better understanding of what drives people to commit crime in the first place. Despite this research, there is very little discussion concerning the potential relationship between emigration and violence within migrant-sending regions around the world. This intellectual lacuna is particularly surprising in Mexico, where emigration rates and crime have increased at similar paces over the last two decades.

Roughly 10 percent of Mexico's 122 million citizens live in a country other than Mexico, and the majority of these individuals have left their country in the last two decades. During this same period, crime rates have increased dramatically, especially in high-migration regions. Between 2005 and 2015 an estimated 164,000 people were victims of homicide, and an additional 26,000 people were disappeared (Breslow 2015). As Table 6.1 reveals, with an average age of twenty-seven, the vast majority of disappeared people during this time frame were of working age, and roughly 72 percent of the victims were men. Although it is impossible to know the exact circumstances surrounding these individuals' disappearances, their basic profiles are very similar to that of many migrants. Consequently, it seems at least plausible that increased levels of violence may in part be related to the fact that the ostensible success of those who are able to emigrate places strain on those left behind to achieve similar levels of success. This may be particularly true in rural areas, where emigration and poverty rates are significantly higher and the culture of emigration is extolled as a principal form of social mobility. To the degree to which this is true, it seems likely that in recent years the lasting effects of emigration have contributed to the number of young people willing to participate in criminal activities such as drug trafficking, extortion, kidnapping, and corruption. In the next section, as a

Table 6.1. Basic profile of disappeared in Mexico, 2005–2015

	Gender	Average age
Male	18,732	28.6
Female	7,186	25.5
Total	25,918	27.4

Source: Registro Nacional de Datos de Personas Extraviados o Desaparecidas (RNPED). https://rnped.segob.gob.mx (last consulted: March 1, 2016).

Note: Data reports through April 2015.

means of further exploring this possibility, I analyze qualitative data gathered in Michoacán, Mexico.

Evidence from the Field: Michoacán, Mexico

Michoacán provides a particularly fitting setting to analyze the relationship between emigration, crime, and human rights violations. Next to Guanajuato, this central Mexican state sends more people to the United States than any other Mexican state, and it typically receives more remittances than other states in Mexico. Michoacán has also experienced a considerable spike in crime in recent years, including homicides, disappearances, and human rights violations.

Two separate episodes in 2015 shed light on the nature of violence occurring in Michoacán. The first took place on January 6, 2015, in Apatzingán, where eight civilians were killed by Federal Police officers who were apparently trying to break up a demonstration by self-defense groups. The second incident occurred on May 22 in Tanhuato, where Federal Police killed forty-two civilians at a compound that was allegedly being held by a criminal organization. Despite clear evidence of extrajudicial killings, no police officers have been charged in either case (Human Rights Watch 2015). Apatzingán and Tanhuato are examples of what the Inter-American Commission on Human Rights (IACHR) recently described as a "serious human rights crisis" (2015: 32). The report details evidence regarding forced disappearances, extrajudicial executions, torture, citizen insecurity, injustice, and widespread impunity (2015).

Events like these lead to an important question. Does mass emigration and the transfer of remittances back to Michoacán contribute to rising violence by reducing pressure on officials to respect and protect human rights? This section attempts to answer this question in two stages. In the first stage, I analyze data trends regarding emigration, homicides, and disappearances across 113 municipalities in Michoacán. In the second stage, I introduce the reader to qualitative evidence from a community named La Peralta, which is located in northern Michoacán near the border with Guanajuato.

Data Trends Across Michoacán

Table 6.2 displays descriptive statistics for the data used in this section. Data is from the National Institute of Statistics and Geography (INEGI) and the National Population Council (CONAPO). There were nearly 1,600 homicides registered in Michoacán between 2005 and 2015, with a mean of more than 8 homicides per 100,000 residents. There was substantial variation across Michoacán's 113 municipalities, with homicide rates ranging from close to 0 all the way up to 177. During this same period just over 1,000 people disappeared in Michoacán, with a mean of 1.5 disappearances per 100,000 inhabitants.

Emigration in the developing world is generally higher in economically deprived regions. Thus, if emigration and crime were to correlate in Michoacán, we might expect that homicide rates would be highest in the state's least developed municipalities. With that in mind, Figure 6.1 plots homicide rates per 100,000 inhabitants with human development levels across Michoacán's municipalities. As expected, homicide rates between 1990 and 2010 are significantly lower in municipalities that have higher levels of well-being. This trend follows general tendencies around the world in which violence drops in

Table 6.2. Descriptive statistics for homicides and disappearances in Michoacán, 2005–2015

	Obs.	Mean	Std. dev.	Max
Homicide Rate per 100,000	1,574	8.59	17.68	177.02
Disappearance Rate per 100,000	1,004	1.52	4.21	41.54

Source: Registro Nacional de Datos de Personas Extraviados o Desaparecidas (RNPED) and the National Institute for Statistics and Geography (INEGI).

Note: Data reports through April 2015.

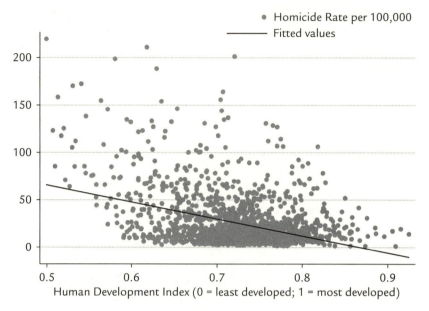

Figure 6.1. Homicide rates per 100,000 by Human Development in Michoacán (1990–2010). Source: Based on date from INEGI.

areas where inhabitants have relatively better access to health care, education, and income.

Michoacán's least-developed municipalities are typically located in rural areas; thus we should expect rural municipalities to have higher homicide rates, which, as Figure 6.2 reveals, is in fact the case. Only 34 percent of Michoacán's municipalities surpassed the state's average of 13 homicides per 100,000 residents during the period 2000–2010. However, among these high-homicide municipalities, nearly 80 percent are located in rural municipalities with less than 58,000 inhabitants. While criminals may prefer to dump bodies in rural locations, it appears that migration rates and remittance flows also play a role in explaining where homicides occur most frequently. Homicide rates are substantially higher in municipalities where more households receive remittances. In fact, while only 31 percent of rural municipalities fall into the high-homicide category (more than 13 per 100,000), an astonishing 84 percent of these are municipalities in which at least 8 percent of homes report receiving remittances. This finding demonstrates that in Michoacán, substantially more homicides occur in municipalities reporting

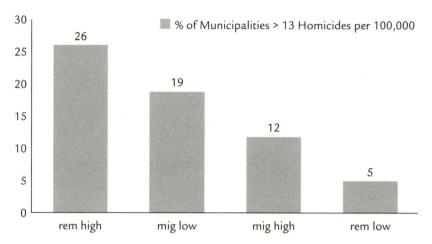

Figure 6.2. Homicide rates across municipalities. Chi^2 significant at p < .001.

above-average remittance flows. This association holds across all municipalities in Michoacán (r = .31; p < .05) and is particularly evident in rural municipalities (r = .42; p < .001). In turn, homicide rates are substantially lower in municipalities where less than 8 percent of homes report having ties to migrants abroad.

La Peralta, Michoacán

In this section I use qualitative evidence from the field to shed light on the potential relationship between mass emigration out of Michoacán and high levels of crime within migrant-sending regions. I draw on interviews conducted in and around a village named La Peralta, which is located in a municipality along the border of Michoacán and Guanajuato. I use pseudonyms for both my interviewees as well as the physical locations that I reference in my discussion. To do otherwise would place the lives of my informants in danger.

La Peralta is a small ranching town located in north-central Michoacán along the border with Guanajuato. The town is near a larger town of nearly seventy thousand inhabitants that serves as a stopover point on the way to Guanajuato. Merchants from both states frequently travel through the village on their way to larger regional markets. Like other towns in the region, migrants have been leaving La Peralta for larger regional cities like Querétaro and Morelia for decades. A smaller percentage of residents go to the United States, but everyone in town knows someone who lives *al otro lado* (on the other side). The town's population hovers around 2,300 people, but approximately 15 percent of the town's native-born population resides in the United States. Most residents have family living in either Michigan or Illinois, but recently, migrants have been settling in less traditional receiving states like Arkansas, North Carolina, and Georgia. *Los paisanos,* or migrants, have played a fundamental role in local development. In addition to the support family members receive from remittances, the town has several Home Town Association groups that have contributed substantial amounts of money to public-works projects through the remittance-matching program "3x1 para migrantes." Still, despite these efforts, the majority of residents living in La Peralta are steeped in deep poverty, with few employment options within the legal market. As a result, more and more residents have joined the ranks of criminal organizations operating in the area. This is particularly true for young men. In the space that follows I share excerpts from my interviews in the region, which help shed light on the complex relationship between migration, the state, and criminal organizations.

During a field visit to Mexico in June 2016 I met up with a man named Enrique, who manufactures furniture in northern Michoacán. As he pointed out, tension in the area has been compounded by the war on drugs. We spoke on a street corner in southern Guanajuato, where he was selling wooden chairs and tables. He was sitting in the shade alongside a wall-sized mural that depicted a map of the United States and Mexico upon which the artist had painted *paisanos* harvesting crops. In the Pacific Ocean, in turn, the artist had painted a picture of downtown Chicago, and in the Atlantic Ocean there was a depiction of the small town Enrique and I happened to be in. The mural is representative of the ubiquitous nature of transnational connections within the region, and not surprisingly, Enrique's life was emblematic of such networks. At the time, his son was living in Atlanta, and his daughter, who had recently been deported, was trying to cross back into the United States via Arizona. Enrique and his wife were raising one of their grandchildren, whom his son had left behind but was afraid to try and smuggle into the United States until he was older. According to Enrique, his life has been deeply affected by the federal government's war on drug trafficking, which has completely disrupted the local economy and stripped the market out from under his furniture business.

I used to employ 12 men. We would travel as far as Chiapas to sell our furniture and small tin stoves. A lot of our product would sell here locally but now that it's so hard for migrants to come back, few see any purpose in purchasing material things in Mexico. They still have their houses but they never come anymore and so the economy has been hit hard. Plus, now that the federal government is trying to weed out the *carteles* [and so] the *narcos* are finding other places to wash their money into the legal market and we're left with nothing. But it never occurs to them [the government] that *narcos* are the only ones providing jobs in these areas and that in combating them they are really just taking away good paying jobs and creating more foot soldiers for the *narcos*. Their businesses might just be fronts but they still employ people, they feed families! (June 2016)

Like others I interviewed, Enrique made a point of distinguishing between outside groups, such as the Army and the Federal Police, and the local government. The problem, he pointed out, is that local elites include both government officials as well as *narcos,* and to a certain degree, they depend on one another. This point also came up in a conversation I had with a secondary teacher named Francisco. We met in June 2016 on the side of the road where his sons were selling watermelons in between classes to try and help with the bills. Francisco had taught that morning in Peralta, and he was on his way to a nearby town where he gives a class in the afternoon. Francisco, who worked for years in California, frequently peppered his conversations with English words and phrases. Regarding violence, he made the following point:

Look, everyone knows who they are. It's a small town. Many of the current *narcos* went to school with me or we played *fútbol* together. But there's nothing you can do. The government knows too and they don't do anything because they benefit from cartel wealth in the form of bribes, payoffs, and quality of life. For them it's a win-win. The *narcos* bribe them, plus they spend their money locally and make major investments in businesses, which are all subsidized by *narcódolares,* and government officials and their families are their best clients! Look, for example, someone recently opened a private gym and day spa in town. It's got beautiful marble floors and stunning Turkish baths in the changing rooms. Now, look around this place, who has money to go to a day spa? I can't afford it! I'm selling watermelons just to keep the lights on! Perhaps people like you or *los paisanos* go to these places when they come back but let's be honest, the day-to-day patrons are people working for the government. These are the indirect benefits of money laundering and they may seem inconsequential but for the local elite, many of whom long for the amenities of the city, the benefits are enormous. Plus, it gives the illusion that officials are bringing progress to *el rancho*. (June 2016)

Francisco often returned to his point that local government had a lot to gain by turning a blind eye to *narcos*. However, as one of my informants from the Mexican military clarified, even if officials wanted to combat criminal organizations, they would run up against the blurred lines between law enforcement and the rank and file members of cartels.

The lines between local law enforcement and *los narcos* are very blurry around here. Many of the law enforcement agents work for both sides. A few years ago, the state police made a big deal about the alleged corruption in a municipal police force just down the road from here and so they came in and removed all of the agents. They let more than 100 officers go and they replaced them with state officers for a few weeks. Then they made a big deal about the fact that the new municipal officers would be hired only after taking a lie detector test and going through a whole new series of training sessions. But it's all for show. A few months later most of the officers were back on the force. Who else were they going to hire? This is a small town and only so many people are willing to risk their lives to become a police officer right now. And they all know the truth, if you work for the police, you work for the local *capo* because *el capitán* is on the take and you need the extra cash. That's just the way it is and this is what we're up against when we get sent into these small towns. No one trusts us and no one wants to talk to us and I don't blame them because they have to live here, we don't. (July 2015)

Later, in June 2016, I spoke with a municipal officer named Carlos. He worked the night shift near an OXXO store just off the main plaza. After some small talk, he asked me what I was up to. I explained to him that I was looking into issues related to corruption and violence. He took a look around to see who might be watching, and after a few glances in each direction, he quietly offered up his thoughts on the matter:

It's not just the material benefits that you have to consider. Look, if you ask me, does the government participate in these types of atrocities? Well, in some cases yes but usually it's much more subtle than that. They're complicit in the crimes but not directly. Look, it's like this. You see, government officials and traffickers know each other. Many times they grew up together but even if they didn't, the *narcos* are the only ones with money in these *ranchos* and the government depends on money, right? So of course they know each other! For God's sake, I know who the local players are! Everyone does. But we don't apprehend them. It doesn't work like that. Officials benefit from the *narcos* and the money they spend on all the businesses they set up and who knows how much they benefit from unwritten agreements! But more recently, as things have heated up, officials have also benefited from their *pactos* with *narcos* in the form of security and enforcement. If they're on the take and something happens, they look the other way, and if they need someone to disappear and they've already got a working relationship with someone, well, they can make that happen too. You get the idea. So, you see, it's not like they directly hire *narcos* to take care of their dirty work but they might as well because everyone knows how it works! (June 2016)

What is particularly telling, given the common knowledge most people have in La Peralta regarding the presence of criminal organizations, is the fact that relatively little information ends up in the pages of local newspapers. This is especially true when it comes to the type of investigative journalism that would publicly connect government officials with organized crime. With that in mind, I share an excerpt from an interview I conducted in December 2015 with Claudio, the editor in chief for one of the region's most circulated newspapers.

We know it's going on but we don't ask questions about it. Government officials and *narcos* have worked together for a long time in these regions and now that things are hot [violent] it's not surprising that government officials are being accused of being complicit in murders and human rights violations. I mean, Ayotzinapa is in the news because it was so blatant but those kinds of things happen around here all the time but on a much smaller scale. Someone starts asking the wrong questions and pretty soon they're nowhere to be found. But nobody is looking into these cases because they're fearful they might turn over the wrong stone but if you were to add up all the disappearances, well, they'd probably run into the thousands. We've had to place reporters on paid leave for months at a time because they begin receiving death threats for articles they publish on homicides. Around 2011 we started a policy of only reporting the facts that the government provides us with in homicide cases that we think might be related to *los carteles.* As a consequence, the government has complete control over what the public ends up seeing in these cases, which means that indirectly *los narcos* control what the public ends up reading. It's not right but it's a matter of life or death, so we decided it's just not worth it to do investigative reporting on these issues. (December 2015)

A local journalist, whom I refer to as Roberta here, corroborated Claudio's account. As she pointed out, cartels frequently employ *halcones,* or falcons, to spy on the police and the press.

We never know when they're watching but they are. We all use two cell phones, one for personal use and one for the job and we never give out our personal number under any circumstances but despite that, we've all received death threats on our personal phones. I've also received anonymous tips on my phone. Once a man with a muffled voice called and addressed me by my first name. I started to sweat as he was talking to me but I was afraid to hang up. He told me to go to an abandoned lot, that there was something worth writing about there. I went out there with a colleague and there was nothing to be found. As we were leaving the location I received another call. It was the same voice. He said he was busier than he thought and hadn't got around to our delivery. He told us to come back the next day and so we did and there were two dismembered bodies and a sign with a message for a rival cartel. It was chilling. He was clearly watching us and who knows how he got my private number but he had it. And that's the kind of thing we can't report. Instead, we simply report the basic facts. Two men in their mid-twenties, found dead near such and such place. That's where the story ends. (June 2016)

Another journalist, named Mariana, who has since left the profession but continues to volunteer for an NGO that works with issues related to disappeared journalists, supported Roberta's claims but went a step further in arguing that many government officials are deeply complicit in the crime and human rights violations taking place in central Mexico. We've spoken on multiple occasions, but this is an excerpt from a discussion we had in June 2016.

> I don't have firm numbers but local officials are clearly implicated in these crimes and it runs right up the chain of command. You remember when they detained the attorney general [of Michoacán]? I mean, that's just one example but that's the very individual who should be cracking down on corruption and instead, he's contributing to it! And we know it. Eventually we get to know the *halcones* who work for the *narcos* because we see them at all the crime scenes. We don't know their names but we remember their faces. Occasionally, when we get tips, we're the first ones on the scene and sometimes, in these cases, they're already there. Once, I was at a crime scene before officials ever showed up. Not surprisingly, a *halcon* showed up shortly after me. We exchanged a few words and went about our respective business. My photographer was taking photos of the bodies when I noticed the man send a text. A few minutes later I got a call from [my] editor. He told me to leave immediately. We wouldn't be reporting on the murder. Apparently he'd received a call from above. This type of thing happens a lot.

Mariana's comment refers to one of the federal government's early raids on Michoacán in which federal officers detained the attorney general, twenty high-ranking officials, and at least ten mayors. It's easy to see such apprehensions as progressive steps toward ending drug trafficking in Mexico, but as an informant close to one of the then-detained officials pointed out,

> Many see this and say, "You see, it's all his fault. Now things are going to improve and we'll all be safe again." But it's not that simple. I know this person as a friend and he is a good person but his life was under constant threat. He couldn't go anywhere without his body guards, which usually number between six and ten heavily armed men. Furthermore, he received death threats from rival groups and these are people he knows are capable of carrying out their threats. So what else can he do other than turn a blind eye? What would you do? More

importantly, what will the next person to hold his office do? He's going to face the exact same pressures. (December 2015)

As these interviews reveal, in La Peralta, and likely elsewhere in Michoacán, government officials are at least partially complicit in the crime currently affecting their citizens.

Turning back to migration, in most cases, migrants are not directly involved in the violence unfolding on the ground in places like Michoacán, but as the next exchange clarifies, mass emigration out of Mexico likely contributes to the types of social conditions from which one would expect crime to emerge.

I met Roberto in 2013 during a field visit to a migration-prone town in southern Guanajuato. He works at a local university, where he teaches economics courses. Roberto and I met up again in July 2015 and June 2016. During my most recent field visit, we met up at a restaurant in town, which is alleged to be a front for a criminal organization trying to wash money into the legal system. The establishment was well kept and clearly overstaffed, and despite the rural location and an ample menu, the prices were surprisingly low. Roberto chose a table inside, well removed from the more frequented tables on the cobblestone patio, and as he spoke he kept his head low, and like my other informants, his voice fell into a whisper when he mentioned local officials and individuals purportedly working for cartels. As he pointed out, there is a clear connection in the region between economic decline, migration, and crime.

Money hides corruption and lubricates the system but the machine is run by the foot soldiers. You have to understand, this region's economy was decimated by NAFTA.[1] After 1994 the swine industry all but collapsed and the production of grains and beans was never the same. Nobody was rich but they could make ends meet back then but now, it's nearly impossible. That's why so many left in the 1990s. They went to Chicago, Los Angeles, Tucson, New York, wherever they could find work and they sent money home, which revealed a new way of living to local residents. Suddenly people were building cement homes, watching T.V. on big screens, and driving big trucks. But migration isn't an option for everyone and now the local economy is worse than ever because no one wants to farm or ranch. If you work the fields all day you only get paid $4-5 dollars! And so, you see, not everybody could leave and now it's more difficult for them to go north anyways because of the border security and the higher *coyote* fees. So, for many young people, especially young men, the best option to get their hands on material things is by working for the cartels. It's dangerous work but the *narcos* know that their foot soldiers are replaceable because there are so many young men looking to earn a quick buck. It's a terrible cycle but it shouldn't surprise anyone. (June 2016)

As Roberto shows, migration and remittances introduce conspicuous consumption and inflation into local communities, and in doing so, they fundamentally change the opportunity structures. However, they also create social fissures that have lasting impacts within communities. According to Rodrigo, who teaches social sciences at the same university that Roberto works at, years of emigration contributed to the disintegration of the family unit in many small localities across Mexico, and this, in turn, has left the countryside littered with a generation of young people who lack direction in life.

When you think about it there have been wars over money, so it's not impossible to think that remittances have contributed to violence but not where you might think. Remittances provoke violence in the household. Couples, divided by thousands of miles, fight over how the money should be spent, who can spend it, whether or not to spend it or save it, and many times even though the man isn't present, he administers how the remittances are spent. What is worse is the fact that remittances aggravate an environment that is already marked by domestic violence and a culture of *machismo* that has its roots in *la conquista*. And all of this is related to the current violence we see. In my opinion, it's the root of it. (June 2016)

Shortly after I talked with Rodrigo, I met up with Chucho, whom I'd talked with several times in the past. Chucho, who now lives in Guanajuato near the border with Michoacán, was himself a migrant, but once he had a family he decided to return to his hometown in order to be with his family. As he put it, "I didn't want my children to grow up without a father. I'd seen how poor my friend's relationship with their kids was and I didn't want that to happen to me. So, I came back." Since his return he's found employment working construction and helping out with government development projects. Like

Rodrigo, Chucho feels that family divisions and remittances are related to the recent waves of violence central Mexico has been experiencing.

> There's a great deal of problems within the family. These are kids that grow up without a father or without a mother and then they find themselves of an age when they should be working but they've had everything handed to them because of the remittances and so when it comes down to it they don't want to work. So, they get involved in other forms of contributing to the family and they simply get involved with the wrong people. But once they go that direction there's really no turning back. It's not easy to get out alive. (June 2016)

The case of Rogelio Gutierrez, alias "El Flaco," helps highlight the relationship between migration and violence in the region. El Flaco's father worked for years in the United States. Like many other migrants from his hometown, he was accustomed to working for six months in the United States and then returning home for six months. Then, suddenly, in 2006 he came back for good with a sizable fortune in cash. "He claimed that he was working for a cleanup crew in the aftermath of Hurricane Katrina and one day, to his great fortune, he found a room full of cash that had been abandoned," a local source told me. "But everyone knows the truth. He'd been involved in drug trafficking for years and it appears he simply decided to cut his ties with the organization and return home to ranch." By then, however, El Flaco had gotten involved with local traffickers in order to earn his own money.

> When his father came back with all the money El Flaco started to get a big head. His mom never could control him, and with his father gone for long periods of time, well, he seemed destined for trouble. For a long time he just acted like a *capo* but then he must have decided to try and take control of *la plaza* and that's when things got out of control. When he tried to take over the oil ducts [pipelines] they'd had enough. (June 2016)

Official accounts report that El Flaco was traveling west on a highway near his hometown when an oncoming truck intercepted him. He was kidnapped at gunpoint, but for reasons unclear to the authorities, the kidnapper's vehicle left the highway. With authorities in close pursuit, the kidnappers killed El Flaco in the cab of the car and fled on foot. Authorities were on the scene immediately, and they even apprehended several suspects, but as it turned out, they were merely fieldworkers who happened to be in the area at the time of the shooting. "Well, that's what they printed," said a young woman who grew up just down the street from El Flaco. She went on to explain,

> But that's not what happened. El Flaco was taken from his truck just like they said but a bystander must have called the police because a patrol unit quickly fell into pursuit. The assailants swerved off the road into a nearby field but they killed Flaco before they fled the scene. The authorities were right behind them but somehow the killers managed to simply disappear into thin air. But obviously they didn't get away. The authorities let them go. And that's what they do when they are in on the crime. They just let the criminals go.

I asked her why the authorities would let the aggressors go.

> Look, there is drug trafficking in this area but what the criminals really want to control are the [illegal] oil ducts, and that's what Flaco was trying to do. The problem is that the oil ducts are run by criminal organizations that have deep connections with workers at PEMEX. Insiders let them know when oil will be coming through, what grade [of fuel] it will be, and how much time they'll have to tap the duct before it starts flowing. They say a good milking, as they call it, can net 100,000 US dollars. With so much money at stake, *los carteles* are involved but obviously the government is involved too. So you tell me, why would the authorities let El Flaco's killers go? It's pretty obvious. (June 2016)

I ran my informant's version by several other sources, and they gave similar descriptions of the facts. One, however, drew a connection between El Flaco's upbringing and the eventual unraveling of his family.

> El Flaco's father was one of the few people that I know that was able to clean his hands of whatever he'd been involved in there in the US and come back here and put his money to good use. He bought land, tractors, trucks, and houses, but his family had been unravelling for years in his absence. He died a few years after he came back, then his wife died, and as all this was happening his youngest son, El Flaco, who

had also been the most spoiled, got involved in drugs. They'd always given him everything. His mom bought him everything he wanted with the money his father sent but eventually he wanted things his father's money couldn't buy. He had money but he wanted to control the region it seems. But I think it all started to fall apart when his father began to leave. And it's the same story in all these little towns. Everyone thinks migrants will save the village but that's not how it usually works out. (June 2016)

Together, these excerpts reveal the complex relationship between emigration, crime, and human rights violations in central Mexico. It is unclear to what degree these results can be generalized beyond this region, but at least in the state of Michoacán, it appears that events in La Peralta reflect the types of activities taking place elsewhere in the state. As these accounts demonstrate, decades of emigration appear to have forged the types of social environments from which one might expect relatively more young individuals to turn toward organized crime as a means of getting ahead in life. This, in part, helps account for elevated levels of violence across the state.

Conclusions

In this chapter I provide a theoretical framework for understanding the relationship between mass emigration and violent crime, including human rights violations, in Michoacán, Mexico. Instead of focusing on the types of economic and political factors that researchers generally use to explain state-sponsored violence, I analyze the social conditions from which criminals have emerged in the State of Michoacán, Mexico. My analysis is rooted in the idea that in order to understand fluctuations in crime, one must examine both the perpetrators as well as the shifting social environments from which these individuals emerge (Shaw and McKay 1972). My study relies on qualitative research conducted in central Mexico, where emigration and crime rates have risen precipitously in recent decades. My findings indicate that emigration drains migrant-sending communities of the exact types of economic, human, and social capital that foster government accountability and mitigate crime and human rights violations. Based on this, I argue that emigration has indirectly contributed to rising violence by creating the types of social environments in which crime would be more likely to occur.

This outcome appears to be deeply rooted in the lasting effects of emigration and remittances on small towns. Diaspora communities abroad provide villages with the economic capital they previously lacked, but they simultaneously deprive villages of the type of human capital (education) and social capital (collective engagement) that would best allow those left behind to capitalize on incoming remittances. In effect, mass emigration has peppered the Mexican countryside with thousands of well-maintained ghost towns, in which remittance-funded homes sit empty most of the year and local economies grind to a halt in every month except December, when migrants return home for the holidays. This arrangement might work out all right if all working-age individuals were able to emigrate, but that is not the case. Instead, many individuals—in fact, most individuals—are left behind as local economies stagnate and job sources dry up.

Given this, a large percentage of working-age men and women find themselves trapped in a social environment in which the successful few, namely the families connected to migrants, exhibit their material success to the rest of the village in the form of modern homes, new cars, fancy electronics, new clothes, stories of trips abroad, and, of course, access to basic welfare including health care and education. The stark inequalities introduced to migrant-sending communities through emigration feed a culture of conspicuous consumption in which nonmigrants naturally desire to participate. Given this situation, it is not necessarily surprising that the foot soldiers of cartels, organized crime, and militia groups share a very similar profile with migrants. Cartels typically enlist young males between the ages of eighteen and forty, which is also the general profile for the large majority of the estimated thirty-one thousand people who have gone missing in the last decade, as well as the more than two hundred thousand victims that the war on drugs has left in its wake.

Mexican drug cartels have provided migrant-prone communities with the resources that the government and diaspora communities are unable to deliver (McDonald 2009: 20). This helps explain how cartels have made such quick inroads within communities while concurrently taking control of institutions. The most successful cartels control large percentages of local police forces as well as government institutions at the municipal, state, and federal levels (Castillo García 2009). In turn, collusion between cartels and government officials helps account for Mexico's dismal human rights record.

Still, while conspicuous consumption, social and economic inequalities, and voids of human and social capital likely triggered the deadly wave of violence affecting migrant-sending regions across Mexico, the social conditions necessary for mass violence already existed. As Mexican human rights activist Maria Luisa Ruelas explained to me in October 2015, "It seems much more complex than people leave and as a result there is violence. I mean, I get the connection I just think that local nuances are very important. You have to understand, these are violent places anyways. There is a lot of violence against women in the countryside, and there are countless local aggressions that don't necessarily lead to deaths but there is no lack of violence in these regions, even in areas where migration is less prevalent." What Maria Luisa, who works in Guerrero for the organization Tlachinollan, points out is the fact that even though not all places experience extremely high homicide rates, nonlethal violence is a constant in many parts of rural Mexico.

This leads to an extremely important point, which helps explain why emigration triggers violence in the first place. As Maria Luisa explains, migrants leave highly patriarchal social environments where males are expected to be the sole bread earners and women grow up being told they will stay at home and raise children. And while such norms are not as generalizable as they might have been in the past, by and large males still make up the bulk of Mexican migrants. This is particularly true in the countryside. Thus, emigration provides some males with a means of achieving traditional cultural goals by accessing economic stability in external labor markets. Not everyone is able to emigrate, however. In fact, the large majority don't end up leaving, and unlike their grandparents, who lived in a pre-NAFTA Mexico, many nonmigrants are unable to fall back on traditional means of earning a living, such as farming or ranching. As a result, countless young males grow up in a hypermasculine culture with no means of validating their virility. Capital flight and social emasculation in rural Mexico parallel the situation of millions of young minority males in the United States who grow up in jobless ghettos (Wilson 1996). Like the inner-city joblessness that Wilson describes, young males in migrant-sending regions grow up in highly masculinized social spaces in which there exist few employment alternatives and where, in recent decades, cartels and organized crime are among the few enterprises offering a path to social mobility. With this in mind, until meaningful efforts are made to address the underlying development issues that persist in migrant-sending areas, it may very well be impossible to decrease the current levels of criminal activity.

CHAPTER 7

Bridging Legal Geographies

Contextual Adjudication in Mexican Asylum Claims

Ariadna Estévez

Introduction

The pilot episode of the American TV series *The Bridge*, which addresses drug violence at the El Paso–Ciudad Juárez border, opens with a highly symbolic crime scene: the body of a woman, cut in half, lies across the yellow line geographically separating Mexico from the United States. The torso is in American territory, the hips and legs are on Mexican soil. The legal-geographical consequence of this crime is that both the Juárez and El Paso police departments have jurisdiction and have to work together on the investigation.

When Officer Sonya Cross informs her Mexican counterpart that the torso is that of a local El Paso judge who had ruled against a group of Mexican immigrants, Comandante Marco Ruiz sighs in relief: since the deceased is an American citizen, the case can exclude Mexican law enforcement. However, later that evening the autopsy reveals that the lower half of the body in fact belongs to a young Mexican woman reported as missing: one of the infamous "dead women of Juarez" and a symbol of institutionalized *macho* culture in Mexico.

Neither of the officers is happy about the situation, and their personalities serve as fitting metaphors for their respective judicial systems as portrayed by the American mass media: whereas Cross is methodical and always goes by the book, Ruiz is informal and relaxed. This pilot establishes the series' ongoing tension between the ideology of legal rationality inherent to American legal geography and the corrupted, macho-driven, and informal Mexican legal system.

The Bridge tells us a lot about the clash between American immigration judges and the stories of Mexican asylum seekers in the United States. Like Officer Cross, American judges examining the cases of Mexican men and women fleeing the human rights crisis fail to grasp the complexities of (non-) law enforcement in Mexico. Some judges are even convinced that Mexico is fully dysfunctional due to criminal corruption, although this should have no bearing on asylum decisions, while others believe that the Mexican government possesses a Weberian view of the rule of law and that is why it cooperates with the United States in the drug wars and enforces progressive legislation for the protection of women and minorities. However, in Mexico, legality is heterogeneous, with many uneven layers of corruption and informal rules.

I believe it is necessary for American immigration judges to grasp the complexities of this *gray area of power* (Auyero 2007) where the criminal and the legal coalesce before concluding that the Mexican state is either willing to protect, or capable of protecting, its citizens (both women and men); or that these violations are merely a tragic case of generalized criminal and gender-based violence. The purpose of this chapter is to develop arguments that could help attorneys and judges in general to grasp these complexities while specifically helping sympathetic judges interpret asylum law in the light of the Mexican context, effectively *bridging* Mexican and American legal geographies.

In order to do so, this chapter first describes the phenomenon of Mexican women and men seeking asylum in the United States and the narrow interpretation of asylum law by judges when examining their cases. Second, it describes the features of the clash between Mexican legal geography and its American counterpart. It then outlines the twofold legal-spatial strategy referred to as *bridging legal geographies,* which consists of (a) adapting the idea of a *gray area of power* (Auyero 2007) to explain the legal-spatial site where persecution takes places so that asylum adjudication can be contextualized; and (b) targeting judges in specific circuits in order to improve the possibility of successful contextual adjudication.

Carrying the Human Rights Crisis Across Borders: Mexican Asylum Seekers in the United States

As described in the Introduction to this volume, the human rights toll of the war on drugs represents a human rights crisis. Human rights violations such as killings, forced disappearances, torture, violence against women, cartel terrorism, and human trafficking are also causing internal forced displacement (see Chapters 2 and 3) as well as forced international crossings. In the last few years, thousands of Mexicans have been forced to flee to the United States, seeking international legal protection. Reports by the United Nations High Commissioner for Refugees (UNHCR) from 2007 to mid-2015 indicate a total of 98,547 asylum claims filed by Mexicans in various countries, but mostly in the United States (65.78 percent) and Canada (31.6 percent) (United Nations High Commissioner for Refugees 2007, 2008, 2009, 2010, 2011, 2012, 2013, 2014, 2015).

Although at the beginning of the drug wars most Mexicans fled to Canada, visa requirements by the Canadian government imposed in 2010 changed this trend. From 2006 to 2010, of a total of 44,019 asylum claims, 30,142 were made in Canada and only 13,700 were made in the United States. But in 2011, 8,906 Mexicans applied for asylum in the United States, while only 653 did so in Canada. This trend has continued, with 11,477 asylum claims in the United States and 324 in Canada in 2012; and 9,261 in the United States and 84 in Canada in 2013. In 2014 the United States registered 13,987 out of a total 14,138 claims, while Mexico did not even appear in the figures for Canada for that year. The same is true for figures covering the first six months of 2015: a total of 7,500 Mexicans filed for asylum, but Canada did not even assess Mexico for asylum figures. By mid-2015, a total of 64,831 Mexicans had claimed asylum in the United States, while for Canada the figure was just 31,200 (United Nations High Commissioner for Refugees 2007, 2008, 2009, 2010, 2011, 2012, 2013, 2014, 2015). However, only 1.6 percent of these applicants (about 1,037 people) have been granted refugee status by the United States (Corral-Nava 2014) due to the way the United States generally handles asylum claims (Rosenblum and Salehyan 2004; Ramji-Nogales, Schoenholtz, and Schrag 2007) and as a result of legal issues arising from the specificities of the Mexican human rights crisis vis-à-vis asylum law. Mexicans are not any luckier in Canada. The Canadian government claims that Mexicans have had better acceptance rates since asylum rules were tightened because the acceptance rate went up from 18.8 percent in 2012 to 28.8 percent in 2014. However, this statement is misleading. In 2012 Canada received 322 claims from Mexicans, while in 2014 it received only 80. In absolute terms, Canada granted asylum to sixty Mexicans in 2012 and to only twenty-three in 2014. As we can see, the acceptance in absolute numbers has decreased (Immigration Canada News 2015; Government of Canada 2016).

Although neither the United States nor UNHCR keeps track of gender by nationality in their asylum statistics, the cross-referencing of displacement figures, qualitative information, and case litigation databases helps formulate an informed guess of the different patterns of persecution for men and women. On the one hand, Mexican men are usually displaced for reasons of criminal and state violence; they are frequently informants, business owners refusing to pay extortion to cartels, journalists, activists, victims of crime who decide to seek justice, and victims of drug-related violence such as killings, illegal detention, forced disappearance, forced labor, and torture. On the other hand, the Internal Displacement Monitoring Centre (IDMC) reports that by 2013, 21,500 young people from the Northern Triangle (Guatemala, El Salvador, and Honduras) and Mexico had been forcibly displaced for reasons of rape, gender-based violence, and sexual trafficking; 18,800 of them were women, and 23 percent of these women were girls aged twelve to seventeen years old (International Displacement Monitoring Centre and Norwegian Refugee Council 2015: 17). While women are also victims of drug-related violence, they are targeted as a means of revenge against rival cartels or used as merchandise in the criminal sex market. Therefore, in the context of the drug wars, women are the victims of execution, torture, rape, forced disappearance, and trafficking, but also of a different kind of violence that specifically violates women's rights: domestic violence.

While general figures on the violation of women's rights in the framework of drug-related violence can be found elsewhere (see Chapter 3), violations of women's rights in the context of these two forms of violence—drug-related and domestic—need to be studied in greater detail to provide an understanding of the gender-based asylum claims of Mexican women in the context of the current human rights crisis. The Inter-American Commission on Human Rights (IACHR) claims that by 2012, in Mexico more women than men were the victims of numerous serious crimes violating women's rights to physical integrity and to life: rape (82 percent), human trafficking (82 percent), human smuggling (81 percent), sexual abuse (79 percent), domestic violence (79 percent), statutory rape (71 percent), crimes against the family (56 percent), and crimes against freedom (83 percent) (IACHR 2015). Also, by 2015, 7,185 women were reported as missing, half of them under the age of eighteen (Goche 2015).

In addition, since 1996 more than forty thousand women have been the victims of femicide (women killed because they are women, or because they do not fulfill the social role expected of them) (Rea and Carrión 2015;

Arteaga Botello and Valdés Figueroa 2010). Between 2013 and 2014 a woman was killed every seven minutes (IACHR 2015), while from 2011 to 2013 the states with the highest figures for the murder of women were also those states suffering drug-related violence: Guerrero, Chihuahua, Tamaulipas, Coahuila, Durango, Colima, Nuevo León, Morelos, Zacatecas, Sinaloa, Baja California, and the State of México. As for domestic violence, the most recent official nationwide survey (2011) indicates that 44.8 percent of 24,566,381 married women interviewed have suffered some form of violence in their homes, with 25.8 percent of women reporting physical violence, 11.7 percent sexual violence, 56.4 percent economic violence, and 89.2 percent emotional violence. Domestic violence is becoming increasingly lethal in many parts of the country, including the states of México, Sinaloa, Chihuahua, Guerrero, and Puebla (INEGI 2013; Estrada Mendoza et al. 2014).

The review of asylum cases in general and of specific gender-based persecution databases[1] shows that Mexican women are persecuted for their activism against femicide or because they are the victims of drug-related and domestic violence, frequently involving partners or relatives connected to the drug wars, or law-enforcement officials. Gender-based violence claims include abuse from an intimate partner, including sexual violence; non-domestic sexual violence; repressive social norms; child abuse; and incest. Perpetrators are mostly husbands and fathers, who in some cases are also law-enforcement officials working for cartels or who are protected by corrupt or macho culture–driven civil servants. In all the reviewed cases where women sought justice, they did not find it.

Legal Obstacles to the Right to Asylum

Both women and men suffering persecution in their home country have three possible means of relief in the United States: asylum, defined in terms of the 1951 UN Convention Relating to the Status of Refugees (1951) and its 1967 Protocol; withholding of removal, which implements the obligation of non-refoulement established in the Convention of Refugees; and complementary means of protection under the Convention Against Torture (see Chapter 8). Asylum provides more rights and benefits than the other two options, so the latter are used only if the applicant doesn't qualify for asylum. However, when presenting the case to a judge, attorneys usually state their intention to apply for any of the three forms of protection. The Refugee Act of 1980 and the Immigration and Nationality Act (INA) define political asylum in terms of the UN Convention Relating to the Status of Refugees and its Protocol: "any person who is outside any country of such person's nationality or, in the case of a person having no nationality, is outside any country in which such person last habitually resided, and who is unable or unwilling to return to, and is unable or unwilling to avail himself or herself of the protection of that country because of persecution or a well-founded fear of persecution on account of race, religion, nationality, membership of a particular social group, or political opinion" (INA 101(a) (42)).

The Convention Relating to the Status of Refugees excluded specific forms of persecution suffered by women in the home, as did the INA. However, the United Nations corrected this omission in 1993 by issuing gender guidelines for assessing gender-based persecution. In 1995, the United States responded, issuing its own guidelines, which had little impact since they applied only to the first layer of asylum adjudication—asylum officers—and were optional. In line with these new standards, in 1996 the Board of Immigration Appeals (the Board or the BIA) established that the threat of female genital mutilation constituted a form of persecution against women (*Matter of Kasinga*); shortly after this, a judge applied the same rationale and granted asylum to Rody Alvarado, a Guatemalan woman who suffered extreme domestic violence. The attorney representing the U.S. government appealed the decision, and the Board reversed the decision to grant asylum to Alvarado (*Matter of R-A*). It took thirteen years to reinstate Alvarado's asylum status, and this process involved attorneys general and other trials (Musalo 2015). However, as of 2017, domestic violence as grounds for granting asylum is yet to be recognized, except for the case of a specific group of Guatemalan women, which I address later in this chapter.

Claimants are not considered eligible for asylum if they have participated in the persecution of others on account of one or more of the five protected grounds, remained in the United States for more than a year at the time of the application, or resettled successfully in another country. Once a person proves to be eligible for asylum, his or her claim will be successful if he or she can provide evidence for three interrelated issues: a well-founded fear of persecution; the government's unwillingness or inability to protect the victim from persecutors; and the fact that this persecution is motivated by the victim's race, nationality, religion, political opinion, or membership of a particular social group. In immigration courts, Mexicans face difficulties in proving two of these asylum requirements: (1) the state's unwillingness or inability to protect them; and (2) nexus, that is, proving they are being persecuted because of membership in one or more of the protected categories.

The State's Unwillingness or Inability to Protect

First, fear of persecution is defined as a fear of serious harm and the failure of the state to provide protection vis-à-vis this possibility. Persecution could be understood as the systematic violation of human rights that proves the state's incapability or unwillingness to protect citizens (Price 2006). The level of harm must be considered severe. In order to demonstrate persecution, a person's experience must be more than simple unpleasantness, harassment, or even basic suffering. According to the UN *Handbook and Guidelines on Procedures and Criteria for Determining Refugee Status*, persecution could be an action of the state or could be the result of the inability of the state to control the criminality of nonstate actors (Pickering 2005; García 2011). There are two competing interpretations of persecution by nonstate agents, such as criminals or abusive partners in domestic settings, in cases in which the state is willing but unable to provide protection. One interpretation is that the asylum definition provides protection in situations in which the state of origin is incapable of providing the necessary protection, and a second view insists that refugee status can be established only when the state is directly implicated in the persecution (Bruin 2002).

The involvement of nonstate actors is not the main problem facing Mexican asylum seekers, though as Anna Jessica Cabot, managing attorney at the Las Americas Immigrant Advocacy Center in El Paso, Texas, explains, "That issue, in my opinion at least, is not the most pressing issue because . . . it doesn't even matter for asylum law whether the police are involved or not, to some extent because whether they're involved, maybe they're unwilling to stop the violence, if they're not, maybe they're unable to stop the violence."[2] The nonstate-actor issue is in fact problematic for protection provided under the Convention Against Torture (CAT) (used in cases such as criminals who are excluded from the protection of asylum according to the INA) since protection is only for people who have been tortured or could be tortured by state officials or with the acquiescence of the state. If a claimant cannot prove persecution on account of one of the five protected grounds, this possible venue of protection is also barred if there is no state involvement.

According to Cabot[3] and Nancy Oretskin,[4] attorney and cofounder of the Southwest Asylum and Migration Institute (SAMI), the main issue for Mexican claimants is to prove the inability or unwillingness of the Mexican government to protect its citizens from persecution or torture by state authorities or criminals. As Oretskin puts it, in the end, "the key always is, no matter whether the basis for claiming asylum is political opinion or membership in a social group, the government or representative of the government is incapable or unwilling to protect you. You have to have a tie to the government. . . . So tying the cartels in is the missing piece. . . ."

The difficulty with proving the Mexican government's complicity with drug cartels is the need to prove, for example, that law-enforcement officials are on the payroll of the cartels even though the state enforces the Merida Initiative, among other anti-drug policies. To prove the state's inability or unwillingness to fight the drug cartels, the lawyers for the claimants submit to immigration authorities recommendations from Mexican human rights commissions or news clippings reporting that law-enforcement officials or soldiers directly participated in, or ignored, murders related to the case. However, this type of evidence is not always forthcoming, and testimonies may be the only available proof.

In response, asylum authorities use evidence of Mexican or bilateral policy for the fight against drug trafficking to block claims of government collusion. It is difficult to legally prove there is a gray area where the government and the criminal coalesce, says Cabot, "because there is involvement of the state but clearly the state in Mexico is not a monolithic actor, the state doesn't just do one thing or another, there are loads of different actors within the state itself, you know, the presidency office and the military could be saying conflicting things . . . because there is so much conflicting action within the government, I mean obviously the government is fighting itself at some level, just saying that there is involvement it doesn't prove that there is involvement in a specific person's case."

Nexus Through a Particular Social Group or Political Opinion

Given the characteristics of the Mexican human rights crisis, arguing motivation is never straightforward either. As Cabot claims, "When you're dealing with people who are fleeing from drug violence there's no obvious group, no obvious ground. . . . you know, it's not their race, religion, nationality, so those go out the window." Therefore, asylum claimants have only two category options upon which to base their claims: particular social group, which is the hardest to establish, and political opinion, which is neither easy nor upfront. Given the characteristics of the war on drugs and the legal limitations for gender-based violence, the nexus to a particular social group and/or political opinion is clear only in the most traditional cases, such as those of journalists, human rights activists, and party members suffering from persecution as a result of their social, professional, and political activities.

Establishing motivation based on membership of a particular social group is not easy because in most cases the nexus is not what is *explicitly* indicated by the INA and the UN Refugees Convention, such as women suffering from domestic violence in the home or in relation to drug cartels, people who either refuse to pay extortion or speak out about extortion, former cartel members, informants and witnesses, as well as people resisting recruitment. Membership of a particular social group was defined in 1985 according to the standard established by the *Matter of Acosta*, which called on courts to assess a social group considering a common or immutable characteristic shared by proposed members (*Matter of Acosta*, in Musalo 2015: 1–2), for example, "an innate one such as sex, color, kinship ties, or in some circumstances . . . a shared past experience such as former military leadership or land ownership" (*Matter of Acosta*, in Kurzban 2014: 622).

Immutability applies to people who share an innate or unalterable characteristic such as their past, defined by something as basic as their identity, that they should not be required to abandon (Pickering 2005; Buchanan 2010). For example, police officers (law-enforcement officers in general) could be granted asylum on account of their particular group membership because they have a "shared past experience" and share "a common immutable characteristic," which is that of having been law-enforcement officials, a background that cannot be changed (Buchanan 2010; García 2011).

Nevertheless, since 2008, establishing an acceptable social group as the basis for asylum has become harder in many appellate courts because the Board decided that immutability was just a starting point for assessing a particular social group. The BIA established two additional factors: social visibility and particularity. *Visibility* refers to society's perception of a group as a visible social group: "the extent to which members of a society perceive those with the characteristic in question as members of a social group" (*Matter of S-E-G*, in Frydman and Desai 2012: 2). In 2014, in order to avoid the understanding of "visibility" as "ocular" or "on-sight," the Board established in *Matter of M-E-V-G* and *Matter of W-G-R* that the accurate term should be "social distinction." In order to be socially distinct, "a group need not be seen as society; rather, it must be perceived as a group by society." Under this definition, the important perception is that of the society, not that of the persecutors (*Matter of M-E-V-G*, in Kurzban 2014: 622).

In *Matter of S-E-G*, the Board decided that visibility was a "relevant factor" but defined "particularity" as a requirement. In *Matter of M-E-V-G*, the Board confirmed this requirement, saying, "Particularity requires that a social group have characteristics that provide a clear benchmark for determining who falls within the group. . . . The group must also be discrete and have definable boundaries—it must not be amorphous, overbroad, diffuse, or subjective" (Kurzban 2014: 622–623). According to Cabot, particularity is specifically linked to characteristics unrelated to persecution itself: "The other thing about a social group is, in order to kind of prevent circular logic . . . your social group cannot be defined by the persecution that it suffers, for example, women who suffer domestic violence cannot be a social group because domestic violence is the persecution itself. So Mexican citizens targeted by cartels cannot be a social group because this is being defined by the persecution. That prevents us from using what might be the most obvious social group, a fairly visible thing. That's one problem."

In 2008, *Matter of S-E-G* made social distinction and particularity not only relevant but binding requirements; the matter referred to a case of criminal gang persecution (*Matter of S-E-G*, in Frydman and Desai 2012: 2). These two additional requirements have made the legal construction of social groups a semantics game, in the view of Harvard legal scholar Nicholas R. Bednar. He argues that with these new definitions, "if the applicant defines her group too discretely, the group may fail to satisfy the element of social distinction because the society in question is unlikely to perceive it as a group. But an amorphous or overbroad particular social group, according to BIA precedent, fails the requirement of particularity. To avoid denial of her application due to a lack of either particularity or social distinction, the applicant must define her particular social group with calculated wording" (Bednar 2015: 357).

The situation became even tougher in 2014 with *Matter of W-G-R*, which also referred to gangs. The new precedent established new parameters, "finding 'former members of the Mara 18 gang in El Salvador who have renounced their gang membership' as not constituting a particular social group because it lacks particularity as too diffuse, too broad and too subjective by including any age, sex or background; it is also not a socially distinct group" (Kurzban

2014: 623). *Matter of EAG* had already ruled out engagement in past criminal conduct because this characteristic was not immutable (Kurzban 2014: 623).

In the cases analyzed here, these changes represent a technical obstacle related to the Mexican drug wars because the requirements exclude almost the full range of groups: people who refuse to be recruited by or to pay quotas to drug cartels (First, Fifth, Eighth, and Ninth Circuit Courts of Appeals); informants and witnesses (Fourth and Ninth); and wealthy merchants resisting extortion, because they lack either visibility or particularity. Most circuits explicitly adhered to the new binding nature of particularity and visibility, including the First, Second, Fifth, Eighth, Ninth, Tenth, and Eleventh. However, some circuits explicitly ruled against the 2006 standard (Third and Seventh), while others haven't ruled in favor of or against but treat them simply as requirements (Fourth and Sixth) (Frydman and Desai 2012).

Women who suffer from gender-related violence are also excluded as a specific social group from the outset. Although sex is considered an acceptable immutable feature, it is not enough to prove visibility and particularity because domestic violence occurs in the home, and this could be considered too broad a group in countries with misogynistic legal, social, and political systems. Even women who are victims of violence in the context of criminal gang violence are excluded (First and Tenth Circuits) (Frydman and Desai 2012). In 2014, a small step was taken toward the recognition of gender-based violence when the Board issued *Matter A-R-C-G,* in which it accepted as a particular social group "Guatemalan women who cannot leave their partners" because they belong to a criminal gang. However, the standard applies only to Guatemalan women in those specific circumstances and excludes Mexican and other women (*Matter A-R-C-G,* in Musalo 2015).

A possibility for establishing a particular social group for Mexicans is the family because *family* meets the criteria of a particular social group: "Family membership is a characteristic that a person either cannot change (if he or she is related by blood) or should not be required to change (if he or she is related by marriage)" (U.S. Court of Appeals for the Fifth Circuit 2011: 15). Nevertheless, in circuits such as the Fifth, it is not enough to belong to the family of a persecuted person: persecution on account of family as a social group seeks "to terminate a line of dynastic succession" (7). The Eighth Circuit shares a similar position, whereas the Fourth and Ninth Circuits have opposed the Board's position toward family (Frydman and Desai 2012: 12–13).

As we can see, *particular social group* is not an alternative with potentiality for success in the case of Mexican men and women fleeing drug- and gender-related violence. As a consequence, the other only remaining possibility is *political opinion,* which requires the claimant demonstrate they in fact have a political opinion or that a political opinion has been imputed to them. *Political opinion* should be understood broadly and according to context, as the United Nations recommends. The United Nations states that *political opinion* refers to "any opinion on any matter in which the machinery of the State, government, society and policy may be engaged" (Buchanan 2010: 46). In this sense, political opinions could include a wide range of opinions related to the war on drugs, such as refusing to pay extortion and quotas, to join a cartel or gang, or to become the sexual slave of a drug lord or a gang; or even seeking justice in cases of domestic violence and femicide.

So far, however, people who have managed to demonstrate a well-founded fear of persecution due to their political opinions are those expressing a political opinion in terms of the INA and the UN Convention: "For some people fleeing Mexico there's political opinion, that actually works for them, but that's usually politicians, journalists or human rights activists, so that's specifically for people who speak out, and doesn't apply just to the normal person fleeing violence," says Cabot. Nevertheless, political opinion could be an alternative in circuits that haven't ruled against criminal violence as a source of persecution (Third, Seventh, Fourth, and Sixth) (Frydman and Desai 2012).

To sum up briefly, the possibilities for Mexicans to gain legal relief are blocked by conservative precedent but also narrow interpretations of an anachronistic law, that is, the Refugee Convention and Protocol. While their cases are legitimate, unfortunately, the definition of *refugee* is not context-specific. Frequently, when interpreting the law through originalism and precedent—techniques consisting of going back to the spirit of the law or to similar cases—judges dismiss drug-related violence as generalized criminal violence or as a specific case for which persecution could be prevented by locating somewhere else in the country. Also, they refuse to see violence against women as a legitimate motivation for asylum for a number of reasons that feminist refugee attorney Karen Musalo describes as "a resistance to accepting that women's rights are indeed human rights, and therefore of legitimate concern within a human rights and refugee rights framework. Their remarks frequently demonstrate an adherence to the old public/private sphere approach, stating that one should not 'expect asylum law to address *personal* or *family* issues'" (Musalo 2015: 48).

This is why it is necessary to construct solid but creative legal arguments based on a context-specific analysis of Mexican reality, which in turn could discard internal flight as a solution to supposedly generalized criminal and gender violence, while justifying opposition to drug and gender violence as legitimate political opinions.

Bridging Mexican and American Legal Geographies: Understanding the *Gray Zone of Power*

Bridging legal geographies is an idea that borrows from the work of critical legal geographer[5] David Delaney (2010), who emphasizes the need for the researcher to describe not only what legislation says but how legality—as a geographically specific ideology—shapes places, people, and experiences. In this chapter, bridging legal geographies means bringing the American and Mexican constructions of the legal together by describing how they shape specific places, situations, norms, and legal subjects, and how all of these interact for the construction of versions of legality and illegality. The aim is for judges to understand the differences of the two with reference not only to shared conceptual abstractions but also to how these abstractions shape lives, places, and situations in specific contexts in order to produce legitimate situations of persecution.

On the one hand, American legality is shaped by at least two ideologies: Weberian bureaucratic rationality (Heyman and Campbell 2007), which emphasizes the role of judges and places such as the courts; and legal formalism (Clark 1985), which fetishizes the law in different spaces and situations. These ideologies become stronger vis-à-vis the Mexican construction of legality: "US idea producers construe the US as the home of pure-hearted law enforcement and Mexico as the source of violence and illegality" (Heyman and Campbell 2007: 194).

The ideologies of Weberian rationality and legal formalism are so important in American legality that phenomena such as corruption are thought to be rare if they exist at all and never structural in particular legal spaces. However, corruption exists because norms have limits and are ambiguous, thus pushing individuals to act with pragmatism and cynicism toward the law, as they do everywhere else. The judiciary is a key figure in maintaining those ideologies that shape legal spaces and situations through its supposedly rational and efficient interpretation of norms, an interpretation that is nevertheless discretionary (Heyman and Campbell 2007).

On the other hand, the Mexican construction of legality is defined by two ideologies: legal formalism and macho culture. Mexican legality is far from the Weberian ideal. Mexican legal formalism is characterized by norm production, such as the adherence to most human rights treaties or the construction of new criminal types such as femicide, victimization, and forcible disappearance. However, unlike what happens in the United States, in Mexico legal formalism does not necessarily lead to enforcement, and as argued in different chapters of this volume, impunity has been pervasive (see Chapters 10 and 11). In the words of Villanueva: "Crime victims do not report because they consider it a 'waste of time' (39 percent) or distrust authority (16 percent). Most of the victims who filed a complaint assert 'nothing' happened (33 percent) or that the complaint is 'pending' (23 percent). . . . To summarize, by 2009 the impunity index rises to 98.3 percent, so that for anyone who commits a crime only 1.7 percent of cases will be brought before a judge" (Villanueva 2011: 175).

In the Mexican judicial system there are many permanent irregular legal spaces, which are the plainly illegal but tolerated and well-known spaces such as safe houses, or legal and institutional places used as safe houses by law-enforcement officials working with criminals, like government-run migrant-detention centers where men and women on their transit to the United States are detained and then handed over to criminals for ransom or trafficking purposes. This is possible due to the normalization of illegality, that is, the systematic but not necessarily generalized phenomenon of law-enforcement officials' working for criminals. Permanent operational irregularity in many areas of the judicial system is mostly produced by what Carlos Flores calls the *failure of the state,* which is different from the concept of *failed state.* Flores claims that the Mexican state fails to comply with its basic duty to guarantee security not because of a lack of resources but because one of its pillars, the judicial system, has been widely coopted by criminal activity and reshaped by the institutionalization of corruption. The consequence is that at many uneven levels, organized crime obstructs and diverts the formal operation of the judicial system (Flores Pérez 2013),[6] thereby making its operation irregular on a permanent basis.

For crimes affecting women's rights, macho culture is embedded in impunity too. Macho culture is an ideology shaping the very fabric of the top-down constructed Mexican national identity, according to cultural studies scholar Héctor Domínguez Ruvalcaba, who claims that in its early-postrevolutionary formation the Mexican state used several expressions of Mexican masculinity to construct a social imaginary that could achieve national cultural cohesion: the revolutionary soldier, the *charro,* the working-class man, the womanizer, the drunk Casanova (Domínguez Ruvalcaba 2013). These images served to reinforce violence and the domination of women and children as folkloric features of the Mexican *macho*. A century later, this macho culture seems to have been renovated with images of the drug lord and the *mirrey* (the young children of top-level politicians, corporatist trade-unionists, and the rich and famous) and has sadly moved beyond simple folklore; it has made misogyny a common social practice that is now institutionalized in the judicial system, as the impunity for femicide, rape, and human trafficking shows.

As a consequence of irregularity and the ideologies shaping the Mexican judicial system, such basic concepts as the public/private divide have become so ambiguous that when disturbances appear, it is impossible to determine whether a subject is a *sicario* (hitman), a cartel member, a police officer, or a soldier. This irregular intertwining of the legal and the criminal, expressed in figures such as the *criminal cop,* is what Mafia scholars have termed *intreccio,* which "signifies more than a simple reciprocity between the mafia and the state; it points to a vast gray area where it is impossible to determine where one leaves off and the other begins" (Schneider and Schneider 2003: 33–34).

I believe that the best way to frame this problem for the purpose of legal-spatial explanation is to use Javier Auyero's notion of the *gray area of power.* The *gray area* comes into being when "the activities of those perpetrating the violence and those who presumably seek to control them coalesce" (Auyero 2007: 32). The irregularities of the Mexican legal system occupy a gray area that has devoured black and white areas at many levels of law enforcement and at an uneven rate. However, it is important to point out that while this is systematic, it is not generalized, being found *anywhere* but not *everywhere.* While the system does not lead to generalized criminal violence, it does blur the boundaries between the criminal and the legal and in particular specific situations involving human rights abuses such as persecution. The systematic but not generalized nature of this gray zone makes internal relocation an unviable solution for asylum seekers since the gray zone could be anywhere, leading to specific violence.

Bridging Legal Geographies: Targeting Immigration Judges

The asylum process is divided into affirmative and defensive procedures. On the one hand, affirmative applicants are those who enter the country with or without a valid visa and have not yet been placed in removal proceedings.

These claims are reviewed by an asylum officer from the U.S. Citizenship and Immigration Services (USCIS), and if not approved, they are referred to an immigration judge of the Executive Office for Immigration Review (EOIR), which is a branch of the U.S. Department of Justice, for judicial review. "This is not a denial of your asylum application. You may request asylum again before the immigration judge and your request will be considered (without additional refiling) when you appear before an immigration judge at the date and time listed on the attached charging document," says the standardized asylum-denial template. According to Kurzban (2014: 698), "Applications first filed with AOs (Asylum Officers) are called 'affirmative applications' because they are not filed in removal proceedings as a 'defense' to removal."

Only at this time is the applicant brought before a judge in Immigration Court as part of removal proceedings—therefore, "defensive procedures.. These courts are grouped into thirteen Federal Court Circuits because migration law is federal administrative law, and they belong to the U.S. Department of Justice's EOIR.[7] In EOIR they are accountable to the Office of the Chief Immigration Judge (OCIJ), which establishes their operation and implementation rules. There are some 250 immigration judges located in 57 immigration courts nationwide (Executive Office for Immigration Review 2016). Immigration courts are administrative courtlike settings that fit the legal fetishism of the American formalism explained in the previous section. According to Cabot, immigration courts are "something that is court-like, it's actually an administrative body, and the administrative body says okay, immigration benefits are such important things to people that we should give people a place that looks like a court basically in order to make sure that their rights are more likely to be appealed in this area."

Although immigration courts are administrative bodies that look like courts, law enforcement in them is even more subjective and politicized than in criminal and civil courts, among other reasons because they provide little constitutional due-process protection, according to the Fifth Amendment that refers to persons rather than citizens; nor freedom-of-speech protection, according to the First Amendment that allows nonimmigrants to be members of anarchist and communist parties (*Rafeedie v. INS* 1992, in Kurzban 2014: 159). In fact, says Cabot, the law "can be changed based on the judge who oversees the court . . . each particular judge can alter the rules within their own court and so this gives the judges much more discretionary powers than judges in other courts in the US, criminal courts, civil courts . . . to change the rules to suit their own biases and preconceptions that they do in other arenas." Their decisions are appealed with the BIA, whose published decisions are law throughout the country, not only for the circuit where the claim was based. If the BIA rejects a claim but the asylum seeker's attorney believes that constitutional rights have been violated, the asylum seeker can make constitutional claims at the Court of Appeals.

As for defensive procedures, these were established in the Illegal Immigration Reform and Immigrant Responsibility Act of 1996, which imposes an expedited removal procedure for people with no documents. Undocumented migrants at the border or those denied refugee status by an Asylum Officer are summarily removed unless they claim asylum before a judge. Undocumented migrants at the border must claim asylum and express a fear of persecution before an Asylum Officer who determines whether the person has a "credible fear" of persecution. If claimants prove to have a credible fear of persecution, they can be paroled (a humanitarian permit to stay while their legal status is resolved) after proving their identity and their likelihood to attend hearings and to represent no threat to U.S. security. If credible fear is not proved, claimants may request a review, which takes up to seven days, during which time they are detained. If credible fear is proved this time, they go to a hearing before a judge to claim asylum, withholding of removal, or protection under the Convention Against Torture (Kurzban 2014: 698, 181). If not, claimants remain in detention until they have their hearing, which could take very long to schedule. Although the length of detention is not standardized for all circuits, most of them have precedents establishing that being detained for a "reasonable time" cannot take years, as in some cases in which claimants were detained for up to 4.5 years. In this case, the Ninth Circuit resolved that a reasonable time could not be more than six months (*Nadarajah v. Gonzalez* 2013, in Kurzban 2014).

Crystal Massey, human rights advocate and researcher at SAMI, claims that at least in the case of Mexican asylum seekers, the affirmative/defensive divide has no other purpose than to serve as a filter for the type of Mexicans who can access the asylum system—which does not mean that they are granted asylum, just access to the system. Massey argues that people who hold a visa are usually middle-class, well-informed Mexicans who have the means or the knowledge to obtain a border-crossing document, or know that stating an interest in asylum at the border will lead to their being placed in detention.[8] While awaiting the judge's decision, applicants can request a "credible fear" interview, that is, an interview in which asylum seekers have to provide evidence that their fear of persecution is well founded. The judge then either grants or denies asylum, proceeding to removal if the latter (Rottman, Fariss, and Poe 2009).

Because of the Weberian legal rationality and legal formalism of the legal system in the United States, judges are the privileged figures for law interpretation even in semilegal scenarios like immigration courts. Judges interpret asylum rules using a variety of techniques, the choice of which depends on their scholarly background but also their place in the political spectrum. According to Gordon L. Clark's classic work on the spatial and subjective construction of law enforcement (1985), conservative as well as conservative formalist judges usually opt for originalism, which goes back to the "spirit" of the law; precedent, which is similar to originalism but returns only to precedent without taking into account different contexts; and authoritative approaches, which take as a starting point hard or exemplary cases. More conservative judges use the all-embracing principle that assesses cases in terms of economic rationality and efficiency, while more progressive judges go for contextual adjudication, which allows for "events and circumstances to play the major role in determining outcomes" (Clark 1985: 56).

Since there is no constitutional basis for asylum adjudication, interpretation is arbitrary, and biases such as racism and political background are influential. Take the case of immigration judges within the Fifth Circuit (Texas, Louisiana, and Mississippi). People fleeing violence in Valle de Juárez, Chihuahua, claim asylum at the El Paso port of entry because of its proximity, so if adjudication is rejected in affirmative procedures, or if people are placed in defensive asylum because they claim asylum at the border without a visa, they go to the Fifth Circuit courts.

First, Immigration Judge William L. Abbot, who served in the U.S. Navy for six years and represented the government as a trial attorney in the INS (Immigration and Naturalization Service, now known as USCIS), had a denial rate of 92.3 percent in the asylum cases brought before him in 2014, when the national average was 48.5 percent. In Abbot's court, 35 percent of all asylum claims came from Mexicans—the highest single nationality percentage (Transactional Records Access Clearinghouse 2014e). Second, during that same year Immigration Judge Thomas C. Roepke, of Texas, who used to work for the U.S. attorney and Immigration and Customs Enforcement (ICE), had a denial rate of 99 percent, which was even higher than Abbot's rate; 41 percent of the claimants were Mexicans, the largest group among the nationalities of petitioners (Transactional Records Access Clearinghouse 2014d). Finally, in 2014 Judge Stephen M. Ruhle, who served in the

U.S. Navy and the Army and was a deputy officer for ICE, had a denial rate of 95.9 percent; 24.3 percent of the claimants were Mexicans, and 32 percent were Salvadorans (Transactional Records Access Clearinghouse 2014c). In contrast, also in 2014, in certain immigration courts of Chicago, Illinois (within the Seventh Circuit), Judge Sheila McNulty had a denial rate of 41.3 percent, which was lower than the national average of 48.5 percent. The largest national groups in Judge McNulty's court were Chinese (22.3 percent) and Mexicans (8.7 percent). McNulty previously served the Department of Justice and INS (Transactional Records Access Clearinghouse 2014b). Judge Robert D. Vinikoor had a 54.9 percent denial rate, where Mexicans were the third largest group (3.2 percent) (Transactional Records Access Clearinghouse 2014a).

As can be seen, El Paso is not the best place for Mexicans to seek asylum; having Chicago as their venue improves their chances. We should, therefore, recall the first section of the chapter, where I stated that the Fifth Circuit has the toughest standards for the adjudication of social groups, while the Seventh Circuit has refused to toughen its standards, including in cases of gang violence. The extremes of Chicago and El Paso show that Mexicans could improve their chances of being granted asylum if human rights groups in Mexico and pro bono and low-cost law firms in the United States cooperate in drawing up a map of the courts within a circuit where gender, gang, or cartel violence is not eliminated from the outset as an element of either persecution for political opinion (Third, Fourth, Sixth, and Seventh Circuits) or particular social group (Seventh and Third Circuits, but maybe Fourth and Sixth too) (Frydman and Desai 2012).

In addition, this mapping should include judges who have the professional, ethnic, and political background to use contextual adjudication and be open enough to assess the idea of the gray zone of power as a context-specific feature of the Mexican human rights crisis when adjudicating asylum. Contextual adjudication would allow judges to prioritize the particular nuances of each case instead of assessing them according to universal rules or anachronistic precedent. More important, "the historical contingencies that give rise to disputes over meaning, even the applicability of alternative principles, can also be taken seriously" (Clark 1985: 56). Consequently, the gray zone of power as a historical specificity of the Mexican legal system could be taken as serious grounds for assessing the Mexican state's permanent incapability to protect, and as a nexus based on social group and particular opinion.

Conclusion

According to the United Nations, between 2006 and 2015, 98,547 Mexicans have claimed asylum, mostly in the United States (65.78 percent). However, only 2 percent of them have been granted asylum status. The chapter claims that adjudication fails to take into account the peculiarities of the Mexican legal system, and the discussion develops the arguments that could help attorneys and judges to interpret asylum law in the light of context, effectively *bridging* Mexican and American legal geographies. After characterizing the causes for international forced displacement, the chapter uses the work of Delaney (2010) and Auyero (2007) to draw a legal-spatial strategy referred to as *bridging legal geographies*.

The strategy first proposes to adapt the idea of *gray area of power* (Auyero 2007) to explain how the criminal and the legal are intertwined so systematically at different and uneven levels that internal relocation becomes a death trap. Second, it suggests that asylum seekers target judges in specific circuits in order to improve the chances for successful contextual adjudication. However, the outline of this legal-geographical strategy suggests that further research is needed to draw the maps in more detail.

CHAPTER 8

Mexican Asylum Seekers
and the Convention Against Torture

Susan Gzesh

Introduction

Over the past century, Mexicans have come to the United States for work, to unite with family members, to study, and—some—to seek refuge. Today more than eleven million Mexicans live in the United States, approximately half of them in undocumented status, the remainder as students, temporary workers, lawful residents, or naturalized U.S. citizens (Zong and Batalova 2016). A book on the state of human rights in Mexico is a logical place to explore one aspect of the situation of Mexicans abroad—whether Mexicans fleeing violence can find protection in the United States.

Asylum seekers can raise public awareness in the country of destination about human rights in their country of origin. Would publicity about Mexicans seeking asylum educate the American public about the human rights violations and threats of violence faced by ordinary Mexicans? Would public knowledge of the situation in Mexico counter the anti-Mexican and antirefugee attitudes of the Donald Trump administration or serve to fortify support for the proposed border wall and other exclusionist policies?

The reception of refugees is the ultimate test of the universality of human rights. Can people in danger whose nation-state cannot protect their human rights find refuge, respect for their rights, and safety in another country? As Hannah Arendt observed in 1950 about the widespread rejection of persecuted Jews in 1930s and 1940s Europe,

The incredible plight of an ever-growing group of innocent people was like a practical demonstration of the totalitarian movements' cynical claims that no such thing as inalienable human rights existed and that affirmations of the democracies to the contrary were mere prejudice, hypocrisy, and cowardice. . . . The very phrase "human rights" became for all concerned—victims, persecutors, and onlookers alike—the evidence of hopeless idealism or fumbling feeble-minded hypocrisy. (Arendt 1976: 269)

In the six decades since Arendt wrote, there has been a proliferation of treaties, human rights bodies, and civil society organizations dedicated to their enforcement. The United States has adopted treaties and laws to protect migrants fleeing danger. Will this system protect the rights of Mexicans fleeing violence and threats?

Worldwide, asylum seekers are desperate to escape violence perpetrated by the state, by nonstate actors, and by criminal organizations. Hundreds of thousands flee civil wars, as governments attack their own civilian populations while fighting armed opposition groups. Many flee threats and violence from criminal gangs who have virtual control over their home communities. Others are desperate to escape catastrophic natural disasters and the longer-term impact of climate change, such as flooding and desertification. Many of these situations were not contemplated in the Refugee Convention promulgated in 1951 (Goodwin-Gil and McAdam 2007; McAdam 2012). The existing categories are delineated in Article 1 of the Convention and Protocol Relating to the Status of Refugees, which states,

The term "refugee" shall apply to any person who . . . owing to a well-founded fear of being persecuted for reasons of race, religion, nationality, membership of a particular social group or political opinion, is outside the country of his nationality and is unable or, owing to such fear, is unwilling to avail himself of the protection of that country; or who, not having a nationality and being outside the country of his former habitual residence as a result of such events, is unable or, owing to such fear, is unwilling to return to it. (United Nations General Assembly 1951, 1967)

The protection of Mexicans in the United States falls squarely within the ongoing global discussion of whether the "old" standards for refugee status found in the Refugee Convention and Protocol, or even the newer commitments under the Convention Against Torture, can serve persons fleeing the wide variety of dangers today. At present, many states parties to these treaties seek to avoid their obligation of "non-refoulement"—the obligation not to return migrants to a country where they fear persecution or face a substantial risk of torture, the core protection of both treaties. Article 33 of the Convention and Protocol Relating to the Status of Refugees states, "No Contracting State shall expel or return ('refouler') a refugee in any manner whatsoever to the frontiers of territories where his life or freedom would be threatened on account of his race, religion, nationality, membership of a particular social group or political opinion" (United Nations General Assembly 1967). Similarly, Article 3 of the Convention Against Torture and Other Cruel, Inhuman, or Degrading Treatment of Punishment (Convention Against Torture, or CAT) states, "No State Party shall expel, return ('refouler') or extradite a person to another State where there are substantial grounds for believing that he would be in danger of being subjected to torture" (United Nations General Assembly 1984).

International obligations are complicated by political realities in the case of Mexico and the United States.

International human rights monitoring bodies agree that the human rights situation in Mexico has deteriorated substantially in the last decade (Al Hussein 2015). Meanwhile, the United States and Mexico seek to maintain cordial diplomatic relations, as partners in antinarcotics efforts, trade, and migration control, among other issues. The U.S. Department of State Country Report on Mexico cites persistent human rights violations (U.S. Department of State 2015). U.S. human rights advocates criticize the failure of the U.S. government to exert more pressure on Mexico to investigate noted cases of violations (Washington Office on Latin America 2015). As in any bilateral relationship, a welcome by the United States to Mexican asylum seekers could be considered an explicit condemnation of the sending state—and a diplomatic tool to be used with caution. In earlier periods, the reverse was true as African Americans escaping slavery in the United States, as well as persecuted religious minorities practicing polygamy, fled to Mexico in the nineteenth century. In the 1940s and 1950s, U.S. citizens and lawful residents suspected of Communist ties fled to Mexico to escape aggressive government investigations.

The United States has ratified both the Refugee Convention and Protocol and the Convention Against Torture. As noted, both treaties—and U.S. laws and regulations enacted to implement the treaties—require the United

States not to return persons to countries where they would be subject to persecution or torture. This requires that the United States provide due-process safeguards for applicants, including considering the elements of qualification for asylum status. Over the past thirty-six years, U.S. administrative judges and federal courts have defined critical terms such as "persecution," "particular social group," "political opinion," and "consent or acquiescence [of the state]" to determine who are "deserving" of refuge among those in flight from violence or threats. That Mexico is in a human rights crisis is without doubt. However, the harm or threat that can qualify an applicant for refugee status does not include every possible violation of human rights. There is an ongoing debate about the extent to which "persecution" maps onto "human rights violations" (McAdam 2014).

Mexicans currently have an extremely low rate of acceptance in applications for political asylum or protection under CAT (Cabot 2014). Historically, agency and judicial decision-making in individual cases often follows the Executive's stated general policy with respect to asylum seekers. Salvadoran and Guatemalan asylum seekers successfully challenged biased decision-making in the 1980s, resulting in a settlement that ordered the reconsideration of their claims "without regard to foreign policy interests" (*American Baptist Churches v. Thornburgh* 1991). Of course, agency decision-makers can determine individual cases on humanitarian grounds, and independent federal judges reviewing agency decisions can insist on a reading of the law at odds with the view of executive branch officials.

Should the United States now provide protection to Mexicans fleeing violence? Given the large undocumented Mexican population in the United States, there is hardly the political will to welcome thousands more (Krogstad and Passel 2014). Would generous standards of even temporary shelter strain capacity and public acceptance? There are also moral questions to be considered. Must the United States offer shelter where the violence Mexicans flee is related to the market for illegal drugs in the United States? Does U.S. responsibility for the flow of guns into Mexico further obligate the United States to offer refuge?

This chapter explains the political and legal pathways through which Mexicans seek protection in the United States. The chapter considers, first, the barriers to seeking asylum under U.S. law, and then the possibility of seeking protection under CAT. A review of U.S. case law demonstrates the key issue of the Mexican state's "control and acquiescence" that applicants must prove to gain protection in the United States.

Mexicans and the U.S. Asylum Process

Despite consistently alarming reports from credible sources on the difficult human rights situation in Mexico, it is important to note that there are no "waves" of Mexican refugees coming to the United States at present. U.S. and Mexican scholars agree that, in the past few years, net Mexican migration to the United States has been reduced to zero due to difficult economic circumstances in the United States and increased border and interior enforcement (Gonzales-Barrera and Krogstad 2015). The Obama administration deported record numbers of Mexicans back to Mexico, and the Trump administration will match or exceed those totals. However, the thousands of Mexicans deported or leaving voluntarily are almost matched by thousands who successfully cross into the United States each year—despite the increased cost and danger of illegal crossing (Gonzales-Barrera and Krogstad 2015; U.S. Border Patrol 2015). Something is compelling Mexicans to leave home—and for at least some, the motive is fear.

Among the estimated five million undocumented Mexicans in the United States, relatively few have applied for protection under either political asylum or CAT. Some statistics are available concerning affirmative asylum applications filed with the Asylum Offices, Department of Homeland Security (DHS). A review of several DHS reports shows a slight rise from an average of 528 Mexicans per month affirmatively requesting political asylum in the first quarter of 2015 to 809 in June 2015, an increase of 53 percent per month (U.S. Citizenship and Immigration Services 2015a; U.S. Citizenship and Immigration Services 2015b). If one were to extrapolate from the available figures, assuming an average of around 600 per month, one could conclude that in 2015 approximately 7,200 Mexicans made affirmative applications for political asylum.

Political asylum in the United States leads to lawful permanent residence and ultimately to citizenship, but the path to approval has gotten more difficult even for seemingly worthy applicants. Mexicans may apply for political asylum for a variety of reasons, including threats based on gender identity or because of persistent domestic violence (UC Hastings 2016). Many applications from Mexican nationals involve threats or harm from criminal cartels or corrupt police. Can threats from criminal gangs constitute "persecution" within the meaning of refugee law?

Persecution by nonstate actors (guerrilla movements, political parties, death squads, for example) has long been recognized by U.S. agencies and courts as an appropriate basis for asylum (Aleinikoff et al. 2012). However, the Board of Immigration Appeals (BIA) and the federal courts narrowly construe eligibility when claimants seek protection from retribution from criminal gangs. Courts have refused to recognize "political opinion" or "particular social group" membership, for example, when claimants argue that resistance to recruitment or to sex acts (with gang members) constitutes a political opinion—or that such resisters constitute a "particular social group."

For an applicant to qualify for political asylum, he or she must prove that the motives of criminal actors are not "merely personal" or mainly for illicit financial gain. The BIA and federal courts require that the successful asylum applicant present evidence that the persecutors' motive is based on one of the statutory grounds, most often the victim's membership "of a particular social group" or as having a disfavored "political opinion." The Immigration and Nationality Act (INA) of 1965 states, "To establish that the applicant is a refugee within the meaning of such section, the applicant must establish that race, religion, nationality, membership in a particular social group, or political opinion was or will be at least one central reason for persecuting the applicant" (United States Congress 1965). The BIA has also set restrictive and complex standards of "social distinction" with respect to any claimed social-group membership, although some federal courts have discarded those standards.[1]

In addition, procedural obstacles put in place by U.S. law limit asylum eligibility. Applicants must comply with a one-year filing deadline after entry. For example, in a summary order (no precedential authority), the Second Circuit Court of Appeals upheld a decision by an immigration judge that "changed circumstances" did not justify the applicant's late filing of an asylum application even when "conditions in the relevant region of Mexico allegedly deteriorated" (*Cardona-Contreras v. Lynch* 2015). Advocates report that successful applications for political asylum from Mexicans are increasingly difficult to win (Cabot 2014).

Mexicans Seeking Protection Under the Convention Against Torture

The United States and Mexico are states parties to CAT and, therefore, have committed their governments not to torture persons within their respective territories, nor to send foreign nationals to places where they may be tortured ("non-refoulement"). Article 1 of CAT defines torture as any act by which severe pain or suffering, whether physical or mental, is intentionally inflicted on a person for such purposes as obtaining from him or a third person information or a confession, punishing him for an act he or a third person has committed or is suspected of having committed, or intimidating or coercing him or a third person, or for any reason based on discrimination of any kind, when such pain or suffering is inflicted by or at the instigation of or with the consent or acquiescence of a public official or other person acting in an official capacity.

Article 3 of CAT explicitly and clearly forbids states parties to return persons to a state where they are likely to be tortured:

1. No State Party shall expel, return ("refouler") or extradite a person to another State where there are substantial grounds for believing that he would be in danger of being subjected to torture.

2. For the purpose of determining whether there are such grounds, the competent authorities shall take into account all relevant considerations including, where applicable, the existence in the State concerned of a consistent pattern of gross, flagrant or mass violations of human rights.

CAT provides an alternative to political-asylum status for Mexicans fleeing violence and threats of violence.

After the U.S. Senate ratified CAT in 1998, the Department of Justice promulgated regulations to make protection against torture available to applicants in hearings before immigration judges (8 C.F.R. §§ 208.16, 208.17). The immigration judge may grant protection under CAT as either "withholding of removal" or "deferral of removal." The BIA reviews denials of CAT protection by immigration judges. BIA denials of CAT protection are subject to review by the U.S. Courts of Appeals. A successful claim for protection under CAT does not lead to permanent residence or citizenship, as does political asylum. The remedy granted is only a promise not to deport the applicant, accompanied by authorization to work. The successful claimant has some security in the United States but continues in a liminal status.

Despite the lack of permanent status, CAT claims may prove a promising route for Mexican applicants for three reasons. First, unlike political-asylum claimants, CAT applicants need not prove a political or discriminatory motive on the part of the feared perpetrators. A possibility that it is "more likely than not" that a person will be tortured is enough. Second, there is no one-year deadline after entry for filing CAT claims as there is for asylum claims—often a serious obstacle for traumatized asylum seekers. And third, even applicants with records of convictions for serious crimes are eligible for CAT relief.

As CAT protection is available to aliens regardless of any criminal record, many felons desperate to remain in the United States where their families reside resort to CAT claims as their only possibility to remain in the United States once they have completed their prison sentences. Given the undisputed evidence of the widespread use of torture by Mexican police and in Mexican prisons (see Introduction, this volume), it is quite possible that many of these returned criminals would present valid claims, but it is extremely difficult for incarcerated applicants to get assistance from lawyers.

While there are statistics about CAT applications before immigration judges, the available statistics do not classify them by nationality. In Fiscal Year 2014, 26,294 applications for deferral or withholding of removal under CAT were made to immigration courts by applicants of all nationalities, of which 536 were granted and 10,602 were denied. Of the remaining 15,156, 715 were "Abandoned," 5,203 were "Withdrawn," and 9,338 were classified as "Other" dispositions. Calculating a percentage of successful applications based on just the relative numbers of applications granted or denied, only 5 percent were granted (U.S. Department of Justice 2014). None of the available statistics disaggregates CAT applicants by nationality.

As noted in the Introduction to this volume, international human rights investigators studying Mexico in recent years have uniformly determined that torture and other human rights violations are widespread. Almost all of the acts perpetrated, including extrajudicial killings, enforced disappearances, the use of child soldiers, and systematic rape fit within the CAT definition of torture. The Office of the United Nations High Commissioner for Human Rights (OHCHR), among others, has noted that Mexico's internal failures to protect its citizens contrast with the government's enthusiastic support of human rights rhetoric in international fora (Al Hussein 2015). This basic ineffectiveness in protecting its citizens is increasingly evident even to U.S. federal courts, which are beginning to recognize that the Mexican state, including local officials, is responsible for many cases of torture. This is where the claims of those seeking protection from forced return to

Mexico coincide with those of protesters in the streets of Mexico: *"Fue el estado!"*—"It was the state!"

Procedurally, Mexican applicants for protection under CAT in the United States must meet certain standards. The applicant seeking withholding or deferral of removal under CAT bears the burden of proving that

- it is "more likely than not" that he or she would be
- "tortured," as defined in the regulations; and
- the torture must be inflicted "by or at the instigation of or with the consent or acquiescence of a public official or other person acting in an official capacity."

According to the applicable regulations, "acquiescence" requires that the public official have prior awareness of the activity and "thereafter breach his or her legal responsibility to intervene to prevent such activity" (8 C.F.R. § 1208.16(c)(2); 8 C.F.R. § 1208.18(a)(1); 8 C.F.R. § 1208.18(a)(7)).

The issue of "consent or acquiescence" is, as our Mexican colleagues would say, the *"chiste"* or key to the matter. Once an applicant has proved that he or she is likely to be tortured, the question of state involvement becomes the central issue. Both CAT and U.S. regulations require that the torture be inflicted "by or at the instigation of or with the consent or acquiescence of a public official or other person acting in an official capacity."

Blaming the Mexican government for failing to protect its own citizens from torture is a very serious matter with implications for United States–Mexico diplomatic relations. Combined with implicit fears of numbers ("too many" qualifying), there are many incentives for U.S. decision-makers not to grant protection to Mexicans.

An overview of selected decisions from U.S. Courts of Appeals, later in this chapter, demonstrates judicial interest in the question of state involvement. Similar to U.S. jurisprudence in police-brutality cases brought under federal civil rights statutes,[2] the inquiry in these CAT cases, where police or law enforcement are involved, centers on whether the government employees were "rogue" officers acting without the knowledge of their superiors. To some judges, particularly in the Seventh and Ninth Circuits, the involvement or knowledge of higher-ranking officials or the central government is immaterial to whether there was state "consent or acquiescence": that local police were perpetrators is enough for accountability by the state.

The main challenge in understanding how Mexican applicants for CAT protection fare is that so few of the decisions are available for public scrutiny. Decisions by immigration judges are usually not reduced to writing. Decisions of the BIA are summary and not often published. The best available body of decisions that discuss the situation in Mexico and protection under CAT are those from the U.S. Circuit Courts of Appeals.

The Annual Report of the Executive Office of Immigration Review for 2014 (the most recent available) indicates that 8,840 applications for protection under the Convention Against Torture were filed by Mexicans before immigration judges in Fiscal Year 2014, with only 124 granted. That same year, 1,852 applications by Mexicans were denied, 218 were abandoned, 2,403 were withdrawn, and 3,088 were classified as "other" (U.S. Department of Justice 2014). Those figures account for 7,561 cases, adding 1,279 cases (just of Mexicans who have applied for CAT protection) to the already enormous backlog of cases before immigration judges, a backlog that results in delays of up to three years for applicants waiting for hearings.

Jurisprudence on CAT Within U.S. Immigration Cases

Immigration Judges

Immigration judges in the United States are administrative judges and employees of the Department of Justice, Executive Office for Immigration Review. Petitions for political asylum and protection under CAT are presented in written form and then in trial-type hearings before immigration judges. Applicants themselves testify and may present testimony of other witnesses and documentary evidence, as well as opinions by experts (in the form of testimony or in writing) (National Immigrant Justice Center 2016).

At the conclusion of the hearing, the immigration judge gives an oral decision, which is recorded but not usually transcribed. In certain exceptional cases, a judge may issue a written decision. This reliance on oral decisions significantly hampers research into trends in jurisprudence in the immigration courts (Ramji-Nogales, Schoenholtz, and Schrag 2007). A national survey of lawyers practicing immigration law would be necessary to produce any conclusions regarding what sorts of protection claims from Mexicans have been successful.

Board of Immigration Appeals

If the applicant loses before the immigration judge, he or she may appeal to the BIA, which bases its review only on the evidence submitted before the immigration judge. Not all decisions of the BIA are published, again hampering researchers. The BIA does publish some of its decisions and may designate a given decision as "precedential," that is, binding on all immigration judges.

In only two cases since 2000 has the BIA issued precedential cases to set out standards for CAT claims. Neither case involved a Mexican applicant. In *Matter of Y-L-A-G-,* 23 I&N Dec. 270 (A.G. 2002) and *Matter of S-V-,* 22 I&N Dec. 1306 (BIA 2000), the BIA held that CAT applicants must show that it is "more likely than not" that they would be tortured and that the torture would be done with the "consent or acquiescence" of the state. Under these BIA decisions, the standard for "consent or acquiescence" requires that the applicant present evidence that state authorities actually knew that torture was likely in a particular case and were "willfully blind" to its happening.

Since *Matter of S-V-,* the BIA has followed that strict standard. Given that most human rights agencies agree that the violence and human rights violations in Mexico have increased substantially in the last five years, the author reviewed all twenty-one available BIA decisions on CAT protection claims by Mexican nationals made between 2011 and 2016. The decisions yielded little insight into the BIA's opinions on circumstances in Mexico. Almost none of the decisions addressed the merits of the cases, and none was designated as precedential. Fourteen of the appeals were denied for procedural reasons (failure to file an application, failure to allege a prima facie case to reopen an earlier decision, and so forth); two appeals were granted and remanded for new hearings on denial of the right to have counsel present before the immigration judge.

One case, *In re: Eber Salgado-Gutierres,* 2015 WL 1605446, BIA 2015, was remanded to the immigration judge for presentation of a full application for CAT protection. (After remand and presentation of a full application for CAT relief, the immigration judge and BIA denied the applications for political asylum and CAT relief on the facts, a decision upheld by the Court of Appeals [*Eber Salgado-Gutierrez v. Lynch,* No. 16-1534, 8/24/2016].) In another, *In re: Adrian de Alba Castrejon,* 2015 WL 1208207, BIA 2015, the BIA held that the applicant had not made out a prima facie case that handicapped persons would be tortured in Mexico. In the case of *In re: Federico Salas-Rocha,* 2015

WL 1208076, BIA 2015, the BIA held that an applicant had failed to make a case that he might be subject to torture because it would be known that he had been deported from the United States; and in only one case, *In re: Jose Manuel Bueno-Mercado,* 2010 WL 4509755, BIA 2010, did the BIA state that the applicant was ineligible because the Mexican government would be able to protect the applicant from the feared harm—a finding of no "consent or acquiescence" by the state.

United States Courts of Appeals

As set out in Article III of the U.S. Constitution and the Federal Judiciary Act of 1789, federal judges are lifetime tenured presidential appointments. This allows them to rule on cases without concern for reappointment or reelection. The U.S. Circuit Courts of Appeals have the power to review decisions by the BIA under 8 USC. Sec. 1252 (INA Sec. 242). As the Courts of Appeals issue written decisions, all of which are released to the public, one can observe trends in the jurisprudence in those decisions. The country is divided into twelve judicial circuits with courts having jurisdiction over cases in which the removal hearing was held in their circuit. U.S. Courts of Appeals' decisions are binding precedent on the BIA for cases that arise in the geographical jurisdiction of that particular circuit court. Circuit courts' decisions, particularly those issued by highly regarded judges, can be persuasive (if not precedential) to other Courts of Appeals as well.[3] When a Court of Appeals remands a case to the BIA, a BIA decision in line with the ruling of the court may be designated as precedential for all immigration judges and thereby have national influence on the interpretations of law. There have been some important recent Courts of Appeals opinions on the issue of "consent or acquiescence" (state accountability), which may eventually govern decisions by immigration judges nationwide.

The author reviewed recent trends in two of the most important Courts of Appeals (the Seventh and Ninth Circuits) regarding applications by Mexican nationals for protection under CAT. The Ninth Circuit (comprising Arizona, California, Idaho, Montana, Nevada, Oregon, and Washington states) is particularly important with respect to standards for protection because it is the largest circuit, and its area has the largest population of immigrants and asylum seekers. The Seventh Circuit Court of Appeals (Illinois, Wisconsin, and Indiana) played an important role in the relevant jurisprudence in part because of the eminence of Judge Richard Posner, often characterized as the most cited federal judge in the entire judicial system (Lattman 2006; Shulman 2017).

This overview does not aim to be the definitive word on the current state of the law in each of the twelve Circuit Courts of Appeals, but rather to spotlight interesting decisions and trends. The author reviewed decisions by these courts that involved Mexican applicants for protection under CAT, published from January 2010 to March 2016.

In the years since the precedential BIA decision in *Matter of S-V*, various Courts of Appeals have interpreted "consent or acquiescence" differently. In the last three years, both the Ninth and Seventh Circuit Courts have made important rulings on the "consent or acquiescence" issue.

The leading decision of the Ninth Circuit Court of Appeals is *Victor Hugo Tapia-Madrigal v. Holder*, 716 F.3d at 505 (2013). The applicant had been a member of the Mexican military who participated in an antinarcotics enforcement effort against the Zetas criminal organization in 2007. The applicant appeared in a nationally broadcast television report of the incidents, after which he was kidnapped and beaten by presumed members of the Zetas. The kidnappers released him with a warning that he tell his commander that the arrested Zetas must be released. At that point, Tapia-Madrigal left military service and heard a few months later that the commander had been killed. Following the commander's killing, Tapia-Madrigal was on the run in Mexico, while his family was visited by strangers asking about his whereabouts. In one instance, shots were fired at him from a passing car in the community where he had hidden. At that point, he left for the United States. Since his arrival in the United States, an anonymous written threat against him was left at his mother's home in Mexico.

In interpreting whether the Mexican government could protect Tapia-Madrigal as part of his claim for political asylum, the BIA relied on evidence that the national Mexican government was willing to control the Zetas. However, according to the Ninth Circuit, the BIA "did not examine the efficacy of those efforts" (*Tapia-Madrigal*: 13). The court went on to say with regard to Tapia-Madrigal's claim for political asylum, "Significant evidence . . . calls into doubt the Mexican government's ability to control Los Zetas. The available country conditions evidence demonstrates that violent crime traceable to drug cartels remains high despite the Mexican government's efforts to quell it. . . . Corruption at the state and local levels 'continues to be a problem' [citing a U.S. Department of State report] . . ." (14). Citing the same evidence with respect to the request for CAT protection, the Ninth Circuit declared, "Both [a political asylum decision and a decision on CAT protection] require examining the efficacy of the government's efforts to stop the drug cartels' violence and both are affected by the degree of corruption that exists in Mexico's government" (19). The court went on to state that the successful CAT relief applicant need not prove that the "entire foreign government" would consent to or acquiesce in his torture, but that the acquiescing agent need only be "a public official" (20). Before ordering that the BIA reconsider Tapia-Madrigal's application, the court further found, "Voluminous evidence in the record explains that corruption of public officials in Mexico remains a problem, particularly at the state and local levels of government, with police officers and prison guards frequently working directly on behalf of drug cartels" (20).

In a later decision involving a transgender woman who presented evidence that she was beaten and tortured by local police in Mexico, *Avendano-Hernandez v. Lynch,* No. 13-73744 (9th Cir. 2015), a different panel of the Ninth Circuit followed the standard established in *Tapia-Madrigal.* This panel further elaborated, "We reject the [U.S.] government's attempts to characterize these police and military officers are merely rogue or corrupt officials. . . . It is enough for her to show that she was subject to torture at the hands of local officials" (*Avendano-Hernandez:* 14).

In two recent Seventh Circuit decisions, both authored by Judge Richard Posner (with four other judges on two separate panels), the court overturned findings by the BIA and also set a standard for "consent or acquiescence" that is more generous than that of the BIA. Posner ruled that the "substantial grounds for believing [that an applicant would face torture]" language in CAT required proof only of "likelihood," but not a greater than 50 percent probability, which is what the BIA's "more likely than not" standard requires.

In *Hair Rodriguez-Molinero,* No. 15-1860 (7th Cir. 2015), Judge Posner and two other judges considered the case of a Mexican citizen who had resided in the United States for many years. Involved in selling methamphetamines for the Zetas, he had been previously tortured in Mexico at the Zetas' behest ("to test his loyalty") and feared torture on return for several reasons. He owed the Zetas $30,000 for methamphetamines confiscated on his arrest; he had become an informant for the U.S. Drug Enforcement Administration and Federal Bureau of Investigation; and his uncle had been kidnapped and killed in Mexico by Zetas seeking information about Rodriguez-Molinero. Rodriguez-Molinero's application for CAT protection followed the completion of his sentence for federal drug crimes.

The court ruled that the "more likely than not" standard for CAT eligibility established in U.S. regulations "cannot be and is not taken literally," as it would contradict the CAT standard of "substantial grounds for believing that" the person "would be in danger of being tortured." Posner established a standard for judges to decide if "there is or is not a substantial risk," a more generous standard than "more likely than not" (*Rodriguez-Molinero:* 2). The court further found that "killing whether or not accompanied by torture" constituted torture under both CAT and U.S. regulations (3). Actions by local corrupt police are sufficient to establish government "consent or acquiescence" (8). On the last point, relying on the 2013 Department of State Human Rights Report, the testimony of an expert witness, and academic articles and books submitted by the applicant, Judge Posner found that the immigration judge had erred in her statement that "the infliction, instigation, or acquiescence in torture must be by the Mexican *government* rather than just Mexican police officers or other government employees" (emphasis in original).

In his usual frank language, Judge Posner said,

> Not the issue! . . . The alien need not show that multiple government officials are complicit. Nor is the issue . . . whether police officers who tortured the petitioner were rogue officers individually compensated by [the criminal cartel] to engage in isolated incidents of retaliatory brutality, rather than evidence of a broader pattern of governmental acquiescence in torture. It is irrelevant whether the police were rogue (in the sense of not serving the interests of the Mexican government) or not. The petitioner did not have to show that the entire Mexican government is complicit in the misconduct of individual police officers. (9)

Judge Posner discounted the position that efforts by the central Mexican government to combat cartels would nullify a claim that the government would "consent or acquiesce," saying, "That the Mexican government may be trying, though apparently without much success, to prevent police from torturing citizens at the behest of drug gangs is irrelevant to this case" (9).

A week later, on December 23, 2015, in *Martin Mendoza-Sanchez v. Loretta Lynch,* F.3d 1182, at 880 (7th Cir. 2015), Judge Posner explicitly directed the BIA to reconsider its standard for "acquiescence." Mendoza-Sanchez had been selling cocaine for a Mexican cartel known as "La Linea." Arrested and convicted of drug dealing in the United States, he was attacked and injured in prison by a member of La Linea who told him that the cartel believed Mendoza-Sanchez had informed on other members and that they would kill him when he returned to Mexico.

The government had not questioned the credibility of the applicant, nor his story of likely killing or torture by a cartel. Rather, the immigration judge and the BIA found that he had not established that "'a Mexican public official would acquiesce (or be wilfully blind) to such harm'" (*Mendoza-Sanchez:* 2). Judge Posner went on to say, "The Board did this in the face of evidence . . . that police officers routinely collaborate with and protect drug cartels in Mexico" (4). The judge also quoted extensively from the U.S. Department of State 2013 Report on human rights in Mexico, which stated that there is widespread impunity among both the military and the police, that investigations are insufficient, and that there is police involvement in kidnapping and the torture of prisoners. Judge Posner also explicitly found that "contrary to what the Board thought, the presence of the Mexican army in Matamoros supports rather than undermines Mendoza Sanchez's claim that local police will acquiesce in his torture; had the police been protecting the city, the army would have no reason to be there" (5).

In *Mendoza-Sanchez,* Judge Posner urged that the BIA adopt a standard for CAT petitions that applicants "need not prove that the Mexican government is complicit in the misconduct of its police officers." With the agreement of the U.S. government attorneys, Judge Posner remanded the case to the BIA for reconsideration of its analysis of standards for CAT applications. Judge Posner urged the BIA "pay careful heed to the analysis in this opinion and in *Rodriguez-Molinero*" (8). In effect, Judge Posner urged the BIA to take the Seventh Circuit standard and make it the national rule for all immigration courts. It is important to note, however, that a subsequent decision by a panel of the Seventh Circuit, without Judge Posner's participation, denied a Mexican applicant for CAT relief, holding him to a very strict level of proof (*Lozano-Zuniga v. Lynch,* 832 F 3d 822 (7th Cir. 2016)).

Later in 2016, in yet another decision, Judge Posner reiterated his support of the standard above but held that the applicant in the case before the court had not met the factual burden of showing likely torture. (*Eber Salgado-Gutierrez v. Lynch,* No. 16-1534, 8/24/2016.) Judge Posner retired from the bench in September 2017.

Conclusions

The stories of Mexicans applying for protection in the United States are evidence of widespread torture and other human rights violations, of the impunity that protects perpetrators, and of the inability of the government to control powerful criminal gangs or its own corrupt officials. Given the numbers of Mexicans impacted by such conduct—and Mexico's proximity to the United States—it is not surprising that many U.S. decision-makers may be reluctant to recognize eligibility for political asylum or protection under CAT. In the meantime, it is hoped that U.S. adjudicators will, in the words of Judge Posner, "pay careful heed" to both the applicable legal standards and the testimony of Mexican asylum seekers themselves.

Certainly, Mexicans seeking protection in the United States and their lawyers would benefit by increased access to Mexican analysts of the human rights situation in Mexico, as they prepare applications and seek to advance the U.S. jurisprudence to provide protection where needed. Cross-border communication and collaboration between human rights advocates will benefit individuals seeking protection and, hopefully, influence public policy on both sides of the border.

It is doubtful that the human rights situation in Mexico will improve in the near future, and the U.S. obligation to provide protection will continue. As the Mexican Nobel laureate Carlos Fuentes wrote,

> *Al norte del río grande*
> *al sur del río bravo,*
> *que vuelen las palabras,*
> *pobre México,*
> *pobre Estados Unidos,*
> *tan lejos de Dios,*
> *tan cerca el uno del otro.*
> (North of the Rio Grande
> South of the Rio Bravo [the Mexican name for the Rio Grande],
> the words fly,
> poor Mexico,
> poor United States,
> so far from God,
> so close to each other.)

PART III

The Institutional Crisis

CHAPTER 9

=====

Democracia a la Mexicana

A Framework Conducive
to Human Rights Violations

Daniel Vázquez

Introduction

We were wrong to believe that human rights violations in Mexico would end with the transition to democracy. Violations did not end with democracy, but instead merely shifted their patterns.[1]

An analysis of the characteristics, logic, and trends of Latin American democracies is necessary to understand whether, within a democratic context, human rights violations decrease, are modified, or increase. Mexico is a good case for this type of analysis because it has experienced a lengthy transition, starting with the student movement of 1968. After multiple electoral reforms, in 1997 the Institutional Revolutionary Party (PRI)—which had governed since it was founded in 1929—lost control of the Chamber of Deputies and in 2000 lost the presidential election to the National Action Party (PAN), led by Vicente Fox. After two PAN governments—2000–2006 with Fox and 2006–2012 with Felipe Calderón Hinojosa as presidents—in 2012 the PRI returned to the presidency.

Even in this new context of alternating political power between Mexico's political parties, human rights violations continue to be serious. The Inter-American Commission on Human Rights (IACHR) classified the Mexican situation as a generalized crisis (IACHR 2015). In 2014 and 2015, the United

Nation's Special Rapporteur on Torture (Human Rights Council 2014) and the United Nation's Committee on Enforced Disappearances (Committee on Enforced Disappearances 2014) also rated the practices of torture and enforced disappearances in the country as widespread.

The use of the term "widespread" as a qualifier of these abuses is not innocuous, as it speaks to a legal category. Human rights violations can be isolated, widespread, or systematic. When these violations are pronounced as "widespread," it means that distinct governmental bodies (federal, local, or municipal) follow the same patterns in their abuse of human rights throughout the entire national territory. This occurs not only with civil and political rights. The Permanent People's Tribunal (TPP 2012) came to the same conclusion in its prehearing final ruling, which analyzed the violations of the rights of indigenous communities and towns in the construction of dams. Regardless of whether the dams were constructed in the north, center, or south of the country, the violations of these indigenous communities' rights followed the same patterns.

Finally, for the purpose of this introduction, and to provide space for a brief consideration of social and economic rights, it is worthwhile to review the data on peoples in conditions of poverty and vulnerability, issued by the National Council for the Evaluation of Social Development (CONEVAL). This organization assesses poverty in Mexico in a multidimensional way that includes in its calculations various human rights, such as access to education, health services, social security, food, and housing, as well as housing quality and conditions. When one of these rights is not met, a person is considered to be suffering a social deprivation. People who are considered extremely poor, poor, or in a vulnerable situation necessarily suffer from at least one form of social deprivation, which is to say that at least one of their six social and economic rights is being violated. The three calculations provided by CONEVAL show that in 2010 at least 74.9 percent of the population had at least one of these economic and social rights violated; this figure changed to 74.1 percent in 2012 and 72.5 percent in 2014 (CONEVAL 2011, 2012, 2015). In other words, ten years after Mexico's transition, more than two-thirds of the population experiences the daily violation of at least one economic or social right.

Based on this assessment, this chapter considers the following questions: What patterns characterize Mexican democracy after its transition? Do these patterns tend to eliminate human rights violations, or rather, are they frameworks conducive to their repetition?

The Transition to Democracy
and Human Rights Expectations

Negative correlations have been found between the level of development, investment flow, the democratization process, and human rights violations, though the causal direction of this relationship remains uncertain (Landman 2005; Freeman 2002). For the purposes of this text, the correlation between democratization and human rights violations is of particular interest.

The relationship between these two factors became particularly evident during democracy's third wave, which began in Portugal and Spain then passed through various African countries, various Latin American military dictatorships, and the Communist bloc. This growing interest regarding the link between democratic transitions and human rights is largely due to two factors: First, all of these countries transitioned from military dictatorships or authoritarian governments known for carrying out systematic human rights violations. Second, human rights discourse had become institutionalized in International Human Rights Law. This human rights discourse began to gain relevance at the international level, as well as within social movements that advocated for the end of military dictatorships and their systematic human rights violations.

Despite this apparent linkage, human rights do not play a fundamental role in transitional justice theory.[2] The principal factor in transitions to democracy tends to be the consolidation of party and electoral systems, as well as the celebration of competitive elections. In some cases, the opening up and liberalization of dictatorial or democratic regimes are analyzed as a preliminary step toward democratization, but even in these cases the role of human rights appears as secondary.

Often it is assumed that democracy is the regime best constituted to respect, protect, and guarantee human rights. This is not to say that there are no human rights violations under democracies, but rather their systematic occurrence is less probable since citizens have more tools to assert their rights. This is due to the conceptual relationship that often forms between democracy and the rule of law based on the tight links between liberalism and democracy. In this way, a representative government will not generate systematic human rights violations for three reasons. In order for democracy to exist, certain civil and political rights must necessarily exist as a precondition.[3] Theoretically, the government that systematically violates human rights should be punished at the ballot boxes in the following election (vertical accountability). In addition to elections, citizens may turn to other governmental organizations to stop these human rights violations and start a process that seeks to investigate, sanction, and ask for reparations (horizontal accountability). Furthermore, people are able to organize in order to defend their rights (social or extra-institutional human rights mechanisms, or societal accountability). These are the key components of a democracy—horizontal, vertical, and social accountability—that are expected to preclude the widespread or systematic violation of human rights and to reduce the occurrence of random violations.

A series of studies analyzes this relationship between the transition to democracy and human rights violations. Most of this research identifies only transgressions of physical-integrity rights as human rights violations—torture, inhumane treatment, enforced disappearance, and extrajudicial executions. Additionally, the majority of the databases that are commonly used in statistical models take into account only these physical-integrity rights violations and do not attempt to measure or analyze political, economic, social, cultural, or environmental rights. The initial premise of these studies was that one should expect to find a negative statistical correlation between a democratic regime and human rights violations. However, this correlation does not always exist.

The *More Murder in the Middle* model maintains that the majority of human rights violations do not occur in consolidated military dictatorships nor in consolidated democracies but, rather, in weakened military dictatorships and young democracies (Fein 1995; King 1998; Regan and Henderson 2002). The reason for this effect is found in a concept referred to as "systematic incoherencies." In consolidated democracies as in consolidated dictatorships, the rules of the game (formal and informal) and the incentives, rewards, and punishments are clearly established. In democracies, the governments will know how to behave in order to avoid horizontal, vertical, or societal accountability and to stay in power. In consolidated dictatorships, citizens will be hesitant to openly present their complaints before the government to avoid being repressed, disappeared, or assassinated. Whereas in weak dictatorships, citizens have more incentives to organize and protest as their governments may either respond violently or give in when faced with protests. Something similar occurs in unconsolidated democracies, where the citizens assume that they are living under a liberal, pluralistic government, but authoritarian enclaves remain and may produce authoritarian responses. While the rules of the game are clear at the extremes, there is a systematic incoherence in the center.

Davenport and Armstrong (2004) arrive at similar conclusions, using a different statistical model (local regressions, a nonparametric method that allows for the identification of nonlinear influences) that allows them to identify the threshold where the inflection point appears. Their statistical results indicate that at the initial stages of the democratization process there is no impact on the reduction of human rights violations, but after reaching a certain threshold (7 on a scale from 1 to 10), the progress toward democratic consolidation has a major impact on the reduction of these human rights violations. On these bases, they conclude that there are, at least, three distinct categories of democratization processes that distinctly impact state repression: one in which the regime change makes no difference (from 0 to 7 on the democratization scale), another in which there is a certain degree of negative impact (from 8 to 9), and one in which there is a strong negative trend (10).

We know that in reality it will not be democratic transition but, rather, democratic consolidation that will probably have a larger impact on the reduction of human rights violations. Under this criteria, Mexico might be considered a classic example of this process. There was a democratic transition, understood as the regular execution of competitive elections; and, in fact, there were already two changes in the political party in power at the federal level. However, many government institutions are far from meeting the standards and expectations generated by the transition. Nevertheless, the Mexico case study allows us to observe whether the patterns of democracy (a) lead us to democratic consolidation and (b) are a framework for the reduction of human rights violations. This study's contribution can thus be found in its detailed analysis of the processes that constitute the actual logic of democracy in the Mexican case: *democracia a la mexicana* (Mexican-style democracy).

Democracia a la Mexicana

Mexican-style democracy is a political process made up of diverse mechanisms, some inherently related to democracy's third wave and others to Mexico. In Figure 9.1, the outer circle refers to those mechanisms inherent in the third wave, while the inner circle corresponds to Mexican aspects.

Of the eight elements that form the logic of Mexican-style democracy, three stem from the way in which the transition was carried out during the third wave, and five are related to the informal and formal rules with which Mexico

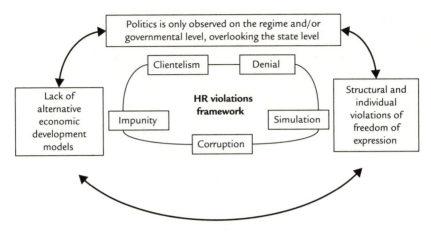

Figure 9.1. The logic of democracy in Mexico.

is governed. This chapter now focuses on the mechanisms that are inherent to Mexico's style of democracy, starting with some brief comments regarding the three elements that correspond to the transitional logic of the third wave.

In Mexico's transition, state-level politics received less attention than meso-level politics—that is, institutions inherent to the political regime. To a certain degree, this approach facilitated the transition—a significant improvement for those people who personally suffered under the dictatorships because it promised them the opportunity to exercise their basic civil and physical-integrity rights.[4] But it obscured assessments of the governing political-economic coalition's structure, which determines the informal and formal rules of political recognition and economic distribution,[5] many of which were not structurally modified with the democratic transition. Worse still, the problem was not only that the transition was focused on the regime level, but rather, once the rules of the game for political power were established, the political debate took place largely, at the federal level to the neglect of state-level politics. In contrast, thinking about democracy at the state-level allows us to formulate crucial questions. Who is included in the current governing political-economic coalition in Mexico? What are the most influential factions at the state and federal levels? What are the fundamental political decisions defined by this set of relationships? And how open/closed is the current political arena in Mexico?

The next characteristic related to democracy's third wave is that there is no systematic analysis of the preconditions for the proper operation of multiparty electoral oversight; in particular, there is no analysis of the institutionalization of freedom of expression. To actualize the multiparty electoral process, free and fair elections, the availability of more than one programmatic proposal from which to choose, and freedom of expression are all required. The form in which freedom of expression has been established in Mexico prevents the realization of multiparty electoral oversight (Vázquez 2007, 2008, 2010a).

The main restriction to the proper functioning of vertical accountability comes from the structural violations to the institutionalization of freedom of expression carried out by the market. We know that the market, by its own logic, is not a suitable mechanism for exercising rights: it reacts to monetary demands and not to a universal logic as is required to protect human rights, and at the same time the actors that make up the market maintain a strong asymmetry of political and economic power. Thus, a concentrated media market that is incapable of reproducing the plurality of voices that make up Mexico's current civil society[6] has emerged (Mastrini and Becerra 2006). The right to freedom of expression not only encompasses freedom from censorship but also requires sufficient media outlets for all voices to be heard. This is one of the main debates currently taking place in Latin America, namely, how to institutionalize freedom of expression to ensure plurality (Serrano and Vázquez 2013).

It is not only the inability to reproduce this plurality but also a problem of institutional and at other times structural bias. To the degree that the owners of large media companies belong to some faction of the governing coalition, and considering that the plurality includes only the factions of the governing coalition, those who continue to be excluded are those who do not belong to any of these factions. Further, to the extent that it concerns business owners, any economic model that critiques the capitalist model in general and the neoliberal approach in particular is totally cast out due to its potential opposition to corporate interests.

Finally, the third characteristic typical of democracy's third wave is the absence of alternatives to the neoliberal development model (whether it be extractionist or dependent on *maquiladoras*—factories with very low production value added) (Cavarozzi 1991; Constantino and Cantamutto 2015). The "consensus" adoption of the capitalist model in general and neoliberalism in particular limits the existence of programmatic proposals, at least in reference to Mexico's economic model. This restriction comes, to a large degree, from the fact that the democratic transition as part of the third wave focused on the regime, and thus, no change was proposed to the existing rules that governed the distribution of economic power at the state level.

Alternative Forms of Intermediation: Clientelism

With the advent of democratic transitions, it was taken as given that the main mechanism of intermediation and governmental control would be free and secret ballots. Instead, far from this expectation was a reality, frequently and persuasively documented, involving the creation of other mechanisms of political intermediation (Isunza and Gurza 2010; Olvera 2010; Cameron, Hershberg, and Sharpe 2012). One of the mechanisms, emphasized here, is clientelism, explained as follows. In Mexico, the abstention rate in elections averages 40 percent (sixty of every one hundred Mexicans vote). Additionally, because of Mexico's current political party system, the candidate who can secure 30 percent of the vote practically has the election in the bag; that is to say, that he/she needs the votes of only eighteen of the sixty voters who actually go to the polls. The point here is not so much to describe how specific clientelist mechanisms work on election day to buy votes. Because much of politics today is local, the key question is whether governors and municipal presidents have the capacity to weave together a clientelist network that can be mobilized on election day to obtain eighteen out of every one hundred possible voters. Unfortunately, despite the ever-increasing host of studies on clientelism, we do not have a figure on the size of the clientelist networks that are able to be mobilized on election day. Nonetheless, we can lay the foundation for some insights. We begin with the fact that the ground in Mexico for the practice of clientelism is fertile because there are 86.8 million Mexicans living in conditions of poverty or vulnerability (see Figure 9.2).

CONEVAL itself, in its evaluations of social policy, explains that thousands of social programs exist on the federal, local, and municipal levels. To be more exact, during 2011 there were 273 federal programs and 2,391 state programs (the number of municipal programs was not recorded for this year) (CONEVAL 2012). By 2014, the figure had grown to 278 federal programs and 2,849 state programs (almost 500 more than the previous year), and for the first time municipal programs were reviewed, showing that there were 1,883 (CONEVAL 2015).

The problem is not that, according to the logic of public policy rationality, having more programs is an error, but that, as the executive secretary of

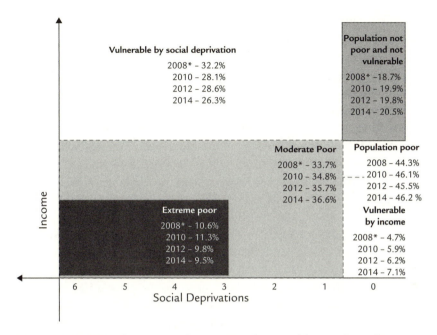

Figure 9.2. CONEVAL's poverty indicators. Distribution of the population by poverty or vulnerability (2008, 2010, 2012). Source: Based on data from http://www .coneval.org.mx/Medicion/MP/Paginas/Pobreza_2014.aspx.

CONEVAL pointed out, having a social policy composed of 5,010 programs is a mess:

- Coordination and complementarity are weak (there are programs with overlapping objectives);
- At the local level, there is no evaluation system, and therefore the results of these programs are unknown;
- Many of them do not have any operational regulations, nor is there any certainty regarding their continuity; they are temporary programs.

The absence of specific operational regulations (that is to say, technical regulatory criteria) and the uncertainty surrounding the continuity of these various programs are two factors that demonstrate the opportunities for clientelist management to benefit from the discretionary use of the "petty cash" they generate.

One additional data point to reinforce this particular insight is to ask, for whom are the most impoverished citizens voting? In accordance with the polling group Parametría (Redacción 2015; Abundis 2015), based on the data from the 2015 elections, the first group of voters who supported the PRI included those with the lowest level of formal education (49 percent with no formal instruction, 42 percent with primary-school education, and 39 percent with secondary-school education), and the second were those with the lowest level of income (48 percent of the people who earn less than $1,517 pesos a month prefer the PRI).

Thus, the combination of widespread conditions of poverty and vulnerability, the creation of clientelist networks as a mechanism for political intermediation, the multiplication of municipal and local social programs without operational regulations and without measures for control or accountability, composes substantial grounds for obtaining eighteen out of every one hundred votes.

The clientelist networks supplant voting as the mechanism of political representation in Mexico and make vertical accountability inoperative. The political parties, as they stand, no longer care about expanding the vote among "free" citizens but instead focus much more attention on maintaining their clentelist networks. Citizens lose one of the accountability mechanisms that, inter alia, could be used to reduce systematic, widespread, or grave human rights violations—rewards and punishments through voting at the polls. The possibility that clientelism displaces vertical accountability is more clearly understood if we relate it to the other elements that compose Mexican-style democracy—particularly denial and impunity. Governments deny the existence of clientelism, and the institutional authorities do not investigate it. Thus, political parties are not held to account, through vertical mechanisms, for human rights violations perpetrated while they are in office.

Denial and Simulation as Political Systems

Denial as Political Action

Denial has become a form of political action in the face of criticism. This includes the denial of the real conditions of poverty (and the attempt to push authorities such as CONEVAL to modify their measurement systems). Another example is the denial of the disruption of different governmental bodies due to organized crime and generalized corruption, based on the notion that corruption is just part of the human condition. The denial extends to the findings of the United Nation's Special Rapporteur that torture is widespread in Mexico; and the denial of the United Nation's Committee on Enforced Disappearance's conclusions that disappearances are also widespread. The government denies the conclusions of the IAHCR and the Office of the UN High Commissioner for Human Rights, which during a visit to Mexico, concluded that there is a human rights crisis in Mexico.

Denial as a form of political action has two consequences: (1) it generates incorrect political assessments, which bring about erroneous or deliberately diverted political actions; and (2) far from allowing for reasoned public deliberation, it allows politics to operate under the principle "If you criticize me, you are my enemy."

The first of the consequences is evident in matters such as what was known as the "historic truth" elaborated by the Federal Attorney General's Office (PGR) regarding the disappearance of the forty-three students in Iguala in 2014. The report presented in September 2015 by the Interdisciplinary Group of Independent Experts of the IACHR (GIEI 2015) made clear not only that there were serious errors in the PGR's investigations but also that the institution was manipulated in order to hide the connection or interdependence between municipal, state, and federal authorities and drug-trafficking organizations in Guerrero.

Institutional denial results in a lack of recognition of the problems that effectively exist in Mexico—among them, human rights violations—and, for that matter, the lack of solutions, proposals, analyses, or public policies that directly confront these problems.

Simulation as a Routine Political Action

Together with the denial of some of the problems associated with structural human rights violations, we have simulation: the production of actions that do not directly impact the root of the problems that produce human rights violations, or actions that are implemented in such a way that their final objective becomes totally distorted. What we observe in these cases are simulated solutions. Consider simulation in the following two examples: the appointment of persons loyal to the government to head diverse governmental agencies, and the forms of negotiation adopted when dealing with social movements.

The Secretariat of Public Offices (Secretaría de la Función Pública) is the federal government's agency in charge of investigating acts of corruption. Probably the most evident recent case of simulation has been the appointment of Virgilio Andrade, a close aide to President Peña Nieto, to lead this secretariat during the latter's government, including the special task of investigating the *"la Casa Blanca"* case.[7] No one was surprised when in August 2015 Virgilio Andrade concluded that his friends Enrique Peña Nieto, First Lady Angélica Rivera Hurtado, and Luis Videgaray (at the time Finance Secretary) had not participated in any type of administrative or legal misconduct.[8]

These types of simulations in appointments are to be expected in the centralized agencies that, in the end, remain under the executive power's domain. However, does the same happen in agencies that are supposed to be autonomous? There are several examples of simulation in autonomous agencies: the appointment of Eduardo Medina-Mora to the Supreme Court,[9] that of Perla Gómez to lead the Federal District's Human Rights Commission,[10] and even the withdrawal of Miguel Sarre's candidacy for the United Nation's Committee Against Torture, with the goal of also colonizing international human rights organs that have recently caused various setbacks for the Mexican government.[11]

Autonomous agencies are supposed to function as a system of checks and balances necessary for horizontal accountability. To the extent that appointments are made to undermine the objectivity of these agencies, they ensure the ineffectiveness of this control mechanism and its corresponding impact on the protection of human rights (Frey 2015).

Let us move on to the second example: negotiating with social movements. At this point, I am less interested in the general framework of collective action as "modular repertoire"[12] of tactics such as marches, meetings, and strikes, than in making explicit the different possible governmental simulation responses. It would not be strange to think that a more democratic, more representative government would be one that includes and articulates the largest number of possible social demands. Also, collective action's modular repertoire is obviously not an end in itself. Exercising one's right to protest is always a means to make public those demands that have not been institutionally articulated.

When facing the successful birth of a social movement that raises a demand—for example, calling for the right to fair wages by rural day laborers, the emergence alive of disappeared family members, an increase in the education budget, or changes to a security policy—some reaction on the part of the government may be expected. This reaction may vary along the following lines:

1) Repression of the modular repertoire;
2) Allowing collective action, but not establishing a direct dialogue with social forces;
3) Opening a dialogue by means of the executive or legislative branches or both, but reaching only general guidelines, not specific agreements;
4) Reaching specific agreements, but not establishing verifiable goals to be reached within a specific time line;
5) Establishing verifiable goals within a time line that will later be violated by the government, taking advantage of a key level of organizational weariness and arguing the impossibility of goal compliance.

The basis of these five possibilities is the bureaucratic script used to guide the simulated negotiations between governments and social movements. This framework has been used in the administration of key social protests, such as the students' strike at Mexico's National Autonomous University (UNAM) in 1999, the Popular Assembly of the Peoples of Oaxaca in 2006, the protests by the National Coordinator of Education Workers against the education reform in 2013 and 2014, and the mobilization around the disappearance of the Ayotzinapa students in 2014. In each of these cases, the script—government responses that alternated between permitting mobilization, opening up spaces for dialogue, and criminalizing social protest—prolonged the conflict and led to the denial of the demands at the core of the mobilization.

Corruption and Impunity: Tightening the Grasp

Our definition of corruption draws from the World Bank's conceptualization, adopted by Transparency International: corruption is the abuse of entrusted power for private gain.[13] Corruption supposes the appropriation of that which is public for private ends; in other words, the cooptation of the government, or the loss of government "publicness." To address impunity, we will look at the concept elaborated by the United Nation's Commission on Human Rights in the *Set of principles for the protection and promotion of human rights through action to combat impunity,* created in 1997 and updated in 2005. This instrument defines impunity as "the impossibility, de jure or de facto, of bringing the perpetrators of violations to account—whether in criminal, civil, administrative or disciplinary proceedings—since they are not subject to any inquiry that might lead to their being accused, arrested, tried and, if found guilty, sentenced to appropriate penalties, and to making reparations to their victims" (OHCHR 2005: para. A).

Corruption as Political Action and Human Rights Violations

In the 1990s boom in studies regarding corruption, the economics of corruption was the primary theme. This literature directed its specific attention to payments made to public servants that led them to ignore the interests of their constituents and to favor private interests (Rose-Ackerman 2009). In fact, if there were something called "corruptology," these studies, dominated by economic approaches, would be at its core. There are three good reviews of the studies published on the economics of corruption: one by Abed and Davoodi, published by the IMF (International Monetary Fund) under the title *Governance, Corruption, and Economic Performance;* a second titled *International Handbook on the Economics of Corruption,* which was edited in 2006 by Susan Rose-Ackerman; and a further one edited by the Inter-American Development Bank, coordinated by José Antonio Alonso and Carlos Mulas-Granados, under the title *Corrupción, cohesión social y desarrollo. El caso de Iberoamérica.* While a wide array of research expands on the economics of corruption, fewer works discuss corruption in relation to human rights.[14] Nevertheless, we can identify human rights violations committed by means of corruption in the following instances:

- Political corruption distorts public policy's design processes (ICHRP 2009), leading to the privatization of that which is public.
- Bribes allow for prohibited actions that openly violate human rights (ICHRP 2009), such as the infringement of worker-safety measures, evident in the *Pasta de Conchos* case, in which a mining company violated various safety measures. Another example is the execution of megaprojects related to tourism, the construction of dams, the oversight of the mining sector, or the generation of wind power, all of which frequently falsify environmental-impact studies through bribery (TPP 2012).

- The solicitation of bribes conditions the access to rights (ICHRP 2009), which fundamentally impedes the access to justice and social services.
- Acts of corruption that divert public resources allow for the private appropriation of public resources or, through bribes, allow for over-payments associated with the procurement of goods and services, thus diminishing public resources (ICHRP 2009). As a result, people receive fewer goods and worse services, in open violation of the government's obligations to protect, guarantee, and promote human rights, as well as the obligations to realize economic and social rights progressively and to the maximum of available resources.
- The lack of transparency (considered a component of corruption) prevents the monitoring of the obligations to realize progressively, to prevent regression, and to use resources to their maximum available levels to fulfill human rights (González and Nash 2011: 30).

The most serious violations of human rights resulting from corruption occur when corruption is endemic and structural in form. In the words of Zalaquet (2007), corruption can be a sporadic practice or an endemic phenomenon. The latter can be particularized (for example, in the police, the judiciary, or customs) or generalized (a major part of government). Evidently, wherever corruption is an endemic phenomenon, whether it be particularized or generalized, it is accompanied by structural problems, with institutional, social, and cultural dimensions (Zalaquet 2007: 19). These manifestations of corruption have also been referred to as structural corruption—a practice that defines how certain institutions function, operating through power networks designed to shield corruption and maintain impunity for the group (Nash 2014: 70). The most common example of this type of corruption is the "capture" and cooptation of the state. In this case, corrupt interests influence the production of state norms and public policies, creating a normative framework that legalizes exclusion and secures illegitimate benefits.

Insofar as corruption is carried out in a concealed fashion, there is regrettably no objective data about it. The best known indicators for measuring corruption actually measure the perception of corruption, as is the case of the indexes generated by Transparency International, the World Bank, and Country Risk. For example, the National Survey of Public Safety, by the National Institute of Statistics and Geography (INEGI), gives an account of

Table 9.1. Perception of corruption and human rights violations

Institution	% of population that views as corrupt	% of population that views as violating HR
State police (Mexico City not included)	70.2	59.2
Municipal police (preventative DF)	68.9	59.6
Attorney General of the state or the DF	68.6	52.3
Attorney General of the Republic	66.7	56.0
Investigative police	60.2	47.9
Federal Police	60.2	48.7
Army	43.4	36.4
Navy	37.5	31.3

Source: Pulido 2016.

the perception of corruption and the violation of human rights by public security forces, as described in Table 9.1.

Impunity as Political Action and Human Rights Violations

Studies on impunity fall into three categories: the general causes of impunity, which concentrate much more on security and legal systems; impunity in the context of democratic transitions; and impunity for serious human rights violations. The relationship between impunity and human rights violations stems from the expectation that prosecuting the guilty deters them from recidivating and, what is more, makes clear for others that human rights violations will not be tolerated (Amnesty International 2010b: 11, specifically referring to torture).

Analyzing violence against women in Mexico, Andión (2012) proposes some guidelines or analytical categories for thinking about the impunity that surrounds serious human rights violations committed under democracy:

- Deficiencies and gaps in the normative framework;
- Deficiencies in the application of the normative framework at all levels of government, including the judicial and executive branches;
- Failure of policies, programs, and institutions created to prevent, penalize, and eradicate violence against women;
- Failure of the justice system;

- Lack of suitable information and lack of access to existing information;
- Lack of actions directed at addressing the structural causes of violence against women.

General information regarding impunity can be found in the indexes created by the United Nations and the World Justice Project. In the 2016 index, Mexico ranked 88th of the 113 countries analyzed (and 24th of the 30 included Latin American countries) (World Justice Project 2016).

According to INEGI, in 2014 more than 33 million crimes were committed, of which only 10.7 percent were reported, meaning that Mexico's unreported crime rate is on average 89.3 percent (varies by state). When those surveyed were asked why they had not reported the crimes, 32.2 percent answered that it was a waste of time, and 16.8 percent distrusted the authorities. That is to say, 49 percent of the victims of crime believe that there is no point in reporting crimes (INEGI 2015b).

A review of the impunity that surrounds serious human rights violations reveals similar patterns. For example, during Mexico's appearance before the United Nation's Committee on Enforced Disappearances in 2015, of the 25,000 cases of enforced disappearance reported, the government acknowledged that only 313 suspects had been investigated by the federal courts for this crime, which resulted in 13 guilty verdicts, including the sentencing of 1 member of the military. According to Special Rapporteur Juan Mendez's report (Human Rights Council 2014), between 2005 and 2013, the National Human Rights Commission (CNDH) received 11,254 torture-related complaints[15] and issued 223 recommendations, but there had not been a single criminal sentence for torture. Furthermore, Mexico's Federal Judiciary Council had issued only seven sentences for torture from 1991 to 2013, while INEGI identified only five sentences for torture at the state level between 1965 and 2012 (Díaz 2014).

Finally, looking jointly at the problems of corruption and impunity, we can see how these problems reinforce each other. For example, during 2014 the National Audit Office of Mexico (Auditoría Superior de la Federación—ASF), a technical body charged with monitoring national accounts and sanctioning wrongdoers, established that, after 14 years of operation (1998–2012) and the initiation of 457 criminal proceedings, only in 19 cases had it imposed sanctions, and those were only minor sanctions on mid- and low-ranking officials. In other words, there was no repercussion in 96 percent of the proceedings initiated by ASF (Chávez 2014).

The main problem of corruption and impunity as generalized frameworks for action is their connection to systematic and repeated human rights violations, perpetrated under the knowledge that there will be no punishment. For this reason, it is not unusual for serious human rights violations to become structural and constant. Recent high-profile atrocities such as the massacre in Tlatlaya (Mexico State) and the disappearance of the forty-three teachers in training in Ayotzinapa (Guerrero), as well as the cases of Apatzingan (Michoacán), Villa Purificación (Jalisco), and Tanhuato (Michoacán), all involved enforced disappearances, extrajudicial killings, torture, and due-process violations. Not surprisingly, such events had occurred previously in the areas surrounding Tlatlaya and Ayotzinapa.

In the case of Tlatlaya, twenty-three civilians were assassinated in a market in 2008. The case was left unresolved. As the initial journalistic accounts of the 2014 executions in Tlatlaya were published (they reported a confrontation between military forces and members of organized-crime organizations), both the PGR and the Attorney General of the State of Mexico had already completed their investigations, which supported the initial account by the Army (that is, that a confrontation with criminals had taken place). It was not until after receiving the testimony of one of the survivors that the PGR reopened its investigation and eventually issued an arrest warrant. What credibility can an investigation have in these conditions? How can one objectively investigate a totally neglected crime scene? In what way has the existing evidence's chain of custody been assured? What investigative hypotheses have been explored, and how was a conclusion drawn? What responsibility do the high-ranking officials have in the case? What about the responsibility of the civil authorities who were tasked with promptly investigating these extrajudicial killings? For all these reasons, it is no coincidence that organizations like Amnesty International demanded a prompt, impartial, independent, and exhaustive investigation without the PGR's participation.

The region surrounding Ayotzinapa also has a history marked by impunity and the repetition of serious human rights violations. In 2011, during a blockade of the Mexico City–Acapulco highway, a clash between protesters and security forces resulted in three people being extrajudicially killed, three more suffering gunshot injuries, and at least fourteen being arbitrarily arrested. One case of torture and seven other cases of inhumane treatment were also documented. Only two police officers were indicted for these incidents, and both were later set free.

Conclusions: *Democracia a la Mexicana:*
A Framework Conducive to Human Rights Violations

Mexican democracy has formal and informal norms that stem, in part, from traits associated with democracy's third wave and, in part, from Mexican particularities. The lack of attention to state-level political power, the structural violations of freedom of expression, and the absence of alternative development models stem from the third wave. Clientelism as a mechanism of political intermediation, denial, simulation, corruption, and impunity are distinctive Mexican particularities. Together, all of these norms and practices establish the patterns that shape Mexican-style democracy, which has as its main objective the neutralization of vertical, horizontal, and societal accountability. These kinds of accountability mechanisms, which serve as a check upon the government, are also critical for the defense of human rights. They generate the expectation that democracy is the best political regime for the respect of human rights. So if these mechanisms are neutralized, what incentives does the democracy in Mexico provide to convince the political class to modify their standards of action and to encourage respect for human rights? None.

Democracy in Mexico not only remains unconsolidated, but its own logic prevents it from moving in any way toward democratic consolidation. Worse still, due to the way in which democracy operates in Mexico, it has become one of the main obstacles to the full enjoyment of human rights. If what one is looking for is a fuller enjoyment and exercise of human rights, the first thing that should be dismantled is the logic of Mexican-style democracy. Even if Mexico's particular kind of democracy seems to lead us into a dead end, it also points toward the way out—the struggle against impunity. Inasmuch as there is a serious process of investigation and punishment of clientelism and corruption, the two key features of *democracia a la mexicana* will be dismantled, and denial and simulation will receive a hard blow. It is not by chance that the Inter-American Commission on Human Rights stressed in its 2016 country report on Mexico the negative consequences of a "situation of structural impunity."

A successful policy against impunity must address, at a minimum, at least two lines of inquiry—on corruption (including the construction of clientelist networks) and on the networks of macrocriminality that generate severe violations of human rights, but whose existence is denied by the government.

The human rights movement in Mexico has identified this challenge. Since 2015, civil society has created two spaces—the Front and the Platform—both of which advocate against corruption and impunity. These coalitions are composed of anticorruption organizations, human rights groups, activists, journalists, and academics. In this context of strategic alliances, the government is creating the National Anti-Corruption System, with more participation from citizens. In addition, anticorruption advocates are pushing for the establishment of a new and autonomous Attorney General's Office (Fiscalía General) to replace the PGR through the #fiscaliaquesirva coalition. This coalition is giving special attention to the need for technical capacity and for autonomy in order to tackle impunity.

The road ahead is long and difficult, but the first step toward guaranteeing the effective exercise of human rights in Mexico is to break the logic of *democracia a la mexicana*. That step must serve to defeat impunity.

CHAPTER 10

Factors Blocking the Compliance with International Human Rights Norms in Mexico

Alejandro Anaya-Muñoz and Natalia Saltalamacchia

Introduction

Mexico has been the focus of a long process of pressure "from above." For nearly twenty-five years, international nongovernmental organizations (NGOs), human rights organs, and bodies of the United Nations and Inter-American human rights regimes, and even (occasionally) government actors from democratic countries, have exerted pressure on Mexico for its human rights shortcomings. In this framework of transnational activism and in the midst of important domestic changes, the Mexican government has promoted reforms to the country's constitutional and legal frameworks, adopted numerous international legally binding commitments, cooperated with and engaged in intense communication with international actors, and designed human rights–oriented public-policy initiatives. All these actions suggest that a socialization process has been under way—that is, that the Mexican government has come to appreciate the merits of international human rights norms and to internalize them as legitimate constraints and benchmarks of behavior (Saltalamacchia Ziccardi and Covarrubias 2011; Anaya Muñoz 2009, 2012). However, for a socialization process to be complete, it is necessary that states habitually comply with international human rights norms in practice (Checkel 2005; Risse and Sikkink 1999). This has not been the case in Mexico. Governments have "talked the talk" and formally committed to the norms, but—as clearly shown throughout this book—it still is quite far away from "walking the walk" (see also Anaya Muñoz 2014a). The socialization process posited by the "spiral model" of human rights change (Risse, Ropp, and Sikkink 1999) has been clearly incomplete in Mexico, which seems to be very good at committing, but very bad at complying. How can we explain this gap between commitment and compliance?

This question leads current debates in the international relations human rights literature. After the seminal contribution of *The Power of Human Rights* (Risse, Ropp, and Sikkink 1999), there has been much theoretical fine-tuning. A good number of academic works are now devoted to understanding (non) compliance by looking into domestic factors and conditions (Cardenas 2007; Simmons 2009; Cavallaro and Brewer 2008; Davis and Murdie 2012). In general, this research posits that unless internal circumstances are propitious, international dynamics (boomerangs and spirals) cannot really have great impact. The authors of the spiral model have acknowledged this and have revisited their original model, highlighting a series of scope conditions for the difficult transition from commitment to compliance (Risse, Ropp, and Sikkink 2013). Closely following this debate in the international relations literature, we explore whether a specific set of conditions has blocked the socialization process and thus precluded the transition from commitment to compliance in Mexico. In this way, this chapter seeks not only to explain the Mexican case but to contribute to broader debates.

First, we review the literature and develop our working hypothesis—namely, that limited statehood, decentralization, and securitization have hindered the socialization process and precluded the transition from commitment to compliance. After this, we trace evidence regarding three key variables—limited statehood, decentralization, and securitization. We then present our conclusions. We find evidence that suggests possible blocking effects caused by limited statehood and by securitization. However, we do not find evidence for decentralization. Drawing on our observations, we conclude the chapter by developing a critique of the argument that differentiates between "voluntary" and "involuntary" sources of noncompliance, posed by Risse and his colleagues in the revised version of the spiral model (Risse and Ropp 2013; Börzel and Risse 2013).

The Difficult Transition from Commitment to Compliance: Key Scope Conditions

After the publication of *The Power of Human Rights*, the spiral model was scrutinized and its arguments contested by different authors. The spiral model postulates a five-staged process of human rights change. According to the model, if Transnational Advocacy Networks (TANs) exert consistent and significant pressure over repressive governments and if argumentation processes occur, a socialization process will take place, and the situation in the country in question will evolve from "repression" (phase one of the model) to "rule consistent behaviour" (phase five) (Risse, Ropp, and Sikkink 1999). The central criticism made reference to the lack of convincing empirical evidence that confirmed the transition from commitment to compliance (Jetschke and Liese 2013). This is very important because the core claim of the spiral model was that persistent pressure and argumentation by transnational advocates would lead to significant improvements in the human rights behavior of repressive states. But as stressed by Jetschke and Liese (2013: 27), "the transition from phase four (prescriptive status) to five (rule-consistent behavior) [is] a bottleneck that only few states pass." In their recent revision of the original model, Risse, Ropp, and Sikkink (2013) took stock of the arguments of their critics and acknowledged that the transition from commitment to compliance was undertheorized and that it was then necessary to specify the scope conditions under which it could take place.

The first condition proposed by Risse and his colleagues is regime type—the democratic or autocratic character of countries is expected to be strongly related to the likelihood of moving from commitment to compliance (Risse and Ropp 2013). Indeed, inserting regime type into the explanatory picture puts the spiral model in tune with a vast human rights literature that has found systematic evidence for the strong connection between democracy and human rights behavior (see Chapter 9). More consolidated democracies tend to have a better human rights performance. However, the human rights behavior of consolidated democracies might or might not relate to the influences of international norms and the pressures applied by transnational advocates. Consolidated democracies might have good human rights regardless of their international commitments. Beth Simmons (2009) has convincingly argued that transitional democracies, or democracies "in flux"—like Mexico, one could say—are more prone to be influenced by international human rights normative dynamics because it is precisely in such transitional contexts that domestic advocates have both the means and the incentives to mobilize and litigate effectively for human rights. What international norms and the dynamics of pressure and persuasion around them do is to improve the political, legal, and institutional framework (the domestic "rules of the game") in which local actors set agendas, mobilize, and litigate in favor of human rights (Simmons 2009).

The authors of the spiral model recall the "managerial" approach to international institutions and argue that not all states possess the administrative and institutional structures required to enforce the decisions and implement the policies preferred by central authorities (Risse and Ropp 2013; Börzel and Risse 2013). Thus, a second scope condition is the degree of "statehood." Many states suffer from limited statehood—that is, there are "parts of a country's territory or policy areas where central state authorities cannot effectively implement or enforce central decisions or even lack the monopoly over the means of violence" (Risse and Ropp 2013: 3). Lack of compliance might not be a question of lack of willingness but of lack of capacities. So human rights violations might continue and endure in specific regions or in concrete policy areas within a country even if central authorities have the will to comply. "If the primary cause for rights violations is limited statehood and lack of capacity to enforce the law, positive incentives, sanctions or persuasion will not do the trick" (Börzel and Risse 2013: 83). In other studies, Risse and his colleagues speak of "voluntary" versus "involuntary" sources of noncompliance (Risse and Ropp 2013).

The degree of decentralization in decision-making and the implementation of government policy is another key domestic scope condition for compliance with international human rights norms. Risse and his colleagues have opened up the black box of the state, recognizing that states are not unitary actors; "compliance is more difficult to achieve if it has to result from collaborative or conflict-ridden negotiations between different decentralized actors" (Risse and Ropp 2013: 19).This scope condition is related to limited statehood in the sense that it makes explicit reference to the actual capacity of the central authorities to implement policies and enforce decisions in the (often distant) places where violations of human rights take place (see, for example, Chapters 5 and 6). A central government with the will to make significant changes might find it difficult to implement its decisions if the authorities at the local level have other interests, incentives, or preferences or if they hold different values or beliefs. So the revised spiral model suggests that the combination of limited statehood and decentralized administrative structures creates a toxic mix of conditions that will block the transition from commitment to compliance.

Finally, two scope conditions included in the original spiral model are highlighted again in the revised version—material and social vulnerability (Risse and Sikkink 1999; Risse and Ropp 2013). Highly interdependent states can be more vulnerable to transnational pressures that link trade, investment, or aid to human rights behavior. For example, trade agreements that include human rights clauses are effective in influencing the human rights behavior of participating states (Hafner-Burton 2005). In this sense, countries with open (dependent) economies are deemed to be more vulnerable to the dynamics of the spiral model and, thus, more likely to complete the transition from commitment to compliance (Risse and Ropp 2013). Social vulnerability, on the other hand, is the central element of the spiral model and its predecessor, the "boomerang effect" (Keck and Sikkink 1998). The "boomerang effect" preceded the spiral model as an analytical devise in the study of transnational human rights pressure and its effects. The model describes the way Transnational Advocacy Networks (TANs) are created and how they exert pressure "from above" (Brysk 1993) over repressive governments. The metaphor of the boomerang implies that given that domestic dissidents cannot influence their own governments directly, pressure flows outward, gathering more strength and then "hitting" repressive governments harder when it comes back down, as a boomerang does (Keck and Sikkink 1998; a modified version of the "boomerang effect" is presented in Chapter 12). The notion of social vulnerability is fundamental for the key mechanism of shaming (Risse, Ropp, and Sikkink 1999; Keck and Sikkink 1998). All else being equal, countries that want to be accepted as "worthy" members of "the club of civilized nations"—like most transitioning democracies, Mexico included—are socially vulnerable and, therefore, more likely to be influenced by transnational pressures and will thus move toward compliance.

Beyond the spiral model, quantitative studies have consistently found a strong significant association between armed conflict (domestic or international) and the violation of human rights (Neumayer 2005; Landman 2005; Simmons 2009; Hafner-Burton 2013). It is not difficult to imagine why human rights violations flourish in the midst of armed conflicts—the availability of firearms, the incentives (or lack of disincentives) to resort to the excessive use of force, and the general context of violence and lawlessness can facilitate or trigger violations by all parties. In armed conflicts, furthermore, the territorial integrity and/or the integrity or even the continuation of state institutions is challenged. A related but broader argument is that violations of human rights proliferate in contexts of real and/or perceived threats to national or public security. In these situations of highly securitized agendas, the incentives for incumbent authorities to resort to repression or to seek security "at any cost," and to develop "counter-frames" to justify their rights-violating actions, are reinforced (Jetschke and Liese 2013; Cardenas 2007; Cavallaro and Mohamedou 2005; Anaya Munoz 2012b).

The above considerations are relevant to Mexico. The Mexican economy is extremely open to international financial and trade flows. In this sense, we could expect the country to be highly vulnerable, from a material perspective, to transnational human rights pressures. However, Mexico has not been subject to meaningful material pressures as a result of its human rights behavior. Mexico's main economic partners (the United States and the European Union) have not linked human rights to trade or foreign direct-investment flows. There has not been a serious process of conditionality.[1] Mexico is highly dependent on foreign trade and foreign investment, but not on foreign aid. For all these reasons, we argue that this scope condition is not particularly relevant to our case study, and thus we do not trace it in further detail. On the other hand, the literature has already shown that Mexico is "socially vulnerable" to external human rights pressures, given its desire to be identified as a member of the club of democratic, "civilized" countries. Shaming, in this sense, has been an important factor in Mexico's human rights processes in the recent past (Anaya Muñoz 2009, 2012a; Saltalamacchia and Covarrubias 2011). The question is, precisely, why a socially vulnerable transitioning democracy that has been subjected to intense and longstanding socialization dynamics and that has taken numerous commitment-oriented measures is far from behaving in accordance to the norms. Do the "blocking factors" identified above help us to develop a convincing answer to this question?

We assume that the blocking factors that are relevant to Mexico are limited statehood, decentralization, and conflict and securitization.Our working hypothesis is that the poor results of the socialization process in Mexico are (at least in part) explained by these three specific factors. In the following three sections we empirically explore this argument.

Areas of Limited Statehood

Mexico is a vast and complex country—nearly 2 million square kilometers in territory, a population of over 120 million, nearly half of it living in poverty (see Chapter 9), over 4 thousand kilometers of international borders, 11 million kilometers of coastline, 32 states, 2,457 municipalities, and an intricate, often knotty geography (INEGI 2015a). The country's political agenda is broad and entangled—including a diverse array of issues, from food self-sufficiency and the provision of health and education to investment in the energy sector and free trade—not to mention inequality, corruption, sluggish economic growth, ethnic and gender inequalities, obesity and malnutrition, pollution and environmental degradation, rampant violence, and all the human rights problems addressed in this volume. In this context of multiple and diverse interests, problems, objectives, needs, and wants, different social groups follow their interests, present claims, expose grievances, or demand the provision of specific public goods, protesting in the streets and squares, lobbying and/or corrupting political elites, or exerting pressure through the media. This is not to suggest that Mexico is particularly unique in this respect, but to stress that the Mexican state has a very large territorial space and quite multifaceted spectrum of areas of public policy to cover. Developing the administrative and institutional structure required to govern the country does not seem to be an easy task, and at first sight, Mexico has limited financial resources to do so properly. Mexico is a middle-income country, with around $15,000 in per-capita national income, significantly below the $32,000 average for the members of the Organization for Economic Cooperation and Development (OECD) (OECD n/d). It collects only a meager 19 percent of its GDP in taxes (OECD 2015, 24–25).

If compared to low-income or other middle-income countries, however, Mexico as a state appears to be in relatively decent shape. The *Index of State Weakness in the Developing World* measures the extent to which states perform "responsibilities commonly considered core functions of statehood" (Rice and Patrick 2008: 8). The index is composed of twenty indicators pertaining to the economy, government, security, and social welfare.[2] Mexico has a score of 7.83 (on a scale in which 0 is the lowest and 10 the highest score) and is located in the top quintile of the 141 included developing countries, far away from being a failed or even a "critically weak" state (Rice and Patrick 2008: 13). Interestingly, the indicators in which Mexico performs more poorly are directly or indirectly related to human rights—GDP growth (with a 3.3 score), income inequality (5.83), rule of law (5.53), political stability and absence of violence (5.83), and gross human rights abuses (4.57) (Rice and Patrick 2008: 42, 47).

The *Index of State Weakness* includes some of the indicators generated by the World Bank in its *Worldwide Governance Indicators,* which include aggregate measures related to (a) voice and accountability, (b) political stability and absence of violence/terrorism, (c) government effectiveness, (d) regulatory quality, (e) rule of law, and (f) control of corruption (World Bank 2017). These indicators report "percentile ranks" that indicate the percentage of countries that rank lower than the country in question. So stronger governance scores are those that are close to one hundred. The indicators that seem to be more relevant for our discussion on statehood are "government effectiveness," "regulatory quality," "rule of law," and "control of corruption"— and Mexico's percentile ranks for 2016 were 59.62, 64.42, 33.17, and 23.08, respectively (World Bank 2017). It seems that, while Mexico's institutions seem to be mediocre in terms of "government effectiveness" and "regulatory capacities," they are clearly deficient in enforcing the law and controlling corruption. Whereas both the absence of the rule of law and corruption can also be seen as causes of poor institutional capacity, they can be interpreted primarily as signs of limited statehood.[3]

Impunity or the "un-rule of law" has been repeatedly considered by qualified observers as a key cause of Mexico's severe and entrenched human rights problems, as stressed in the Introduction and numerous chapters in this volume (see also Americas Watch 1990; Human Rights Watch 2009; Acosta 2012; Human Rights Watch 2009; CMDPDH and IMDHD n/d). Levels of impunity in Mexico in criminal cases are close to 99 percent (see the Introduction to this volume). Although lower than in relation to all crimes taken together, impunity in the case of murder is also extremely high, reaching over 80 percent in 2010, according to the National Institute on Statistics and Geography (INEGI).[4] This locates Mexico well above the international median of 24 percent.

Impunity in cases of murder, furthermore, has clearly increased in the recent past, as the number of killings has multiplied (Mexico Evalúa 2012: 16–19; Institute for Economics and Peace 2016: 23–24). Mexico's institutional structure for the administration of criminal justice blatantly fails to prosecute and punish those responsible for all types of crimes, including those related to the violation of human rights (Anaya Munoz 2013: 185–189). Of course, impunity is not necessarily an indicator of limited capacities for the administration of criminal justice. Strong and/or capable institutions could "decide" or be ordered not to investigate and prosecute. This possibility, however, can hardly be the case in Mexico. Deliberate failure could explain a limited number or a particular category of cases, but we can hardly find good reasons to suppose that any kind of government would deliberately opt not to punish 99 percent of criminals, having the capacity to do so. An explanation based on lack of capacities seems to be clearly more plausible in this case.

In a report published in 2012, the Mexican think-tank México Evalúa compiled data on twenty-five indicators related to institutional weakness in the security and criminal justice system, focusing at the level of state governments.

Even if the details vary across the different states, the overall conclusion of the report is the "weakness, lack of capacities [and] low performance" of the system throughout the country (México Evalúa 2012: 2). Drawing on the conclusions of comparative research, México Evalúa notes that at the international level, the average number of police officers per 100,000 inhabitants is 340. In 2002, Mexico had an average of 486, and in 2011 an average of 354 (in this latter year, without including the Federal Police). So in general, Mexico has an above-average police force in quantitative terms. However, 24 of the 32 states of Mexico fall under the benchmark of 340 police officers per 100,000 inhabitants (México Evalúa 2012: 22–24). From a qualitative perspective, in 2011, half of the states did not have the institutional machinery to evaluate and certify their police officers (México Evalúa 2012: 24–29).

The México Evalúa report also finds severe limitations in the institutional structure of public prosecutors (*ministerios públicos),* who deliver extremely poor results. On average, only 13 percent of the investigations they initiate are completed, while in most states, prosecutors do not implement more than half of the arrest warrants granted by judges. In this dismaying context, understandably enough, less than 10 percent of Mexicans trust the *ministerios publicos* to do their job in delivering justice (México Evalúa 2012: 5, 32–35). This view on the shortcomings of the system of public prosecutors in Mexico is confirmed by academic research that has found clear indicators of inefficiency, which is in turn directly related to low technical capacities, the lack of a professional system for criminal investigations, and pervasive corruption (Magaloni Kerpel 2007).

In addition to the capacity problems related to prosecutors, the justice system lacks sufficient magistrates and judges. On average, Mexico has only 3.5 magistrates and judges per 100,000 persons. The average in a global comparative study of forty-nine countries is sixteen (Le Clercq and Rodriguez 2016). In sum, as put by close observers, "[f]or decades, a host of problems— resource deficits, corruption, and a general lack of professionalization—have undermined Mexico's criminal courts, police agencies, penitentiary facilities, and other vital aspects of the criminal justice system" (Ingram and Shirk 2012: 119).

From a different perspective, an analysis of the limits of statehood can also look at one of the key consequences of limited statehood—the inability to maintain the monopoly of the means of violence and the lack of control of nonstate actors. The recognition by the Mexican government regarding the absence of the rule of law in specific regions or the "invasion" or "kidnapping" of public spaces by organized crime was one of the factors that initially motivated or justified the militarized response to organized crime launched by President Calderón (2006–2012) (Presidencia de la República 2007: 44–46, 58–59). Almost a decade later, the capacity of criminal organizations (and other groups, such as "self-defense" militias in Michoacán) to challenge the state's monopoly over the means of violence has not waned. Repeatedly, federal forces are sent to different cities or regions of the country to restore "law and order" and to control rampant violence and abuses by organized crime. This process seems like an endless, almost circular effort to cover emerging holes of statelessness—just when one particular situation seems to be taken under relative control, a new "hole" will (re)emerge elsewhere in the vast territorial extension of the country, from Ciudad Juárez, Chihuahua, to "Tierra Caliente," in Michoacán, or from Monterrey, Nuevo León, to Iguala, in Guerrero. As a result, statehood in Mexico adopts an unstable and ever-changing Swiss cheese–like pattern[5]—one marked by shifting pockets of lawlessness and uncontrolled violence by nonstate actors (Astorga and Shrik 2010: 28–29; Heinle, Molzahan, and Shirk 2015: 12–20, 29–34; Heine, Rodriguez Ferreira, and Shirk 2013: 22–29).

Decentralization

As argued earlier in this chapter, the literature proposes that the transition from commitment to compliance will be more difficult in contexts of decentralized adoption and implementation of decisions and policies. This implies an assumption that central authorities will have a harder time implementing policy and behavioral changes that lead to improved human rights practices in decentralized contexts where they have to negotiate with or impose new ideas and policies on subnational governments. Formally, Mexico is a federal republic, composed of thirty-one states and Mexico City (formerly the Federal District). States, on their part, are made up by municipalities. State governments have the faculty to investigate and prosecute most crimes, and state courts are charged with administering justice, while policing is a function of all three levels, including the municipalities. This means that issues closely related to the human rights crisis addressed in this book, such as the administration of justice and the use of force, might be affected by the centralization/decentralization equation (see, for instance, Chapters 5, 6, and 12). The Mexican state is not a unified actor, with three levels of government participating in decision-making and the implementation of public policies that affect human rights.

Nevertheless, even if formally a federal republic, Mexico has been historically extremely centralized in practice—the federal government (and more particularly, the president) has overwhelmingly monopolized political and administrative power (Rodriguez 1997: 17–37; Selee 2011: 27–46). Starting in the early 1980s, however, facing pressures for democratization and empowerment from emerging dissident political forces at the local level and in the midst of growing economic and financial strains, the PRI (Institutional Revolutionary Party) regime embarked on a slow and painstaking but ultimately moderately effective process of political and administrative decentralization. Progressively, state and municipal governments obtained some of the political space and the financial resources needed to actually put in practice their formal functions for decision- and policymaking, including the procurement of public security and the administration of criminal justice (Rodriguez 1997; Selee 2011: 47–70). Consequently, around 13 percent of the federal budget for security and rule-of-law issues for Fiscal Year 2016 was allocated to states and municipalities (Tepach and Quintero 2015). The security and rule-of-law budget includes allocations for the federal judicial power, the armed forces, and the Federal Police, among other entities, so the amount to be spent by state and municipal governments in public security is by no means irrelevant.

In the midst of growing insecurity and organized crime–related violence, at least since the Calderón administration, the federal government has argued in favor of the dissolution of municipal police forces. The argument, in general terms, has been that these local forces are the least able and most poorly equipped to face organized crime and, particularly, the most vulnerable to the latter's corruptive powers (Astorga and Shirk 2010: 33; Heinle, Molzahn, and Shirk 2015: 34–35). Furthermore, having only 32 (state-level) police forces, instead of more than 1,800 municipal corporations, facilitates coordination efforts and mechanisms to monitor, supervise, and certify officers. The discussion about municipal police forces and a more centralized policing model gained a higher profile after the disappearance of the forty-three students of the Ayotzinapa teacher-training college in 2014. As the reader might recall, the Iguala municipal police force played an infamous role in the case, reportedly detaining and then handing the students over to organized crime. For those advancing the case against municipal police, the Iguala tragedy stressed the point that municipal police forces are indeed "the weakest link" and that, therefore, they should be absorbed by state-level police corporations.

After the disappearance of the students, in late 2014 President Peña Nieto presented a "10 point proposal" to fight insecurity. One of the ten points was the elimination of municipal police forces. President Peña Nieto sent a bill to Congress, proposing to strip municipal governments of their current public-security functions, except for the "non-policial" prevention of crime. The proposal went well beyond the establishment of a "*mando único*" (or central-ized command) at the state-level and implied the elimination of municipal police forces altogether. The bill reproduced the arguments just mentioned about institutional weakness, vulnerability to corruption, certification, and other problems of municipal police forces. Beyond the issue of policing and public security, the bill also proposed that, under certain circumstances, the federal government could take over some or all governance functions in municipalities "infiltrated" by organized crime (Presidencia de la República 2014). At the moment of writing, the bill had not yet been approved, and it faced significant opposition in Congress.

The centralization argument makes some intuitive sense. But the prob-lem of corruption and infiltration by criminal organizations is not unique to municipal authorities, often also affecting state and federal security forces and authorities (Cardenas 2016; Chabat 2002; Astorga and Shrik 2010: 29–30; Heinle, Molzahn, and Shirk 2015: 35–36). In addition, there is evidence of good practices and encouraging results in specific initiatives to strengthen the capacities and reliability of police forces in some municipalities, and observers have convincingly concluded that centralization is by no means a "silver bullet" to tackle the severe problems faced by the policing structure in Mexico (Cardenas 2016).

Similar arguments could be advanced regarding the violation of human rights. Recalling the Ayotzinapa case, some could argue that given their insti-tutional weakness and their vulnerability to organized crime and the interests and whims of local rulers, municipal police forces are indeed an important part of the country's human rights crisis. It could be argued that having only 32 police forces to work with in terms of socialization, training, and oversight might make more sense for a central government willing to pursue a human rights agenda, than trying to socialize and monitor the behavior of more than 1,800 disperse and highly dissimilar corporations. But again, there are no compelling reasons to expect a priori that centralization might advance sub-stantive change. The evidence of the violation of human rights by federal or state-level security forces is overwhelming (Human Rights Watch 2009, 2011; CNDH 2015b, 2014a; Anaya Munoz 2014b; Astorga and Shrik 2010: 29). For example, in the disappearance of five young persons in Tierra Blanca, Vera-cruz, in 2016, it was the state police forces who detained the victims and handed them over to organized crime (Cisneros 2016).

The state-level system of administering criminal justice prosecutes around 93 percent of the crimes reported in Mexico. Since a small proportion of all crimes are prosecuted and judged by federal authorities (México Evalúa 2012: 4), the severe impunity problem identified earlier in this chapter largely resides in state-level institutions. Would the problems related to the adminis-tration of criminal justice be more easily tackled in a centralized framework of prosecutors and courts? Someone could argue that the difficult coordina-tion and negotiations between the central government and its thirty-two sub-national counterparts make change more difficult to implement. Of course, in spite of the recent adoption of a National Criminal Proceedings Code, nobody in Mexico is currently talking about eliminating state prosecutors or courts and creating a centralized or unitary system for the administration of criminal justice.

This chapter's analysis of impunity and institutional capacities related to the administration of criminal justice is based on state-level indicators. Unfortunately, to the best of our knowledge, there is a gap in the analysis of the (much smaller) system of federal prosecutors and courts. In any case, the pervasive impunity in issues pertaining to drug trafficking or to torture by federal agents (both of which fall under the jurisdiction of federal authori-ties) suggests that federal authorities are not significantly more efficient than their state-level counterparts. In human rights issues, the Federal Attorney General's Office (PGR) is often identified as part of the problem or as directly responsible for the violation of rights. Between 2007 and 2014, the National Human Rights Commission (CNDH) issued 33 recommendations to the PGR, representing 5 percent of the total number of recommendations issued by CNDH in the period (see also Anaya Muñoz 2014b). Another case in point regarding the centralization/decentralization discussion is the imple-mentation of the 2008 reform of the system of administration of criminal justice that, inter alia, replaced the traditional inquisitorial procedural sys-tem with an adversarial and oral one (Shirk 2011; Chapter 11, this volume). The new system had to be implemented at both the federal and state levels within a period of eight years, and the differences in the time it has taken state governments to implement the reform demonstrate a stark variation in capacities and/or willingness to do so across states. In any case, the imple-mentation of the reform by federal authorities has been even slower and more painstaking than in many states (Shirk 2011; Rodriguez Ferreira and Shirk 2016), showing that federal authorities responsible for the administration of criminal justice do not seem to perform much better than their state-level counterparts. These examples suggest that the elimination of coordination and negotiation problems between levels of government does not seem to make a clear and significant difference, and thus there appears to be no a priori reason to expect that centralization would improve the chances for a more effective process of human rights change in Mexico.

Securitization

As advanced in the Introduction to this volume, in the midst of an increasingly violent confrontation between drug-trafficking organizations, President Calderón securitized Mexico's public agenda and launched his "war on drugs." His government's National Development Plan (PND, the six-year master policy plan of the federal government) set the course of action. The first idea in the PND's "vision for Mexico in 2030," for example, envisaged "a country of laws, where our families and our property are safe" (Gobierno de la República 2007: 25). The PND's first chapter focused on the rule of law and security. The PND saw organized crime as the cause not only of violence and insecurity but also of lawlessness in the country. Furthermore, it explicitly understood drug-trafficking organizations as one of the most violent and harmful manifestations of organized crime, as a direct challenge to the state, and as a threat to national security (Gobierno de la República 2007: 41–80). So the PND established as one of its explicit objectives to "recover the strength of the State and safety in social interactions through the direct and efficient combat to drug trafficking and other expressions of organized crime" (Gobierno de la República 2007: 59). The PND, therefore, called for a reform of the system of criminal justice, inter alia by giving constitutional standing to the controversial practice of *arraigo* (the prolonged detention of suspects without charge) and by granting public prosecutors the authority to conduct house searches and to intercept personal communications, without judicial control (Gobierno de la República 2007: 50–53). On the other hand, the PND committed to allocate more resources to the armed forces, to support their role "as keepers of the internal security of the country and specifically in the combat against organized crime" (Gobierno de la República 2007: 59).

A systematic review of Calderón's discourse in his annual Informes de Gobierno (the equivalent in Mexico to the state of the union address in the United States) shows that throughout his term in office, Calderón developed a narrative on the country's security challenges and the ways to address them. For example, in his Informes, Calderón consistently highlighted the unprecedented efforts by his government to give "frontal battle" or "frontal combat" to organized crime (Calderón 2008, 2009) and explicitly characterized this task as "the national priority" (Calderón 2008). The president also highlighted the fact that his government had identified a "deep backlog" in security matters, which severely affected the quality of life of the population and the development of the country (Calderón 2011). He repeatedly offered data and nuanced information about his government's achievements in the fight against drug trafficking (the number of criminals arrested, weapons seized, or drugs confiscated) and the new policies implemented to buttress the operational and technological capacities of the security forces. He also underlined efforts to enhance the tools and powers available to institutions to investigate and prosecute organized crime (Calderón 2009, 2012).

Beyond discourse, Calderón followed in practice a highly securitized policy agenda. In early 2007, he sent to Congress the aforementioned bill to reform the system of criminal justice, following the blueprint advanced in the PND. The bill also featured other issues welcomed by the human rights community. However, it was highly controversial because it also included provisions that would undermine due-process guarantees in criminal investigations, particularly those related to organized crime. The justification for this change, explicitly stated in the text of the proposed bill, was the unprecedented challenge to security posed by organized crime and the need to "protect society" (Anaya Muñoz 2012b: 124–126). An amended version of the bill was adopted by Congress in early 2008. Mexico's constitutional and legal framework was modified to sanction the practice of *arraigo*. But contrary to Calderón's wishes, the approved bill included clear judicial controls over *arraigo* and other investigatory practices, such as the interception of personal communications (Anaya Muñoz 2012b: 124–126). In any case, in the terms of scholar Alejandro Madrazo, the 2008 reform implied significant "constitutional costs" through the establishment of a "special regime of reduced rights and extraordinary police faculties" in the investigation of organized crime. All this in the name of security (Madrazo 2014: 8–11).

As already underlined, the other characteristic of Calderón's reaction to what he perceived as an extraordinary national-security challenge was a militarized face-off with organized crime. It is true that Mexico's public-security policies and institutions started to be militarized in the 1980s, leading to a growing presence of military personnel (active or retired) in police forces at the federal, state, and municipal levels. However, this approach was taken to unprecedented extremes in the Calderón term, in which tens of thousands of troops were deployed to directly combat organized crime (Freeman and Sierra 2005; Astorga and Shirk 2010: 2–3, 27–30). Just as the aforementioned legal reforms imposed high "constitutional costs," the militarization of law enforcement generated important costs for human rights in practice (see Chapter 1). Between 2008 and 2011 the number of complaints against the Army and the Navy for the presumed violation of human rights registered by Mexico's CNDH and the number of cases in which the latter actually confirmed the violations increased dramatically (Anaya Muñoz 2014b).

Meanwhile, violent confrontations between criminal organizations did not recede, and perhaps even increased as a result of the government's strategy to target the leaders of criminal groups. So throughout the Calderón *sexenio* (the presidential six-year period), a virulent "drug war" stained Mexico's security environment—members of criminal organizations fought and killed one another, and they fought, killed, and were killed by government forces, resulting in an unprecedented rise of violent deaths (Introduction and Chapter 1; Astorga and Shirk 2010; Heinle, Molzahn, and Shirk 2015; Heine, Rodriguez Ferreira, and Shirk 2013).

President Peña Nieto (2012–2018) attempted to distance himself from his predecessor's securitized discourse and his "war on drugs," particularly by changing the communications strategy. The new government attempted to "de-securitize" the public agenda, emphasizing the so-called strategic reforms (regarding the economic, education, and energy sectors) (Crowley 2014; Heinle, Molzahn, and Shirk 2015: 38). His administration's PND explicitly considered violence and crime as a matter of "public" not "national" security, stressing the role of social development, prevention, and intelligence, as opposed to outright direct confrontation. However, Peña Nieto's PND was framed around five "great National Goals," the first of which was labeled "Mexico in Peace" (Gobierno de la República 2013). Furthermore, the PND acknowledged that Mexico faced "unprecedented" and severe crime and violence problems and recognized that insecurity was the main concern for large sectors of the population. His PND highlighted the "predominant role" of the armed forces in the government's efforts to address the country's security problems (Gobierno de la República 2013).

The issue of insecurity and its challenges could not be avoided in Peña Nieto's Informes de Gobierno. Following the framework established in his PND, his *informes* have so far addressed explicitly five "great National Goals," the first of which, as already stressed, is labeled "Mexico in Peace" (Peña Nieto 2013, 2014, 2015). In his first Informe, for example, the president recognized that "one of the central demands of society is to achieve a Mexico in peace." In addition, once again he acknowledged the key role played by the armed forces in securing the "aspirations and the right of Mexicans to live in a setting of peace and tranquility" (Peña Nieto 2013: 17, 23; see also Peña Nieto 2015: 29). In his second Informe, he stressed that "Mexico has faced grave problems of public security, characterized by generalized presence of violence and crime, which generates high social and economic costs" (Peña Nieto 2014: 27). Furthermore, as Calderón used to do, Peña Nieto provided detailed accounts of the specific actions taken by his government, in particular by the armed forces, in the struggle against drug trafficking (Peña Nieto 2013: 46–54; Peña Nieto 2014: 27, 53–54, 69; Peña Nieto 2015: 55–59). So, not unlike Calderón's, Peña Nieto's public discourse emphasized the existence of an outstanding challenge to security, giving the armed forces a leading role in the government's efforts to address it.

The homicide rate modestly declined in Mexico between 2012 (the last year of Calderón's sexenio) and 2014, only to rise again in 2015 (Martínez 2016). As stressed in the Introduction to this volume, 2017 was the most violent year in Mexico's recent history, more so than 2011. Overall, organized-crime violence has remained unabated, and Peña Nieto was not ultimately able to change the dominant, securitized public narrative of the country's situation. The challenges generated by a seemingly endless turf war between drug-trafficking organizations remain. Furthermore, the armed forces are still out "in the streets," leading the government's response—his government has not called off the "war on drugs." The security challenges under Peña Nieto remain as real and daunting as under Calderón, and the key features of the government's response remain largely the same. As noted in the Introduction to this volume, more than 209,000 people were murdered in Mexico between 2007 and 2016. More than 20,000 persons were murdered in the country in 2014 alone, and the rate of homicides per 100,000 inhabitants remains very high (18.7 in 2013). Although it is not possible to know exactly how many of these deaths can be directly attributed to organized crime, qualified observers have estimated that between a third to half of them are related to drug trafficking. The impact of organized crime–related violence over security is even starker if we consider the particular situation in states such as Guerrero, México, Michoacán, and Tamaulipas, where the levels of violence have spiraled during the Peña Nieto administration (Heinle, Molzahan, and Shirk 2015).

In sum, during the past decade, Mexico has experienced an extremely violent conflict around drugs and their trade. Tens of thousands of people have been violently killed, disappeared, or tortured in the midst of the "drug war" (Introduction, this volume). As stressed earlier in this chapter, the existence of conflict in and of itself constitutes a powerful blocking factor—regardless of the accumulation of pressure and persuasion efforts, violations of human rights are prone to be severe in conflict situations. The securitization of the public agenda and the resulting militarized response of the government to the evident security threats have significantly contributed to the appalling rights-violations toll (Chapter 1, this volume; Anaya Munoz 2012b, 2014b; Madrazo 2014; Perez Correa, Silva Forne, and Gutierrez Rivas 2011, 2015; Deaton and Rodriguez Ferreira 2015; Human Rights Watch 2011; Amnesty International 2009a). Furthermore, the Calderón government developed (and the Peña Nieto administration sustained) an official discourse that has nurtured a limited conception of human rights—a "counter-frame" that legitimizes *"mano dura"* (iron fist) responses, weakens the overall social standing of the human rights agenda, and blocks the effects of the socialization process.

Conclusions

We have explored whether limited statehood, decentralization, and conflict and securitization might be related to Mexico's human rights shortcomings and its compliance deficit. We find evidence that clearly shows a framework of limited capacities of state institutions for policing and the administration of criminal justice, and the result has been almost total impunity. This "unrule of law" is said to lie at the heart of the overall human rights problems in the country. We also observe the daunting effects of securitization on human rights. We, therefore, have reasons to conclude that limited statehood and securitization have contributed to Mexico's poor compliance with human rights. We do not find similar evidence for decentralization. It is true that decentralization is a feature of Mexico's political and administrative structure, including in policing and the administration of criminal justice. However, the preliminary evidence we have gathered suggests that federal authorities show the same kind of poor results as their state- and municipal-level counterparts. The situation would not be considerably different in a centralized setting.

From a methodological standpoint, Mexico is a useful case study to think about a theory on the scope conditions or blocking factors of compliance with international norms, like the one recently proposed by Risse and his colleagues (Risse and Ropp 2013). Mexico represents a case in which "something" has blocked the socializing effects of a long and persistent process of transnational pressure and argumentation, or the transition from commitment to compliance. It is a socially vulnerable country characterized by limited statehood, decentralization, and conflict and challenges to security. It is also a democracy "in flux." This chapter, being a sort of "most likely" case study and a "disciplined-configurative" study (Eckstein 1975: 99–104, 118–119), can impugn existing theoretical arguments and offer alternatives and feedback. Although comparative research or further case studies are necessary, our research on Mexico seems to confirm the blocking effects of limited statehood and securitization, but questions those of decentralization.

However, regarding the statehood or capacities argument, the chapter argues that federal or central authorities do not show significantly better human rights records than their state- or municipal-level counterparts. This suggests that the federal government has lacked the will and/or the capacities to pursue meaningful human rights change. It seems, therefore, that the effects of centralization are mediated by two prior scope conditions: governmental will to actually pursue change and institutional capacities. This leads us to consider explicitly a discussion on the distinction between "voluntary" or "involuntary" sources of noncompliance (or "lack of willingness" or "lack of capacities"), highlighted by Risse and his colleagues (Börzel and Risse 2013; Risse and Ropp 2013; see also Cole 2015; Engleheart 2009).

We agree that explicitly recognizing capacity-related causes of noncompliance (or "involuntary" sources) is important, as it might help to better define actions, priorities, and strategies to address specific human rights problems and shortcomings. However, the lack-of-capacities argument and particularly the notion of "involuntary" sources of noncompliance can have perverse policy consequences. Talk of "involuntary" noncompliance might help legitimize rights-violating governments, shielding them from the criticism and pressure so important for local and international advocates who on a daily basis face "denial" responses by the governments they criticize. The notion of "involuntary" noncompliance (imported by Risse and his colleagues from literature that addresses issues quite different from that of human rights) could be used by rights-violating governments as part of their already broad spectrum of denial techniques (Cohen 1996). In the case of Mexico, for example, talk of "involuntary" violations of human rights (or even "lack of capacities") could be used to dilute the responsibility of the federal government for the human rights abuses presented in this volume.

We concede that, from an analytical perspective, the difference between lack of will and lack of capacity is highly important. However, our research on Mexico suggests that a framework that explicitly incorporates these two types of blocking factors needs to be theorized more carefully. In the case of limited statehood in Mexico, could we really argue that noncompliance is really "involuntary," after decades of lost opportunities to strengthen the capacities of police forces, prosecutors, and courts? There is, clearly, a limited statehood and, therefore, a lack-of-capacities problem—but have the different Mexican governments during the past two decades shown the will to address the problem and boost institutional capacity? More research is needed, but many observers of human rights in Mexico would probably argue that the different governments have done too little, too late. Granted, the role of limited statehood and even decentralization might be quite different in settings in which the central authorities authentically have tried to address human rights shortcomings—that is, in cases in which "willingness" has clearly been present. In this sense, the distinction between "lack of will" and "lack of capacities" (or "voluntary" and "involuntary" sources of violations) is analytically valuable. But an empirical examination of "willingness" seems to have analytical priority—there seems to be little point in discussing capacities if we do not show first that governments have really tried to implement change.

Willingness, in this sense, is the key scope condition for human rights change. The spiral model and similar approaches that emphasize the role of pressure "from above" suppose that willingness is generated by pressure and argumentation. It is striking, however, that willingness seems to be taken for granted in the presence of pressure and argumentation or other conditions and that, therefore, it is not explicitly examined empirically. Cases like that of Mexico, in which the government has shown remarkable skills to "talk the talk" without "walking the walk" and grows more and more resilient to transnational pressures, suggest that theories that do not explicitly theorize willingness are flawed.

CHAPTER 11

Human Rights and Justice in Mexico

An Analysis of Judicial Functions

Karina Ansolabehere

Introduction

This chapter analyzes the behavior of the federal judicial branch of Mexico in response to the country's human rights crisis. The puzzle the chapter examines is why, even when one can identify changes in judicial ideas regarding international human rights law, judicial accountability for rights violations remains poor.

This study complicates the shared assertion that a situation of systematic impunity prevails in Mexico by suggesting that there is a decoupling of the Federal Judiciary's active role in the diffusion of international human rights norms and the pursuit of accountability for human rights violations. This discrepancy presents a real danger: the trivialization of legal human rights discourse. To understand the discrepancy between the diffusion and the application of human rights norms, this study makes the claim that the Mexican Federal Judiciary is charged with handling two processes that have different dynamics. The first is related to the dissemination of international human rights norms as legal tools, and the second to the establishment of accountability for human rights violations, which is in turn influenced by other actors of the justice system (strictly speaking, the law-enforcement system) and by the prior record of impunity. While these two judicial processes are not unrelated, they do not converge perfectly because they arise from different logics and dynamics. Thus, they are decoupled.

This calls us to examine the existing literature on judicial proceedings in human rights, specifically to problematize the assumption that when judiciaries exercise judicial power with regard to rights, the key variable is whether they are pro-rights or not (Gauri and Brinks 2008; Helmke and Rios-Figueroa 2011). This chapter stresses that judiciaries can exercise different functions when it comes to human rights and that these functions are not necessarily aligned due to unique institutional responses to different processes, which impact judicial structures in distinct ways (Kapiszewski, Silverstein, and Kagan 2013). These functions are a collective/institutional construction, and they go beyond the individual preferences of the judges.

In this way, this chapter not only contributes to the understanding of the judicial function as it relates to human rights in Mexico but also proposes to complement the existing literature on activist judiciaries by considering the multiple pro-rights functions of judicial powers and their connection with the overarching processes in which these tasks are anchored and to which they are related. Additionally, the chapter contributes to understanding what mechanisms need to be monitored and reformed to improve the legal accountability of the judiciary for human rights violations.

The chapter begins with a review of the relevant literature on the judiciary's human rights functions. Then it outlines the methodology that supports the analysis, followed by a brief description of the characteristics of Mexico's Federal Judiciary and its relationship to human rights. Finally, the chapter analyzes the two processes in question—the dissemination of human rights ideas and accountability for human rights violations.

Pro-Rights Judiciaries

To gain insight into the relationship between judicial powers and human rights accountability, it is important to first examine and account for the ways in which judiciaries are connected with human rights protections in general. Understanding the relationship between judiciaries and the protection of human rights in accordance with the literature leads us to pose two related questions: What does it mean to say that a judiciary is pro-rights? And why are judiciaries able to adopt a pro-rights perspective?

The meaning associated with being a pro-rights judiciary differs in accordance with the perspective that one adopts, and why this particular perspective is adopted.

Literature on the study of human rights from within the field of political science has recognized three main functions of all judiciaries in relation to human rights:

a) the *dissemination* of international human rights norms (Simmons 2009; Hathaway 2002; Risse, Ropp, and Sikkink 1999; Huneeus 2010; Powell and Staton 2009; Dancy and Sikkink 2012)—which has received special attention from international relations studies;
b) the pursuit of *accountability* for human rights violations, particularly in situations of political regime change or in postconflict scenarios—a topic that includes the vast body of literature on transitional and post-conflict justice (Elster 2006; Naomi 2006; Call 2007; Bell 2009; Collins 2010; Lessa et al. 2014; Sikkink 2011; Michel and Sikkink 2012; Olsen, Payne, and Reiter 2010);
c) the *judicialization of social rights* (Uvin 2004; Hamm 2001; Cornwall and Nyamu-Musembi 2004; Abramovich and Courtis 2002; Gauri and Brinks 2008).

Given these alternatives, specifying what constitutes a judicial power committed to the protection of human rights must take into consideration the function one looks to explore. One could say that a judiciary performs the function of *dissemination* when the international human rights norms and their specific legal tools take part in motivating judicial decisions. Empirically, this can be measured by analyzing how much attention international human rights norms have received in setting legal precedents. For its part, a judiciary performs the human rights *accountability* function when it has issued rulings on this issue, whether referring to the victims or the perpetrators. Empirically, this would be measured by the quantity of cases of human rights violations that go to trial and are sentenced, as well as by the content of these decisions. Finally, a judiciary operates as a guarantee and protection of *social rights* when it has addressed these topics in its decisions, and this function can be measured via the quantity and content of judgments rendered.

The answer to the second question—why are judiciaries able to adopt a pro-rights perspective?—is based on discussions of judicial politics and the factors that influence judicial decisions. Although no consensus exists, judicial pro-rights decisions are associated with one or various of the following factors: the interests of the judges (Gely and Spiller 2012; Helmke 2002), the predominant judicial culture or professional ideologies (Couso and Hilbink

2011; Hilbink 2007; Couso 2005; Couso, Huneeus, and Sieder 2010), the political attitudes of the judges prior to their appointment (Segal and Spaeth 2002), the institutional design for accessing justice (Navia and Ríos-Fugueroa 2005; Wilson 2009; Smulovitz 2013; Ríos-Figueroa 2010; Ríos-Figueroa and Pozos-Loyo 2010), the operation of the judicial hierarchy and the characteristics of constitutional control (Ansolabehere 2007a; Shapiro and Stone Sweet 2002; Navia and Ríos-Figueroa 2005), civil society's capacity to initiate strategic litigation (Epp 1998; Smulovitz 2010), the public visibility of judicial decisions (Staton 2010), the distribution of political power between the executive and legislative branches (Ríos-Figueroa 2007; Chavez 2004), the institutional history of the judiciary (Ansolabehere 2010; Kapiszewski 2012b), and nongovernmental organizations' pedagogical initiatives to change judicial culture (Gonzalez Ocantos 2014).

In response to this diversity of explanations, a body of scholarship looks to explain the complexity of judicial policymaking, advancing multidimensional approaches (Gloppen et al. 2010) based upon a multiplicity of factors that intervene: litigants' opportunity structures and judges' opportunity structures (sociopolitical context, legal cultural, institutional framework)— or, rather, a procedural analysis that takes into account the different moments of the judicial process from litigation to the implementation of court sentences (Yamin and Gloppin 2011; Glauri and Brinks 2008).

This chapter complements this last group of the literature by focusing not solely on one of the human rights–related functions performed by the judiciaries but on two of them, and by further including in this analysis an investigation of the specific processes that connect them and how they relate to each other.

The research approach adopted in this chapter and its methodology are both constructed from within the historical institutionalist approach to judicial decision-making. According to this analytical perspective, in order to thoroughly understand judicial institutions, one needs to look past the idea that their operation can be attributed to the behavior of their individual members. On the contrary, judiciaries should be seen as socially constructed spaces in which the personal preferences and values of their members are the product of the dynamics and institutional practices of the present and the inertia of the past (Gillman and Clayton 1999).

This chapter also makes an additional contribution to this field by advancing our understanding of the dynamics of federal judiciaries, and thus expands current research that focuses primarily on the highest courts or the constitutional courts, which are the judicial authorities that have received the greatest attention in Latin America.

Dimensions of Analysis

The particular import of this chapter lies in its explanation of the performance of two functions of Mexico's Federal Judiciary—the dissemination of human rights ideas and the establishment of accountability for human rights violations, viewed as processes configured by factors that are both internal and external to the judiciary and that, in turn, have become entrenched in relevant events. The analysis will demonstrate the degree to which domestic law's reference to the role of international human rights law pervades the construction of legal precedents in Mexico, including precedents regarding the role of international human rights law within domestic law, as well as tools used to harmonize both legal orders—domestic and international. Among these tools are the obligation to review domestic law through the standards of the American Convention on Human Rights or "control of conventionality"; the need to expand the interpretation of the constitution in order to conform to international human rights law standards (the so-called principle of conforming interpretation); or the mandate to choose the most protective legal criteria (domestic or international) in cases of human rights conflicts, called the pro-person principle. In accordance with this perspective, this paper hypothesizes that a greater quantity of precedents linked to these issues will engender a more intense diffusion of international human rights law.

To gain a deeper understanding of the exercise of these judicial functions in the current human rights context in Mexico, this study assesses the significance of relevant events by using primary and secondary sources that explain the dissemination of international human rights norms in general, and within the judiciary in particular.

To evaluate the judicial function of pursuing accountability for human rights violations, the chapter concentrates on one type of grave abuse: the enforced disappearance of persons. In this case, the assumption is that a greater intensity in the performance of this function is evidenced by the number of open trials and rulings directly related to this issue in the Federal Judiciary. The accountability function should be seen in relation to previous efforts to address human rights violations in Mexico, the dynamics among the various branches of the Federal Judiciary, in particular the criminal courts, and the role of law-enforcement agencies that operate as prosecutors. In assessing the accountability function, one must pay particular attention to the effectiveness of these institutions in carrying out criminal investigations and the resulting criminal proceedings.

The sources of information used to assess the accountability function include official reports, reports by official and unofficial international human rights organizations and domestic civil society organizations, transitional justice databases, and legal precedents on the justiciable nature of human rights violations in Mexico.

The objective of this chapter is not only to analyze the performance of each one of these two functions—dissemination and accountability—but also to consider the ways in which they are linked to each other.

Given the idiosyncrasies of the Mexican case, the tracking of these processes will begin in 1995 and end in 2015. In 1995, Mexico implemented a constitutional reform of the Federal Judiciary, increasing its power, privileges, and level of autonomy with respect to the executive branch. This event was a watershed in the relationship between the Federal Judiciary, political power, and society and, as such, was seen as part of the process of political liberalization that culminated in the exchange of political power in 2000. The following section presents an analysis of the characteristics of the Mexican judiciary and the most significant milestones in its development within the confines of the period being studied.

The Mexican Judiciary After 1995

Only at the end of the 1990s did the judiciaries in Latin America begin to garner the attention of political scientists (Helmke and Rios-Figueroa 2011; Kapiszewski, Silverstein, and Kagan 2013) as a result of two processes: the democratic transition from authoritarian governments and the structural reforms aimed at allowing for an economic opening of the countries (Ansolabehere 2007b; Kapiszewski 2012a). Mexico was no exception. Reforms to the Federal Judiciary were pursued from the beginning of the 1980s, with the country's 1982 external debt crisis, but even more so since 1995 as part of the process of political liberalization and the "citizenization" and "judicialization" of the electoral institutions (Merino and Valenzeula 2003; Valdés Ugalde 2010). These reforms increased the judiciary's autonomy from political power as well as the power of the judiciary itself as a way to consolidate the Supreme

Court as arbitrator of the political conflicts of the new political landscape (Ansolabehere 2007b).

To explain the characteristics of Mexico's current Federal Judiciary, I first consider the system in 1995 as a baseline and then identify milestones leading up to 2015. The analysis reviews the changes in relation to political power, law-enforcement agencies, lower-level institutions under the purview of the Federal Judiciary, and society in general.

From 1995 to 2015 the judiciary in Mexico became more public, influential, autonomous from the political system, and powerful within the political and social landscape. During this period one of the main changes in the judicial role was the improvement of its social legitimacy through the adoption of some causes like same-sex marriage, abortion, and so on.

In its evolution, the judiciary faced three different moments regarding human rights. The first was in 1995, when the Supreme Court became arbitrator of the political conflict between different branches of government and between political minorities and majorities, resulting in the need to take control of the lower courts where the human rights agenda was hardly present. The second started in 2008, when the reform of the criminal justice system was approved, bringing the rights of both the victims and the accused to the center of the discussion. The third occurred after 2009, when the Federal Judiciary assumed the agenda of international human rights law after the *Radilla Pacheco v. Mexico* ruling of the Inter-American Court of Human Rights (IACtHR).

Atop the hierarchy of Mexico's Federal Judiciary is the Supreme Court of the Nation, consisting of eleven judges. The other parts include (a) the Council of the Federal Judiciary,[1] presided over by the President of the Supreme Court, and charged with the administration of the courts and tribunals, as well as with the administration of the profession and judicial conduct; (b) the Federal Election Tribunal, charged with the resolution of conflicts associated with electoral processes; and (c) jurisdictional agencies such as the collegiate and single-judge circuit courts, the district courts, and regional auxiliary centers.

The 1995 constitutional reform was a key to the redefinition of the role of the Federal Judiciary, especially the Supreme Court, and of Mexico's political system at large (Ríos-Figueroa 2007; Finkel 2008). Via this reform, (a) the authority of the Supreme Court was strengthened in order to resolve conflicts between the three branches of government, as well as between political majorities and minorities via constitutional claims; (b) the Council of the Federal Judiciary was created to manage the judiciary and the conduct of judges and magistrates, modifying the responsibilities of the Supreme Court on that matter; (c) a new division in labor, to overcome the backlog of cases, was created between the Supreme Court and the collegiate circuit courts, through which the first would attend to questions of constitutionality and legality when the cases involved establishing new legal precedents, and the circuit courts would deal with questions of legality in cases in which the Supreme Court had already established legal criteria.

Although this era led the way for the "judicialization" of political conflict, it did not result in important modifications to the mechanisms necessary for offering citizens access to justice. Two indicators illustrated this lack of access. First, only the branches of government (or one of their agencies), political parties, and legislative minorities had the authority to operate the concentrated mechanisms of constitutional control (Constitutional Claim and the Action of Unconstitutionality). Second, the resource par excellence for the defense of rights in Mexico, the writ of *amparo*, was not subject to the necessary modifications that would improve its accessibility and effectiveness until 2011, when a constitutional reform (Diario Oficial de la Federación 2011b) was passed on this matter. This reform reduced some of the barriers to access by incorporating an avenue for presenting writs of *amparo* due to omissions by authorities or due to the noncompliance with international human rights–related treaties, and also by legitimizing interested third parties (not only those affected directly) to utilize this resource.

Meanwhile, from the judicial hierarchy's point of view, the 1995 reform, with its creation of the Council of the Federal Judiciary, changed the procedures used to select and promote judges and magistrates. It incorporated more actors into the process, which up until this point had depended solely on the Supreme Court justices. Nevertheless, the obligatory nature of the rules that reduced the scope of interpretation of the lower courts in the settlement of judicial cases regarding legal precedents—also known as binding legal precedent—was not changed[2] (Ansolabehere 2007b).

The second milestone occurred in 2008 with the approval of the reform to the criminal justice system. This penal reform entailed Mexico's move from an inquisitorial system in which law enforcement acted as the system's center of gravity to a system characterized as adversarial, defined by (1) equal procedural roles for the prosecution and the defense, (2) oral public proceedings, and (3) the centrality of the judge in managing the legal criminal procedure. This reform required the adjustment of all the national criminal justice systems, state and federal, by its June 2016 deadline.

In order to adjust its procedures and train its personnel in the implementation of this new criminal justice system, in 2015 the Federal Judiciary created an implementation unit, which initiated a plan for the gradual implementation of the reform. The plan had seven stages, starting in November 2015 in the states of Durango and Puebla. By December 2015, the new federal system was operating in twenty-four states.

The third milestone for the Federal Judiciary took place in 2009 when Mexico was held accountable by the IACtHR for a crime that occurred during the "Dirty War" against the armed socialist movement of the 1970s, in the case of *Rosendo Radilla Pacheco v. Mexico*. In this case, the IACtHR held the Mexican government responsible for the forced disappearance of Radilla Pacheco. Some of the actions requested by the IACtHR in this ruling were specific to Mexico's judiciary: to investigate with due diligence and, if possible, undertake criminal proceedings related to illegal detention and forced disappearance; to conduct training for the judiciary's personnel on the IACtHR's jurisprudence; and to make public any information relevant to the investigation of cases of disappearance. This ruling and the resulting actions, as noted in the next section of this chapter, triggered a discussion within Mexico's Supreme Court about its relationship with the IACtHR.

The fourth milestone, which cannot be separated from the third, was the approval of the 2011 constitutional reforms regarding human rights and the writ of *amparo* (Diario Oficial de la Federación 2011a, 2011b). Via this reform, international treaties that have human rights clauses were incorporated into Mexico's national legal system with the same legal force as the Constitution, and the "*pro-hominem* principle"[3] was established as a hermeneutic tool for deciding human rights cases. For its part, the *amparo* reform moderately expanded access to justice by adopting the rule that any party may use the writ regarding the violation of a right legally declared of legitimate interest, even if they are not directly affected by the rights-violating act of authority. Both modifications opened the door to the judicialization of conflicts over rights.

By 2015, these key moments modified the face and practices of the judiciary, making it a more visible arena in which conflicts were discussed through the language of human rights not only at the level of the Supreme Court but also within the lower courts. Finally, the judiciary had become slightly more accessible.

These transformations were not produced in a political and social vacuum. Between 1995 and 2000, the Federal Judiciary operated in a context of political liberalization and the unprecedented exchange of power in 2000, marking the end of the hegemonic party's presidential control. Economically, the era was marked by the crisis of 1995, and socially, by the general increase in the number of civil society organizations, specifically the increase of those organizations dedicated to human rights (Olvera and Olvera 2003; Frey 2015), many of which used litigation as a tool for the defense and protection of human rights. Additionally, since the Zapatista National Liberation Army's uprising in Chiapas in 1994, there had been an increase in international pressure on Mexico regarding its human rights record (Anaya Muñoz 2012). Within this context, there was a notable increase in civil society's demands for improving due-process guarantees and protections for civil and political rights (Estévez López 2007). This mobilization, however, resulted in only limited judicialization of demands for human rights protection (Ansolabehere 2003; Magaloni and Zaldivar 2006).

From 2000 until 2006, in the context of the nation's partisan shift in the presidency, Mexico assumed a new openness to international scrutiny of its human rights record. For example, in 2001, President Vicente Fox signed an agreement to establish an office in Mexico of the UN High Commissioner for Human Rights and to develop, in association with this agency, the first National Human Rights Program (Anaya Muñoz 2009). Also during this period, the government made an ultimately failed attempt to account for the human rights violations committed during the period of the Dirty War and the acts of repression committed against the student movement in 1968 and 1978, when the Attorney General created the Special Prosecutor's Office for Political and Social Movements from the Past (FEMOSPP).

Since the start of President Calderón's six-year term in 2006, the turn away from even these small steps toward accountability for human rights violations has been dramatic. As stressed throughout this volume, President Calderón's strategy to combat drug trafficking coincided with an escalation in violence in Mexico and a corresponding increase in human rights violations, which in turn have come to characterize the country's human rights crisis. The country's openness to international scrutiny came sharply into tension with policies oriented toward security and the maintenance of law and order, which were often presented as a zero-sum game.

The human rights crisis continued into the administration of President Enrique Peña Nieto. As noted in this volume's Introduction, official statistics show that there have been 209,401 homicides in Mexico between 2007 and 2016. Furthermore, 30,123 disappearances were recorded in the same period. It is clear from these observations that in the last two six-year presidential terms, the problem of violence in Mexico has not improved.

In short, the Federal Judiciary operates in a context marked by an ongoing cascade of human rights violations. Although it is not the principal forum in which cases of human rights violations are processed, due to the fact that a large number of these cases are processed in each individual state's judicial branch, the Federal Judiciary faces (and will continue to face) the challenge of ensuring accountability for human rights violations whether directly or through *amparo* proceedings.

Having established the panorama of the characteristics and conditions in which the Federal Judiciary operates, this chapter next analyzes the two central processes under focus, the dissemination of international human rights norms and the (practically nonexistent) function of ensuring accountability for human rights violations.

The Dissemination of International Human Rights Norms: The Inclination to Establish the Meaning, Reach, and Limits of the Law

While the Mexican government exhibited changes in its foreign policy concerning international human rights norms and increased its openness to international scrutiny starting in 2000, with the exchange of parties in power (Saltalamacchia Ziccardi and Covarrubias Velasco 2011), the Federal Judiciary entered late into this international arena. The discussion surrounding the hierarchy of international law within the domestic legal order was not new for the Supreme Court, but its centrality as a topic of discussion intensified and expanded as of 2011.

Figure 11.1 provides an account of the evolution and intensity of this function during the period under investigation.

As is regularly debated in the field of international relations, the processes by which human rights norms are disseminated include different moments and actors (Keck and Sikkink 1998). These processes may include the ratification of international treaties (Lutz and Sikkink 2000) or may depend on the relative openness to international oversight (Saltamacchia Ziccardia and Covarrubias Velasco 2011) and the development of public policies guided by international human rights standards, which had their heyday between 2000 and 2004 (Anaya Muñoz 2009). Finally, diffusion requires the standardization of legislation and the incorporation of these norms into legal decisions (Ansolabehere, Valdés Ugalde, and Vázquez Valencia 2015).

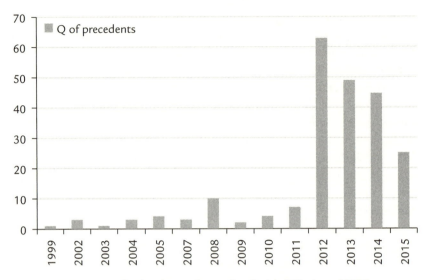

Figure 11.1. Quantity of judicial precedents related with diffusion of IHRL (1995–2005). Source: Based on data on settled case law and nonbinding judicial precedents from the *Semanario Judicial de la Federación* (Federal Judiciary Weekly Journal).

While Mexico has a long tradition of ratifying international human rights treaties, one cannot overlook the fact that ratifications reached their peak intensity between 2001 and 2002. In addition to ratifications, the most innovative move in the early years of the period studied for this chapter (1995–2015) was the design and implementation (not without problems) of the National Human Rights Program in 2004 (Anaya Muñoz 2009). This program was a preliminary attempt to promote international human rights norms within public policies developed by the federal government.

The early 2000s, therefore, represented a period of relative political openness to the international scrutiny of Mexico's human rights record. Yet the Federal Judiciary, apart from its initiation of a collaborative program with the OHCHR, stayed distant from the processes of norm diffusion (Ansolabehere 2015). Instead, it was the configuration of two previously cited events—the IACtHR's ruling in the 2009 *Radilla Pacheco* case[4] and the June 2011 constitutional reform—that triggered more intense internal discussions within the judiciary about the role of international human rights treaties and other resolutions of international agencies, including a reconsideration of the IACtHR's rulings as sources of law.

In *Radilla Pacheco,* the Supreme Court found the Mexican state responsible for violating the rights to liberty, humane treatment, life, and recognition as a person before the law, as well as the rights to physical and mental integrity, to judicial guarantees, and to the judicial protection of family members. Similarly, the court ruled that the proceedings brought before Mexico's military courts failed to respect the standards of due process established in international law (IACtHR 2009). After the court's ruling, the President of the Mexican Supreme Court "made a request to the full Court asking for them to determine the procedure that might best correspond to the pronounced ruling in the *Radilla Pacheco* case against the United States of Mexico" (Diario Oficial de la Federación 2011c). The request made by the president of the highest court to the rest of his colleagues signaled a change in the way that the Supreme Court interacted with the Inter-American Human Rights System. Despite the fact that the ruling was generically addressed to the Mexican state as a whole, the Supreme Court directly initiated a deliberative process on the reach and limits of this judicial decision for the Federal Judiciary itself.

As a result of the plenary consultation, the Supreme Court decided, by an 8–3 majority,[5] that (a) despite not receiving express notification regarding the court's responsibilities relative to this ruling, it could proceed as an institution, *motu propio,* to comply without taking further steps to coordinate with other branches of the Mexican state (Acuerdo 482/2010); and (b) for this endeavor it should take into account the *Radilla Pacheco* ruling in its totality, and not merely the operative paragraphs that corresponded to the judiciary. In its decision, the court elaborated the process through which it would articulate its relationship with the Inter-American Human Rights System. Specifically, the process would consider the manner in which the Mexican state's exclusions under the IACtHR's jurisdiction would be interpreted, including the reservations and interpretive declarations of the Mexican state under the American Convention on Human Rights (ACHR) and the American Convention on Forced Disappearances of Persons, as well as the government's concrete obligations under this ruling (Diario Oficial de la Federación 2011c). The Supreme Court's decision effectively challenged the existing relationship between the national legal order and international human rights law, as well as between domestic legal institutions and international human rights institutions. The Supreme Court's decision opened the door for the judiciary to act as a sounding board for international human rights norms.

This resolution, known as Expediente Varios (Diario Oficial de la Federación 2011c), which established the responsibility of the Federal Judiciary regarding rulings of the IACtHR, set forth several foundational principles with regard to this responsibility. Expediente Varios determined, inter alia, that (a) caveats and restrictions could not be carried out by the Mexican government to diminish the rulings of the IACtHR directed to it; (b) rulings against Mexico are obligatory for the Federal Judiciary; (c) the interpretive criteria found within the IACtHR's case law will guide the nation's judicial branch; and (d) the judiciary should exercise ex officio the ability to review the laws of compliance between the ACHR and internal legal norms.[6]

Among judicial actors, the Supreme Court's decision in the *Radilla Pacheco* case was seen as a turning point for the institution. For example, a circuit-court magistrate defined the Supreme Court's decisions on the *Radilla* case as a "wake up call" for the Federal Judiciary.[7]

Another fortuitous event for the dissemination of international human rights norms was the constitutional reform on human rights published in the Diario Oficial de la Federación (Official Federal Journal) on June 10, 2011. These events worked as catalysts for an extensive discussion in the Federal Judiciary in general, and in the Supreme Court in particular, about the status of international human rights law, about the ways to align domestic law with external sources, about the specific interpretative techniques for achieving these ends, and about the authority held by lower-level judges not to enforce domestic legal norms if they are found contrary to the ACHR.

Despite these important institutional events, the process of disseminating human rights norms on the part of the Federal Judiciary is not complete; the guiding principles of the dissemination process are still being adapted and rearranged. The resolution of the Conflicting Lines of Precedent 293/2011 is an example of these tensions. "Conflicting Lines of Precedent" defined the procedure by which the Supreme Court would resolve different outcomes by lower courts and unified the criteria for interpretation. This decision arose out of a conflict regarding the legal interpretation of two courts of appeals concerning the reach of international treaties in the domestic legal order and the legal enforceability of the IACtHR's settled case law. In the end, the Supreme Court established by a majority of ten votes that (a) the international treaties that include human rights provisions have the same rank as the Political Constitution of Mexico, except when the Political Constitution contains a restriction regarding said treaty, in which case the constitutional provision takes precedence; and (b) the IACtHR's settled case law is binding for Mexico provided that it is the most favorable case law for the person concerned. The resolution received four votes in favor (Minister Jorge Pardo

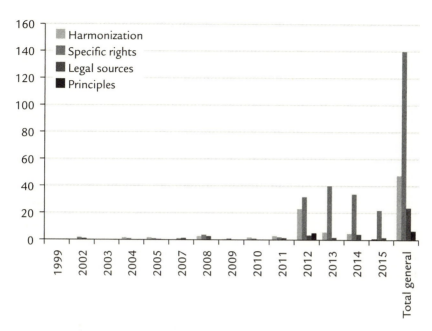

Figure 11.2. Thematic evolution of the judicial precedents related to the dissemination of international human rights norms. Source: Based on an existing database on judicial precedents regarding the dissemination of human rights ideas developed by the Federal Judiciary Weekly Journal.

Rebolledo, Minister Arturo Zaldívar, Minster Olga Sánchez Cordero, and Minister Alfredo Gutiérrez Ortiz Mena) and two dissenting votes (Minister Luis María Aguilar and Minister José Ramón Cossío). More than half of the ministers established their particular position on the matter, which in itself demonstrated that deliberations on this matter were dynamic and not uniform. The decision set forth four overarching themes strengthening the function of disseminating international human rights norms (see Figure 11.2):

a) Harmonization: A concern for the mechanisms used to align domestic law with international law, such as the review of compliance, the principle of conforming interpretation, and the pro-person principle.

b) Specific rights: A concern for the interpretation of specific rights, especially the scope of these rights in accordance with the nation's new legal framework and the principles applicable to their interpretation.

c) Legal sources: A concern for the status of the sources of international law within the domestic legal order.

d) Principles: A concern for the legal remedies available to protect human rights.

As seen in Figure 11.3, after 2011, not only did the number of precedents increase, but the number of themes these precedents talked about increased too. The function of dissemination is strengthened by the increase in the quantity of precedents and by the diversity of topics these precedents focus on. For example, while in 1999 only one theme was addressed in a judicial precedent, in 2012, 2013, and 2014 as many as four themes were addressed by the Federal Judiciary in its precedents.

One of the most interesting findings from this study of judicial human rights decisions is that this function of dissemination is not spread uniformly among judicial agencies. Within the Supreme Court, the Plenary and the First Chamber are the judicial bodies in which the process of dissemination is concentrated.

For their part, the circuit courts had a comprehensive discussion regarding the dissemination of international human rights norms, which covered

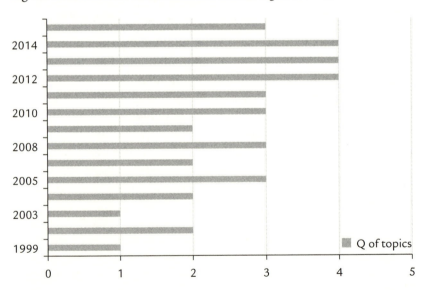

Figure 11.3. Quantity of topics treated per year, 1995–2015. Source: Based on data on binding and nonbinding judicial precedents found in the Federal Judiciary Weekly Journal.

all of the previously referenced topics. The dissemination function was concentrated in three particular circuit courts. The first circuit court (Mexico City) was responsible for 40.2 percent of the judicial precedents, followed by the fourth circuit court (Nuevo León) with 10 percent of the precedents, and the third circuit court (Jalisco) with 7 percent. The remaining 29 percent of precedents were distributed among the remaining circuit courts. In other words, at the lower-court level, the production of judicial precedents regarding international human rights norms has been concentrated in less than half of the country's circuit courts.

Table 11.1 illustrates the level of dissent found within the judiciary, specifically with regard to the function of disseminating human rights norms. The level of dissent is low, as observed in the unanimous votes that dominate the decisions. Approximately 90 percent passed with consensus. Regardless of this tendency, however, there were other topics and spaces on which dissent was greater, for example, in cases including an analysis of specific rights.

In sum, I observed two extremes in implementing the dissemination function: the absence of such implementation in 1995 and intense implementation in 2015. These extremes, nevertheless, were triggered by two events outside of the judiciary, which had repercussions in Mexico's Federal Judiciary: the IACtHR's ruling on the *Rosendo Radilla Pacheco* case in 2009 and the constitutional reform on human rights in 2011. These events created a

Table 11.1. Dissent in the legal decisions concerning the different topics associated with the dissemination of international human rights norms

Vote	*Topics*				
	Harmonization	*Interpretation of rights*	*Legal sources*	*Principles legal remedies*	*Total*
Divided Vote	5	22	6	—	33
Concurring Vote	—	1	1	—	2
Unanimous Vote	43	118	17	7	185
Total	48	141	24	7	220

Source: Based on data from the Federal Judiciary Weekly Journal, which corresponds to the analysis of binding and nonbinding legal precedents from 1995–2015.

structure of opportunity, energizing discussions about the dissemination of human rights norms in the Federal Judiciary.

The Accountability Function:
Many Allegations but Few Trials

Evidence shows that, in the Latin American region, judicial accountability for serious human rights violations in past decades has not led to increases in armed conflicts or other serious violations, nor has it had a destabilizing effect on democracy (Sikkink and Walling 2007). Despite this finding, the path toward accountability for human rights violations is not one that Mexico has chosen to travel. Instead, the country has been characterized by a "justice filter"—which has resulted in the prosecution of an extremely small number of cases despite the magnitude and seriousness of reported violations. Sources concur that there exists a pattern of impunity in the cases of present and past human rights violations (IACHR 2015a; Human Rights Watch 2016; Committee on Enforced Disappearances 2015). This point is emphasized in this volume's Introduction and repeated within many of its chapters. This consensus places the justice system's operations in general (including local judiciaries and the Federal Judiciary as well as the Federal Attorney General's Office and state offices), and the judiciary's operations in particular, at the center of a debate about the effectiveness of its operations.

According to official data, more than thirty-one thousand cases of missing and disappeared persons were registered between 2006 and 2016. Furthermore, in accordance with the information presented by the Mexican government before the Committee on Enforced Disappearances (Committee on Enforced Disappearances 2014), since 2006, only 99 cases of forced disappearance were investigated at the federal level and 192 by local judiciaries. Of these, six cases have reached final judgment and sentences for convicted perpetrators—one of these for a crime committed decades earlier, in the times of the Dirty War. This data highlights a key characteristic of Mexico's accountability process for human rights violations. As shown through these limited convictions in cases of disappearances, for instance, there is a filtering process in the justice system that allows for the engagement of the judicial system in only about 1 percent of all human rights crimes. This dynamic highlights that the entity where these cases continue to pile up and stall is law enforcement, which is in itself tasked with carrying out the preliminary investigation of each case in order to initiate criminal proceedings.

Similar to the case of norm dissemination, the exercise of the accountability function cannot be separated from two factors that highlight the particularities of the relationship between law enforcement and the judiciary: (a) the (failed) experience of accountability focused, as of 2001, on human rights violations carried out during Mexico's Dirty War, as well as those violations arising from the repression of the student movement in 1968 and 1971; and (b) the implementation of the 2008 criminal justice reforms. The latter reform was to be completely implemented in both the federal and state judiciary systems by June 2016.

The most visible experience in terms of accountability for human rights violations was the FEMOSPP, discussed earlier in this chapter. The FEMOSPP had authority to investigate cases of human rights violations from the past, specifically the forced disappearance of members of the political opposition, particularly from armed leftist movements, as well as the repression of the student movement in 1968 and 1971 (Dutrenit Bielous and Varela Petito 2010; Dutrenit Bielous and Argüeyo 2011; Aguayo and Treviño 2007). Mexico initiated this process when other Latin American countries had already widely advanced their investigations regarding human rights crimes and even begun so-called posttransitional justice processes (Collins 2010).

Despite the accumulated regional experiences and the intervention of international organizations with specific recommendations—such as the International Center for Transitional Justice (ICTJ) (ICTJ 2008; Seils 2004) and Human Rights Watch (Human Rights Watch 2003)—the results of the FEMOSPP process in terms of truth, justice, and reparation were almost nonexistent. The International Center for Transitional Justice concluded, "Results were meager regarding truth-seeking. It has been impossible to bring to trial those responsible for past crimes, and no reparations have been made to victims" (ICTJ 2008: 1).

This pro-accountability agenda was driven by human rights organizations, victims, and their family members. The main strategy adopted by these organizations was increasing the visibility of the fate of different types of political opposition in different moments: guerillas, student movements, left-wing militants, and so forth. Despite the agreement of the Fox administration to create an accountability mechanism, the decision to place the prosecutor's office within the Federal Attorney General's Office (PGR) rapidly weakened its legitimacy among the very family members, victims, and organizations that had demanded it. The PGR has been the government agency with the largest number of complaints registered against it for human rights violations (see Chapter 10), and also, at the time of FEMOSPP's creation, the General Prosecutor was a military veteran whose motivation to try his peers was questionable. Furthermore, this institutional decision generated a polemic among a sector of the intelligentsia that had advocated for the creation of a truth commission (Aguayo and Treviño 2007). Additionally, there were inconsistencies in the appointments of the special prosecutor's office. Ignacio Carillo Prieto was appointed head of the FEMOSPP despite having limited experience in the subject matter and almost no public recognition to aid him with such a significant undertaking. The principal characteristic of this prosecutor's office was thus its weakness and lack of credibility (Dutrenit and Argüello 2011; Dutrenit and Varela 2010; ICTJ 2008; Comité 68 et al. 2006; Acosta and Ennelin 2006).

As with the cases of disappearance in recent years, the accountability experience of FEMOSPP also operated as a justice filter. According to ICTJ, FEMOSPP initiated 1,000 investigations but "it brought only 10 charges in 19 cases; it issued 20 arrest warrants and brought 8 indictments" (ICTJ 2008: 3). Through 2009, there was not a single conviction by a circuit court or a district court of the Federal Judiciary regarding these cases. The Special Prosecutor's Office was finally shut down on March 26, 2007.

From the Federal Judiciary's point of view, its ability to exercise the accountability function for past human rights violations was restricted by FEMOSPP's performance. The meager results were indicative of two problems: the incapability of law-enforcement agencies to undertake investigations in complex cases, and the absence of a human rights framework by the judges who considered them. Only the Supreme Court's intervention altered this approach, providing interesting cues to the lower courts to establish, for example, that the disappearance of persons was a continuous crime and, therefore, that the statute of limitations was triggered only by the location of a body or proof of the crime.[8]

This dynamic had, and has, as its gravitational center the agencies of the PGR, which control the ability to bring criminal charges and to investigate them. The proposed criminal justice reform, driven by a broad coalition of academics, civil society organizations, and international development agencies, represented an attempt to change this dynamic, at least formally (Ansolabehere 2014). Still, more than a decade after the failed experience of the FEMOSPP, accountability for crimes such as forced disappearances has not increased.

The law enforcement–judiciary relationship highlights the dissonance between the enormous numbers of reported disappearances and the judiciary's lack of response to them. The limitations on the Federal Judiciary's exercise of the accountability function is directly linked to a law-enforcement system characterized by large levels of inefficiency. A review of Supreme Court–settled case law and nonbinding court precedents from 1995 until 2015 finds nine precedents that directly referenced forced disappearances. These cases were related to the following situations: (a) a 2002 constitutional claim, related to the Dirty War, in which the Supreme Court acknowledged forced disappearance as a continuous crime,[9] and (b) legal complaints and writs of *amparo* filed after the 2011 constitutional reform, which were resolved by circuit courts in which advocacy attempts within law-enforcement bodies were observed on the part of judges.[10] These cases established that a judge, in cases of forced disappearances, could take formal action to find the disappeared persons and, moreover, that the victims in these cases had the right to access information about the investigative efforts undertaken by the prosecutors. Notably, these judicial rulings referenced international human rights standards and, thus, serve as a model for bringing together the dissemination function and the accountability function in the judiciary's response to the crime of forced disappearance.

The temporal analysis of the exercise of the accountability function for human rights violations and the disseminating function for international norms, and of the processes with which each of these functions are linked, allows us to understand the reasons for the uncoupling of these two functions. Nevertheless, it should be emphasized that ever since the IACtHR's ruling in the *Radilla* case, an event that connected these two processes, there has been mutual engagement between these two human rights functions. However, due to the relatively small number of cases that bring together these two functions, it still cannot be considered a consistent trend.

Conclusions

This chapter addresses the significance of separately analyzing some of the different functions that judiciaries can exercise when confronting human rights issues. The objective is to understand the relationship between two specific judicial functions: the dissemination of international human rights norms and the accountability for human rights violations. In Mexico, these functions have operated separately, and this separation might trivialize human rights discourse and the legal tools put in place to protect human rights.

The strengthening of the dissemination function can be observed in Mexico, while the exercise of the accountability function is basically nonexistent. This distinction helps explain the particularities of the relationship between the two functions, characterized by the processes with which each of these functions is related. This approach thus allows this chapter to identify the following:

a) The dissemination of international human rights norms was strengthened in a concentrated way (in some governmental bodies and regions) after 2011 as part of Mexico's slow process of opening up to international scrutiny. This opening in turn linked the country with international human rights protection agencies and culminated in a ruling against Mexico by the IACtHR, which, together with a constitutional reform consistent with this spirit, operated to trigger the dissemination function by the Federal Judiciary.

   It is important to monitor why this concentrated diffusion takes place, and to promote different initiatives to train members of the judiciary in international human rights law, beyond the more populated judicial circuits of the country.

b) The accountability function in the Mexican judiciary is limited, operating as what I have called a justice filter. In the cases related to disappearances, for example, more than 99 percent of them have stalled in the preliminary investigation stage and lack the investigative momentum to advance into the following stages of the judicial process.

   It is important to know, in that regard, the main obstacles to investigations and to develop strategies for overcoming them.

This pattern is persistent: it was seen in the failed experience of accountability for past human rights violations within the FEMOSPP, whose results have been almost nonexistent, and it continues to be seen in cases of forced disappearances today. There is an expectation that the 2016 reform of the criminal justice system will open new windows of opportunity for defense lawyers and judges to begin to undo this failed accountability dynamic by rebalancing the powers of the prosecutor and the defense within criminal proceedings. To do so, it will be fundamental not only to identify the mechanisms that perpetuate a situation of impunity but also to focus attention on those mechanisms that may be able to undo the justice filter.

This chapter makes clear that one item of unfinished business for the Mexican justice system is the development of effective mechanisms that ensure accountability for human rights violations. This is critical to avoid the consequences of decoupling the dissemination and accountability functions of the judiciary and, therefore, to avert the risks associated with the hollowing out of the human rights discourse. There is still much work to do in Mexico, including identifying the causal mechanisms related to the dissemination of international norms in the judiciary in order to restructure the mechanisms that currently restrict the judicialization of grave human rights violations, but also to reorganize those that allow for it.

CHAPTER 12

The Judicial Breakthrough Model

Transnational Advocacy Networks and Lethal Violence

Janice Gallagher

Introduction

Lower courts in Mexico have long been regarded as corrupt, inefficient, and incapable of carrying out their basic functions by scholars and citizens (Cornelius and Shirk 2007; Morris and Klesner 2010; Davis 2006; Taylor 1997). Crucially, as stressed in the Introduction of this volume, the lower courts routinely fail to hold those who violate the most basic human right—the right to life—accountable more than 80 percent of the time (Introduction, this volume; Mexico Evalúa 2012: 16). Despite these failings, the lower courts are still, with few exceptions, citizens' primary recourse when they seek justice. While Mexico has territorial pockets in which the justice system is complemented by indigenous systems of justice (Anaya Muñoz 2006), and its Supreme Court has opened itself to a human rights discourse (Chapter 11), citizens in most of the country—including the northern states, which are the focus of this chapter—rely overwhelmingly on broken state-level systems of justice when seeking legal redress for rights violations.

Citizens' frustration with this failed system has generated ongoing social movements and demands for "justice" on the streets and at the ballot box (Ley 2014). In 2011, these calls for justice coalesced in a nationwide movement, "The Movement for Peace with Justice and Dignity," which in turn inspired new, local victim-led movements throughout Mexico (Gallagher

2012). Frustrated with the failures of their justice system, Mexican citizens have also sought external allies' assistance as they seek to activate investigations into serious crimes (for example, Anaya Muñoz 2011). What has been the role of external and transnational actors in Mexico since 2006, specifically around issues of gross human rights violations? Has the intervention of external state and nonstate actors facilitated greater accountability for human rights violations—or conversely, have external actors at times unwittingly worked against local struggles for justice?

In this chapter, I argue that external groups have the greatest positive impact on domestic judicial outcomes when they broker local groups into productive relationships with investigatory officials, and when they concentrate on exerting pressure at the physical location where key investigative and prosecutory decisions are made, which I call the judicial decision-making site (JDMS). I build on my previous findings that locate a judicial bottleneck between the reporting and investigation of disappearances and homicides (Gallagher 2017). I have argued that a combination of confrontational activist tactics and advocacy strategies facilitates the flow of investigative information between victims of violence and state investigators, doubling the likelihood that a case will be investigated. Departing from most analyses of judicial outcomes, which measure "success" in a conviction/nonconviction binary, I use the linear concept of judicial progress. I argue that there are distinct phases in the judicial process—reporting a case, investigating the case, passing the case to a judge, initiating the trial, and obtaining a verdict—and that we should think about judicial progress as the progression of judicial cases through these distinct judicial phases.

In the first section of this chapter, I briefly review my findings that activists and advocates in northern Mexico significantly impact judicial progress in cases of lethal violence. I next clarify that I am departing from standard human rights frameworks by arguing for the importance of the more inclusive term "lethal violence" as opposed to "enforced disappearances" and "extrajudicial executions." Next, I develop a modification to the foundational theories of transnational advocacy networks (TANs) (Keck and Sikkink 1998; Ropp and Sikkink 1999). While the boomerang and spiral models rightly emphasize the importance of citizen action in changing the human rights behavior of states, they leave open the questions of whether political pressure works differently depending on the targeted state institution and official, and how this external intervention affects local human rights groups. I suggest several modifications to the boomerang model in the context of local struggles to achieve judicial progress in Mexican lower courts, and go on to analyze the struggles for justice of local human rights groups in two northern Mexican states. I highlight how the involvement of international or externally located human rights groups has impacted human rights outcomes, and draw out lessons for external actors.

Mexican Context and Concepts: Domestic Courts, Lethal Violence, and Human Rights

Civil Society Groups Improve Judicial Progress: Chihuahua and Nuevo León

Chihuahua and Nuevo León are two northern border states that have been controlled by Mexico's corporatist party, the Institutional Revolutionary Party (PRI), since 2003, and that have experienced dramatic increases in drug trafficking organization (DTO)–spurred lethal violence between 2006 and 2012. Most of these crimes go unpunished and show no signs that they have been investigated: in Nuevo León, 66 percent of all homicides and 71 percent of disappearances show no evidence of investigatory activity. In Chihuahua, 84 percent of homicides and 95 percent of disappearances show no evidence of investigatory activity. In both states, there are civil society organizations that dedicate themselves to pursuing justice in cases of disappearances and/or homicides. By comparing the judicial progress of all cases of homicides and disappearances filed with state officials to a small number of cases represented or accompanied by NGOs (slightly more than 100 cases in Chihuahua; 212 in Nuevo León as of 2013), I find that more than 75 percent of NGO-accompanied cases report concrete investigatory advances as compared to fewer than 35 percent of average cases in both states (Gallagher 2017). The investigation of these cases is a crucial and largely overlooked outcome. Investigations push cases into the judicial pipeline where it is possible (though still unlikely) that a perpetrator will be charged, tried, and punished. Investigating a case means this first tenacious barrier to obtaining justice— that the state actually opens the case file—has been overcome.

While some cases accompanied by civil society organizations make significant judicial progress beyond the investigatory stage, including the credible conviction of guilty parties, I argue that rates of judicial progress vary significantly depending on the strategies, relationships, and political positioning of the accompanying organization. While these civil society organizations are usually classified together under the broad category of human rights organization, I argue that these organizations engage in quite different, though complementary, activities. I classify organizations as either *activists* or *advocates* based on the types of activities in which they engage.

Activists name, shame, critique, and confront the state while contradicting governmental narratives that blame victims. They are usually institutional outsiders who publicly and regularly denounce impunity, demand structural change, and take a consistently and vocally critical role of the justice system. They may have little contact with government officials, or the contact they have may be hostile and contentious. Activists produce the strongest political cost when they maintain a permanent presence at the location where judicial decisions are made, while also building national and international ties. Activists are also key actors in identity transformation. Leveraging the persuasive mechanisms of symbolic politics (Keck and Sikkink 1998), activists claim that victims of violence are deserving of justice and challenge government narratives that the victims are complicit in their own victimization because of their politics or affiliations with criminal groups.

Advocates facilitate communication and the sharing of investigatory information between judicial officials and the family members of victims. They build relationships with investigatory officials, human rights NGOs, and the family members of victims of violent crime. Advocates use their access to state officials to push for investigations and prosecutions to stay on track and to call for rapid state responses to new threats and violent events. They serve as a bridge, or interlocutor, between the government officials and those directly affected by violence, and advocates must have legitimacy with both of these constituencies to effectively occupy this role. Advocates must have an ongoing physical presence at the JDMS and are the key to embedding judicial actors in civil society networks. Advocates can have different institutional homes: family members of victims, local NGOs, cause lawyers, and international organizations all play this role in the different cases I document. Advocates exist only if the political opportunity structure (Tarrow 1994) is open enough to facilitate relationship building with state officials.

Ideally, activists and advocates have a complementary political dynamic: activists impose a political cost to impunity, and advocates channel this pressure into concrete judicial advances. When only activists are present, the state often takes symbolic actions that do not translate into concrete judicial progress; when only advocates are present, there is not the necessary political pressure to meaningfully promote judicial accountability. Later in this chapter I return to these civil society categories. In my case studies, I illustrate how external actors affect the configuration of activists and advocates within Chihuahua and Nuevo León.

"Lethal Violence" vs. "Enforced Disappearances" and "Extrajudicial Killings"

In the statistics cited above, I analyze disappearances and homicides, as opposed to "enforced disappearances" and "extrajudicial killings." This is a departure from standard approaches within human rights literature and international human rights law, which separate these crimes based on the presumed identity of the perpetrator. Human rights and transitional justice scholars analyze state-perpetrated lethal violence (categorized as extrajudicial killings and enforced disappearances under international law) separately from lethal violence perpetrated by civilians. Why do I choose a different approach?

Human rights violations in Mexico are not classified as such within the legal system. Under nearly any definition, a person who is, for example, disappeared at the hands of the police or military is a human rights violation. Yet since the state of Nuevo León did not have the crime of enforced disappearance[1] on the books until 2012, and even after this time was reluctant to classify disappearances as "enforced" because of the implication of state involvement, disappearance at the hands of state officials would not be apparent from the way that this crime was registered in the justice system, nor in the crimes that the perpetrators were found guilty of.

Relatedly, many cases of lethal violence in Mexico include involvement by both criminals and state agents and blur the line between state-perpetrated human rights violations and criminal violence. The legal charges filed against perpetrators that work for the Mexican government—homicide, kidnapping, and aggravated kidnapping—are the same as those filed against civilian perpetrators. In other words, human rights violations, which are understood as perpetrated by state officials, are often not meaningfully distinguishable from criminal violence in terms of how the cases are filed in the legal system, nor in the facts of their commission. Determining the identity of the perpetrators of violence as opposed to the material authors of a crime is often practically impossible, and in many cases I documented, it was difficult to distinguish between the actions, identities, and roles of criminals and state agents. Finally, it is also important to note that the vast majority of cases of lethal violence in Mexico are tried in the state-level court system. That lethal violence committed by state agents is not legally classified in Mexico as a human rights violation; that the lines of culpability between state and nonstate perpetrators of violence are blurred and often crimes are committed with the complicity of both; and finally, that these cases are overwhelmingly tried in state-level courts, as opposed to in international judicial contexts or even in Mexico's federal system, highlight the relevance of understanding local systems of justice in Mexico as we seek to understand the nature and status of human rights violations. By focusing on the lower-level courts with jurisdiction over the majority of cases of disappearances and homicides, I shift the focus to the location at which most Mexican citizens experience justice—or more often the lack thereof—and ask how international actors affect these locales.

Relationship Politics: Theorizing TANs in Local Judicial Systems

The foundational work of the transnational politics literature (Keck and Sikkink 1998: 204–205) has argued that human rights violations that take a life (a central, grave category of bodily harm) have been a central focus of claims made by TANs. These claims are ubiquitous, in part, because the right to life—or as it is referred to in international treaties, the right to physical integrity—is enshrined in every democracy. TANs have been increasingly successful at providing credible documentation of homicides and disappearances, pushing states to adopt pro-justice discourse, promoting policies aimed at decreasing these violations, and placing the killings of civilians on the local, national, and international agenda in cases of grievous violations.

Despite extensive TAN and governmental focus on lethal violence, understanding how to change state behavior—how do you get states to protect the right to physical integrity and punish those states that violate this right?—has remained fairly elusive. Keck and Sikkink (1998) argue that TANs seek to persuade, socialize, and exert pressure in order to improve a state's human rights behavior using four tactics: (1) information politics; (2) symbolic politics; (3) leverage politics; and (4) accountability politics. When TANs focus on improving judicial progress in local courts, I find that an additional tactic is often used to change state behavior, what I call *relationship politics*. I define this as the ability to locate strategically positioned

judicial decision-makers and influence their actions through repeated interactions with TAN members.

In this section I first argue against thinking about the state as a coher-
ent unitary actor and, instead, highlight the distinct identities, incentives,
and positionalities of state investigators—who comprise the strategically
positioned judicial decision-makers just cited. Next, I argue that since most
judicial decisions are made within the justice systems of Mexico's thirty-two
states, we cannot understand TANs' impact on human rights and justice
without looking closely at the JDMS. I emphasize the difficulties in accessing
justice that citizens face when they do not happen to live in the state capital.
Finally, I discuss the importance of relationships between investigators and
the family members of victims to investigations.

Judicial Actors Have Different Incentives
and Challenges than Other State Officials

The effectiveness of TANs is often thought to hinge on the persuasion of powerful actors. Command and control is often assumed: if orders from top officials call for a change in behavior—the end of enforced disappearances, for
example—the expectation is that in both authoritarian regimes and democracies there will be means of enforcing orders. In most democracies, elections
and performance-based assessments of state officials are considered mechanisms by which political appointees and bureaucrats can be incentivized to
carry out the orders of the higher-ups. See Figure 12.1.

In judicial bureaucracies where impunity is the norm, I argue that these
mechanisms are largely absent. Though the vocal support of high-level officials is most often a necessary condition for eroding impunity, I argue that it is
almost never sufficient. Judicial bureaucrats who are key to successful investigations are usually quite insulated from the boomerang of international political pressure. Police officers and members of the state and Federal Attorney
General's Offices and other investigative units are often lifelong bureaucrats
who are untouched by electoral cycles. While performance-based assessments
may exist on paper, they are often rare or nonexistent in practice. In Mexico,
even the most basic steps of an investigation—interviewing family members
or witnesses; gathering a victim's cell phone records; looking for a disappeared
person in morgues, hospitals, or jails—are exceedingly rare. It is difficult to
imagine a performance-based assessment of judicial bureaucrats having integrity with overall rates of judicial inaction at such high levels. Finally, these

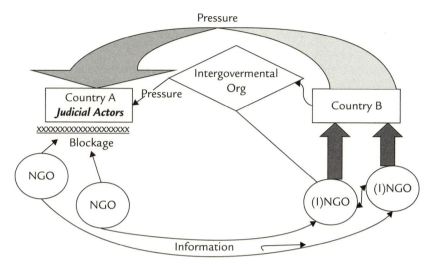

Figure 12.1. Boomerang Iteration 1: Judicial Actors. Source: Based on Keck and Sikkink 1998.

public officials may face loss of employment or threats to their own and their families' physical safety if they do proceed with investigations. Their key role in investigations together with their low profile (and lack of access to protective measures) makes them highly vulnerable to physical attack.

Given these circumstances, it is no surprise that both individuals and groups of judicial actors play a key role in producing and maintaining impunity at the local level—especially local and low-level members of the state judicial bureaucracy. Improving judicial success entails changing the actions of these state agents who are often anonymous and who make decisions that are opaque both to the public and to those who might seek to pressure them. Despite their anonymity and relatively low rank in the political hierarchy, in most countries these state officials process the vast majority of cases of violations of citizens' most serious rights—yet we know little about how or how well they work.

Location Matters: The Judicial Decision-Making Site—JDMS

Leverage politics remains a central tactic in understanding how TANs succeed in changing states' human rights behavior. This leverage is most often understood as international pressure leveraged from powerful external actors to promote compliance, led by powerful actors in the rights-violating country. Following Simmons (2009), however, I argue that the key site of contention, or "blockage" in the language of the boomerang, in the struggle over impunity is within the target country, at the JDMS, whereas the boomerang/spiral actors could be said to focus on the political decision-making site, which is nearly always presumed to be at the highest levels of government—at the presidency or perhaps the national legislature. I define the JDMS as the physical location in which those with the authority to make key decisions about the investigation and prosecution of the case (for example, which personnel will be assigned to the case) reside. The location of the judicial decision-making site varies by country. In Mexico, a federal system, this authority resides for most crimes in the state capitals. Decisions about investigative personnel are generally taken by the governor or the State Attorney General. See Figure 12.2.

The highlighted section in Figure 12.2 is the JDMS. In the cases I consider in this chapter, the judicial decision-making sites are in Monterrey, Nuevo León, and Chihuahua City, Chihuahua. As I discuss at length at the end of the chapter, the effectiveness of mobilization outside of the JDMS is drawn into sharp relief by the failures of mobilization and advocacy in Ciudad Juárez. Juárez is the largest city in the state of Chihuahua, but it is not the capital: Chihuahua City is. While I discuss how Juárez mobilizations were dealt a blow by the intervention of an external actor, efforts to advocate for justice

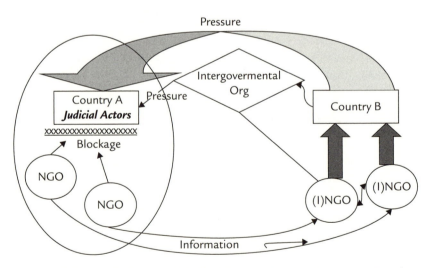

Figure 12.2. Boomerang Iteration 2: Judicial Decision-Making Site. Source: Based on Keck and Sikkink 1998.

were also made more difficult by the city's physical distance from Chihuahua City. Advocates from Juárez were not able to build the same types of relationships with investigators or be present at the judicial proceedings as their colleagues and allies in Chihuahua City. I argue that the distance has contributed significantly to the tenaciousness of impunity in the cases of disappearances and homicides in Juárez.

Relationships Between Investigatory Officials and Victims

The dynamics between activists, advocates, and state officials are key to explaining how mobilization and political pressure can, under certain circumstances, break through judicial inaction. In Mexico, there is deep mistrust between the citizens and their government, and this is especially true of judicial officials. The implicit message from government officials has often been that if a person became a victim of disappearance or homicide, it was because *estaban en algo*—he or she most probably was involved in some criminal activity. Under this logic, the victim's guilt excuses the lack of investigation and judicial progress. The governor's spokesperson in Nuevo León explained that he stopped pursuing an investigation into his own nephew's disappearance after he learned that his nephew had gambling debts: he must have been up to no good, so what was the use of investigating? Citizens, for their part, answer in survey after survey that they mistrust government generally, and police and public prosecutors are viewed by 66 percent and 43 percent of Mexicans, respectively, as frequently engaged in corruption.[2]

This mutual mistrust often results in a tense, silent standoff between judicial officials and citizens—including the family members and friends of victims of homicides and disappearances who might have relevant information about the investigation. I find that in cases in which advocates successfully establish relationships with judicial officials, it may be possible for investigators to gain key investigative information by establishing dialogue with the family members of victims and their advocates, and in several positive cases, these officials report that they have also shifted their views and beliefs about victims of violent crime. A head of state investigations in Nuevo León told me that meeting with the victim-advocacy group convinced him that family members could often supply important investigatory leads, and he also came to see victims differently. By getting to know their families, he had begun to work all of his cases differently—and now routinely asks to meet with the family members of disappeared victims. While the importance of the relationship between state investigators and the victims of crime is largely absent from the literature on judicial politics, literature on state-society relations (for example, on participatory budgeting: Baiocchi, Heller, and Silva 2011; Amengual 2016) argues that embedding state officials in civil society networks shifts their affective environment and should shift their actions as well. In other words, a concrete set of connections between the state and particular social groups is necessary for a functioning state (Evans 1995).

Given the importance of building relationships at the JDMS with the state officials involved in the investigation and prosecution of crimes, what does this imply for TANs, and especially for TAN members located externally, and those that identify as international NGOs or organizations? I will draw out these implications in the final section of this chapter.

External Intervention in Northern Mexico:
Different Impacts

The iterative model presented in Figures 12.1 and 12.2 was derived from my fieldwork, conducted intensively in Mexico between 2010 and 2013, with additional research trips in 2014–2016. In this section, I first highlight how external actors legitimated and strengthened the local human rights organization in Nuevo León. I recount how a national group was able to broker the local organization into an advocacy role. Next, I analyze the role of external intervention in Chihuahua. The particular dynamics of external intervention in Ciudad Juárez can serve as a cautionary tale of what happens when external intervention is not attuned to local organizing dynamics. While I am primarily thinking about the impact of external actors in terms of their effect on judicial progress in cases of lethal violence in domestic courts, these findings also speak to the ways in which external actors can strengthen (or undermine) local organizing efforts.

Nuevo León: External Groups Legitimate
and Broker Local Efforts

When I walked into Sanchez's[3] office, one of the state coordinators of investigations in Nuevo León, he had the recently issued Human Rights Watch report on enforced disappearance in Mexico pulled up on his computer screen. Though the meeting was to focus on the advances in cases of disappearances that would be the focus of the collaborative investigatory sessions that coming week, Sanchez first wanted to share his critique of the report. He complained that even if the report had gotten most things right, it hadn't fully recognized his personal role in moving a certain case forward in the justice system. He wondered if CADHAC (Citizens in Support of Human Rights), the local human rights organization that had asked for the meeting, could help him fix the error in the report.

It's worth dwelling on this snapshot in Sanchez's office and thinking about how it reflects the ways in which international actors influence local judicial processes. First, it highlights how local judicial investigators are increasingly attuned to the reputation costs of their actions in the international arena, and shows that they understand implicitly that local organizations are not only part of a larger human rights network, but that what the local organizations say holds weight with international actors. In other words, they understand that information flows up to the national and international levels from the local organizations.

Sanchez's vision—of CADHAC as a nationally and internationally connected organization—is hard-won. CADHAC is a small organization (one office, approximately five to ten employees) in Monterrey, Nuevo León, that regularly sends cases that show evidence of state involvement in a disappearance to the UN Special Rapporteur on Enforced Disappearances (UNSRED). CADHAC receives regular visits from the Office of the United Nations High Commissioner for Human Rights (OHCHR), Human Rights Watch, Amnesty International, and other transnational human rights advocates. When CADHAC launched an ultimately successful campaign to make enforced disappearance illegal in Nuevo León, most of these actors came in person to Nuevo León to help persuade state legislators and the state governor—the kind of international attention local elected officials are not accustomed to getting. These international networks also assisted in the drafting of this enforced-disappearance law and in the development of an investigatory protocol in the case of disappearances.

While this international legitimacy is important for CADHAC's ongoing interaction with state prosecutors, the tone and scene in Sanchez's office would raise a series of questions for most people familiar with the justice system in Mexico: namely, how did the local NGO end up conversing comfortably with the investigator's office in the first place? What kind of collaborative investigatory meeting are they preparing for? Beyond this, why would the state investigator think that the NGO would assist him in setting the record straight about his performance—rather than condemning him? To answer these questions, it is necessary to look more in depth at the trajectory of CADHAC particularly, and at the context of both violence and civil society in the state of Nuevo León.

CADHAC initially concentrated on documenting human rights abuses suffered by prisoners in the state's many prisons, and used the classic activist strategies of naming and shaming. As violence in Nuevo León worsened, CADHAC—Nuevo León's only NGO dedicated to defending civil and political human rights at the time—shifted its focus to disappearances. This shift was spurred by the demand of the people who came to CADHAC to ask for help: in 2009 and 2010, the organization received fewer than 15 reports of disappearances; in 2011, 105 cases; and in 2012, more than 215. CADHAC's relationship with the state, however, was nonexistent. As the director told me, "We had the idea that the investigators were incapable and overwhelmed. We saw working with them as impossible . . . let's not even talk about *resolving* these cases—there was no *movement* in any of them." In short, in the summer of 2011, you would not have found human rights leaders, lawyers, family members of victims, nor international researchers in Sanchez's office. What changed this?

The Movement for Peace with Justice and Dignity (MPJD) emerged in Mexico in the spring of 2011 in the wake of the murder of Javier Sicilia's son, Juan. Sicilia is a nationally known and respected poet in Mexico, and his son's murder was testament that many innocent people were suffering the consequences of the government's war on drugs. Sicilia emerged as a leading voice articulating a critique of this war, and in 2011 he led two national caravans to publicize the costs of this ill-conceived war. These caravans, made up of hundreds of people traveling in buses throughout Mexico, went to smaller towns and cities affected by drug-war violence in order to expose the violence and make space for the family members of victims of the drug war to share their testimonies. The MPJD's Northern Caravan arrived in Nuevo León in early June 2011. After being greeted by more than 1,500 people from more than 30 civil society organizations in the main square of the city, the State Attorney General welcomed Sicilia, other movement leaders, and CADHAC's founder into his office. After a midnight meeting, the attorney general gave an impromptu press conference at which he promised the assembled press, family members, and civil society that he would be personally accountable for doing everything possible to seek justice in cases of disappearances. CADHAC began to hold bimonthly meetings with the State Attorney General's Office in July 2011. The MPJD leadership flew in to Monterrey from Mexico City to attend the majority of the early meetings, and their presence summoned the media and served to remind the State Attorney General of the commitment he had made to personally oversee the investigations of disappearances. Their presence also made it clear that they regarded CADHAC as the legitimate interlocutor between victims and the state. CADHAC also credits the MPJD leadership with shifting their own beliefs about the state, and specifically teaching CADHAC members the value of dialogue. As a result of these meetings, the cases accompanied by CADHAC are being investigated at more than double the rate of similar cases in Nuevo León, four local police officers were detained for the enforced disappearance of a civilian,[4] and collaborative investigations between civil society and investigators are ongoing in Nuevo León.

CADHAC's physical proximity to the JDMS has been key to this progress. CADHAC is only about a ten-minute walk from the State Attorney General's Office, allowing members both to regularly march to the offices and to meet with the officials inside. The location also has impacted who was able to take advantage of the organization's services: a majority of the family members of victims who remained active with CADHAC over the long term lived closer to Monterrey, while those that lived farther away from the city found it arduous to travel to the city to participate in the many activities that CADHAC organized.

Juárez and Chihuahua City: External Actors and the JDMS

The State of Chihuahua has two large economically and politically important cities, Chihuahua City and Juárez. While they are similar in many ways, there has been considerably more international human rights attention focused on Juárez than Chihuahua City, due largely to the well-publicized killings of women, or femicides (Anaya Muñoz 2011). Juárez also sits on the U.S. border, with El Paso on the other side, and is, therefore, more visible and accessible to United States–based activists than Chihuahua City. If, as the boomerang model would suggest, TAN pressure was able to change the human rights behavior of states by improving judicial progress, we would expect there to be greater judicial success in Juárez than in Chihuahua City. I find that, to the contrary, civil society groups in Juárez have experienced lower levels of relative judicial success, while organizations in Chihuahua City have experienced significant judicial progress. I argue that the comparative judicial progress of the Chihuahua City–based advocates is due to two primary factors: (1) their location at the JDMS has enabled them to build strong relationships with state officials; (2) external intervention has played a brokering, legitimating role in Chihuahua City, while in Juárez it has been disruptive to local organizing.

Chihuahua City

One employee of the local NGO, Justicia para Nuestras Hijas (Justice for Our Daughters), located in Chihuahua City, explained that the NGO's director, Norma Ledezma, really has two offices: one in the small NGO, and one in the state prosecutor's office. As I spent several days shadowing the director, I found that we spent more time inside the prosecutor's office than in her office, attending two oral trials and having several meetings in the state prosecutor's office. Perhaps equally important, she informally greeted many judicial officials by name—stopping to talk with them briefly about pending investigatory activity. How did this happen? And what are the measurable consequences of these relationships?

Activist organizations were well established in Chihuahua City in the early 2000s, with an organization called El Barzón gaining significant statewide power. El Barzón started to mobilize in response to the suffering of farmers from the peso crisis in 1994 and grew into a partisan, pro-PRD social movement with diverse rural and urban constituencies. When Norma Ledezma's daughter was disappeared in 2002, she joined with a prominent El Barzón lawyer. Together, they founded Justicia para Nuestras Hijas. Like their counterparts in Nuevo León, they initially had very little judicial success and had difficulty accessing state officials. A turning point came in 2007. After intense activist pressure, the governor of Chihuahua agreed to bring in outside experts to review the case files of murdered and disappeared women. These experts, trained in Chile and Colombia in forensic science and investigation, sat down with Ledezma and taught her not only how to read a case file but what actions to ask state authorities to take in order to solve the cases, and how to look for investigatory leads. Using this training, Justicia began to analyze case files in a much more rigorous way than before. Ledezma asked for and received monthly meetings with the prosecutors, and in these meetings they began to review cases in detail. Ledezma also began to "give instructions" to the investigators as to how to advance investigations and follow leads.

In 2011, the informal structures and relationships that Ledezma had nurtured were institutionalized with the creation of a special investigative unit inside the State Attorney General's Office. While "special units" had been created previously, this one differed in a crucial way: Ledezma selected all twenty-seven of the staff and investigators to be assigned to this unit, with the agreement that these investigators, psychologists, and administrators would devote all of their time to working on the cases that Justicia presented to them. According to my original analyses of their cases, their results have been remarkable: in 105 cases of disappearances over the course of five years, 23 percent of cases have perpetrators indicted, and 12 percent have guilty verdicts. This differs markedly from the dire statistics in Chihuahua overall—in which 95 percent of the cases of disappearances show no sign that they are being investigated in any way.

Activists and advocates were solidly established in Chihuahua City in 2011. When the MPJD caravan came to town, Justicia, El Barzón, the Center for Women's Human Rights (CEDEHM),[5] and other local allies were able to organize a series of events to receive them. The caravan's arrival did not significantly tax these organizations and provided some benefit in terms of publicizing the violence in the state—Chihuahua City was also in the midst of a wave of violence, and the MPJD visit garnered national attention. The MPJD visit did not, however, fundamentally alter local organizing dynamics.

Ciudad Juárez

Unlike in Chihuahua, the MPJD's impact in Juárez ultimately contributed to a schism in the nascent coalition of civil society groups organizing to confront the historically high levels of violence in the city. In 2010, Juárez was famously the most dangerous city in the world. The number of homicides exploded in the early years of the Calderón administration: there were 1,500 in 2008; in 2009, 2,500; and in 2010, more than 3,000.[6] While the numbers of disappearances are less knowable, civil society organizations reported that these too increased.

How did civil society organize to advocate for justice in the wake of these killings and disappearances in Ciudad Juárez? Victim-led organizations in Juárez were exhausted in 2008. Many organizations had emerged in response to the femicides of the late 1990s and early 2000s, but internal conflict, the limited attention span of the international funding and solidarity community, and the brutality of the violence they confronted had created an organizational vacuum. In 2008, this meant that no group had the capacity to confront the brutal wave of homicides. Civil society organizations born previously were focused almost exclusively on violence against women, but the vast majority of the victims of the post-2008 homicides were men. These dynamics meant that in the most violent city in the world in 2010, there was not a single civil society organization that was capable of providing legal and psycho-social support to the family members of the murdered or disappeared male victims.

Recognizing this shortcoming, in 2010 a local human rights organization, the Paso del Norte Human Rights Center, which had played a fairly marginal role during the height of the femicides, began to accept a small number of cases of torture and enforced disappearance. Unlike their counterparts in Nuevo León and Chihuahua City, groups in Juárez did not have nor seek relationships or ask for meetings with government officials. As one staff member told me, "We thought—what are we going to gain from sitting down with the state? For us, it [was] different because the victimizer . . . was the state itself." Was the state more responsible for violence in Juárez than in Chihuahua City and Nuevo León? While this is an open question, I believe Paso del Norte's physical distance from the JDMS was an important factor in the organization's view of the government: the staff's lack of regular contact with investigatory officials facilitated the ability to dismiss them as just another part of the violent state. While activists and advocates in Monterrey and Chihuahua City also saw state officials as primary perpetrators of violence, their proximity to the JDMS meant that they were able to locate individual allies within the state investigatory apparatus and forge relationships with them.

In 2009 Paso del Norte joined with eighteen other groups in Juárez to confront the growing crisis of violence in the city. These groups—some of which were among the exhausted victim-led groups, but most of which were traditionally apolitical service-providing organizations—decided that they had three central beliefs in common: the need to demilitarize the city; the importance of justice and truth around violence; and the improving of governance. When President Calderón came to Juárez for the first time as president in 2010, this group was invited to a large public meeting to discuss the human rights situation in Juárez. The group decided to take a hard line, and famously, a member of the coalition, a mother of two teenagers killed in the brutal 2010 Villas de Salvárcar massacre, stood up in front of the group and told President Calderón that she could not welcome him to Juárez because "Juárez is in mourning." As a result of these critical comments, the president excluded the human rights coalition from subsequent meetings. For the Juárez human rights community, this was a defining moment: it would no longer dialogue with the Calderón administration and would broaden an activist repertoire of contention to include direct action and hunger strikes.

During this time, several of the Juárez groups were in close contact with Mexico City–based organizations. When the MPJD emerged in the spring of 2011, these relationships became politically key: Juárez activists played central roles in early MPJD events, and when the MPJD proposed ending a large national action called a caravan in Juárez, the groups there were eager to bring the national spotlight to Juárez. They had two conditions, however, for the caravan. First, there would not be a dialogue held with government authorities. Second, the caravan would need to call for the immediate demilitarization—the removal of the Mexican Army—from Chihuahua. As one member of the planning committee stated, "We told him [Javier Sicilia] that this wasn't the place for dialogue with authorities—we told him that we were at a point where we wanted to call for an immediate end to militarization. So we thought that this was the agreement—that the Caravan would come, but that it was clear that here we didn't want to have the fight over [these basic understandings]" (author interview, February 2013). The MPJD seemed to agree with this condition, and the intensive planning effort to host the caravan commenced. To prepare for the caravan, the nascent group of human rights organizations worked hard to bring together a very broad coalition of organizations. When the caravan of more than five hundred people arrived in Juárez in June 2011, caravan participants were met by at least as many locals, and together they engaged in two intensive days of reflection and drafting of a joint agenda for the MPJD and the Juárez coalition. As more than one thousand people worked to come to consensus, the result was somewhat predictably chaotic: a document containing 460 points was drafted. Overall, the document was much more antigovernment than the MPJD had previously articulated. Most important, this document called for the immediate withdrawal of the Mexican Army from Chihuahua—a demand that had been central to the Juárez coalition groups but not to the MPJD. The next day, in an impromptu press conference just across the border in El Paso, MPJD leader Sicilia disavowed the new document.

Sicilia's disavowal of the joint statement angered and alienated many of the assembled groups and led directly to a breakdown in the relationship among the Juárez organizations. Paso del Norte was caught in an untenable position between its local allies and the MPJD. This division would undermine Paso del

Norte's viability as a coalition leader for years. For Juárez, a city in the midst of a terrible wave of violence, the MPJD's visit resulted in the schism of a nascent coalition of human rights activists– something the city could ill afford.

Implications for External Actors

What can we learn from these brief case studies about the role of external actors in Mexico, and in particular their possible role in strengthening local struggles for justice in cases of lethal violence?

Groups Outside JDMS Can Broker Locals into Advocacy Roles

While groups located outside of the JDMS cannot play primary roles as advocates or activists, local human rights NGOs and victims' organizations in Mexico needed to be brokered into advocacy roles by externally located actors. State officials were suspicious of local actors and reported that they were hesitant to build relationships with groups that had been critical of them in the past, and that they deemed to be associated with politically and socially undesirable groups. This resistance on the part of state officials was overcome in the Nuevo León case by the MPJD delegation, and in Chihuahua City by the international forensic experts. Local public officials in these cases were receptive to meeting with international actors, who in turn explicitly conferred legitimacy onto local groups. The international actors asked state officials to continue to meet with the local groups and to regard them as worthy interlocutors. As externally based actors consider their possible role in fighting impunity, they should assess whether they are politically positioned to facilitate productive relationships between locally based nonstate actors and state judicial officials.

External Groups' Impact Depends on Local
Activist/Advocate Dynamics in Local Efforts

The central work of externally located TAN members—documenting human rights abuses, diffusing this knowledge, and exerting pressure on state officials to change policies and practices—remains an important part of

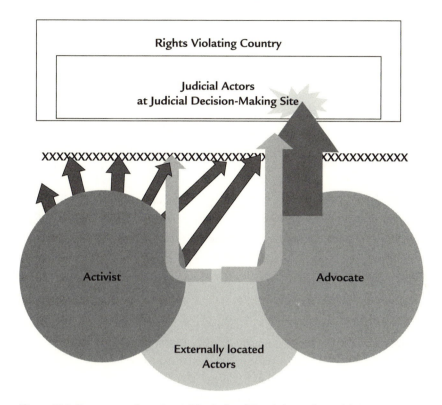

Figure 12.3. Boomerang Iteration 3: The Judicial Breakthrough Model. Source: Based on Keck and Sikkink 1998.

supporting both activists and advocates struggling against impunity on the ground. However, these actions are best understood as accompanying and strengthening the efforts of advocates and activists and should be undertaken in coordination with groups based at the JDMS. In this final iteration of the boomerang model, I theorize that advocates are best positioned to break the judicial blockage and build relationships with judicial actors, and that this breakthrough is key in changing judicial behavior and improving the provision of justice. Activists, on the other hand, play an important role in chipping away at the judicial blockage, creating the political pressure necessary for advocates to be able to break through the blockage of impunity. Externally located actors can strengthen activists by legitimating and publicizing their critiques of the state, and can strengthen advocates by brokering them into new relationships with state actors, funding their efforts, and conferring legitimacy on them by making it known that the advocacy groups bring inter-national visibility and the endorsement of the international human rights community. See Figure 12.3.

With this in mind, the Juárez case is instructive and cautionary in two ways. First, despite historically strong international mobilization in the wake of femicide killings (Anaya Muñoz 2011), there was not a focus on building relationships and shifting behavior at the JDMS. While it can be persuasively argued that the levels of violence and corruption in the state of Chihuahua at the time effectively precluded effective advocacy and judicial progress, it is notable that Chihuahua City–based organizations were able to establish themselves and build relationships with state investigators, while Juárez-based organizations lacked these relationships. If the JDMS is acknowledged as strategically important in the fight against impunity, more conscious efforts could be made to formalize cooperation with Chihuahua City–based groups (these collaborations did happen more informally). Second, the Juárez case reminds external actors of the importance of understanding the local orga-nizing context and of identifying the activist/advocate dynamics. Since brief interventions can have a lasting impact on the organizing capacity of local coalitions, strategic considerations of local conditions are vital.

Conclusion

As the human cost of violence in Mexico continues to grow, it is clear that Mex-ico is in crisis. While it is much more difficult to see the opportunities, this chapter draws lessons learned from past collaborations between local, national, and international actors committed to addressing impunity. I argue that by clarifying certain concepts and reconceptualizing the boomerang model, we may be able to see opportunities for productive action by external actors.

I argue that conceptual clarity is important in three ways. First, I propose a more inclusive definition of what constitutes a "human rights violation" in the current Mexican context. I make the case that fuzzy legal categories and shared identity and activities between state and nonstate perpetrators of lethal violence make homicides indistinguishable from extrajudicial killings and disappearances indistinguishable from enforced disappearances. Con-sequently, I argue that we must think broadly about the category of lethal violence as the target of human rights activist and advocacy efforts. Second, after highlighting the vital role of local organizations in the struggle against impunity, I differentiate the actions of civil society organizations between activists, who use confrontational, critical tactics and contradict state narratives that blame the victim, and advocates, who serve as interlocutors able to facilitate the sharing of investigatory information between the state investigators and civil society actors. Third, I argue for the importance of locating the JDMS, or the physical location in which key decisions are made and decisive battles are fought over the judicial fate of cases; and I argue that relationship politics—specifically, the relationships between the family members of the victims of violent crimes and their civil society allies—can be definitive in the provision of justice in local courts.

Using these concepts, I draw concrete lessons for external actors who are interested in strengthening the efforts of local organizations that are combating impunity. I discuss the important ways that groups outside the JDMS can broker locals into advocacy roles. Finally, I use case evidence from Mexico to illustrate how external groups can either strengthen, legitimize, and enable local advocacy work or play the role of spoiler if they are not attuned to local needs and political dynamics.

NOTES

Introduction

1. World Bank data: https://data.worldbank.org/indicator/VC.IHR.PSRC.P5 (consulted: October 20, 2017).

Chapter 1

We thank Alonso Rodriguez, Karen Silva, Fernando Gómez, and José Luis Torres for their collaboration. We also thank Hilary Burke for her translation. A previous version of this text was published in *Perfiles Latinoamericanos* in 2017.

1. *Favelas* is used to refer to the shanty towns, in or outside the city, in Rio.

2. To build the press database, we reviewed the digital archives of two nationally distributed newspapers: *El Universal* and *La Jornada*. If the figures for the dead and wounded did not coincide in the two newspapers, a third nationally distributed paper was consulted *(Reforma)* or a fourth *(La Crónica de Hoy)*. If the figures continued to differ, the lowest number of deaths and the highest number of wounded would be recorded (see Silva Forné, Pérez Correa, and Gutiérrez).

3. Information in the press regarding clashes tends to privilege the most violent cases with the greatest number of deaths and to exclude those that resulted only in injuries. This bias increases the value of the lethality index.

4. More than three-fourths of the clashes registered in the press database involved the participation of the Army, so in the previous study, information was requested only from that institution.

5. These indexes were obtained from official data.

6. INFOMEX is Mexico's electronic system by which people can ask for information from public institutions.

7. Information requests were made to the following federal offices: SEDENA, the Ministry of the Navy (SEMAR), and the Federal Police. In this chapter, for the years 2007 and 2013, the information requests used were 0413100088114 (Federal Police) and 0001300092314 (Navy). For the years 2014 and 2015, the information requests used were 0413100158815 (Federal Police) and 0001300105915 (Navy).

For the Army, we used information request 0000700211714 for the years 2007–2014, as information about civilians killed and wounded was denied after April 2014. Information regarding clashes (shoot-outs) was given and included in this text.

8. For the methodology followed to build the press database, see note 2.

9. The press information reviewed for this study reflected only 15 percent of the clashes reported by the official figures for this period. However, trends are the same. In the case of the

Army, 26 clashes were reported in 2008, and that figure rose as high as 129 in 2011, later falling to 43 in 2014.

10. We take the figure of civilians killed from 2013 since SEDENA provided figures on the dead and wounded in 2014 only up to the month of March. Regarding the press information, the trend is similar to what appears in SEDENA's data: the annual total of civilians killed in clashes with the Army went from 653 in 2011 to 238 in 2014. As stated earlier, the figures on civilians killed in clashes that were culled from the press represent about 50 percent of the official figures. The fact that the national press under review captured 15 percent of the clashes but 50 percent of the deaths of civilians reflects the press's selection of the most violent cases, making evident the implicit difficulties and caution required in using that source.

11. The number of dead civilians decreased in 2013 and 2014 from the peaks reached in 2011 and 2012, but it is striking that the Federal Police's official figures indicated fewer civilians killed in clashes in 2014 (forty-one) than those registered by the national press (fifty-one), which reported on a significantly smaller number of clashes. This fact underscores the need to continue obtaining information from different sources to build this and other indicators and compare their evolution in the coming years.

12. The differences between the press's and official data in the case of the Navy are very high. According to official data, only six and eight civilians died during clashes in 2011 and 2012, respectively. However, according to the press, during these clashes, fifty-two civilians were killed in 2011 and thirty-six in 2012.

13. The lethality indexes calculated in this chapter include only civilians reported as suspected or "probable" members of organized crime. We do not take into account the individuals killed or wounded who were reported as bystanders (in Spanish, reported as *probables civiles*). The categories that both the police and the Navy use to divide combatants from civilians, however, are important in terms of understanding the context of war in which these institutions operate and use lethal force.

14. Attorney General's Office (PGR), request 0001700326814.

15. Article 7 of the Federal Transparency and Access to Public Government Information Law. Furthermore, the Army's decision not to gather information also violates the institution's own regulations on the use of force.

16. The prologue to the *Manual on the Use of Force to be Applied to the Three Armed Forces* establishes that the use of force must be governed by "the principles of opportuneness, proportionality, rationality and legality" Diario Oficial de la Federación.

17. Resolution 34/169 of the UN General Assembly, approved on December 17, 1979.

18. Adopted by the Eighth UN Congress on the Prevention of Crime and the Treatment of Offenders on September 7, 1990, in Havana, Cuba.

19. Published in the Diario Oficial de la Federación on April 23, 2012.

20. Published on May 30, 2014, in the Diario Oficial de la Federación.

21. Article 13 of the Directive establishes that the bodies that constitute the Army should draft manuals and protocols about when the use of force would be appropriate for specific circumstances, as well as the measures needed to avoid collateral damage due to the illegitimate use of force.

22. The notion of rationality is linked in the Manual to an assessment of the objectives that are being pursued with the use of force, the circumstances of the aggression, and the aggressor's personal characteristics and capacities. That is to say, the Manual reiterates that when faced with a hostile situation, the federal forces can resort to the use of force only if they cannot adopt

other alternative means. Finally, with regard to the principle of legality, the Manual replicates the criteria found in the Directive without adding new elements: the use of force must adhere to the current rules and regulations and must protect human rights.

Chapter 2

1. The cases of middle- and upper-class cattle breeders and walnut farmers of Chihuahua stand out. Also, the cases of leaders of mid-sized businesses from Nuevo León and Michoacán; doctors from Guerrero; and teachers from Tamaulipas. Their financial situations were stable before they were victimized and had to pay large sums of money to criminal gangs in protection quotas or ransoms for the release of kidnapped relatives.

2. The author has monitored violence-induced internal displacement in Mexico and elsewhere in Latin America systematically since February 2011. She collaborates with CMDPDH on fieldwork, data collection, and assistance to IDPs. The results of this monitoring work have been included in IDMC 2015 and 2016.

3. Full names are avoided to protect their identities.

4. Prospera is a program of social inclusion launched in September 2014, implemented by the Ministry of Social Development (SEDESOL), which provides underprivileged families with education, access to health care, economic and productive opportunities, help with housing, and a small stipend for food. The stipend is normally based on the economic conditions of the area where the beneficiary lives; these are called priority areas. Many IDPs stated that when they were displaced, they tried to claim their Prospera stipend, but it was denied to them because they could not provide a local address, and when they could, their new address was in an area with a lower stipend or was not included in the program at all.

5. Since 2014, Mayor Juan Raúl Acosta Salas of Choix has supported IDPs living within his jurisdiction with money for rent for the poorest families, food, school enrollment for IDP children, and water.

6. IACHR 149 periods of sessions, available at http://www.youtube.com/watch?v=S -tPYwm8asE.

7. Under-Secretary Campa holds this view, along with other officials: Alejandro Alday (former Director General of Human Rights within the Ministry of Foreign Affairs, SRE), interviewed in June 2015. A former member of the Executive Commission of Assistance to Victims (CEAV), Carlos Rios Pieter, also expressed concern with this definition.

8. For information on the composition of CEAV, see http://www.ceav.gob.mx/comites -integrados-en-la-ceav/.

9. At a meeting at CEAV on June 17, 2015, President Jaime Rochín mentioned CEAV's incapacity to act upon that decision because of persisting legal discrepancies and disagreements among the commissioners.

10. SEDESOL announced that IDPs could receive assistance through some of its social programs (Prospera), provided that they were registered beforehand at RENAVI.

11. Questions like this already appeared in the 2000 population census; however, for the 2010 census, the question asking respondents to specify the municipality from which they fled was eliminated; so the 2010 census gives us information only if the respondent left the state or the country within five years; the causes of migration are not very specific, and a general question of insecurity was introduced.

12. The author requested to participate by e-mail and in telephone conversations with members of INEGI's board; no other scholars who have been doing research on forced internal

displacement were invited either; and CMDPDH, which made the formal request for the inclusion of the questions, was not informed that the consultations were taking place.

13. As a result of recommendations by the special rapporteurs on the rights of the internally displaced and the rights of indigenous peoples, in 2004 Mexican authorities presented an action plan with its commitments to improve the situation of displaced communities and create an office to oversee the protection of and assistance to IDPs. The creation of the interministerial Working Group and the sponsoring of a seminar on forced displacement are the only "tangible" actions taken by the government in more than ten years.

14. The first meeting was on February 18, 2015, and the second on March 20, 2015. The participants were representatives of SEGOB, the Federal Attorney General's Office (PGR), INFONAVIT and the National Council on Housing, SEDESOL, CONAPO, CEAV, CMDPDH, and Mexico's Autonomous Technologic Institute.

15. CMDPDH, the Internal Displacement Monitoring Center, the Center for Justice and International Law, and the Loyola Law School in Los Angeles signed the petition.

16. For photographs, see Rubio 2014.

Chapter 3

A special thanks to Jairo Antonio López for comments and suggestions on the preliminary version of this chapter.

1. The then-governor of Chihuahua minimized and even justified the killings, citing the inappropriate conduct of the murdered women, leading the National Human Rights Commission (CNDH) to issue Recommendation 44/98.

2. In 2001, the bodies of eight women were found in a zone outside Ciudad Juárez. The Red de Mujeres de Ciudad Juárez, backed by the Center for the Integral Development of Women, filed a case before the Inter-American Commission on Human Rights (IACHR) in 2002, resulting in a sentence against the state by the Inter-American Court on Human Rights (IACtHR) in 2009. The IACtHR's sentence recognized that the women's murders took place in a context of violence and impunity regarding gender violence in Ciudad Juárez and required the Mexican government to take special measures to address this phenomenon (IACtHR 2009).

3. The local campaigns of family-member collectives linked up with national nongovernmental organizations to create, toward the end of 2015, the Movimiento por Nuestros Desaparecidos (Movement for Our Disappeared) in Mexico, in which all of the local campaigns previously mentioned participate, as well as many other campaigns that are in large part composed of women. In 2016, they launched the campaign "#SinLasFamiliasNo," which calls for a General Law on Forced Disappearance that would be based on, among other things, the experiences of the families, as well as their active participation in the development and monitoring of public policies on this topic. With regard to this campaign, see www.sinlasfamiliasno.org.

4. An example of this occurred in the city of Tijuana, one of the places identified as a center for the trafficking of women and girls, when in October 2015, the mayor of the city, Jorge Astiazarán, presented the a campaign to promote the city, "Tijuana Coqueta" ("Flirty Tijuana"), denounced by civil society organizations as a decision that promotes sexual tourism despite its categorization as a crime (Heras 2015; SDPnoticias.com 2015).

5. The Inter-Ministerial Commission to Prevent, Punish, and Eradicate Crimes in Trafficking in Persons is the authority in charge of defining and coordinating the implementation of a state policy regarding human trafficking, laid out in the General Law to Prevent, Sanction, and

Eradicate Crime in Trafficking in Persons and Protecting and Assisting the Victims of These Crimes (Article 84).

Chapter 4

In developing the ideas presented here, I have used the research and work carried out by the Information Group on Reproductive Choice (www.gire.org.mx).

1. Yucatán, Chiapas, Tabasco, Guerrero, Michoacán, Tamaulipas, Baja California, Morelos, Mexico City, State of México, Querétaro, Veracruz, Puebla, Sinaloa, Durango, and Chihuahua.

2. Baja California, Baja California Sur, Durango, Zacatecas, Aguascalientes, Colima, Hidalgo, Puebla, State of México, Mexico City, Guerrero, Oaxaca, Campache, and Quintana Roo.

3. Baja California, Baja California Sur, Chihuahua, Durango, Zacatecas, San Luis Potosí, Aguascalientes, Hidalgo, Colima, State of México, Mexico City, Puebla, Guerrero, Oaxaca, Tabasco, Campeche, and Quintana Roo.

4. Mexico City (30), Baja California (3), Guerrero (3), Oaxaca (2), and Durango (1).

5. Baja California (1), Chihuahua (2), Mexico City (2), Oaxaca (4), Puebla (1), and San Luis Potosí (2).

6. Baja California (2), Baja California Sur (1), Durango (1), Mexico City (18), Querétaro (1), State of México (33), and Tlaxcala (3).

7. Baja California (2), State of México (9), Oaxaca (1), Puebla (1), and Tlaxcala (2).

Chapter 5

I conducted part of this research while serving as consultant for El Colegio de la Frontera Norte in Tijuana, Mexico, and The Ford Foundation in Mexico City, between 2013 and 2015. Kim Krasevac, Dolores Paris, Rene Zenteno, and Sonja Wolf shared insightful remarks and constructive comments on earlier versions of some of the arguments presented here. I wrote this chapter while a visiting fellow at the Centre for the Study of Human Rights at the London School of Economics. Professor Chetan Bhatt, Dr. Margot Salomon, and Dr, Claire Moon made this possible. I am indebted to them. Sara Ulfsparre and Heidi El-Megrisi helped me overcome unimaginable bureaucratic complications. I would also like to thank Daniela Melisa Gómez, Alfonso Moreno, and Mitzi Muñoz for their help with research. Finally, I would like to thank Alejandro Anaya-Muñoz and Barbara Frey for detailed comments.

1. I conducted twenty of these interviews as a consultant to the Ford Foundation between December 2012 and March 2013. Another sixty-two interviews were carried out as part of the research study "An Analysis of Political Actors in the Design and Implementation of Migration Policy and Management in Mexico," directed by Dolores Paris at El Colegio de la Frontera Norte, between July 2013 and July 2014. For security reasons, I opted to preserve the confidentiality of the interviewees. I conducted one last interview in 2016.

2. This chapter focuses primarily on the immigration policy of the Felipe Calderón administration (2006–2012). The situation of transmigrants has changed little in the present administration of President Peña Nieto (2012–2018). In fact, for the majority of human rights activists, the human rights crisis has worsened. But this is a topic I address in the conclusion.

3. The numbers reported by CNDH correspond to 2009 and 2010 only. Had the situation improved, the government would surely have published some reports on this issue, primarily in order to respond to criticism from the international human rights community. The lack of transparency in information related to the kidnapping of migrants in transit in Mexico offers

an indicator of the continuing seriousness of this problem. Can we extrapolate the 2010 data to explain what is happening in 2016? Methodologically, we cannot argue that the number of migrants kidnapped in 2010 is exactly the same as in 2016. However, it would be difficult to infer that the number of kidnappings has decreased. Multiple migrant-rights organizations and transnational human rights bodies have recently shown that, far from improving, the situation faced by migrants continues to worsen. Furthermore, there are other unsettling figures that, while not specific to the migrant situation, help further illuminate how the security situation in the country has continued to deteriorate. During the first two years of the Enrique Peña Nieto administration (2012–2014), the yearly average of people murdered was greater than the yearly average reported during the government of Felipe Calderón (Hope 2016). The number of kidnappings in Mexico increased by 52 percent (Martínez 2015). Did the number of kidnapped migrants increase by the same percentage?

4. Interview with a human rights activist of the Program on Migrants of the Human Rights Institute of the Central American University, El Salvador, August 22, 2013.

5. Ibid.

6. Interview with an officer of the Local Human Rights Commission in the southeast of Mexico, May 13, 2013.

7. Interview with a Guatemalan migrant. Guatemala City, August 19, 2013.

8. Ibid.

9. Interview with a journalist and expert on transmigrants. Mexico City, April 8, 2016.

10. Ibid.

11. Interview with a Guatemalan migrant.

12. This section of the chapter explores how different state actors take part in the migration industry. This section shows that securitization theories cannot explain why there are migrants who pass through Mexico without being perceived by the authorities as a "threat" and then reach the United States without being detained or deported. This chapter focuses on undocumented transit migration. However, it can also help to shed light on the structuring of social relations between authorities and (documented and undocumented) foreigners. The discriminatory treatment of certain foreigners is based not only on racial prejudice but also on economic factors.

13. Ordinary Mexicans are beyond securitization theories because these theories talk about "the state" and its agents. These theories ignore the fact that ordinary citizens also commit atrocities. Analysis of the reasons why so many ordinary Mexicans are involved in committing abuses in the context of the war on drugs is beyond the scope of this chapter.

14. Interview with a Guatemalan consular official. The State of México, March 19, 2014.

15. Interview with Federico Mastrogiovanni, Journalist. Mexico City, February 25, 2014. (He agreed to be quoted).

16. Interview with a member of Congress and of the Commission on Migrant Affairs of the House of Representatives. Mexico City, January 2014.

17. See note 3.

18. Interview with a former member of the United Nations and expert on the human rights of migrants. May 29, 2014.

Chapter 6

1. Here Roberto is referring to the North American Free Trade Agreement (NAFTA), which was signed into law on January 1, 1994. NAFTA opened Mexico's economy to competition with

Canada and the United States by lowering barriers to trade including quotas and tariffs. While NAFTA has helped Mexico's industrial sector, it has decimated much of the country's agriculture sector, as many small and medium-size farmers and ranchers are simply unable to compete with their highly subsidized counterparts in the United States and Canada.

Chapter 7

1. In the United States, the specificities of cases are not made public. The only available data is that provided by civil organizations and legal firms litigating cases, which provide case summaries and sometimes copies of the legal rulings issued by the courts. For this chapter, the gender-based cases analyzed were the thirty-one cases made available by the Center for Gender & Refugee Studies (San Francisco, California), which also included persecution and sexual violence involving two gay men. The period covered is 1998–2014. Other less formal databases consulted were those of the New Mexico–based Southwest Asylum and Migration Institute (SAMI) and the Texas-based Carlos Spector Law Firm, both from 2006 to 2012.

2. Author interview with Anna Jessica Cabot, managing attorney at Las Americas Immigrant Advocacy Center. El Paso, Texas, June 25, 2012.

3. Ibid.

4. Author interview with Nancy Oretskin, attorney and cofounder of SAMI. El Paso, Texas, June 24, 2012.

5. Critical legal geography is a critical framework based on the idea that legal meaning produces social space, not only in material but also in symbolic ways. In addition, this approach assumes that the legal is not static but constantly made and unmade by subjects that perform law (Delaney 2010).

6. The empirical data supporting this assertion are abundant. First, the merging of criminals and law-enforcement officials in criminal gangs such as Los Zetas, a drug cartel formed by former and active soldiers; La Línea, a gang of active police officers who commit murders for the Juárez Cartel; and the local police in the Ayotzinapa case, who kill for Guerreros Unidos cartel. Second, the impunity of high-level politicians from all political parties accused of links to drug cartels and money laundering, such as Humberto Moreira (Coahuila), Tomás Yarrington (Tamaulipas), and Mario Villanueva (Quintana Roo). Not to mention the recurrence of forced disappearances and femicide in states where governors have been linked to criminal gangs profiting from sexual trafficking, human smuggling, and drug trafficking (notably Veracruz, Puebla, and Tlaxcala).

7. The Federal Courts' Circuits are geographically distributed as follows:

First Circuit: Maine, Massachusetts, New Hampshire, Puerto Rico, and Rhode Island
Second Circuit: Connecticut, New York, and Vermont
Third Circuit: Delaware, New Jersey, Pennsylvania, and Virgin Islands
Fourth Circuit: Maryland, North Carolina, South Carolina, and Virginia
Fifth Circuit: Louisiana, Mississippi, and Texas
Sixth Circuit: Kentucky, Michigan, Ohio, and Tennessee
Seventh Circuit: Illinois, Indiana, and Wisconsin
Eighth Circuit: Arkansas, Iowa, Minnesota, Missouri, Nebraska, North Dakota, and South Dakota
Ninth Circuit: Alaska, Arizona, California, Guam, Hawaii, Idaho, Montana, Nevada, Northern Mariana Islands, Oregon, and Washington

Tenth Circuit: Colorado, Kansas, New Mexico, Oklahoma, Utah, and Wyoming
Eleventh Circuit: Alabama, Florida, and Georgia
Federal Circuit: Washington, D.C. and federal agencies

8. Author interview with Crystal F. Massey, researcher/human rights advocate and cofounder of the New Mexico–based SAMI. El Paso, Texas, June 23, 2012.

Chapter 8

1. See, e.g., *Matter of S-E-G-*, 24 I&N Dec. 579 (BIA 2008); *Matter of E-A-G-*, 24 I&N Dec. 591 (BIA 2008); *Matter of M-E-V-G-*, 26 I&N Dec (BIA 2014); *Matter of W-G-R-*, 26 I& N Dec. 208 (BIA 2014).

2. See extensive litigation and academic analysis of this issue over the past four decades, following the U.S. Supreme Court case that set standards for holding municipalities liable for the actions of their police officers, *Monell v. Department of Social Services of the City of New York*, 436 US 658 (1978).

3. For more information, see the official website of the federal courts, http://www.uscourts .gov/judges-judgeships/authorized-judgeships/judgeship-appointments-president, or the official website of the Department of Justice, https://www.justice.gov/eoir/board-of-immigration -appeals.

Chapter 9

My sincere thanks to Barbara Frey and Alejandro Anaya-Muñoz for their support in the translation and copyediting of this text.

1. For more about the relationship between democracy and human rights, see Vázquez 2010b and 2013.

2. This literature is particularly well known due to the four-volume work coordinated by Guillermo O'Donnell, Philippe Schmitter, and Laurence Whitehead (1986a, 1986b, 1986c, and 1986d), crossing later into the work of Juan Linz, and to the Mexican scholarship produced by José Woldenberg and Leonardo Valdés.

3. There has been much theoretical development on this point stemming from the investigation of liberal democracy by Dahl, Bobbio, and Sartori, to name only a few.

4. This is not to say that there are no violations of these rights today in Latin America, but rather that the pattern of such violations has changed.

5. Conceptualizations regarding the rule of law or state organization are not neutral. When the structural relations that compose a state are obscured, one loses sight of this lack of neutrality (Santos 2009; Stammers 2007, 2009).

6. In fact, just in March 2015, a group of Latin American human rights organizations specializing in freedom of expression requested a hearing with IACHR about diversity, pluralism, and media concentration in Latin America (AAVV 2015).

7. This refers to an alleged act of corruption performed by Mexico's president involving one of the business groups that has most benefited during this administration: Grupo Higa. This case involved not only the president and his wife but also an important media group, Televisa, as well as the Secretary of Finance and presidential hopeful Luis Videgaray.

8. Virgilio Andrade also served as a member of Mexico's Federal Electoral Institute between 2003 and 2010, an agency that is supposed to have an autonomous institutional standing.

9. Beyond the dispute that exists within the judicial branch between pro-human rights and pro-sovereignty magistrates, the appointment of Eduardo Medina-Mora—former director of the Center for Intelligence and National Security (2000–2005), former Secretary of Public Security (2005), former Attorney General (2006–2009), and former ambassador to the United Kingdom and the United States (2009–2015)—was interpreted as the incorporation of a minister who had as his principal goal the increase of conservative and anti–human rights views on the Supreme Court. In particular, his appointment was seen as a way of supporting impunity for human rights violations, itself a product of the security policies introduced by Calderón and continued by Peña Nieto. This fear was borne out by his deciding vote in April 2015, when the Supreme Court decided that *arraigo* (prolonged pretrial detention without charges) was constitutional. Another example was his vote against the right of same-sex couples to adopt children, in August 2015.

10. The Federal District's Human Rights Commission had previous presidents (Emilio Álvarez Icaza and Luis González Plasencia) who had tense relationships with the city's government. In this context, Mayor Miguel Ángel Mancera decided to avoid such tensions with an autonomous agency by securing the appointment of a party loyalist, losing all of the organizational presence, ability to summon, and legitimacy that the commission had gained. It is worth mentioning that in this case the simulation was carried out by the governing party in Mexico City, the Party of the Democratic Revolution (PRD). However, my critical argument on simulation and democracy in Mexico refers to all actors that make up the party system.

11. The Mexican government declared that the nominations to occupy these positions would be for retired diplomats. It is important to highlight that diplomats have the task of defending the government, but not human rights.

12. For further development of this point, see Vázquez 2008.

13. In a similar vein, Zalaquet understands corruption as a practice or phenomenon that involves the use or abuse of power and public functions to improperly generate wealth or private benefits (Zalaquet 2007: 19).

14. For an analysis of the current status of corruption studies, and of the relationship between corruption and human rights, see Vázquez 2016.

15. Various sources have documented security forces' continued use of torture as a mechanism for obtaining self-incriminating confessions. In fact, the bulk of the instances of torture happen between the time of arrest and the detained person's presentation before a judge, a period that may itself exceed twenty-four hours. This explains the pervasiveness of the logic in Mexico, as described in the 2014 Amnesty International report, which argues that 64 percent of people in Mexico fear being tortured if they are detained—a number that is higher only in Brazil, with 80 percent (Díaz 2014).

Chapter 10

1. The United States has recently tied some funds of the security-aid package to Mexico known as the "Merida Initiative" to some particular human rights issues. In October 2015, in the midst of the current human rights crisis, the U.S. State Department withheld $5 million of Merida Initiative aid (Partlow 2015). This amount, however, seems insignificant for a country like Mexico, with over $6 billion budgeted for its armed forces in 2015 (Secretaria de Hacienda y Credito Publico 2015).

2. The complete list of indicators can be seen at Rice and Patrick 2008: 9.

3. For the effects of corruption on state capacities, see Chabat 2002: 138–139.

4. In some states—Chihuahua, Durango, Sinaloa, and Guerrero—impunity in murders reached over 90 percent in 2010 (México Evalúa 2012: 16–19).

5. We borrow the Swiss cheese metaphor from Jeffrey Rubin's highly influential account on the patched and uneven presence of power of the Partido Revolucionario Institucional (PRI) regime in postrevolutionary Mexico (Rubin 1997).

Chapter 11

This work was carried out with the support of Diana Mora and María José Urzúa, who in their roles as research assistants contributed to the collection and systematization of much of the information presented here.

1. This Council has subsidiary bodies: The Federal Judicial, the Federal Institute of Public Defense, the Federal Institute of Specialists in Bankruptcy Proceedings, the Judicial Inspection Unit, and the Federal Prosecutor's Office.

2. In Mexico, the legal precedents developed by the Plenary of the Supreme Court or in its Chambers or its Tribunals are binding for lower agencies when the same criteria are used to decide five consecutive court rulings in the exact same way. In the case of the Supreme Court, all precedents are binding in Constitutional Claims and Actions of Unconstitutionality when these decisions have been made with a majority of eight or more votes. http://www.juridicas.unam.mx /publica/rev/boletin/cont/83/art/art3.htm (consulted: April 12, 2016).

3. This principle states that in any case, the legal norm that must be applied will be the more protective one for the person who suffered a grievance related to her/his rights.

4. The *Radilla Pacheco* case was quickly followed by three others: the *Rosendo Cantú* case, the *Fernández Ortega* case, and the *Cabrera García and Montiel Flores* case, better known as the *campesino* environmentalists case.

5. In favor: Ministers Cossío Díaz, Luna Ramos, Franco González Salas, Zaldívar Lelo de Larrea, Sánchez Cordero de García Villegas, Silva Meza, and President Ortiz Mayagoitia.

6. 912/2010 Supreme Court of Justice agreement. http://www2.scjn.gob.mx/AsuntosRelevantes /pagina/SeguimientoAsuntosRelevantesPub.aspx?ID=121589&SeguimientoID=225 (consulted: May 30, 2016).

7. Court of Appeals Judge Interview. November 19, 2015.

8. Settled Case Law P 87/2004 corresponding to the Constitutional Claim 33/2002.

9. Settled case law P/J/86/2004; P/J/87/2004; P/J/49/2004; P/J/48/2004, corresponding to the Constitutional Claim 33/2002.

10. Nonbinding Court Settlements VIII.2doPA.2P and VII.2doPA.3P, corresponding to the *Incidente de Suspensión* 38/2012; Court Settlements I.9no.P60.P and I.9no.P61.P, corresponding to the Legal Complaint 29/2014.

Chapter 12

1. See Article 2 of the International Convention for the Protection of All Persons from Enforced Disappearance (2006).

2. Gobierno Federal de Mexico, Instituto Nacional de Estadística y Geografía (INEGI), "Presenta Inegi Encuesta Sobre Calidad de Trámites y Servicios del Gobierno." Press release, October 16, 2012.

3. Name changed.

4. http://www.milenio.com/policia/detienen_oficiales_fuerza_civil-desaparicion_forzada _fuerza_civil_0_754724602.html (last consulted April 16, 2018).

5. CEDEHM is a human rights organization founded in 2006 by several well-known activists, including Luz Estela "Lucha" Castro, the El Barzón lawyer who assisted Ledezma initially. See Michel 2011.

6. These numbers are supported by the INEGI and were cited repeatedly by Juárez civil society organizations during interviews there in January 2013. For an analysis of the dynamics that led to this violence, see Meyer 2010. Joint Operation Chihuahua, launched in 2008, deployed more than two thousand members of the military to Juarez; in 2009 Calderón sent five thousand more soldiers. These deployments are seen by most analysts as a primary cause of the violence, as they served to fortify one side of a territorial war over the city.

BIBLIOGRAPHY

AAVV. 2015. *Diversidad, pluralismo y concentración de los medios de comunicación en América Latina.* Unpublished manuscript.

Abed, George T., and Hamid R. Davoodi. 2002. *Governance, Corruption and Economic Performance.* Washington, D.C.: International Monetary Fund.

Abramovich, Victor, and Christian Courtis. 2002. *Los derechos sociales como derechos exigibles.* Madrid: Trotta.

Abundis, Francisco. 2015. "Universitarios votan por el PAN; los de menor escolaridad, por el PRI." *El Financiero,* May 3. http://www.elfinanciero.com.mx/nacional/universitarios-votan -por-pan-los-de-menor-escolaridad-por-el-pri.html (last consulted: October 30, 2017).

Acosta, Mariclaire, ed. 2012. *La impunidad cronica de Mexico. Una aproximacion desde los derechos humanos.* Mexico City: Comisión de Derechos Humanos del Distrito Federal.

Acosta, Mariclaire, and Esa Ennelin. 2006. "The Mexican Solution to Transitional Justice." In *Transitional Justice in the Twenty-Century: Beyond Trust versus Justice,* edited by Naomi Roht Arriaza and Javier Mariezcurrena, 94–119. Cambridge, UK: Cambridge University Press.

Adams, Richard H. Jr. 1989. "Worker Remittances and Inequality in Rural Egypt." *Economic Development and Cultural Change* 38, 1: 45–71.

Adams, Richard H. Jr., Alfredo Cuecuecha, and John Page. 2008. "The Impact of Remittances on Poverty and Inequality in Ghana." Policy Research Working Paper No. WPS4732, World Bank.

Adida, Claire L., and Desha M. Girod. 2011. "Do Migrants Improve Their Hometowns? Remittances and Access to Public Services in Mexico, 1995–2000." *Comparative Political Studies* 44, 3: 3–27.

Aikin, Olga, and Alejandro Anaya Muñoz. 2013. "Crisis de derechos humanos de las personas migrantes en tránsito por México: redes y presión transnacional." *Foro Internacional* 53, 1: 143–181.

Aimar, Verónica. 2005. "Política, policía y violencia en la provincia de Santa Fe." In *Policía, violencia, democracia. Ensayos sociológicos,* edited by Máximo Sozzo, 15–46. Santa Fe, Argentina: Ediciones UNL.

Albuja, Sebastián, and Laura Rubio Díaz-Leal. 2011. "Los Olvidados de la guerra contra el narcotráfico en México: Los desplazados internos." *Foreign Affairs Latinoamérica* 11, 4: 23–31.

Aleinikoff, Thomas, David Martin, Hiroshi Motomura, and Maryellen Fullerton. 2012. *Immigration and Citizenship: Process and Policy,* 7th ed. Eagan, MN: West Publishing.

Al Hussein, Zeid Ra`ad. 2015. "Statement on His Visit to Mexico." *UN High Commissioner for Human Rights.* October 7. http://www.ohchr.org/EN/NewsEvents/Pages/DisplayNews.aspx ?NewsID=16578&LangID=E (last consulted: July 19, 2016).

Almazán, Alejandro. 2013. "Liberar Almas . . . y migrantes del narco." *El diario,* April 20. http://diario.mx/Nacional/2013-04-20_f9986a69/libera-almas-y-a-migrantes-de-narcos/ (last consulted: October 30, 2017).

Alonso, José, and Carlos Mulas-Granados, eds. 2011. *Corrupción, cohesión social y desarrollo. El caso de Iberoamérica.* Madrid: Fondo de Cultura Económica.

Álvarez, Rosa María, and Alicia Elena Pérez, eds. 2010. *Modelos para prevenir, atender, sancionar y erradicar la violencia contra las mujeres.* Mexico City: Instituto de Investigaciones Jurídicas-Universidad Nacional Autónoma de México, Consejo Nacional de Ciencia y Tecnología.

Amengual, M. 2016. *Politicized Enforcement in Argentina: Labor and Environmental Regulation.* New York: Cambridge University Press.

Americas Watch. 1990. *Human Rights in Mexico. A Policy of Impunity.* Washington, D.C.: Americas Watch.

Amnesty International. 2009a. *Mexico: New Reports of Human Rights Violations by the Military.* London: Amnesty International.

———. 2009b. *Whose Justice? Bosnia and Herzegovina's Women Still Waiting.* London: Amnesty International.

———. 2010a. *Invisible Victims. Migrants on the Move in Mexico.* London: Amnesty International.

———. 2010b. *Acabar con la impunidad. Justicia para las víctimas de tortura.* Madrid: Amnesty International.

———. 2014. *Out of Control. Torture and Other Ill-Treatment in Mexico.* London: Amnesty International.

———. 2015. *Paper Promises, Daily Impunity: Mexico's Torture Epidemic.* London: Amnesty International.

———. 2016. *Surviving Death. Police and Military Torture of Women in Mexico.* London: Amnesty International.

Anaya Muñoz, Alejandro. 2006. *Autonomía indígena, gobernabilidad y legitimidad en México: la legalización de los usos y costumbres electorales en Oaxaca.* Mexico City: Universidad Iberoamericana.

———. 2009. "Transnational and Domestic Processes in the Definition of Human Rights Policies in Mexico." *Human Rights Quarterly* 31, 1: 35–58.

———. 2011. "Explaining High Levels of Transnational Pressure over Mexico: The Case of the Disappearances and Killings of Women in Ciudad Juárez." *The International Journal of Human Rights* 15, 3: 339–358.

———. 2012a. *El país bajo presión. Debatiendo el papel del escrutinio internacional de derechos humanos sobre México.* México: CIDE.

———. 2012b. "Security Versus Human Rights. The Case of Contemporary Mexico." In *Mexico's Security Failure. Collapse into Criminal Violence,* edited by Paul Kenny and Monica Serrano (with Arturo Sotomayor), 122–140. New York and London: Routledge.

———. 2014a. "Communicative Interaction Between Mexico and Its International Critics Around the Issue of Military Jurisdiction: 'Rhetorical Action' or 'Truth Seeking Arguing'?" *Journal of Human Rights* 13, 4: 434–455.

———. 2014b. *Violaciones a los derechos humanos en el marco de la estrategia militarizada de lucha contra el narcotráfico en México. 2007 a 2012.* Mexico City: CIDE-Programa de Política de Drogas.

Andión, Ximena. 2012. "Entre dos fuegos: la impunidad sistemática de la violencia contra las mujeres en México." In *La impunidad crónica de México. Una aproximación desde los derechos humanos,* edited by Mariclaire Acosta, 239–292. Mexico City: Comisión de Derechos Humanos del Distrito Federal.

Ansolabehere, Karina. 2003. *Los efectos de la justicia sobre el proceso político democrático. Cortes supremas, gobierno y democracia.* Mexico: Flacso.

———. 2007. *La política desde la justicia: Cortes supremas, gobierno y democracia en Argentina y México.* Mexico City: Flacso.

———. 2010. "More Power, More Rights? The Supreme Court and Society in Mexico." In *Cultures of Legality: Judicialization and Political Activism in Latin America,* edited by Javier Couso, Alexandra Huneeus, and Rachel Seider, 78–111. New York: Cambridge University Press.

———. 2014. "Impotentes optimistas y controlados preocupados. La reforma de la justicia penal en el Distrito Federal desde el punto de vista de los defensores públicos, los ministerios públicos y los policías de investigación." In *Reformas judiciales, prácticas sociales y legitimidad democrática en América Latina,* edited by Angélica Cuellar Vázquez and I. García Gárate, 25–52. Mexico City: UNAM.

———. 2015. "La respuesta a la violencia. El caso de la Oficina de la Alta Comisionada para los Derechos Humanos en México." In *Derechos humanos y transformación política en contextos de violencia,* edited by A. Estévez López and L. D. Vazquéz Valencia, 165–196. Mexico City: CISAN-FLACSO.

Ansolabehere, Karina, et al. 2017. *Informe sobre Desapariciones en el estado de Nuevo León con información de CADHAC.* Mexico City: FLACSO-México.

Ansolabehere, Karina, Francisco Valdés Ugalde, and Luis Daniel Vázquez Valencia. 2015. *Entre el pesimismo y la esperanza: Los derechos humanos en América Latina. Metodología para su estudio y medición.* Mexico: FLACSO-México.

Arana, Marcos, and María Teresa Del Riego. 2012. *Estudio sobre los Desplazados Internos por el Conflicto Zapatista en Chiapas.* Mexico City: Programa Conjunto por una Cultura de Paz.

Aranda, Jesús. 2010. "Zetas ejecutaron por la espalda a los 72 migrantes; no pudieron pagar rescate." *La Jornada,* August 26.

Arendt, Hannah. 1976. *The Origins of Totalitarianism.* New York: Harcourt, Inc.

Aristegui Noticias. 2018. "En 2017, más de 29 mil asesinatos en México; 671 fueron feminicidios," January 21. https://aristeguinoticias.com/2101/mexico/en-2017-mas-de-29-mil-asesinatos-en-mexico-671-fueron-feminicidios/ (last consulted: March 23, 2018).

Armijo, Natalia. 2011. "Introducción." In *Migración y seguridad: nuevo desafío en México,* edited by Natalia Armijo, 5–10. Mexico City: Colectivo de Análisis de la Seguridad con Deéocracia.

Arteaga Botello, Nelson, and Jimena Valdés Figueroa. 2010. "Contextos socioculturales de los feminicidios en el Estado de México: nuevas subjetividades femeninas." *Revista Mexicana de Sociología* 72, 1: 5–35.

Astorga, Luis, and David Shirk. 2010. "Drug Trafficking Organizations and Counter Drug Strategies in the U.S.-Mexican Context, Center for US-Mexican Studies, University of San Diego, Working Paper USMEX WP 10-01." San Diego, CA: University of San Diego. https://escholarship.org/uc/item/8j647429#page-2 (last consulted: November 19, 2015).

Auyero, Javier. 2007. *Routine Politics and Violence in Argentina: The Gray Zone of State Power,* Cambridge Studies in Contentious Politics. Cambridge, UK: Cambridge University Press.

Azam, Jean-Paul, and Flore Gubert. 2005. "Those in Kayes: The Impact of Remittances on Their Recipients in Africa." *Revue Economique* 56, 6: 1,331–1,358.

Baiocchi, G., P. Heller, and M. K. Silva. 2011. *Bootstrapping Democracy: Transforming Local Governance and Civil Society in Brazil.* Palo Alto, CA: Stanford University Press.

Barham, B., and S. Boucher. 1998. "Migration, Remittances, and Inequality: Estimating the Net Effects of Migration on Income Distribution." *Journal of Development Economics* 55, 2: 307–331.

Barrios, David. 2013. "Madres de desaparecidas en Juárez contra la ineptitud del gobierno." *Des Informémonos,* June 24. http://desinformemonos.org/2013/06/madres-dedesaparecidas-en -juarez-contra-la-ineptitud-delgobierno/ (last consulted: July 10, 2013).

Barrow, Amy. 2009. "'It's Like a Rubber Band.' Assessing UNSCR 1325 as a Gender Mainstreaming Process." *International Journal of Law in Context* 5, 1: 51–68.

Bauman, Zygmunt. 2003. "From Bystander to Actor." *Journal of Human Rights* 2, 2: 137–151.

Bednar, Nicholas R. 2015. "Social Group Semantics: The Evidentiary Requirements of 'Particularity' and 'Social Distinction' in Pro Se Asylum Adjudications." *Minnesota Law Review* 100, 1: 355–403.

Beittel, J. 2015. *Mexico: Organized Crime and Drug Trafficking Organizations.* Washington, D.C.: Congressional Research Service.

Belén, Posada del Migrante, Humanidad Sin Fronteras, and Fronteras con Justicia. 2009. *Quinto Informe sobre la situación de los derechos humanos de las personas migrantes en tránsito por México.* Saltillo, Mexico: Belén, Posada del Migrante, Humanidad Sin Fronteras y Fronteras con Justicia.

Bell, Christine. 2009. "Transitional Justice, Interdisciplinarity and the State of the 'Field' or 'Non-field.'" *International Journal of Transitional Justice* 3, 1: 5–27.

Bell, Christine, and Catherine O'Rourke. 2010. "Peace Agreements or Pieces of Paper? The Impact of UNSC Resolution 1325 on Peace Processes and Their Agreements." *International and Comparative Law Quarterly* 59, 4: 941–980.

Belur, Jyoti. 2010. *Permission to Shoot? Police Use of Deadly Force in Democracies.* New York: Springer.

Berber, Miguel Ánge. 2016. "Trayectorias de violencia. Homicidios 2008–2014" *Nexos,* July 1. http://www.nexos.com.mx/?p=28803 (last consulted: October 30, 2017).

Birkbeck, Christopher, and Luis G. Gabaldón. 2002. "Estableciendo la verdad sobre el uso de la fuerza en la Policía Venezolana." *Nueva Sociedad* 182: 47–58.

Börzel, Tanja, and Thomas Risse. 2013. "Human Rights in Areas of Limited Statehood: The New Agenda." In *The Persistent Power of Human Rights: From Commitment to Compliance,* edited by Thomas Risse, Stephen Ropp, and Kathryn Sikkink, 3–84. Cambridge, UK: Cambridge University Press.

Bourbeau, Philippe. 2011. *The Securitization of Migration. A Study of Movement and Order.* London: Routledge.

Breslow, Jason. 2015. "The Staggering Death Toll of Mexico's Drug War." *PBS Frontline,* July 27. http://www.pbs.org/wgbh/frontline/article/the-staggering-death-toll-of-mexicos-drug -war/ (last consulted: October 20, 2017).

Bruin, Roland H. M. 2002. "Working Party on Non-State Agents of Persecution: 2002 Report." Haarlem, The Netherlands: International Association of Refugee Law Judges.

Brysk, Alison. 2005. *Human Rights and Private Wrongs: Constructing Global Civil Society.* New York: Routledge.

Buchanan, Holly. 2010. "Fleeing the Drug War Next Door: Drug-related Violence as a Basis for Refugee Protection for Mexican Asylum-Seekers." *Merkourios. Utrecht Journal of International and European Law* 27, 72: 28–60.

Bustamante, Jorge. 2012. "¿Son nuestros muertos?" *Reforma,* March 28.

Butcher, K. F., and A. M. Piehl. 1998. "Recent Immigrants: Unexpected Implications for Crime and Incarceration." *Industrial and Labor Relations Review* 51, 4: 654–679.

———. 1998. "Cross-city Evidence on the Relationship Between Immigration and Crime." *Journal of Policy Analysis and Management* 17: 457–493.

Butler, Judith. 2009. *Frames of War: When Is Life Grievable?* London: Verso.

Cabot, J. Anna. 2014. "Problems Faced by Mexican Asylum Seekers in the U.S." *Journal on Migration and Human Security* 2, 4: 361–377.

Calderón, Felipe. 2007. Primer Informe de Gobierno. http://calderon.presidencia.gob.mx/informe/primer/informe/index.html (last consulted: November 25, 2015).

———. 2008. Segundo Informe de Gobierno. http://calderon.presidencia.gob.mx/informe/segundo/resumen/index.html (last consulted: November 25, 2015).

———. 2009. Tercer Informe de Gobierno. http://calderon.presidencia.gob.mx/informe/tercer/resumen/indexd8ce.html?contenido=61 (last consulted: November 25, 2015).

———. 2011. Quinto Informe de Gobierno. http://calderon.presidencia.gob.mx/informe/quinto/resumen-ejecutivo/estado-de-derecho-y-seguridad/ (last consulted: November 25, 2015).

———. 2012. Sexto Informe de Gobierno. http://calderon.presidencia.gob.mx/informe/sexto/sexto_informe.html (last consulted: November 25, 2015).

Call, Charles. 2007. *Constructing Justice and Security After War.* Washington, D.C.: United States Institute of Peace Press.

Cameron, Maxwell, Eric Hershberg, and Kenneth Sharpe, eds. 2012. *Nuevas instituciones de democracia participativa en América Latina: la voz y sus consecuencias.* Mexico City: FLACSO-México.

Cano, Ignacio. 1997. *Letalidade da Ação Policial no Rio de Janeiro.* Rio de Janeiro: ISER.

———. 2003. *La Policía y su evaluación. Propuestas para la construcción de indicadores de evaluación en el trabajo policial.* Santiago de Chile: Centro de Estudios para el Desarrollo, Área de Seguridad Ciudadana.

———. 2010. "Racial Bias in Police Use of Lethal Force in Brazil." *Police Practice and Research* 11, 1: 31–43.

Cardenas, Ana. 2016. "Mando Unico: Solucion a los problemas de seguridad y corrupcion policial?" *Mexico Evalua,* February 11. http://mexicoevalua.org/2016/02/mando-unico-solucion-a-los-problemas-de-seguridad-y-corrupcion-policial/ (last consulted: February 22, 2016).

Cardenas, Sonia. 2007. *Conflict and Compliance: State Responses to International Human Rights Pressure.* Philadelphia: University of Pennsylvania Press.

Carrasco, Jorge. 2010. "Familiares de víctimas del narco en Sinaloa se manifiestan en el DF." *Demócrata Norte de México,* June 10.

Carter, K. R. 2010. "Should International Relations Consider Rape a Weapon of War." *Politics & Gender* 6, 3: 341–371.

Castañeda, Martha Patricia, Patricia Ravelo, and Teresa Pérez. 2013. "Feminicidio y violencia de género en México: omisiones del Estado y exigencia civil de justicia." *Iztapalapa Revista de Ciencias Sociales y Humanidades* 34, 74: 11–39.

Castillo, Manuel Ángel, and Mónica Toussaint. 2010. "Seguridad y migración en la frontera sur." In *Seguridad nacional y seguridad interior, Los grandes problemas de México,* edited by Arturo Alvarado and Mónica Serrano, 269–300. Mexico City: El Colegio de México.

Castillo García, Gustavo. 2009. "Controla el narco a 62% de los policías del país, dice informe." *La Jornada,* January 2. http://www.jornada.unam.mx/2009/02/01/index.php?section=politica&article=009n1pol (last consulted: October 23, 2017).

———. 2016. "Cienfuegos ofrece disculpa pública por tortura que cometieron militares." *La Jornada*, April 17. http://www.jornada.unam.mx/2016/04/17/politica/003n1pol (last consulted: April 18, 2016).

Cavallaro, James, and Stephenie E. Brewer. 2008. "Reevaluating Regional Human Rights Litigation in the Twenty-First Century: The Case of the Inter-American Court." *The American Journal of International Law* 102, 4: 768–827.

Cavarozzi, Marcelo. 1991. "Más allá de las transiciones a la democracia en América Latina." *Revista de Estudios Políticos* 74: 85–111.

Centro de Estudios Legales y Sociales (CELS). 2002. *Violencia y enfrentamientos policiales.* Buenos Aires: Centro de Estudios Legales y Sociales.

Cervantes Loredo, María Teresa. 2015. "La participación social en familias víctimas de desaparición involuntaria." *RISCH Revista Iberoamericana de las Ciencias Sociales y Humanísticas* 4, 8: 48–59.

Cervera Flores, Miguel. 2015. "Respuesta a Dr. José Antonio Guevara Bermúdez, Director Ejecutivo de la Comisión Mexicana de Defensa y Promoción de los Derechos Humanos, por parte del Director General de INEGI." January 20, Aguascalientes, 200/009/2015, INEGI. ESD2.01.

Chabat, Jorge. 2002. "Mexico's War on Drugs: No Margin for Maneuver." *The Annals of the American Academy of Political and Social Science* 582: 134–148.

Chavez, R. B. 2004. *The Rule of Law in Nascent Democracies: Judicial Politics in Argentina.* Palo Alto, CA: Stanford University Press.

Chávez, Víctor. 2014. "Al vacío 96% de las denuncias de la Auditoría Superior." *El Financiero*, February 24. http://www.elfinanciero.com.mx/politica/al-vacio-96-de-las-denuncias-de-la-auditoria-superior.html (last consulted: October 30, 2017).

Chayes, Abram, and Antonia Handler Chayes. 1993. "On Compliance." *International Organization* 47, 2: 175–205.

Checkel, Jeffrey. 2005. "International Institutions and Socialization in Europe: Introduction and Framework." *International Organization* 59, 4: 801–826.

Chevigny, Paul. 1987. *Police Abuse in Brazil: Summary Executions and Torture in São Paulo and Rio de Janeiro.* Washington, D.C.: Americas Watch.

———. 1990. "Police Deadly Force as Social Control: Jamaica, Brazil and Argentina." *Criminal Law Forum* 1, 3: 389–425.

———. 1993. *Urban Police Violence in Brazil: Torture and Police Killings in São Paulo and Rio de Janeiro After Five Years.* Washington, D.C., and São Paulo, Brazil: Americas Watch and the Center for the Study of Violence at the University of São Paulo.

Cisneros, Jose Roberto. 2016. "Tierra Blanca, Veracruz, un caso más de desaparición forzada." *CNN Expansion,* January 27. http://www.cnnexpansion.com/economia/2016/01/27/tierra-blanca-veracruz-un-caso-mas-de-desaparicion-forzada (last consulted: February 23, 2016).

Clark, Gordon L. 1985. *Judges and the Cities: Interpreting Local Autonomy.* Chicago: University of Chicago Press.

CNDH and CIESAS. 2017. *El derecho a la protección a la salud de las mujeres indígenas en México: análisis nacional y de casos desde una perspectiva de derechos humanos.* http://www.cndh.org.mx/sites/all/doc/Informes/Especiales/Informe-Derecho-Proteccion-Salud.pdf (last consulted: October 30, 2017).

CNN México. 2013. "Masacres en México: Recuento de la violencia." *CNN*, November 18. http://mexico.cnn.com/nacional/2011/11/24/villas-de-salvarcar (last consulted: April 3, 2018).

Cobo, Rosa. 2011. *Hacia una nueva política sexual. Las mujeres ante la reacción patriarcal.* Madrid: Los Libros de la Catarata.

Cohen, Stanley. 1996. "Government Responses to Human Rights Reports: Claims, Denials and Counterclaims." *Human Rights Quarterly* 18, 3: 517–543.

Cole, Wade M. 2015. "Mind the Gap: State Capacity and the Implementation of Human Rights Treaties." *International Organization* 69, 2: 405–441.

Collier, Paul, and Anke Hoeffler. 2004. "Greed and Grievance in Civil War." *Oxford Economic Papers* 56, 4: 563–595.

Collins, C. 2010. *Post-transitional Justice. Human Rights Trials in Chile and El Salvador.* State College: Pennsylvania State University Press.

Comisión de Derechos Humanos de las Naciones Unidas (CDHNU). 1997. *La administración de justicia y los derechos humanos de los detenidos. Informe final revisado acerca de la cuestión de la impunidad de los autores de violaciones de los derechos humanos (derechos civiles y políticos) preparado por el Sr. L. Joinet de conformidad con la resolución 1996/119 de la Subcomisión.* E/CN.4/Sub. 2/1997/20/Rev.1 S/P. October 2.

Comisión Ejecutiva de Atención a Víctimas (CEAV). 2014. "Acta de la Cuadragésima Tercera Sesión del Pleno de la Comisión Ejecutiva de Atención a Víctimas." *CEAV,* July 29. http://www .ceav.gob.mx/wp-content/uploads/2014/04/AO-43.pdf (last consulted: February 7, 2016).

———. 2016a. "Comunicado de Prensa, Fallan a la gente los estados que no han creado sus comisiones de Atención a Víctimas." *CEAV,* January 14. http://www.ceav.gob.mx/2016/01 /fallan-a-la-gente-los-estados-que-no-han-creado-sus-comisiones-de-atencion-a-victimas -ceav/ (last consulted: February 9, 2016).

———. 2016b. "Las otras víctimas invisibles." March 14. Mexico City: Comisión Nacional de Atención a Víctimas (CEAV).

Comisión Mexicana de Defensa y Promoción de los Derechos Humanos (CMDPDH) and IMDHD (Instituto Mexicano de Derechos Humanos y Democracia). n/d. "Access to Justice in Mexico: The Incessant Impunity on Human Rights Violations Report Presented Before the Human Rights Council on the Occasion of Mexico's Universal Periodic Review." http:// www.iccnow.org/documents/Access_to_Justice_in_Mexico_-_English.pdf (last consulted: February 17, 2016).

Comisión Mexicana de Defensa y Promoción de los Derechos Humanos (CMDPDH). 2015. *Propuestas para la conformación de una ley eficaz de aplicación nacional sobre tortura, tratos y penal crueles, inhumanos o degradantes.* Mexico City: CMDPDH.

Comisión Nacional de los Derechos Humanos (CNDH). 2009. *Informe Especial sobre los casos de secuestro en contra de migrantes.* Mexico City: Comisión Nacional de los Derechos Humanos.

———. 2013. *Diagnóstico sobre la situación de la trata de personas en México.* México: Comisión Nacional de Derechos Humanos.

———. 2014a. Recommendation 51/2014. http://www.cndh.org.mx/sites/all/fuentes/documentos /Recomendaciones/2014/REC_2014_051.pdf (last consulted: October 30, 2017).

———. 2014b. Recommendation 01/2014. http://www.cndh.org.mx/sites/all/doc/Recomendaciones /2014/Rec_2014_001.pdf (last consulted: October 30, 2017).

———. 2014c. Recommendation 29/2014. http://www.cndh.org.mx/sites/all/doc/Recomendaciones /2014/Rec_2014_029.pdf (last consulted: October 30, 2017).

———. 2015a. Informe Anual de Actividades 2014. http://www.cndh.org.mx/Informes_Anuales _Actividades (last consulted: October 23, 2017).

———. 2015b. Recommendation 3VG/2015. http://www.cndh.org.mx/sites/all/doc
/Recomendaciones/ViolacionesGraves/RecVG_003.pdf (last consulted: February 23, 2016).

———. 2016. Recomendación 15/2016. http://www.cndh.org.mx/sites/all/doc/Recomendaciones
/2016/Rec_2016_015.pdfhttp://www.cndh.org.mx/sites/all/doc/Recomendaciones/2016
/Rec_2016_015.pdf (last consulted: October 8, 2017).

Comité 68, et al. 2006. "Esclarecimiento y sanción de los delitos del pasado en el sexenio 2000-
2006. Compromisos quebrantados y Justicia Aplazada." http://catedraunescodh.unam.mx
/catedra/mujeres/menu_superior/Doc_basicos/5_biblioteca_virtual/9_informes/ONG/49
.pdf (last consulted: October 2, 2017).

Committee on Enforced Disappearances. 2014. "Consideration of Reports Submitted by States
Parties Under Article 20, Paragraph 1, of the Convention. Reports of States Parties Due in
2012." Mexico. U.N. Doc. CED/MEX/1. April 17.

———. 2015. Concluding Observations on the Report Submitted by Mexico. CED/C/MEX/CO/1.
March 5.

Committee on the Elimination of Discrimination Against Women (CEDAW). 2011. "Alyne da
Silva Pimentel vs. Brazil. Communication N° 17/2008." U.N. Doc. CEDAW/C/49/D/17/2008,
August 10.

Committee on the Elimination of Discrimination against Women. 2012. "Concluding Observations: Mexico." U.N. Doc. CEDAW/C/MEX/CO/7-8, July 27.

Committee on the Rights of the Child. 2015. Concluding Observations on the Combined Fourth
and Fifth Periodic Reports of Mexico. U.N. Doc. CRC/C/MEX/CO/4-5, June 8.

Consejo Nacional de Evaluación de la Política Social (CONEVAL). 2011. Informe de evaluación
de la política de desarrollo social en México. Mexico City: CONEVAL.

———. 2012. Informe de evaluación de la política de desarrollo social en México, 2012. Noviembre.
Mexico City: CONEVAL.

———. 2015. Informe de evaluación de la política de desarrollo social en México, 2014. Febrero.
Mexico City: CONEVAL.

Coria, Carlos. 2013. "Madres de desaparecidas caminan de Ciudad Juárez a Chihuahua." Excelsior, January 16. http://www.excelsior.com.mx/2013/01/16/879692 (last consulted: October 30, 2017).

Cornelius, W. A., and D. A. Shirk, eds. 2007. Reforming the Administration of Justice in Mexico.
Notre Dame, IN: University of Notre Dame Press.

Cornett, Linda, Peter Haschke, and Mark Gibney. 2016. "Introduction to the Societal Violence
Scale: Physical Integrity Rights Violations and Non-State Actors." Human Rights Quarterly
38, 4: 1,102–1,108.

Cornwall, A., and C. Nyamu-Musembi. 2004. "Putting the 'Rights-based Approach' to Development into Perspective." Third World Quarterly 25, 8: 1,415–1,437.

Corral-Nava, Valori. 2014. "Only 1.6 Percent of Mexicans Seeking Political Asylum Are Accepted
by U.S. Courts." Borderzine.com, June 27. http://borderzine.com/2014/06/only-1-6-percent
-of-mexicans-seeking-political-asylum-are-accepted-by-u-s-courts/ (last consulted: March
16, 2016.)

Cortes, Rosalia. 2008. "Children and Women Left Behind in Labour Sending Countries: An
Appraisal of Social Risks." Working Paper, United Nations Children's Fund. New York:
United Nations Children's Fund (UNICEF), Policy, Advocacy and Knowledge Management
Section, Division of Policy and Practice.

Costantino, Agostina, and Francisco Cantamutto. 2015. "Modos de desarrollo y realización de
derechos en América Latina." In Entre el pesimismo y la esperanza: los derechos humanos en

América Latina. Metodología para su estudio y medición, edited by Karina Ansolabehere, Francisco Valdés Ugalde, and Daniel Vázquez, 181–214. Mexico City: FLACSO-México.

Coupland, Robin. M., and David R. Meddings. 1999. "Mortality Associated with Use of Weapons in Armed Conflicts, Wartime Atrocities, and Civilian Mass Shootings: Literature Review." *BMJ* 319, 7207: 407–410.

Couso, Javier A. 2005. "The Judicialization of Chilean Politics. The Rights Revolution that Never Was." In *The Judicialization of Politics in Latin America,* edited by R. Sieder, L. Schjolden, and A. Angell Houndsmill, 105–129. New York: Palgrave McMillan.

Couso, Javier A., Alexandra Huneeus, and Rachel Sieder. 2010. *Cultures of Legality: Judicialization and Political Activism in Latin America.* New York: Cambridge University Press.

Couso, Javier A., and Lisa Hilbink. 2011. "From Quietism to Incipient Activism." In *Courts in Latin America,* edited by Gretchen Helmke and Julio Ríos-Figueroa, 99–127. New York: Cambridge University Press.

Crawford, Neta C. 2013. *Civilian Death and Injury in the Iraq War, 2003–2013,* available at http://watson.brown.edu/costsofwar/files/cow/imce/papers/2013/Civilian%20Death %20and%20Injury%20in%20the%20Iraq%20War%2C%202003-2013.pdf (last consulted: April 3, 2018).

Crowley, Michael. 2014. "The Committee to Save Mexico." *Time Magazine,* 183, 7: 36–39.

Dancy, G., and K. Sikkink. 2012. "Ratification and Human Rights Prosecutions: Toward a Transitional Theory of Treaty Compliance." *Journal of International Law and Politics* 44, 3: 751–790.

D'Auberterre, M. 2000. "Mujeres y espacio transnacional: maniobras para renegociar el vínculo conyugal." In *Migración y relaciones de género en México,* edited by D. Bassols and C. Oehmichen, 63–85. Mexico City: UNAM.

Davenport, Christian, and David Armstrong. 2004. "Democracy and the Violation of Human Rights: A Statistical Analysis from 1976 to 1996." *American Journal of Political Science* 48, 3: 538–554.

David, Steven R. 1997. "Internal War: Causes and Cures." *World Politics* 49, 4: 552–576.

Davis, David R., and Amanda Murdie. 2012. "Shaming and Blaming: Using Events Data to Assess the Impact of Human Right INGOs." *International Studies Quarterly* 56, 1: 1–16.

Davis, D. E. 2006. "Undermining the Rule of Law: Democratization and the Dark Side of Police Reform in Mexico." *Latin American Politics and Society* 48, 1: 55–86.

Deaton, Janice, and Octavio Rodriguez Ferreira. 2015. "Detention Without Charge. The Use of Arraigo for Criminal Investigations in Mexico, Special Report, Justice in Mexico Project, Department of Political Science and International Relations, University of San Diego." https://justiceinmexico.org/wp-content/uploads/2015/01/150113_ARRAIGO _Coverthumb.png (last consulted: December 18, 2015).

Delaney, David. 2010. *The Spatial, the Legal and the Pragmatics of World-making: Nomospheric Investigations.* London: Routledge.

Del Olmo, R. 1990. *Segunda ruptura criminológica.* Caracas: Universidad Central de Venezuela, 37–68.

De Marinis, Natalia. 2011. "Breaking the Silence: State Violence Towards Triqui Women of Oaxaca, Mexico." *Development* 54, 4: 480–484.

Diario Oficial de la Federación. 2011a. "Decreto por el que se modifica la denominación del Capítulo I del Título Primero y reforma diversos artículos de la Constitución Política de los Estados Unidos Mexicanos." June 10. http://dof.gob.mx/nota_detalle.php?codigo=5194486 &fecha=10/06/2011 (last consulted: October 2, 2017).

———. 2011b. "Decreto por el que se reforman, adicionan y derogan diversas disposiciones de los artículos 94, 103, 104 y 107 de la Constitución Política de los Estados Unidos Mexicanos." June 6. http://dof.gob.mx/nota_detalle.php?codigo=5193266&fecha=06/06/2011 (last consulted: October 2, 2017).

———. 2011c. "Resolución dictada por el Tribunal Pleno en el expediente varios 912/2010 y Votos Particulares formulados por los Ministros Margarita Beatriz Luna Ramos, Sergio Salvador Aguirre Anguiano y Luis María Aguilar Morales; así como Votos Particulares y Concurrentes de los Ministros Arturo Zaldívar Lelo de Larrea y Jorge Mario Pardo Rebolledo." October 4. http://dof.gob.mx/nota_detalle.php?codigo=5212527&fecha=04/10/2011 (last consulted: October 2, 2017).

———. 2014. "Manual del Uso de la Fuerza, de Aplicación Común a las Tres Fuerzas Armadas." May 30. http://dof.gob.mx/nota_detalle.php?codigo=5346857&fecha=30/05/2014 (last consulted: October 18, 2017).

Díaz, Gloria. 2014. "Temen ser torturados 64% de los mexicanos: Amnistía." *Proceso,* May 13. http://www.proceso.com.mx/?p=372072 (last consulted: November 8, 2017).

Domínguez Ruvalcaba, Héctor. 2013. *De la sensualidad a la violencia de género. La Modernidad y la Nación en las representaciones de la masculinidad en el México contemporáneo, Publicaciones de la Casa Chata.* Ciudad de México: CIESAS-Conacyt.

Dorff, Robert. 2005. "Failed States After 9/11: What Did We Know and What Have We Learned?" *International Studies Perspectives* 6, 1: 20–34.

Doyle, David. 2013. "Remittances and Social Spending." Manuscript, Oxford University. http://nebula.wsimg.com/f806a014499af3c53362d4bed802b7f6?AccessKeyId=ED2D6EE708C991B3B60B&disposition=0 (last consulted: May 25, 2015).

Durin, Séverin. 2013. "Los desplazados por la guerra contra el crimen organizado en México. Reconocer, diagnosticar y atender." In *El desplazamiento interno forzado en México. Un acercamiento para su reflexión y análisis,* edited by Oscar Tórrens, 155–194. Mexico City: CIESAS, Colegio de Sonora, Senado de la República.

Durkheim, Émile. [1883] 1984. *The Division of Labour in Society.* New York: Free Press.

———. [1897] 1951. *Suicide: A Study in Sociology.* New York: Free Press.

Dutrenit Bielous, Silvia, and Gonzalo Varela Petito. 2010. *Tramitando el pasado. Violaciones de los derechos humanos y agendas gubernamentales en casos latinoamericanos.* Mexico City: FLACSO/CLACSO.

Dutrenit Bielous, Silvia, and Libertad Argüeyo. 2011. "Una gestión atrapada. El caso de FEM-OSPP." In *La crisis de las instituciones políticas en México,* edited by Fernando Castañeda, Angélica Cuellar, and Edith Kuri, 111–114. Mexico City. UNAM-Facultad de Ciencias Políticas y Sociales.

Eckstein, Harry. 1975. "Case Studies and Theory in Political Science." In *Handbook of Political Science. Political Science: Scope and Theory,* edited by F. I. Greenstein and N.W. Polsby, 94–137. Reading, MA: Addison-Wesley Educational Publishers Inc.

Elster, Jon. 2006. *Rendición de cuentas: La justicia transicional en perspectiva histórica.* Buenos Aires: Katz Editores.

Englehart, Neil A. 2009. "State Capacity, State Failure, and Human Rights." *Journal of Peace Research* 46, 2: 163–180.

Epp, C. R. 1997. *The Rights Revolution: Lawyers, Activists, and Supreme Courts in Comparative Perspective.* Chicago: University of Chicago Press.

Eriksson, Mikael, and Peter Wallensteen. 2004. "Armed Conflict, 1989–2003." *Journal of Peace Research* 41, 5: 625–636.

Escalante, Fernando. 2011. "Homicidios 2008–2009. La muerte tiene permiso." *Nexos,* January 1. http://www.nexos.com.mx/?p=14089 (last consulted: October 30, 2017).

Estévez López, Ariadna. 2007. "Transición a la democracia y derechos humanos en México: la pérdida de integralidad en el discurso." *Andamios* 3, 6: 7–32.

Estrada Mendoza, María de la Luz, Martha Yuriria Rodríguez Estrada, Gabriela Rivera Díaz, Rodolfo Manuel Domínguez Márquez, and Anayeli Pérez Garrido. 2014. *Estudio de la implementación del tipo penal de feminicidio en México: Causas y consecuencias 2012–2013.* Mexico City: Observatorio Ciudadano Nacional del Feminicidio.

Evans, Michael. 2014. "Los Zetas Drug Cartel Linked San Fernando Police to Migrant Massacres." *The National Security Archive,* December 22. http://nsarchive.gwu.edu (last consulted: October 30, 2017).

Evans, Peter B. 1995. *Embedded Autonomy: States and Industrial Transformation.* Princeton, NJ: Princeton University Press.

Excelsior. 2015. "Feminicidios evidencian pornografía sádica en Juárez: estudio." July 16. http://www.excelsior.com.mx/nacional/2015/07/16/1035059 (last consulted: October 30, 2017).

Executive Office for Immigration Review. 2016. "About the Office: Office of the Chief Immigration Judge." The United States Department of Justice. https://www.justice.gov/eoir/office-of-the-chief-immigration-judge (last consulted: May 27, 2016).

Fajnzylber, P., and H. Lopez. 2007. *Close to Home: The Development Impact of Remittances in Latin America.* Washington, D.C.: World Bank.

Fearon, James D., and Laitin, David. 2003. "Ethnicity, Insurgency, and Civil War." *American Political Science Review* 97, 1: 75–90.

Fein, Helen. 1995. "More Murder in the Middle: Life-integrity Violations and Democracy in the World." *Human Rights Quarterly* 17, 1: 170–191.

Ferri, Pablo. 2014. "Cronología del caso Tlatlaya." *Esquire Latinoamérica,* October. http://www.esquirelat.com/reportajes/14/10/23/Cronologia-del-caso-Tlatlaya (last consulted: October 30, 2017).

Finkel, Jodi S. 2008. *Judicial Reform as Political Insurance.* Notre Dame, IN: University of Notre Dame Press.

Finklea, Kristin M., et al. 2010. *Southwest Border Violence: Issues in Identifying and Measuring Spillover Violence.* Washington, D.C.: Congressional Research Service.

Flores, Raúl. 2014. "Se dedican a la trata 47 grupos criminales." *Excelsior,* July 30. http://www.excelsior.com.mx/nacional/2014/07/30/973599 (last consulted: October 30, 2017).

———. 2016. "Militares y federales torturan a mujer en Guerrero." *Excelsior,* April 14. http://www.excelsior.com.mx/nacional/2016/04/14/1086518 (last consulted: October 30, 2017).

Flores Pérez, Carlos Antonio. 2013. *Historias de polvo y sangre: génesis y evolución del tráfico de drogas en el estado de Tamaulipas.* Mexico City: CIESAS.

Fray Matías de Córdova, Refugio Hogar de la Misericordia. 2008. *La crisis de derechos humanos en la frontera sur de México.* Tapachula, Chiapas, Mexico: Fray Matías de Córdova.

Freeman, Laurie, and Jose Luis Sierra. 2005. "Mexico: The Militarization Trap." In *Drugs and Democracy in Latin America: The Impact of U.S. Foreign Policy,* edited by Coletta A. Youngers and Eileen Rosin, 263–302. Boulder, CO: Lynne Rienner Publishers.

Freeman, Michael. 2002. *Human Rights. An Interdisciplinary Approach.* Cambridge, UK: Polity Press.

Frey, Barbara. 2015. "Uneven Ground: Asymmetries of Power in Human Rights Advocacy in Mexico." In *The Social Practice of Human Rights,* edited by J. Pruce, 121–139. Basingstoke, UK: Palgrave-MacMillan.

Freyermuth, Graciela, Marisol Luna, and José A. Muños. 2016. *Indicadores 2014*. Mexico City: Centro de Investigaciones y Estudios Superiores en Antropología Social (CIESAS), Observatorio de Mortalidad Materna en México (OMM).

Frydman, Lisa, and Neha Desai. 2012. "Beacon of Hope or Failure of Protection? US Treatment of Asylum Claims Based on Persecution by Organized Gangs." In *Immigration Briefings*, vol. 12, no. 10, 1–51. St. Paul, MN: Westlaw.

Gallagher, Janice. 2012. "Mobilization in Mexico 2012: The Movement for Peace and the Struggle for Justice." *Anuari del Conflicte Social* 12, 1: 1,235–1,260.

———. 2017. "The Last Mile Problem: Activists, Advocates and the Struggle for Justice in Domestic Courts." *Comparative Political Studies* 50: 1,666–1,698.

García, Sergio. 2011. "Asylum for Former Mexican Police Officers Persecuted by the Narcos." *Boston College Third World Law Journal* 31, 2: 245–267.

Gauri, V., and D. M. Brinks. 2008. *Courting Social Justice: Judicial Enforcement of Social and Economic Rights in the Developing World*. Cambridge, UK: Cambridge University Press.

Gely, R., and P. T. Spiller. 2012. "The Political Economy of Supreme Court Constitutional Decisions: The Case of Roosevelt's Court-packing Plan." *International Review of Law and Economics* 12, 1: 45–67.

Germenji, E., and J. Swinnen. 2004. "Impact of Remittances on Household-based Farms in Rural Albania." Paper presented at the: International Conference on New Perspectives on Albanian Migration and Development, Korçë, Albania.

Giannou, C., and M. Baldan. 2010. "War Surgery, Working with Limited Resources in Armed Conflict and Other Situations of Violence." International Committee of the Red Cross (ICRC). https://www.icrc.org/eng/assets/files/other/icrc-002-0973.pdf (last consulted: October 30, 2017).

Gillman, H., and C. W. Clayton. 1999. *The Supreme Court in American Politics: New Institutionalist Interpretations*. Lawrence: University Press of Kansas.

Gloppen, Siri, Bruce M. Wilson, Roberto Gargarella, Elin Skaar, and Morten Kinander. 2010. *Courts and Power in Latin America and Africa*. New York: Palgrave Macmillan.

Gobierno de la República. 2007. *Plan Nacional de Desarrollo 2007–2012*. Mexico City: Gobierno de los Estados Unidos Mexicanos, Presidencia de la República.

———. 2013. *Plan Nacional de Desarrollo 2013–2018*. Mexico City: Gobierno de los Estados Unidos Mexicanos, Presidencia de la República.

Goche, Flor. 2015. "Más de 7 mil desaparecidas en México." *Contralínea*, September 13. http://www.contralinea.com.mx/archivo-revista/index.php/2015/09/13/mas-de-7-mil-desaparecidas-en-mexico/ (last consulted: September 13, 2015).

Gonzales Barrera, Ana, and Jens Manuel Krogstad. 2015. *What We Know About Illegal Migration from Mexico*. Washington, D.C.: Pew Research Center.

González, Marianne, and Claudio Nash. 2011. *Transparencia, lucha contra la corrupción y el sistema interamericano de derechos humanos*. Santiago, Chile: Centro de Derechos Humanos, Universidad de Chile.

González, Wilberth. 2014. "Sin tierra, sin casa, sin Gobierno." *Río Doce*, January 27. http://riodoce.mx/noticias/sociedad/sin-tierra-sin-casa-sin-gobierno (last consulted: February 2, 2016).

Gonzalez Ocantos, Ezequiel. 2014. "Persuade Them or Oust Them: Crafting Judicial Change and Transitional Justice in Argentina." *Comparative Politics, Forthcoming* 46, 4: 479–498.

Goodman, Gary L., and Jonathan T. Hiskey. 2008. "Exit Without Leaving: Political Disengagement in High Migration Municipalities in Mexico." *Comparative Politics* 40, 2: 169–188.

Goodwin-Gill, Guy S., and Jane McAdam. 2007. *The Refugee in International Law,* 3rd ed. Oxford: Oxford University Press.

Government of Canada. 2016. Data base 10.2. "Refugee Claimants by Top 50 Countries of Citizenship, 2005 to 2014. Facts and Figures 2014: Immigration Overview: Temporary Residents." Government of Canada. February. http://www.cic.gc.ca/english/resources/statistics/menu-fact.asp (last consulted: May 26, 2016).

Grayson, G., and S. Logan. 2012. *The Executioner's Men: Los Zetas, Rogue Soldiers, Criminal Entrepreneurs, and the Shadow State They Created.* Piscataway, New Jersey: Transaction.

Grupo de Información en Reproducción Elegida (GIRE). 2013. *Omisión e Indiferencia: Derechos Reproductivos en México.* Mexico City: GIRE.

———. 2015a. *Violencia Obstétrica: Un Enfoque de Derechos Humanos.* Mexico City: GIRE.

———. 2015b. *Niñas y Mujeres sin Justicia: Derechos Reproductivos en México.* Mexico City: GIRE.

Grupo Interdisciplinario de Expertos Independientes (GIEI). 2015. *Informe Ayotzinapa. Investigación y primeras conclusiones de las desapariciones y homicidios de los normalistas de Ayotzinapa.* Mexico City: GIEI.

Gubert, F. 2000. "Migration, Remittances and Moral Hazard. Evidence from the Kayes Area." *CERDI, Etudes et Documents 2000* 17: 32.

Guerrero, Eduardo. 2011. "La Raíz de La Violencia." *Nexos,* June 1. http://www.nexos.com.mx/?p=14318 (last consulted: October 20, 2018).

Guevara, José Antonio. 2014. "Conexiones entre los derechos humanos de las personas migrantes y la seguridad. ¿Es posible afirmar que el derecho mexicano criminaliza la migración indocumentada?" *Cuestiones constitucionales. Revista mexicana de derechos constitucional* 31: 81–117.

Gurney, Kyra. 2014. "Red de trata de personas en México revela cambio en el papel de los carteles." *InSight Crime,* July 31. http://es.insightcrime.org/noticias-del-dia/red-trata-personas-mexico-revela-cambio-papel-carteles (last consulted: October 30, 2017).

Gutiérrez, Edith, and Estela Rivero. 2012. "Diagnóstico estadístico sobre desplazamiento interno por violencia." In *Forced Displacement Linked to Transnational Organised Crime in Mexico,* edited by Laura Rubio, 8–15. Geneva, Switzerland: Internal Displacement Monitoring Center–Norwegian Refugee Council.

Haeri, Medina, and Puechguirbal, Nadine. 2010. "From Helplessness to Agency: Examining the Plurality of Women's Experiences in Armed Conflict." *International Review of the Red Cross* 92, 877: 103–122.

Hafner-Burton, Emilie. 2005. "Trading Human Rights: How Preferential Trade Agreements Influence Government Repression." *International Organization* 59, 3: 593–629.

———. 2013. *Making Human Rights a Reality.* Princeton, NJ: Princeton University Press.

Hamm, Brigitte. 2001. "A Human Rights Approach to Development." *Human Rights Quarterly* 23, 4: 1,005–1,031.

Hathaway, Oona. 2002. "Do Human Rights Treaties Make a Difference?" *Yale Law Journal* 111, 8: 1,935–2,042.

Hegre, Håvard, and Nicholas Sambanis. 2006. "Sensitivity Analysis of Empirical Results on Civil War Onset." *Journal of Conflict Resolution* 50, 4: 508–535.

Heinle, Kimberly, Corey Molzahn, and David A. Shirk. 2015. *Drug Violence in Mexico. Data and Analysis Through 2014, Special Report, Justice in Mexico Project.* San Diego, CA: Department of Political Science and International Relations, University of San Diego.

Heinle, Kimberly, Octavio Rodriguez Ferreira, and David A. Shirk. 2013. *Drug Violence in Mexico. Data and Analysis Through 2013, Special Report, Justice in Mexico Project.* San Diego, CA: Department of Political Science and International Relations, University of San Diego.

Helmke, Gretchen. 2002. "The Logic of Strategic Defection: Court-Executive Relations in Argentina Under Dictatorship and Democracy." *American Political Science Review* 96, 2: 291–303.

Helmke, Gretchen, and Julio Rios-Figueroa. 2011. *Courts in Latin America.* New York: Cambridge University Press.

Heras, Antonio. 2015. "Critican a alcalde de Tijuana por promover el turismo sexual." *La Jornada Baja California,* October 24. http://jornadabc.mx/tijuana/24-10-2015/critican-alcalde -de-tijuana-por-promover-el-turismo-sexual (last consulted: October 30, 2017).

Hernández, Evangelina. 2015. *Tierra de padrotes: Tenancingo, Tlaxcala, un velo de impunidad.* Mexico City: Tusquets Editores.

Hessbruegge, Jan Arno. 2005. "Human Rights Violations Rising from Conduct of Non-state Actors." *Buffalo Human Rights Law Review* 11: 21–88.

Heyman, Josiah McC., and Howard Campbell. 2007. "Corruption in the U.S. Borderlands with Mexico: The 'Purity' of Society and the 'Perversity' of Borders." In *Corruption and the Secret of Law: A Legal Anthropological Perspective,* edited by Monique Nuijten and Gerhard Anders, 191–217. Aldershot, UK: Ashgate.

Hilbink, Lisa. 2007. *Judges Beyond Politics in Democracy and Dictatorship: Lessons from Chile.* New York: Cambridge University Press.

Hill, Felicity, Mikele Aboitiz, and Sara Poehlman-Doumbouya. 2003. "Nongovernmental Organizations' Role in the Buildup and Implementation of Security Council Resolution 1325." *Signs* 28, 4: 1,255–1,269.

Hincapié, Sandra. 2015. "Estado y crisis de derechos humanos en México. Claves analíticas para su interpretación." *El Cotidiano* 193: 89–96.

Hincapié, Sandra, and Jairo López. 2016. "Ciclos de movilización y crisis de derechos humanos. La acción colectiva de las ONG nacionales y los derechos humanos en México." *Revista de Estudios Sociales* 56: 26–38.

Hope, Alejandro. 2016. "Para entender la espiral de violencia." *El Universal,* September 26. http://www.eluniversal.com.mx/entrada-de-opinion/columna/alejandro-hope/nacion /2016/09/26/para-entender-la-espiral-de-violencia (last consulted: October 30, 2017).

Human Rights Council. 2007. *Report of the Special Rapporteur on Extrajudicial, Summary or Arbitrary Executions, Philip Alston, Addendum, Mission to Guatemala.* A/HRC/4/20/Add.2, February 19.

———. 2009. "Resolution 11/8. Preventable Maternal Mortality and Morbidity and Human Rights." Adopted June 17.

———. 2010. *Report of the Special Rapporteur on Extrajudicial, Summary or Arbitrary Executions, Philip Alston, Addendum, Study on Targeted Killings.* A/HRC/14/24/Add.6, May 28.

———. 2013a. *Report of the Special Rapporteur on Torture and Other Cruel, Inhuman or Degrading Treatment or Punishment, Juan E. Méndez.* A/HRC/22/53, February 1.

———. 2013b. *Report of the Working Group on the Universal Periodic Review: México.* A/HRC/25/7, December 11.

———. 2014. *Report of the Special Raporteur on Torture, and Other Cruel, Inhuman or Degrading Treatment or Punishment, Juan E. Méndez. Addendum. Mission to Mexico.* A/HRC/28/68/ Add.3, December 29.

Human Rights Watch. 2003. *World Report 2003*. New York: Human Rights Watch.

———. 2009. *Uniform Impunity. Mexico's Misuse of Military Justice to Prosecute Abuses in Counternarcotics and Public Security Operations.* Washington, D.C., and New York: Human Rights Watch.

———. 2011. *Neither Rights nor Security. Killings, Torture and Disappearances in Mexico's "War on Drugs."* Washington, D.C., and New York: Human Rights Watch.

———. 2014. "Mexico. Resumen de país." https://www.hrw.org/sites/default/files/related_material/mexico_sp_4.pdf (last consulted: October 18, 2017).

———. 2015. "Mexico: Police Killings in Michoacán." October 28. https://www.hrw.org/news/2015/10/28/mexico-police-killings-michoacan (last consulted: October 18, 2017).

———. 2016. *World Report 2016: Mexico.* https://www.hrw.org/world-report/2016/country-chapters/mexico (last consulted: November 2, 2017).

———. 2017. *World Report 2017. Mexico.* https://www.hrw.org/es/world-report/2017/country-chapters/298379 (last consulted: October 23, 2017).

Huneeus, Alexandra. 2010. "Judging from a Guilty Conscience: The Chilean Judiciary's Human Rights Turn." *Law & Social Inquiry* 35, 1: 99–135.

Huntington, Thomas. 1968. *Political Order in Changing Societies.* New Haven, CT: Yale University Press.

Immigration Canada News. 2015. "Refugee Acceptance Up in Canada Despite Stricter Asylum Conditions." *Immigration Canada,* March. http://www.immigration.ca/en/quebecimmigration-topmenu/181-canada-immigration-news-articles/2015/march/1256-refugee-acceptance-canada-stricter-asylum-conditions.html (last consulted: May 26, 2016).

Ingram, Matthew C., and David A. Shirk. 2012. "Building Institutional Capacity in Mexico's Criminal Justice System." In *Mexico's Struggle for Public Security. Organized Crime and State Response,* edited by George Philip and Susana Berruecos, 119–145. New York: Palgrave MacMillan.

Institute for Economics and Peace. 2016. *Mexico Peace Index 2016. Mapping the Evolution of Peace and Its Drivers.* Sydney, New York, Brussels, and Mexico City: Institute for Economics and Peace.

Instituto Nacional de Estadística y Geografía (INEGI). 2011. "Encuesta Nacional de Ocupación y Empleo (ENOE) 2010." http://www.beta.inegi.org.mx/app/biblioteca/ficha.html?upc=702825445072 (last consulted: November 3, 2017).

———. 2013a. "Panorama de violencia contra las mujeres en México. ENDIREH 2011." http://internet.contenidos.inegi.org.mx/contenidos/productos/prod_serv/contenidos/espanol/bvinegi/productos/estudios/sociodemografico/mujeresrural/2011/702825048327.pdf (last consulted: October 18, 2017).

———. 2013b. "Encuesta Nacional de Víctimización y Percepción sobre seguridad pública (ENVIPE) 2013." http://www.beta.inegi.org.mx/proyectos/enchogares/regulares/envipe/2013/default.html (last consulted: October 18, 2017).

———. 2014a. "Encuesta Nacional de la Dinámica Demográfica (ENADI) 2014." http://www.beta.inegi.org.mx/proyectos/enchogares/especiales/enadid/2014/ (last consulted: October 18, 2017).

———. 2014b. "Encuesta Nacional de Víctimización y Percepción sobre seguridad pública (ENVIPE) 2014." http://www.beta.inegi.org.mx/proyectos/enchogares/regulares/envipe/2014/default.html (last consulted: October 18, 2017).

———. 2015a. "Anuario estadístico y geográfico de los Estados Unidos Mexicanos 2015." http:// www3.inegi.org.mx/sistemas/biblioteca/ficha.aspx?upc=702825077280 (last consulted: February 11, 2016).

———. 2015b. "Encuesta Nacional de Víctimización y Percepción sobre seguridad pública (ENVIPE) 2015." http://www.beta.inegi.org.mx/proyectos/enchogares/regulares/envipe /2015/ (last consulted: October 18, 2017).

———. 2017. "Encuesta Nacional sobre la Dinámica de las Relaciones en los Hogares 2016 (ENDI-REH-2016)." http://www.beta.inegi.org.mx/proyectos/enchogares/especiales/endireh/2016/ (last consulted: October 30, 2017).

Inter-American Commission on Human Rights (IACHR). 2003. *The Situation of the Rights of Women in Ciudad Juárez, Mexico: The Right to Be Free from Violence and Discrimination.* OEA/Ser.L/V/II.117. Doc. 44, March 7.

———. 2009. *Report on Citizen Security and Human Rights.* OEA/Ser.L/V/II. Doc. 57, December 31.

———. 2010. *Access to Maternal Health Services from a Human Rights Perspective.* OEA/Ser.L/V/ II. Doc. 69, June 7.

———. 2013. *Human Rights of Migrants and Other Persons in the Context of Human Mobility in Mexico.* OEA/Ser.L/V/II. Doc. 48/13, December 30.

———. 2015a. *Situation of Human Rights in Mexico.* OEA/Ser.L/V/II. Doc. 44/15, December 31.

———. 2015b. "Resolución 14/15, Medida Cautelar No. 77-15, Asunto: Defensoras E. y K. y sus familiares, respecto de México." April 27. http://www.oas.org/es/cidh/decisiones/pdf/2015 /MC77-15-ES.pdf (last consulted: February 14, 2016).

Inter-American Court of Human Rights (IACtHR). 2009. *Case of Radilla Pacheco v. Mexico. Preliminary Objections, Merits, Reparations, and Costs.* November 23. Series C No. 209.

International Center for Transitional Justice (ICTJ). 2008. "Mexico. Submission to the Universal Periodic Review of the UN Human Rights Council. Fourth Session: February 2–13, 2009." September 8. https://www.ictj.org/sites/default/files/ICTJ-Mexico-Periodic-Review-2008 -English.pdf (last consulted: October 2, 2017).

International Council on Human Rights Policy (ICHRP). 2009. *La Corrupción y los Derechos Humanos. Estableciendo el Vínculo.* Geneva and Monterrey, Mexico City: International Council on Human Rights Policy and Tecnológico de Monterrey-EGAP.

International Displacement Monitoring Center (IDMC). 2012. *Forced Displacement Linked to Transnational Organised Crime in Mexico.* Geneva: Norwegian Refugee Council-Internal Displacement Monitoring Centre.

———. 2015. *People Internally Displaced by Violence and Conflict.* Geneva: Norwegian Refugee Council-Internal Displacement Monitoring Centre.

———. 2016. *Global Report on Internal Displacement (2016).* Geneva: Norwegian Refugee Council-Internal Displacement Monitoring Centre.

———. 2017. *Global Report on Internal Displacement (2017).* Geneva: Norwegian Refugee Council-Internal Displacement Monitoring Centre.

Isacson, Adam, and Maureen Meyer. 2012. *Beyond the Border Buildup: Security and Migrants Along the U.S.-Mexico Border.* Washington, D.C.: Washington Office on Latin America.

Isunza, Ernesto, and Adrián Gurza. 2010. *La innovación democrática en América Latina. Tramas y nudos de la representación, la participación y el control social.* Mexico City: CIESAS/Universidad Veracruzana.

Jetschke, Anja, and Andrea Liese. 2013. "The Power of Human Rights a Decade After: From Euphoria to Contestation." In *The Persistent Power of Human Rights: From Commitment to Compliance,* edited by Thomas Risse, Stephen Ropp, and Kathryn Sikkink, 26–42. New York: Cambridge University Press.

Kaldor, Mary. 2001. *Las nuevas guerras: la violencia organizada en la era global.* Barcelona: Tusquets.

Kalyvas, Stathis. 2003. "The Ontology of ` Political Violence ': Action and Identity in Civil Wars." *Perspectives on Politics* 1, 3: 475–494.

Kapiszewski, Diana. 2012a. *High Courts and Economic Governance in Argentina and Brazil,* 1st ed. Cambridge, UK: Cambridge University Press.

Kapiszewski, Diana, Gordon Silverstein, and Robert A. Kagan. 2013. *Consequential Courts: Judicial Roles in Global Perspective.* Cambridge, UK: Cambridge University Press.

Keck, Margaret E., and Kathryn Sikkink. 2014. *Activists Beyond Borders: Advocacy Networks in International Politics.* Ithaca, NY: Cornell University Press.

Kerry, John. 2016. *"Letter From Secretary Kerry" Trafficking in Persons Report 2016.* Washington, D.C.: U.S. Department of State.

Kimmerle, Erin, and Jose Skeletal Baraybar. 2008. *Trauma: Identification of Injuries Resulting from Human Rights Abuse and Armed Conflict.* Boca Raton, FL: CRC Press.

King, John C. 1988. "Repression, Domestic Threat, and Interactions in Argentina and Chile." *Journal of Political & Military Sociology* 26, 2: 1,991–1,211.

Krogstad, Jens Manuel, and Jeffrey S. Passel. 2014. *U.S. Border Apprehensions of Mexicans Fall to Historic Lows.* Washington, D.C.: Pew Research Center.

Kurzban, Ira J. 2014. *Kurzban's Immigration Law Sourcebook,* 14th ed. Washington, D.C.: American Immigration Council.

Lachaud, J. P. 1999. *Pauvreté, Ménages et Genre en Afrique Subsaharienne.* Bordeaux: Centre d'Economie du Developpement de l'Universite Montesquieu Bordeaux IV.

Lagarde, Marcela. 2011. "Prefacio: claves feministas en torno al feminicidio. Construcción teorica, politica y juridica." In *Feminicidio en América Latina,* edited by Rosa-Linda Fregoso, 11–14. México: Centro de Investigaciones Interdisciplinarias en Ciencias y Humanidades (CEIICH)-UNAM, Red de Investigadoras por la Vida y la Libertad de las Mujeres (Diversidad Feminista).

La Jornada. 2010. "Nos empiezan a cansar cantaletas contra el ejército, dice Calderón." *La Jornada,* August 27.

Landman, Todd. 2005. *Protecting Human Rights: A Comparative Study.* Washington, D.C.: Georgetown University Press.

———. 2006. *Studying Human Rights.* New York: Routledge.

Lanier, Mark M., Staurt Henry, and Desiré J. M. Anastasia. 2015. *Essential Criminology.* Boulder, CO: Westview Press.

Lattman, Peter. 2006. "A Paean to the Opinions of the Prolific Judge Posner." *The Wall Street Journal Law Blog,* October 6.

Le Clercq, Jose Antonio, and Gerardo Rodriguez. 2016. *Indice Global de Impunidad Mexico 2016.* Puebla, Mexico: Universidad de las Americas Puebla.

Lee, Matthew T., Ramiro Martinez Jr., and Richard Rosenfeld. 2001. "Does Immigration Increase Homicide Rates? Negative Evidence from Three Border Cities." *Sociological Quarterly* 42: 559–580.

León, Miguel Ángel. 2016a. "Los feminicidios con Duarte aumentan a 509: la impunidad los alienta, acusa académica de la UV." *Sinembargo.mx*, July 2. http://www.sinembargo.mx/02 -07-2016/3061849 (last consulted: October 30, 2017).

———. 2016b. "Y en Veracruz, sin ayuda oficial, la Brigada halla a flor de tierra más fosas y cuerpos carbonizados." *Sinembargo.mx*, August 10. http://www.sinembargo.mx/10-08-2016 /3078333http://www.sinembargo.mx/10-08-2016/3078333 (last consulted: October 30, 2017).

Lessa, Francesca, Tricia D. Olsen, Leigh A. Payne, Gabriel Pereira, and Andrew G. Reiter. 2014. "Overcoming Impunity: Pathways to Accountability in Latin America." *International Journal of Transitional Justice* 8, 1: 75–98.

Levi, Primo. 1987. *If This Is a Man*. London: Abacus.

Loche, Adriana. 2010. "A letalidade da ação policial: parâmetros para análise." *Revista do Núcleo de Pós-Graduação e Pesquisa em Ciências Sociais* 17: 39–56.

Long, Kathy. 2010. *Home Alone? A Review of the Relationship Between Repatriation, Mobility and Durable Solutions for Refugees*. Geneva: UNHCR.

Lutz, E., and K. Sikkink. 2000. "International Human Rights Law and Practice in Latin America." *International Organization* 54, 3: 633–659.

Lyons, Christopher J., María B. Vélez, and Wayne A. Santoro. 2013. "Neighborhood Immigration, Violence, and City-Level Immigrant Political Opportunities." *American Sociological Review* 78, 4: 604–632.

Madrazo Lajous, Alejandro. 2014. "Los costos constitucionales de la guerra contra las drogas: Una primera aproximación desde México, Cuaderno de Trabajo No. 12, Programa de Política de Drogas del Centro de Investigación y Docencia Económicas (CIDE), Región Centro." Aguascalientes, Mexico: CIDE.

Magaloni, Ana Laura, and Arturo Zaldivar. 2006. "El ciudadano olvidado." *Nexos*, June 1. http:// www.nexos.com.mx/?p=11915 (last consulted: October 30, 2017).

Magaloni Kerpel, Ana Laura. 2007. "Arbitrariedad e ineficiencia de la procuracion de justicia: Dos caras de la misma moneda, Working Paper No 26." Mexico City: Department of Juridical Studies, Centro de Investigación y Docencia Económica (CIDE).

Manjarrés, Azucena. 2013. "El silencio que reclama justicia." *El Universal*, January 21. http:// www.noroeste.com.mx/publicaciones.php?id=841539 (last consulted: October 30, 2017).

Mars, Joan R. 2002. *Deadly Force, Colonialism, and the Rule of Law: Police Violence in Guyana*. Westport, CT: Greenwood.

Martínez, Diana. 2016. "Alerta de Género: una esperanza aún lejana para las mujeres." *Expansión*, March 8. http://expansion.mx/economia/2016/03/08/alerta-de-genero-una-esperanza -contra-los-feminicidios (last consulted: October 30, 2017).

Martínez, Lupita. 2016. "Torturan militares y federales a una mujer." *SDPnoticias.com*, April 14. http://www.sdpnoticias.com/nacional/2016/04/14/torturan-militares-y-federales-a-una -mujer-video (last consulted: October 30, 2017).

Martinez, Ramiro Jr. 2002. *Latino Homicide: Immigration, Violence and Community*. New York: Routledge Press.

Martinez, Ramiro Jr., Matthew T. Lee, and Amie L. Nielsen. 2004. "A Segmented Assimilation, Local Context and Determinants of Drug Violence in Miami and San Diego: Does Ethnicity and Immigration Matter?" *International Migration Review* 38: 131–157.

Martinez Ahrens, Jan. 2016. "El Ejército mexicano se disculpa por primera vez por un caso de torturas." *El País*, April 17. http://internacional.elpais.com/internacional/2016/04/16 /mexico/1460834706_958329.html (last consulted: April 18, 2016).

Massey, Douglas S., and Lawrence C. Basem. 1992. "Determinants of Savings, Remittances, and Spending Patterns Among U.S. Migrants in Four Mexican Communities." *Sociological Inquiry* 62, 2: 185–207.

Massey, Douglas, Luin Goldring, and Jorge Durand. 1994. "Continuities in Transnational Migration: An Analysis of Nineteen Mexican Communities." *American Journal of Sociology* 99, 6: 1,492–1,533.

Mastrogiovanni, Federico. 2013. "El negocio de la migración. Migrantes centroamericanos en tránsito por México hacia Estados Unidos." MA thesis, Universidad Nacional Autónoma de México (UNAM), Mexico City.

McAdam, Jane. 2012. *Climate Change, Forced Migration, and International Law.* Oxford: Oxford University Press.

———. 2014. "Human Rights and Forced Migration." In *The Oxford Handbook of Refugee and Forced Migration Studies,* edited by Gil Loescher, Katy Long, Nando Sigona, and Elena Fiddian-Qasmiyeh, 203–214. Oxford: Oxford University Press.

Mckenzie, David, and Hillel Rapoport. 2006. "Network Effects and the Dynamics of Migration and Inequality: Theory and Evidence from Mexico." *Journal of Development Economics* 84, 1: 1–24.

Mejía, Alberto. 2016. "Colectivo Familias de Desaparecidos Orizaba-Córdoba hallan restos óseos calcinados." *AGN Veracruz,* August 9. http://elinformantedeveracruz.com/single.php?id=11675 (last consulted: April 7, 2018).

Merino, Mauricio. 2003. *La transición votada: crítica a la interpretación del cambio político en México.* Mexico City: Fondo de Cultura Económica.

Merton, Robert K. 1938. "Social Structure and Anomie." *American Sociological Review* 3, 5: 672–682.

México Evalúa. 2012. *Seguridad y Justicia Penal en los Estados: 25 Indicadores de Nuestra Debilidad Institucional.* Mexico City: México Evalúa Centro de Análisis de Políticas Públicas.

Meyer, Maureen. 2010. "Abused and Afraid in Ciudad Juarez: An Analysis of Human Rights Violations by the Military in Mexico." Washington Office on Latin America and Center PRODH, September. https://www.wola.org/sites/default/files/downloadable/Mexico/2010/WOLA_RPT_Juarez_FNL2-color.pdf (last consulted: April 17, 2018).

Michel, Veronica, and Kathryn Sikkink. 2013. "Participation Rights of Victims in Criminal Proceedings and Human Rights Prosecutions." *Law and Society Review* 47, 4: 873–907.

Milanovic, Branko. 1987. "Remittances and Income Distribution." *Journal of Economic Studies* 14, 5: 24–37.

Mines, Richard, and Alain de Janvry. 1982. "Migration to the United States and Mexican Rural Development—A Case Study." *American Journal of Agricultural Economics* 64, 3: 444–454.

Mitchell, Neil J., and James M. McCormick. 1988. "Economic and Political Explanations of Human Rights Violations." *World Politics* 40, 4: 476–498.

Morris, Stephen D., and Joseph L. Klesner. 2010. "Corruption and Trust: Theoretical Considerations and Evidence from Mexico." *Comparative Political Studies* 43, 10: 1,258–1,285.

Movimiento Migrante Centroamericano. 2016. "Madres de migrantes desaparecidos envían carta al Papa Francisco." *Movimiento migrante mesoamericano,* February 11. https://movimientomigrantemesoamericano.org/2016/02/11/madres-de-migrantes-desaparecidos-envian-carta-al-papa-francisco/ (last consulted: October 30, 2017).

MundoFox. 2014. "La Tuta: Incómodo y acusador, lo que no se vio." January 21. https://www.youtube.com/watch?v=bwUHxfGZI-0 (last consulted: April 7, 2018).

Musalo, Karen. 2015. "Personal Violence, Public Matter: Evolving Standards in Gender-Based Asylum Law." *Harvard International Review* 36, 2: 45–48.

Nash, Claudio. 2014. *Corrupción y derechos humanos: una mirada desde la jurisprudencia de la Corte Interamericana de Derechos Humanos.* Santiago, Chile: Centro de Derechos Humanos—Universidad de Chile.

National Immigrant Justice Center. 2016. *Basic Procedural Manual for Asylum Representation.* https://www.immigrantjustice.org/resources/procedural-manual-asylum-representation (last consulted: October 30, 2017).

Navia, Patricio, and Julio Ríos-Figueroa. 2005. "The Constitutional Adjudication Mosaic of Latin America." *Comparative Political Studies* 38, 2: 189–217.

Neumayer, Erick. 2005. "Do International Human Rights Treaties Improve Respect for Human Rights?" *The Journal of Conflict Resolution* 49, 6: 925–953.

Nobles, Jenna. 2011. "Parenting from Abroad: Migration, Nonresident Father Involvement, and Children's Education in Mexico." *Journal of Marriage and Family* 73, 4: 729–746.

Nowrojee, Binaifer. 2003. "Your Justice Is Too Slow: Will the ICTR Fail Rwanda's Rape Victims?" Consortium on Gender, Security and Human Rights, Working Paper No. 105. Boston: University of Massachusetts–Boston.

Observatorio Ciudadano del Sistema de Justicia (OCSJ). Arraigo, Medidas Cautelares y Ejecución Penal. 2015. *El uso del arraigo a nivel federal, en el estado de Nuevo León y el Distrito Federal: Análisis de constitucionalidad, legislación y práctica.* Mexico City: OCSJ.

O'Donnell, Guillermo. 2004. "Why the Rule of Law Matters." *Journal of Democracy* 15, 4: 32–46.

O'Donnell, Guillermo, Philippe C. Schmitter, and Laurence Whitehead, eds. 1986a. *Transitions from Authoritarian Rule. Comparative Perspectives.* Baltimore and London: The Johns Hopkins University Press.

———. 1986b. *Transitions from Authoritarian Rule: Latin America.* Baltimore and London: The Johns Hopkins University Press.

———. 1986c. *Transitions from Authoritarian Rule: Southern Europe.* Baltimore and London: The Johns Hopkins University Press.

———. 1986d. *Transitions from Authoritarian Rule: Tentative Conclusions About Uncertain Democracies.* Baltimore and London: The Johns Hopkins University Press.

Office of the United Nations High Commissioner for Human Rights (OHCHR). 2005. *Set of Principles for the Protection and Promotion of Human Rights Through Action to Combat Impunity.* E/CN.4/2005/102/Add.1. February 8.

Olsen, Tricia D., Leigh A. Payne, and Andrew G. Reiter. 2010. *Transitional Justice in Balance: Comparing Processes, Weighing Efficacy.* Washington, D.C.: U.S. Institute of Peace.

Olson, Joy. 2012. "Organized Crime as Human Rights Issue." *Harvard Review of Latin America* 11: 10–12.

Olvera, Alberto. 2003. "Las tendencias generales de desarrollo de la sociedad civil en México." In *Sociedad Civil, esfera pública y democratización en América Latina: Mexico,* edited by Alberto Olvera, 42–70. Mexico City: Fondo de Cultura Económica.

Olvera, Alberto. 2010. *La democratización frustrada. Limitaciones institucionales y colonización política de las instituciones garantes de derechos y de participación ciudadana en México.* Mexico City: CIESAS/Universidad de Veracruz.

Olvera, Dulce. 2016. "Madres toman las calles en 5 estados y la CdMx para reclamar por sus hijos desaparecidos." *Sinembargo.mx,* May 10. http://www.sinembargo.mx/10-05-2016 /1658703 (last consulted: October 30, 2017).

ONU. 2015. "El Alto Comisionado de la ONU para los Derechos Humanos concluye visita a México, October 7." http://www.un.org/spanish/News/story.asp?NewsID=33542#.Vqe_r8eta1V (last consulted: January 30, 2016).

ONU Mujeres. 2012. *México ante la CEDAW.* Mexico City: ONU/ONU-Mujeres/UNFPA.

Open Society Justice Initiative. 2016. *Atrocidades innegables: Confrontando crímenes de lesa humanidad en México.* New York: Open Society Foundations.

Organización de Estados Americanos (OEA). 2014. "Derechos humanos de los migrantes y otras personas en el contexto de la movilidad humana en México." *CIDH,* August 18. http://www.oas.org/es/cidh/prensa/Comunicados/2014/088.asp (last consulted: February 12, 2016.)

———. 2015. "Observaciones Preliminares de la Visita *in Loco* de la CIDH a México, October 2." http://www.oas.org/es/cidh/prensa/comunicados/2015/112A.asp (last consulted: October 15, 2015.)

Organization for Economic Cooperation and Development (OECD). n/d. "OECD Data. National Income." https://data.oecd.org/natincome/net-national-income.htm (last consulted: November 15, 2017).

———. 2015. "Revenue Statistics 1965–2014." OECD Publishing. http://dx.doi.org/10.1787/10.1787/ (last consulted February 11, 2016).

Ousey, G. C., and C. E. Kubrin. 2009. "Exploring the Connection Between Immigration and Violent Crime Rates in U.S. Cities, 1980–2000." *Social Problems* 56, 3: 447–473.

París Pombo, Ma. Dolores. 2012. "Cambio institucional, organización política y migración entre los triquis de Copala." In *Migrantes, Desplazados, Braceros y Deportados: Experiencias Migratorias y Prácticas Políticas,* edited by Ma. Dolores París Pombo, 109–146. México: Colef-UACJ-UAM.

Partlow, Joshua. 2015. "U.S. Blocks Some Anti-drug Funds for Mexico over Human Rights Concerns." *The Washington Post,* October 18. https://www.washingtonpost.com/world/the_americas/us-blocks-some-anti-drug-funds-for-mexico-over-human-rights-concerns/2015/10/18/8fa3925e-710b-11e5-ba14-318f8e87a2fc_story.html (last consulted: December 17, 2015).

Peña Nieto, Enrique. 2013. *Primer Informe de Gobierno.* http://www.presidencia.gob.mx/primerinforme/ (last consulted: November 30, 2015).

———. 2014. *Segundo Informe de Gobierno.* http://www.presidencia.gob.mx/segundoinforme/ (last consulted: December 9, 2015).

———. 2015. *Tercer Informe de Gobierno.* http://www.presidencia.gob.mx/tercerinforme/ (last consulted: December 9, 2015).

———. 2016. *Cuarto Informe de Gobierno.* http://www.presidencia.gob.mx/cuartoinforme/ (last consulted: October 18, 2017).

Perez Correa, Catalina, Carlos Silva Forne, and Rodrigo Gutierrez Rivas. 2011. "Índice letal: los operativos y los muertos." *Nexos,* November 1.

———. 2015. "Índice de letalidad. Menos enfrentamientos mas opacidad." *Nexos,* July 1.

Permanent Council of the Organization of American States, Committee on Juridical and Political Affairs. 2014. *Draft Resolution. Internally Displaced Persons,* OEA/Ser.G. CP/CAJP-3252/14 rev. 2. May 23.

Pickering, Sharon. 2005. "Crimes of the State: The Persecution and Protection of Refugees." *Critical Criminology* 13, 2: 141–163.

Pinker, Steven. 2011. *The Better Angels of Our Nature: Why Violence Has Declined.* New York: Penguin Books.

Powell, Emilia J., and Jeffrey K. Staton. 2009. "Domestic Judicial Institutions and Human Rights Treaty Violation." *International Studies Quarterly* 53, 1: 149–174.

Presidencia de la Republica. 2006. *Plan Nacional de Desarrollo 2006–2012.* Mexico City: Presidencia de la República.

———. 2007. "Plan Nacional de Desarrollo 2007–2012." *Gobierno de los Estados Unidos Mexicanos, Presidencia de la Republica.* http://www.cenidet.edu.mx/docs/pnd_2007_2012.pdf (last consulted: February 17, 2016).

———. 2011. "El Presidente Calderón en la Inauguración de la semana nacional de migración. Derechos humanos de migrantes." October 17. http://calderon.presidencia.gob.mx/?s=migrantes+centroamericanos&tipo_busqueda=2&cat1=1006&dia=0&mes=0&anio=0&dia2=0&mes2=0&anio2=0 (last consulted: February 17, 2016).

Price, Matthew E. 2006. "Persecution Complex: Justifying Asylum Law's Preference for Persecuted People." *Harvard International Law Journal* 47, 2: 413–466.

Procuraduria General de la Republica. n/d. "Información Estadística sobre Desaparición de Personas. Base Personas Desaparecidas 2014–Junio 2015." http://www.pgr.gob.mx/Transparencia/Paginas/desaparicion-personas.aspx (last consulted: April 21, 2016).

Puerchguirbal, Nadine. 2010. "Discourses on Gender, Patriarchy and Resolution 1325: A Textual Analysis of UN Documents." *International Peacekeeping* 17, 2: 172–187.

Pulido, Miguel. 2016. "El arte de negar y negar." *Aristegui Noticias,* March 3. http://aristeguinoticias.com/0303/mexico/el-arte-de-negar-y-negar-negar-y-negar-articulo-de-miguel-pulido/ (last consulted: October 30, 2017).

Radio Fórmula. 2012. "Malova ofrece protección a desplazados por inseguridad." *Radio Fórmula,* May 15. http://radioformula.com.mx/notas.asp?Idn=243616 (last consulted: February 2, 2016).

Ramji-Nogales, Andrew, I. Schoenholtz, and Philip G. Schrag. 2007. "Refugee Roulette: Disparities in Asylum Adjudication." *Stanford Law Review* 60, 295: 295–412.

Rea, Daniela, and Lydiette Carrión. 2015. "Así matan a las mujeres en México." *Liberación mx,* April 28. http://www.liberacionmx.com/nota.php?NotaID=2164 (last consulted: March 15, 2016).

Redacción. 2015. "La gente pobre y sin estudios, el principal activo del PRI: encuesta." *CNN-México,* May 5. http://www.ehui.com/2015/05/la-gente-pobre-y-sin-estudios-el-principal-activo-del-pri-encuesta/ (last consulted: April 7, 2018).

Reforma. 2014. "Sería una excepción el caso Tlatlaya: SEGOB." *Reforma,* September 26. http://www.reforma.com/aplicaciones/articulo/default.aspx?id=350986&impresion=1 (last consulted: November 19, 2016).

Regan Patrick, and Errol Henderson. 2002. "Democracy, Threats and Political Repression in Developing Countries: Are Democracies Internally Less Violent?" *Third World Quarterly* 23, 1: 119–136.

Reichert, Joshua S. 1981. "The Migrant Syndrome: Seasonal U.S. Wage Labor and Rural Development in Central Mexico." *Human Organizations* 40, 1: 56–66.

Reid, Lesley W., Harold E. Weiss, Robert M. Adelman, and Charles Jaret. 2005. "The Immigration-Crime Relationship: Evidence Across US Metropolitan Areas." *Social Science Research* 34, 4: 757–780.

Rice, Susan, and Stewart Patrick. 2008. "Index of State Weakness in the Developing World." The Brookings Institution. http://www.brookings.edu/~/media/Research/Files/Reports/2008/2/weak-states-index/02_weak_states_index.PDF (last consulted: February 11, 2016).

Ríos Figueroa, Julio. 2007. "Fragmentation of Power and the Emergence of an Effective Judiciary in Mexico, 1994–2002." *Latin American Politics and Society* 49, 1: 31–57.

———. 2010. "Justicia constitucional y derechos humanos." *Revista Latinoamericana de Política Comparada* 3: 53–68.

Ríos Figueroa, J., and A. Pozas-Loyo. 2010. "Enacting Constitutionalism: The Origins of Independent Judicial Institutions in Latin America." *Comparative Politics* 42, 3: 293–311.

Risse, Thomas, Stephen Ropp, and Kathryn Sikkink, eds. 1999. *The Power of Human Rights: International Norms and Domestic Change.* Cambridge, UK: Cambridge University Press.

———. 2013. *The Persistent Power of Human Rights: From Commitment to Compliance.* Cambridge, UK: Cambridge University Press.

Risse, Thomas, and Stephen Ropp. 2013. "Introduction and Overview." In *The Persistent Power of Human Rights: From Commitment to Compliance,* edited by Thomas Risse, Stephen Ropp, and Kathryn Sikkink, 3–25. Cambridge, UK: Cambridge University Press.

Rivas, Francisco. 2014. *Estadística sobre la eficiencia en el combate a la trata de personas en México.* Mexico City: Observatorio Nacional Ciudadano.

Robledo Silvestre, Carolina. 2015. "El laberinto de las sombras: desaparecer en el marco de la guerra contra las drogas." *Estudios Políticos* 47: 89–108.

Rodriguez, Victoria E. 1997. *Decentralization in Mexico. From Reforma Municipal to Solidaridad to Nuevo Federalismo.* Boulder, CO: Westview Press.

Rodriguez Ferreira, Octavio, and David Shirk. 2016. *Criminal Procedure Reform in Mexico, 2008–2016. The Final Countdown for Implementation, Special Report Justice in Mexico.* San Diego, CA: University of San Diego.

Rosagel, Shaila. 2016. "La lista de estados donde ser mujer es un riesgo crece, y los gobiernos no oyen, dicen ONGs." *Vanguardia,* March 26. http://www.vanguardia.com.mx/articulo /la-lista-de-estados-donde-ser-mujer-es-un-riesgo-crece-y-los-gobiernos-no-oyen-dicen -ongs (last consulted: October 30, 2017).

Rose-Ackerman, Susan, ed. 2006. *International Handbook on the Economics of Corruption.* Northampton, MA: Edward Elgar Publishing Limited.

Rose-Ackerman, Susan. 2009. "Economía política de las raíces de la corrupción: investigación y políticas públicas." In *Corrupción y transparencia. Debatiendo las fronteras entre Estado, mercado y sociedad,* edited by Irma Erendira Sandoval, 23–43. Mexico City: Instituto de Investigaciones Sociales–UNAM/Siglo XXI.

Rosenblum, Marc R., and Idean Salehyan. 2004. "Norms and Interests in US Asylum Enforcement." *Journal of Peace Research* 41, 6: 677–697.

Roht-Arriaza, Naomi. 2006. "The New Landscape of Transitional Justice." In *Transitional Justice in the Twenty-First Century: Beyond Truth versus Justice,* edited by Naomi Roht-Arriaza and Javier Mariezcurrena, 1–16. New York: Cambridge University Press.

Rottman, Andy, Christopher J. Fariss, and Steven C. Poe. 2009. "The Path to Asylum in the US and the Determinants for Who Gets In and Why." *International Migraton Review* 43, 1: 3–34.

Rubio Díaz-Leal, Laura. 2015. "Desplazamiento interno forzado en México: El debate sobre conceptos, cifras y la responsabilidad del Estado." Paper from workshop "Los Grupos Criminales Organizados y la Nueva Ola de Desplazamiento Forzado en América Latina" (Organised Criminal Groups and the New Wave of Forced Displacement in Latin America), held on May 22–23, 2014, in San Salvador, El Salvador, with Mauricio Gaborit, Universidad Centroamericana (UCA), and David James Cantor, Refugee Law Initiative (RLI), as co-convenors.

——. 2014. *Desplazamiento interno inducido por la violencia: Una experiencia global, una realidad mexicana.* Mexico City: CMDPDH.

Rubio Díaz-Leal, Laura, and Brenda Pérez Vázquez. 2016. "Desplazados por violencia: La tragedia invisible." *Nexos* 457: 30–39.

Rubio Díaz-Leal, Laura, and Daniela Bachi. 2015. "Desplazamiento interno forzado en el multilateralismo: evolución normativa y participación de México." In *México y el multilateralismo en el siglo XXI,* edited by Guadalupe González, Olga Pellicer, and Natalia Saltalamacchia 236–268. Mexico: CIDE- ITAM-Senado de la República.

Rubio Díaz-Leal, Laura, and Sebastián Albuja. 2014. "Criminal Violence and Displacement in Mexico: Evidence, Perceptions and Politics." In *Crisis and Migration. Critical Perspectives,* edited by Anna Lindley, 73–92. London: Routledge.

Rubin, Jeffrey W. 1997. *Decentering the Regime. Ethnicity, Radicalism and Democracy in Juchitán, Mexico.* Durham, NC, and London: Duke University Press.

Sagot, Montserrat, and Ana Carcedo. 2011. "Cuando la violencia contra las mujeres mata: femicidio em Costa Rica, 1990–1999." In *Feminicidio en América Latina,* edited by Rosa-Linda Fregoso, 193–220. Mexico City: Centro de Investigaciones Interdisciplinarias en Ciencias y Humanidades (CEIICH)-UNAM, Red de Investigadoras por la Vida y la Libertad de las Mujeres (Diversidad Feminista).

Saltalamacchia Ziccardi, Natalia, and Ana Covarrubias Velasco. 2011. "La trayectoria de los derechos humanos en la política exterior de México 1945–2006." In *Derechos Humanos en Política Exterior. Seis casos latinoamericanos,* edited by Natalia Saltalamacchia Ziccardi and Ana Covarrubias Velasco, 161–211. Mexico City: Porrúa & ITAM.

Sambanis, Nicholas. 2004. "What Is Civil War? Conceptual and Empirical Complexities of an Operational Definition." *The Journal of Conflict Resolutions* 48, 6: 814–858.

Sampson, Robert J., Jeffrey Morenoff, and Stephen Raudenbush. 2005. "Social Anatomy of Racial and Ethnic Disparities in Violence." *American Journal of Public Health* 95, 2: 224–232.

Sánchez, Paulina, and Carlos de la Rosa. 2015. "Por qué preocuparte aunque no seas periodista." *Animal Político,* September 1. http://www.animalpolitico.com/blogueros-tanque-pensante /2015/09/01/por-que-preocuparte-aunque-no-seas-periodista/ (last consulted: January 30, 2016).

Santos, Boaventura de Sousa. 2009. *Sociología jurídica crítica para un nuevo sentido común en el derecho.* Bogota: Ilsa.

Schedler, Andreas. 2014."The Criminal Subversion of Mexican Democracy." *Journal of Democracy* 25, 1: 5–18.

——. 2016. *En la niebla de la guerra. Los ciudadanos ante la violencia criminal organizada.* Mexico City: CIDE.

Schmeer, Kammi. 2009. "Father Absence Due to Migration and Child Illness in Rural Mexico." *Social Science and Medicine* 69, 8: 1,281–1,286.

Schneider, Jane, and Peter T. Schneider. 2003. *Reversible Destiny: Mafia, Antimafia, and the Struggle for Palermo.* Berkeley: University of California Press.

SDPnoticias.com. 2015. "Acusan a alcalde de promover turismo sexual con proyecto 'Tijuana Coqueta.'" *SDPnoticias.com,* October 26. http://www.sdpnoticias.com/estados/2015/10/26 /acusan-a-alcalde-de-promover-turismo-sexual-con-proyecto-tijuana-coqueta (last consulted: October 30, 2017).

Secretaría de Gobernación. 2014. *Comisión intersecretarial para prevenir, sancionar y erradicar los delitos en materia de trata de personas y para la protección y asistencia a las víctimas de estos delitos. Informe anual 2013.* Mexico: Secretaría de Gobernación.

———. 2016. *Programa Nacional para Prevenir, Sancionar y Erradicar los Delitos en Materia de Trata de Personas y para la Protección y Asistencia a las Víctimas de estos Delitos 2014–2018.* Mexico: Secretaría de Gobernación.

Secretaría de Gobernación, Instituto Nacional de las Mujeres, and ONU Mujeres. 2016. "La violencia feminicida en México, aproximaciones y tendencias 1985–2014, Resumen Ejecutivo, 2016." Mexico City: Secretaría de Gobernación, Instituto Nacional de las Mujeres, and ONU Mujeres.

Secretaria de Hacienda y Crédito Público. 2015. "Paquete económico 2015." http://www .hacienda.gob.mx/ApartadosHaciendaParaTodos/ppef2015/index.html# (last consulted: December 17, 2015).

Secretaría de Salud, Dirección General de Epidemiología. 2014. *Informe semanal de vigilancia epidemiológica: defunciones maternas: semana epidemiológica 53 del 2014.* https://www.gob .mx/cms/uploads/attachment/file/12329/MMAT_2014_SE53.pdf (last consulted: October 30, 2017).

Secretariado Ejecutivo Sistema Nacional de Seguridad Pública (Secretariado Ejecutivo SNSP). 2014. "Cifras de Incidencia Delictiva 1997–2014." http://www.secretariadoejecutivosnsp .gob.mx/work/models/SecretariadoEjecutivo/Resource/1/1/cifras_publicacion_junio14 .pdf (last consulted: January 25, 2016).

Segal, Jeffrey A., and Harold J. Spaeth. 2002. *The Supreme Court and the Attitudinal Model Revisited.* New York: Cambridge University Press.

Segato, Rita Laura. 2006. "Que es un feminicidio. Notas para un debate emergente." *Mora* 12: 3–18.

Seils, Paul. 2004. "A Promise Unfulfilled? The Special Prosecutors Office in Mexico." Occasional Paper Series. New York: International Center for Transitional Justice.

Selee, Andrew. 2011. *Decentralization, Democratization, and Informal Power in Mexico.* University Park, PA: The Pennsylvania State University Press.

Sen, Amartya. 2010. *La idea de la justicia.* Mexico City: Taurus.

Serrano, Sandra, and Daniel Vázquez. 2013. "La postura del Ecuador frente al proceso de fortalecimiento del Sistema Interamericano de Derechos Humanos. La disputa por los conceptos . . . y sus consecuencias." *Pensamiento Propio* 38: 185–234.

Shapiro, Martin M., and Alec Stone Sweet. 2002. *On Law, Politics, and Judicialization.* New York: Oxford.

Shaw, Martin. 1999. "War and Globality: The Role and Character of War in the Global Transition." In *Peace and Conflict: A New Agenda,* edited by Ho-Won Jeong, 61–80. Hampshire, UK: Ashgate Publishing.

Shirk, David. 2011. "Criminal Justice Reform in Mexico: An Overview." *Mexican Law Review* 3, 2: 189–228.

Shor, Eran. 2008. "Conflict, Terrorism, and the Socialization of Human Rights Norms: The Spiral Model Revisited." *Social Problems* 55, 1: 117–138.

Shulman, Steven. 2017. "Judge Posner's Road Map for Convention Against Torture Claims." *Scholar Law Review* 19, 3: 297–319.

Sikkink, Kathryn. 2011. *The Justice Cascade: How Human Rights Prosecutions Are Changing World Politics.* New York: W. W. Norton.

Sikkink, Kathryn, and Carrie B. Walling. 2007. "The Impact of Human Rights Trials in Latin America." *Journal of Peace Research* 44, 4: 427–445.

Silva Forné, Carlos, Catalina Pérez Correa, and Rodrigo Gutiérrez. 2012. "Uso de la fuerza letal. Muertos, heridos y detenidos en enfrentamientos de las fuerzas federales con presuntos miembros de la delincuencia organizada." *Desacatos Revista de Antropología Social* 40: 47–64.

Simmons, Beth. 2009. *Mobilizing for Human Rights. International Law in Domestic Politics.* Cambridge, UK, and New York: Cambridge University Press.

Sin embargo. 2016. "Madres que decidieron buscar a sus hijos por su cuenta viven acoso y amenazas en Veracruz." *SinEmbargo.mx,* May 26. http://www.sinembargo.mx/09-05-2016 /1658290 (last consulted: October 30, 2017).

Smulovitz, Catalina. 2010. "Judicialization in Argentina: Legal Culture, or Opportunities and Support Structures?" In *Cultures of Legality: Judicialization and Political Activism in Latin America,* edited by J. Couso, A. Huneeus, and R. Seider, 234–253. Cambridge, UK: Cambridge University Press.

———. 2013. "Acceso a la justicia: Ampliación de derechos y desigualdad en la protección." *Revista SAAP* 7, 2: 245–254.

Sozzo, Máximo. 2002. "Usos de la violencia y construcción de la actividad policial en la Argentina." In *Violencia, justicia y delito en la Argentina,* edited by Sandra Mayol and Gabriel Kessler, 225–258. Buenos Aires: Ediciones Manantial SRL.

Stammers, Neil. 2007. "La aparición de los derechos humanos en el Norte: hacia una revaloración histórica." In *Ciudadanía incluyente: significados y expresiones,* edited by Naila Caber, 57–64. Mexico City: PUEG-UNAM.

———. 2009. *Human Rights and Social Movements.* London: Pluto Press.

Stanley, Elizabeth. 2009. *Torture, Truth, and Justice: The Case of Timor-Leste.* London: Routledge.

Staton, Jeffrey K. 2010. *Judicial Power and Strategic Communication in Mexico.* Cambridge, UK: Cambridge University Press.

Swaine, Aisling. 2009. "Assessing the Potential of National Action Plans to Advance Implementation of United Nations Security Council Resolution 1325." *Yearbook of International Humanitarian Law* 12: 403–433.

Tamés, Regina. 2014. "Violencia obstétrica: un fenómeno común, pero olvidado." *Foreign Affairs Latinoamérica* 14: 23–28.

Tarrow, Sidney G. 1994. *Power in Movement: Social Movements, Collective Action and Politics.* Cambridge, UK: Cambridge University Press.

Tavera, Pilar, ed. 2015. *Sobreviviendo al riesgo. Personas defensoras de derechos humanos y sus organizaciones.* Mexico City: Centro de Investigación y Capacitación Propuesta Cívica.

Taylor, M. C. 1997. "Why No Rule of Law in Mexico—Explaining the Weaknesses of Mexico's Judicial Branch." *NML Rev* 27, 141: 142–166.

Tepach, Reyes, and Martha Quintero. 2015. "El Presupuesto Público Federal para la Función Seguridad Pública. 2015-2016." Mexico City: Camara de Diputados, Dirección General de Servicios de Documentación, Información y Análisis. http://www.diputados.gob.mx/sedia /sia/se/SAE-ISS-22-15.pdf (last consulted: February 22, 2016).

Tercero, Magali. 2010. "Culiacán, el lugar equivocado." *Letras Libres,* June 2010. http://www .letraslibres.com/sites/default/files/pdfs_articulos/pdf_art_14696_12829.pdf (last consulted: September 22, 2016).

The Transactional Records Access Clearinghouse. 2014a. "Judge Robert D. Vinikoor. FY 2009-2014, Chicago Immigration Court." TRAC-Syracuse University. http://trac.syr.edu /immigration/reports/judgereports/00295ELP/index.html (last consulted: March 15, 2016).

———. 2014b. "Judge Sheila McNulty. FY 2009-2014, Chicago Immigration Court." TRAC-Syracuse University. http://trac.syr.edu/immigration/reports/judgereports/00295ELP/index .html (last consulted: March 15, 2016).

———. 2014c. "Judge Stephen M. Ruhle. FY 2009–2014, El Paso Immigration Court." TRAC-Syracuse University. http://trac.syr.edu/immigration/reports/judgereports/00295ELP/index.html (last consulted: March 15, 2016).

———. 2014d. "Judge Thomas C. Roepke. FY 2009–2014, El Paso Immigration Court." TRAC-Syracuse University. http://trac.syr.edu/immigration/reports/judgereports/00054ELP/index.html (last consulted: March 15, 2016).

———. 2014e. "Judge William L. Abbott. FY 2009–2014, El Paso Immigration Court." TRAC-Syracuse University. http://trac.syr.edu/immigration/reports/judgereports/00051ELP/index.html (last consulted: March 15, 2016).

Thomas, Pedro M. 2011. "Theoretical Articulation on Immigration and Crime." *Homicide Studies* 15, 4: 382–403.

Treviño Rangel, Javier. 2005. "Los hijos del cielo en el infierno: un reporte sobre el racismo hacia las comunidades chinas en México, 1880–1930." *Foro Internacional* 45, 3: 409–444.

———. 2008. "Racismo y nación: comunidades imaginadas en México." *Estudios Sociológicos* 16, 78: 669–694.

———. 2016. "What Do We Mean When We Talk About the 'Securitization' of International Migration in Mexico? A Critique." *Global Governance* 22, 2: 289–306.

Tribunal Permanente de los Pueblos (TPP). 2012. *Dictamen Final de la preaudiencia sobre Presas, derechos de los pueblos e impunidad.* Mexico City: MAPDER.

Tryggestad, Torunn. 2009. "Trick or Threat? The UN and Implementation of Security Council Resolution 1325 on Women, Peace and Security." *Global Governance* 15, 4: 539–557.

Tuckman, Jo. 2010. "Survivor Tells of Escape from Mexican Massacre in Which 72 Were Left Dead." *The Guardian,* August 26.

Turati, Marcela. 2013. "A la luz, los secretos de las matanzas de Tamaulipas." *Proceso,* November 2.

UNODC. 1998. *Economic and Social Consequences of Drug Abuse and Illicit Trafficking.* New York: UNODCCP. https://www.unodc.org/pdf/technical_series_1998-01-01_1.pdf (last consulted: April 7, 2018).

United Nations General Assembly. 1951. *Convention Relating to the Status of Refugees.* Res. 429(V), 189 UNTS 2545, at 145. Geneva: United Nations.

———. 1984. *Convention Against Torture and Other Cruel, Inhuman, or Degrading Treatment or Punishment.* 1465 UNTS 24841, at 85.

———. 2015. "Extrajudicial, Summary or Arbitrary Executions. Note by the Secretary-General." A/69/265, August 6.

United Nations High Commissioner for Refugees. 2007. *Asylum Levels and Trends in Industrialized Countries, 2007. Statistical Overview of Asylum Applications Lodged in Europe and Selected Non-European Countries.* Geneva: United Nations.

———. 2008. *2008 Global Trends: Refugees, Asylum-seekers, Returnees, Internally Displaced and Stateless Persons.* Geneva: United Nations.

———. 2009. *Global Trends: Refugees, Asylum-seekers, Returnees, Internally Displaced and Stateless Persons,* edited by UNHCR. Geneva: United Nations.

———. 2010. *Asylum Levels and Trends in Industrialized Countries, 2010. Statistical Overview of Asylum Applications Lodged in Europe and Selected Non-European Countries.* Geneva: United Nations.

———. 2011. *A Year of Crises. UNHCR Global Trends 2011.* Geneva: United Nations.

———. 2012. *UNDisplacement. The New 21st Century Challenge.* Geneva: United Nations.

———. 2013. *UNHCR Asylum Trends 2013. Levels and Trends in Industrialized Countries.* Geneva: United Nations.

———. 2014. *UNHCR Asylum Trends 2014. Levels and Trends in Industrialized Countries.* Geneva: United Nations.

———. 2015. *UNHCR Mid-Year Trends 2015.* Geneva: UNHCR.

United Nations Office on Drugs and Crime (UNODC). 2014. *Diagnóstico Nacional sobre la Situación de Trata de Personas en México.* Mexico City: UNODC.

United Nations Population Fund. 2013. "Motherhood in Childhood: Facing the Challenge of Adolescent Pregnancy." New York: United Nations Population Fund.

United States Court of Appeals for the Fifth Circuit. 2011. *Demiraj v. Holder.* The United States Court of Appeals for the Fifth Circuit.

Ureste, Manuel. 2016. "Un grupo de mujeres activistas encuentran 75 fosas clandestinas en Veracruz." *Animal Político,* September 5. http://www.animalpolitico.com/2016/09/grupo-mujeres -activistas-fosas-clandestinas-veracruz/?utm_source=Circulo+de+Amigos+Animal&utm _campaign=42c9988bb8-ga&utm_medium=email&utm_term=0_aafc25e12d-42c9988bb8 -392973425 (last consulted: October 30, 2017).

U.S. Border Patrol. 2016. *Sector Profile FY 2015.* January 12. https://www.cbp.gov/sites/default /files/documents/USBP%20Stats%20FY2015%20sector%20profile.pdf (last consulted: April 7, 2018).

U.S. Citizen and Immigration Services. 2015a. *Asylum Office Work Load.* Department of Homeland Security. https://www.uscis.gov/sites/default/files/USCIS/Outreach/Upcoming %20National%20Engagements/PED-Asylum_Office_Workload_June_2015.pdf (last consulted: October 30, 2017).

———. 2015b. *Asylum Applications Filed.* Department of Homeland Security. https://www.uscis .gov/sites/default/files/USCIS/Outreach/PED-2015-01-03-NGO-Asylum-Stats.pdf (last consulted: October 30, 2017).

U.S. Congress. 1965. The Immigration and Nationality Act (INA). 8 U.S.C. 1158.

U.S. Department of Justice. n.d. "Statistical Yearbook 2014." Executive Office of Immigration Review. gov/sites/default/files/eoir/pages/attachments/2015/03/16/fy14syb.pdf (last consulted: October 30, 2017).

U.S. Department of State. 2015. *Mexico 2014 Human Rights Report. Country Reports on Human Rights Practices for 2014.* Washington, D.C.: Bureau of Democracy, Human Rights and Labor.

———. 2016. *Trafficking in Persons Report 2016.* Washington, D.C.: U.S. Department of State.

Uvin, Peter. 2004. *Human Rights and Development.* Bloomfield, CT: Kumarian Press.

Valdés Ugalde, Francisco. 2010. *La regla ausente. democracia y conflicto constitucional en México.* Barcelona: Gedisa.

Valdez Cárdenas, Javier. 2012. "ONG: 30 mil sinaloenses, desplazados por la violencia." *La Jornada,* July 10.

———. 2013. "Julio en Sinaloa: desplazados entre la muerte y la nostalgia." *Nuestra Aparente Rendición,* August 4. http://nuestraaparenterendicion.com/index.php/sinaloa-2/item/1894 -julio-en-sinaloa-desplazados-entre-la-muerte-y-la-nostalgia (last consulted: November 8, 2015).

Van Creveld, Martin. 1991. *The Transformations of War.* New York: The Free Press.

Vázquez, Daniel. 2007. "La democracia, el populismo y los recursos políticos del mercado: déficits democráticos y neopopulismo." In *Vox Populi. Populismo y democracia en América Latina,* edited by Julio Aibar Gaete, 319–363. Mexico City: FLACSO.

———. 2008. "Democracia liberal procedimental y movimientos sociales. Temas pendientes en la democracia mexicana luego del conflicto en Oaxaca." In *Política y Sociedad en México.*

Entre el desencuentro y la ruptura, edited by Julio Aibar and Daniel Vázquez, 259–304. Mexico City: FLACSO.

———. 2010a. "La democracia deliberativa y la confrontación entre poderes fácticos en una decisión gubernamental: modificación al artículo 77 de la Ley de Propiedad Industrial." *Revista Mexicana de Ciencias Política y Sociología* 52: 105–131.

———. 2010b. "Los derechos humanos y la teoría y estudios empíricos sobre la democracia." In *Los derechos humanos en las ciencias sociales: una perspectiva multidisciplinaria,* edited by Ariadna Estévez and Daniel Vázquez, 221–259. Mexico City: Flacso-México/Cisan-UNAM.

———. 2013. "Los límites de la reforma constitucional en materia de derechos humanos en México: por un poder político desconcentrado." *Isonomía. Revista de Teoría y Filosofía del derecho* 39: 161–181.

———. 2016. *Corrupción, impunidad y derechos humanos: ¿dónde quedó el Estado?* Unpublished manuscript presented at the FLACSO Research Seminar "Human Rights and Democracy." Mexico City: FLACSO.

Vázquez, Daniel, and Ariadna Estévez. 2010. *Los derechos humanos y las ciencias sociales. Una perspectiva multidisciplinaria.* Mexico City: FLACSO-CISAN-UNAM.

Vélez, María B. 2009. "Contextualizing the Immigration and Crime Effect: An Analysis of Homicide in Chicago Neighborhoods." *Homicide Studies* 13, 3: 325–335.

Venet Rebiffé, Fabienne, and Irene Palma Calderón. 2011. *Seguridad para el migrante: una agenda por construir. Documento de trabajo núm. 2.* Mexico City: Instituto de Estudios y Divulgación sobre Migración-Instituto Centroamericano de Estudios Sociales y Desarrollo.

Villanueva, Ernesto. 2011. "Seguridad, transparencia y derechos humanos. Notas preliminares de un tema de frontera." *Derecho Comparado de la Información* 17: 165–183.

Villanueva-Egan, Luis Alberto. 2010. "El maltrato en las salas de parto: reflexiones de un gineco-obstetra." *Revista CONAMED* 15, 3: 148–151.

Villarreal Martínez, María Teresa. 2014. "Respuestas ciudadanas ante la desaparición de personas en México (2000–2013)." *Espacios Públicos* 17, 39: 105–135.

Villela, Gema. 2016. "Obstaculizan la Alerta de Violencia de Género como si se atacara a los gobiernos." *Cimacnoticias,* September 2.

Waldmann, Peter. 2012. "El narcotráfico en México: Una escalada de violencia anónima." Documento de Trabajo 3. Puebla, Mexico: Universidad Benemérita de Puebla, Instituto de Ciencias de Gobierno y Desarrollo Estratégico.

Waldmann, Peter, and Reinares, Fernando, eds. 1999. *Sociedades en guerra civil. Conflictos violentos de Europa y América Latina.* Barcelona: Paidós.

Washington Office on Latin America. 2015. "U.S. Congress Members: Human Rights Violations Point to Broader Problem in Mexico." *WOLA,* July 2.

Wiest, Raimond E. 1973. "Wage-Labor Migration and the Household in a Mexican Town." *Journal of Anthropological Research* 29, 3: 180–209.

Wilson, B. 2009. "Rights Revolutions in Unlikely Places: Costa Rica and Colombia." *Journal of Politics in Latin America* 1, 2: 59–85.

Wilson, William Julius. 1996. *When Work Disappears: The World of the New Urban Poor.* New York: Random House.

World Bank. 2017. World Wide Governance Indicators. http://info.worldbank.org/governance/wgi/index.aspx#home (last consulted: November 15, 2017).

World Health Organization (WHO). 1996. "Cuidados en el parto normal: una guía práctica. Informe presentado por el Grupo Técnico de Trabajo." Geneva: World Health

Organization. http://www.index-f.com/lascasas/documentos/lc0063.pdf (last consulted: October 30, 2017).

———. 2009. "Adolescent Pregnancy: A Culturally Complex Issue." *Bulletin of the World Health Organization* 87, June 7.

———. 2014a. "The Prevention and Elimination of Disrespect and Abuse During Facility-based Childbirth." http://apps.who.int/iris/bitstream/10665/134588/1/WHO_RHR_14.23_eng .pdf (last consulted: October 30, 2017).

———. 2014b. *Trends in Maternal Mortality: 1990–2013. Estimates by: WHO, UNICEF, UNFPA, The World Bank and the United Nations Population Division.* Geneva: WHO, UNICEF, UNFPA, The World Bank, and the UN Population Division.

———. 2016. "Maternal Mortality Fact sheet," updated November 2016. http://www.who.int /mediacentre/factsheets/fs348/en/ (last consulted: October 30, 2017).

World Justice Project. 2016. *Rule of Law Index 2016. Mexico.* http://data.worldjusticeproject.org /#/groups/MEX (last consulted: November 15, 2017).

Yamin, Alicia E., and Siri Gloppen. 2011. *Litigating Health Rights: Can Courts Bring More Justice to Health?* Cambridge, MA: Harvard University Press.

Zalaquet, José. 2007. *Transparencia y rendición de cuentas y lucha contra la corrupción en América.* Santiago, Chile: Centro de Derechos Humanos–Universidad de Chile/Chile Transparente.

Zamora, Anaiz. 2015. "Segob se obstina en que Alerta de Género no se aplique." *Cimacnoticias,* April 30. http://www.cimacnoticias.com.mx/node/69538 (last consulted: October 30, 2017).

Zavaleta, Noé. 2017. "Sinaloa: La incasable busqueda de desaparecidos," *Proceso,* January 28. https://www.proceso.com.mx/472199/sinaloa-la-incansable-busqueda-desaparecidos (last consulted: April 8, 2018).

Zepeda Lecuona, Guillermo. 2003. "La Investigación de los Delitos y la Subversión de los Principios del Subsistema Penal en México." USMex 2004-03 Working Paper Series. San Diego, CA: Center for U.S.-Mexican Studies, University of California San Diego.

———. 2005. "Desafíos de la seguridad ciudadana y la justicia penal en México." In *Sociedad Civil y Reforma Judicial en América Latina,* edited by the Due Process of Law Foundation and National Center for State Courts, 293–308. Washington, D.C.: Due Process of Law Foundation and National Center for State Courts. http://www.dplf.org/sites/default/files /1190409065.pdf.

Zinecker, Heidrun. 2007. "From Exodus to Exitus: Causes of Post-war Violence in El Salvador." Frankfurt: Peace Research Institute Frankfurt. https://www.files.ethz.ch/isn/55174/prif80 .pdf (last consulted: October 30, 2017).

Zong, Jie, and Jeanne Batalova. 2014. "Mexican Immigrants in the United States." *Migration Policy,* March 17. http://www.migrationpolicy.org/article/mexican-immigrants-united-states (last consulted: October 30, 2017).

LIST OF CONTRIBUTORS

Alejandro Anaya-Muñoz is a professor-researcher in the Department of Social, Political, and Legal Studies at the Instituto Tecnológico y de Estudios Superiores de Occidente (ITESO), in Guadalajara, Mexico. He has been Fulbright Scholar at the University of Minnesota and Mexico Public Policy Scholar at the Woodrow Wilson International Center for Scholars. His most recent book is *Derechos Humanos en y desde las Relaciones Internacionales (Human Rights in International Relations)* (2014). He is associate editor of the *International Journal of Human Rights*.

Karina Ansolabehere is a researcher at the Institute of Legal Research at Mexico's National Autonomous University (UNAM) and also serves as a part-time researcher and professor at FLACSO-Mexico. She is the author of *La política desde la justicia. Cortes Supremas Gobierno y Democracia en Argentina y México (Politics from Justice. Supreme Courts, Government and Democracy in Argentina and Mexico)* (2007) and coeditor of *Entre el pesimismo y la esperanza: los derechos humanos en América Latina (Between Pessimism and Hope: Human Rights in Latin America)* (2015). She is currently directing the Observatory on Disappearances and Impunity in Mexico, with the Human Rights Program of the University of Minnesota and Oxford University.

Ariadna Estévez works as a full-time researcher (tenured professor) at the Centre for Research on North America of the National Autonomous University of Mexico (UNAM) and teaches human rights and forced migration at UNAM's Faculty of Political and Social Sciences. She is the author of *Human Rights, Migration, and Social Conflict: Towards a Decolonized Global Justice* (2012).

Barbara Frey, J.D., is a senior lecturer in the Institute for Global Studies at the University of Minnesota, where she has served as director of the Human

Rights Program since 2001. She is a research collaborator with the Observatory on Disappearances and Impunity in Mexico, along with colleagues at Oxford University and FLACSO-Mexico. Frey received a Fulbright–García Robles Teaching and Research Award to support her teaching and research in Mexico in 2013. Frey has cofounded several important human rights institutions, including the Minnesota Advocates for Human Rights, where she served as executive director (1985–1997); the Center for Victims of Torture; and the Midwest Coalition for Human Rights. Frey has published on human rights issues including immigration, gender, firearms, and human rights advocacy.

Janice Gallagher is an assistant professor in the Department of Political Science at Rutgers University–Newark. She has conducted more than two years of fieldwork in Mexico and Colombia, and she previously worked as a human rights accompanier in Colombia. Her research has appeared in *Comparative Political Studies,* and she has received funding from the National Science Foundation, the Inter-American Foundation, the Fulbright–García Robles program, and the Social Science Research Council.

Rodrigo Gutiérrez Rivas is a researcher at the Institute of Legal Research at UNAM (IIJ, UNAM). He received his Doctor in Law from the Complutense University in Madrid, with a specialty in Political Science and Constitutional Law from the Center for Constitutional Studies of Madrid. He has edited eight books on constitutional law and human rights and is the author of multiple articles on these same subjects.

Susan Gzesh is a senior lecturer and executive director of the Pozen Center for Human Rights at the University of Chicago. She is also an attorney of counsel with the Chicago firm Hughes Socol Piers Resnick & Dym. She consults on migration policy and law with NGOs, community organizations, and public officials in the United States and Mexico.

Sandra Hincapié is a research professor at the Autonomous University of Zacatecas, Mexico. Her research focuses on social conflicts, human rights, state order, and democratization processes. Her recent publications include "Transnational Legal Activism, the Environment and Diversity: Agendas and Collective Action Support Networks in the Inter-American Human Rights System" (*Análisis Político* 91, 2017); "Between Extractivism and the Democracy Defense: Direct Democracy Mechanisms in Latin America's Socioenvironmental Conflicts" (*Recerca, Revista de pensament i anàlisi* 21, 2017);

and "Society-state Capabilities for Local Democracy in Contexts of Violence in Colombia and Mexico" (*European Review of Latin American and Caribbean Studies* 107, 2017).

Catalina Pérez Correa is a professor and researcher at the Center for Research and Teaching in Economics (CIDE). She studies the Mexican criminal justice system from an interdisciplinary approach, as well as drug policy in Latin America. Her most recent publications include "The Foundations of Modern Criminal Law and Gender Inequality" in the *Seattle Journal for Social Science*; and *Sobredosis Carcelaria y política de drogas en América Latina (Penintentiary Overdose and Drug Policy in Latin America)*, coauthored with Sergio Chaparro (2017).

Laura Rubio Díaz-Leal is an independent consultant and scholar on forced migration. She has taught international relations and forced migration at the Autonomous Technological Institute of Mexico (ITAM) since 2006. She has published extensively in English and Spanish on violence-induced and environmental internal displacement in Mexico and the Americas. Her latest book is *Environmental Displacement: Global Experience, Mexican Reality* (2017). She consults on internal-displacement issues for the Mexican Commission on the Defense and Promotion of Human Rights, the Norwegian Refugee Council's Internal Displacement Monitoring Centre, and Refugees International.

Natalia Saltalamacchia is a full professor in the Department of International Studies at the Instituto Tecnológico Autónomo de México (ITAM). Previously, at ITAM, she was director of the Undergraduate Program in International Relations and director of the Center for Inter-American Studies and Programs (CEPI). Her most recent book (as coeditor) is *México y el multilateralismo del siglo XXI (Mexico and 21st-Century Multilateralism)* (2015).

Carlos Silva Forné is a researcher at the Institute of Legal Research at UNAM (IIJ, UNAM). He received his Doctor in Social Science with a specialty in Sociology from El Colegio de Mexico (COLMEX). His most recent publications include *Percepción del desempeño de las instituciones de seguridad y justicia. Encuesta Nacional de Seguridad* Pública (*[Perceptions on the Performance of Security and Justice Institutions. The National Survey on Public Security), coauthored with René Jiménez Ornelas (2015) and "The Excessive Use of Force by México City Law Enforcement Agencies: Corruption, Normal Abuse and Other Motives" in the *Mexican Law Review* (2016).

Regina Tamés has been the executive director of the Information Group on Reproductive Choice (GIRE) since April 2011. She worked in the Latin American and Caribbean Office of the Planned Parenthood Federation of America (PPFA) and the Office in Mexico of the United Nations High Commissioner for Human Rights (OHCHR) and Mexico's National Commission of Human Rights. She has taught in undergraduate and postgraduate programs on human rights in universities such as Universidad Iberoamericana, ITAM, and FLACSO-Mexico.

Javier Treviño-Rangel is an assistant professor in the Cátedras-CONACYT/ Drug Policy Program at the Center of Research and Teaching in Economics (CIDE) in Aguascalientes, Mexico. He has been a visiting fellow at the Centre for the Study of Human Rights at the London School of Economics and Political Science. He has served as a consultant for the Ford Foundation and for the Office of the United Nations High Commissioner for Human Rights (OHCHR). Currently, he is a research collaborator on the Wellcome Trust–funded grant "Human Rights, Human Remains," hosted by the London School of Economics and Political Science. His most recent publications are forthcoming in the *Journal of Human Rights* and the *International Journal of Human Rights*.

Daniel Vázquez is a professor-researcher at the Institute of Legal Studies of Mexico's National Autonomous University (UNAM) and a collaborator at FLACSO-Mexico. His most recent books include *Corrupción y Derechos Humanos (Corruption and Human Rights)* (2017), *Test de razonabilidad y derechos humanos: instrucciones para armar (Reasonability Test and Human Rights: Building Instructions)* (2016), and *Derechos humanos y restricciones. Los dilemas de la justicia (Human Rights and Restrictions: The Dilemmas of Justice)* (2015), in addition to several books that he has coedited.

Benjamin James Waddell is an assistant professor of International Studies at the Center for Research and Teaching in Economics (CIDE) in Aguascalientes, Mexico. He researches the impact of international migration on human development and crime. He has recent publications in *Sociology of Development, Latin American Research Review,* and *The Social Science Journal.* He teaches in the areas of migration and development, research methods, and international relations.

INDEX

Abbot, William L. (Judge), 164
abduction, 72–73, 111
abortion, 87, 100–103, 233
Acapulco, 47
accountability, 3, 7, 19, 39, 63, 80, 144,
  176, 178, 196, 213, 227–232, 236–237,
  244–249, 251, 254–255; horizontal, 190,
  198, 205; social, 190, 205; vertical, 193,
  196, 205
Acteal, 45
activism, 18, 20, 151, 207
activist judiciaries, 19, 228
advocacy, 12, 18, 20, 44, 64–65, 85, 153, 247,
  251, 258–260, 268–271
Al Hussein, Zeid Ra'ad, 45, 169, 174
Almazan, Alejandro, 118, 120
American Convention on Forced Disappearances of Persons, 239
American Convention on Human Rights
  (ACHR), 19, 67, 231, 239–240
Amnesty International, 8, 65, 74–75,
  107–108, 111, 122, 202, 204, 224, 261, 281
amparo, 234–237, 247
Andrade, Norma, 77, 198
Andrade, Virgilio, 198
Apatzingán, 1, 24, 42, 84, 130, 204
arbitrary executions, 5, 23
armed conflict, 2, 13, 32, 52, 63–79, 84, 211,
  244
Army (Mexican), 2, 11–12, 23–42, 45, 50,
  61, 75–76, 135, 182, 204, 222, 267, 274.
  See also Zapatista National Liberation
  Army
arraigo, 220–221, 281
assault, 84, 101. *See also* sexual abuse; sexual
  violence

asylum, 15–16, 44, 51, 148–155, 158,
  161–183
asylum law, 16, 148–149, 153, 158, 166
Ayotzinapa, 2, 56, 137, 199, 204, 217–218,
  279. *See also* Iguala

Baja California, 45–48, 71, 76, 151
Basic Principles on the Use of Force and
  Firearms by Law Enforcement Officials,
  40–42
Beijing's Fourth World Conference on
  Women, 64, 66
Beta Group, 107
Board of Immigration Appeals (BIA), 152,
  155–156, 163, 172–173, 176–182
Boca del Río, 78
border (Mexico's northern), 15–16, 20, 71,
  73, 75, 141, 147–148, 163–164, 167, 171,
  183, 252, 263, 268
border security, 141
bribe, 114, 135, 200–201
bystanders, 119–121, 143

Cabot, Anna Jessica, 153–154, 156, 158, 162,
  170, 172
Calderón, Felipe, 2, 5, 11, 24, 27–29, 33–36,
  46, 48, 52, 108–116, 122, 187, 216–217,
  220–224, 236, 265–267, 277–278, 281, 283
Camacho, Alma Trinidad, 76–77
Caminata por la Justicia, 80
capo, 15, 136, 142
Carillo Prieto, Ignacio, 246
cartel terrorism, 149
carteles, 135, 138, 143
censorship, 86, 193
checkpoints (military), 29, 117–118

Chiapas, 45, 48–50, 53–56, 71, 87, 92, 95, 97–98, 107, 135, 236
Chiapas Human Rights Commission, 97
Chihuahua, 1, 5, 20, 45–49, 53, 55, 71, 77, 79, 95, 151, 164, 216, 252–254, 258–260, 263–270, 275–276
child abuse, 151
child soldiers, 174
child trafficking, 69
Cienfuegos, Salvador (General), 1
Citizens in Support of Human Rights (CADHAC), 261–263
Ciudad Juárez, 47–48, 71, 75, 77, 79, 81, 87, 147, 216, 258, 260, 265, 276
civil rights, 175, 188–189, 192, 236
civil society organizations (domestic), 11–12, 14, 83, 90, 121, 168, 232, 236, 246, 252–253, 262–263, 264–266, 271
civil war, 68–69, 168
clandestine graveyards, 43,
clashes, 11–12, 23–42, 48, 70, 273–274
clientelism, 17, 125, 194–196, 205
climate change, 168
Coahuila, 1, 46, 48, 71, 79, 95, 151, 279
Code of Conduct for Law Enforcement Officials, 40
Code of Criminal Procedure (Federal), 81
coercion, 72, 86, 91
collective action, 63–65, 75–81, 85, 198–199
collusion (between government and organized crime), 64, 69, 79, 85, 114, 122, 145, 154
Commission for the Prevention and Eradication of Violence against Women in Ciudad Juarez, 81
Committee on the Elimination of Discrimination against Women, 99
Committee on the Rights of the Child, 100
Committee on Sexual Violence of the Executive Commission for Victim's Assistance, 81
communal disputes, 44
compliance, 18, 65, 89, 95, 199, 207–211, 216, 224–226, 240–241, 258
Convention against Torture and Other Cruel, Inhuman or Degrading Treatment (CAT), 16–17, 151, 153, 163, 167–170, 172–177, 180–182
Convention against Transnational Organized Crime, 66–67, 72

Convention and Protocol Relating to the Status of Refugees, 168–169
Convention of Belém do Pará, 64, 66, 68
Convention of Refugees, 151
Convention on the Elimination of All Forms of Discrimination Against Women (CEDAW), 64, 66, 96, 99–100
conventionality (control of), 231
corruption, 10, 17–18, 43–46, 52, 61, 86, 120, 125, 129, 136, 139–140, 148, 160, 179–180, 192, 197–206, 212–215, 218, 259, 270, 281
Cotton Field (case), 75, 87
Council of the Federal Judiciary, 233–234
coyote, 141
crimes against freedom, 150
crimes against the family, 150
criminal gang violence, 157
criminal violence, 1, 12, 43–45, 64, 76, 158, 161, 254
Culiacán, 47, 49, 57, 76–77
culpability, 255

death threats, 57–58, 138–139
decentralization, 18, 208, 210, 212, 216–219, 224–226
dehumanization, 114–115, 122
democracy, 17–18, 122, 124–125, 187–196, 202, 205, 209, 212, 225, 244, 255
democratization, 124–125, 189, 191, 217
denial, 16–17, 87, 91, 93, 123, 162, 164–165, 173, 177, 205, 225–226; as political action, 196–199
Department of Homeland Security (DHS), 171
detention, 43, 111, 114, 150, 160, 163, 220, 235
Diagnostic on the Situation of Human Trafficking in Mexico, 82
Díaz Genao, Lucía, 77
dignity, 40, 91, 92, 109, 114
Directive that Regulates the Legitimate Use of Force by Personnel from the Mexican Military and Air Force, 40–41
disappearances, 1, 5–10, 13–16, 19–20, 43, 56, 72, 78–79, 81, 86–87, 114, 117, 122, 129–131, 138, 197, 199, 204, 217–219, 235–236, 244, 246–248, 251–252, 254–255, 259, 261–263, 265, 270; enforced, 3, 7–8, 73, 174, 188, 190, 203–204, 231, 251,

254, 256, 261, 263, 266, 270; forced, 7, 45, 72, 80, 111, 130, 149–150, 160, 235, 244–248, 279. *See also* extrajudicial killings

discrimination, 65, 86–87, 96–98, 111, 173; non-discrimination, 95–96, 103

displaced (rights of the), 53, 57, 59, 276

displacements (massive), 48

disposable commodities, 109, 113–115, 119, 121–122

dissemination (judiciary function), 227–229, 231–232, 237, 240–249

domestic courts, 19, 252, 260

domestic violence, 141, 150–152, 155–158, 171

drug cartels, 2, 16, 145, 154–157, 179–182, 279. *See also* carteles

drug crimes, 180

drug gang activity, 45

drug trafficking, 13, 26, 29, 69, 76, 118, 129, 134, 139, 142–143, 154, 219–223, 236, 252

drug trafficking organization, 252

drug war, 2–3, 148–151, 157, 222–224, 262. *See also* "war on drugs"

due process (lack of), 111, 239

Durango, 92, 235

economic deprivation, 46

economic development, 124–127, 192

economic insecurity, 45

economic migrants, 57

ejidatarios, 45

ejidos, 57

El Paso, 147, 153, 164–165, 263, 267

El Salvador, 80, 109, 115–117, 128, 150, 156

election, 17, 187, 189–196, 256

emigration, 15, 124–132, 140–146

enforced disappearances. *See* disappearances

equality, 102

erga omnes obligations, 68

Esparza Castro, Mónica, 74

Esparza, Olga, 77

exceptionality (principle of), 40, 42

Executive Commission of Assistance to Victims (CEAV), 53, 59–60, 81–82, 99

Executive Office for Immigration Review (EOIR), 162, 176

extortions, 45, 107, 111, 114, 122, 129, 150, 155, 157–158

extrajudicial executions, 8, 12, 23, 26, 36, 39, 42, 81, 130, 190, 251

extrajudicial killings, 2–3, 26, 30, 45, 130, 174, 204, 254, 270

Federal Attorney General's Office (PGR), 5, 58, 73, 197, 219, 244–245, 256

Federal Bureau of Investigation, 180

Federal Election Tribunal (Mexico), 233

Federal Health Ministry, 89

Federal Judiciary, 19, 203, 227–248

Federal Police, 1–2, 11–12, 24–39, 58, 113–114, 118–119, 130, 135, 202, 215–217

Federal Public Administration, 53, 60

femicide, 1, 13, 45, 69–73, 78–79, 81–88, 150–151, 158, 160–161, 263, 265–266, 270, 279

First Amendment, 162

forced international crossings, 149

foreign policy, 51, 170, 237

Fox, Vicente, 2, 167, 236, 245

freedom of expression, 17, 192–193, 205

freedom of movement, 50, 119

García Villegas, Paula María, 84

Gender Alert System, 83–84

gender identity, 171

gender violence, 15, 63, 69, 71–72, 75, 85, 148, 150–151, 155, 157, 158–159

gender-based homicide, 13. *See also* femicide

General Law for Victims of Crime, 53

General Law on Women's Access to a Life Free of Violence, 69, 81, 83, 88

General Population Law, 55

Golden Triangle, 46

Gómez, Perla, 198

gray areas of power, 9, 148, 154, 159–161, 165–166

grievance mechanisms, 87, 89

Guatemala, 80, 109, 115–116, 119–120, 150, 152, 157, 170

Guerrero, 1, 12, 24, 26, 37–38, 44, 46–50, 53–54, 56, 60, 69, 73, 80, 92, 95, 146, 151, 197, 204, 216, 224

Guerreros Unidos, 73, 279

guerrilla, 171

Guiding Principles on Internal Displacement, 51–52, 55, 60

Gulf Cartel, 73

Gulf of Mexico, 46

halcones, 138–139
harmonization, 241, 243
healthcare, 88
Home of Mercy, 107
homicides, 3–5, 9, 13, 20, 25, 43, 45, 47, 57, 69–70, 81, 129–133, 138, 146, 223, 236, 251–255, 259, 265–266, 270
housing, 49, 56, 58–61, 90, 129, 188, 275
Human Rights Watch, 3, 131, 214, 218, 224, 244–245, 260–261
human trafficking, 63, 69, 72–73, 82–85, 111, 149–150, 161, 276
humanitarian assistance, 44, 107
humanitarian crisis, 43, 121
humanitarian protection, 46

Ibarra, Bárbara, 77–78
identity transformation, 253
Iguala, 1, 197, 216–217
Illegal Immigration Reform and Immigrant Responsibility Act of 1996, 163
Immigration and Nationality Act (INA), 152–153, 155, 158, 172, 178
immigration courts, 152, 162, 164–164, 174, 176, 182
immutability, 155
imprisonment, 128
impunity, 1–3, 7, 10–12, 18–20, 26, 39, 43, 45–48, 52, 61, 67, 69, 78, 80, 85–86, 130, 160–161, 182–183, 192, 196, 199–206, 214, 219, 224, 227, 244, 249, 253, 256–259, 268–271, 276, 279, 281
in loco visit, 45
incommunicado, 108
indigenous communities, 46, 188
indigenous women, 96
inequality, 125, 128, 212–213
INFOMEX, 27
Information Group on Reproductive Choice (GIRE), 89–90, 92–94, 97–98, 101–103
inhumane treatment, 88, 93, 190, 204
insecurity, 2, 11–12, 43–48, 59, 61, 130, 217–223
Institutional Revolutionary Party (PRI), 187, 196, 217, 252
institutional weakness, 214, 218
Inter-American Commission on Human Rights (IACHR), 1, 3, 5, 7, 9, 43–45, 50–58, 62, 67–68, 74–75, 95, 110–111, 114, 121, 130, 150–151, 187, 197–199, 205, 244, 248

Inter-American Court of Human Rights (IACtHR), 19, 67, 87, 233, 235, 238–240, 243, 247, 276
Inter-American Development Bank, 200
Interdisciplinary Group of Independent Experts of the Inter-American Commission on Human Rights (GIEI), 197
internal armed conflict, 68
internal displacement, 10, 12, 43–63
Internal Displacement Monitoring Centre, 150
Internal Displacement Working Group, 58
internal forced displacement, 149
internally displaced person (IDP), 12, 44–45, 48–62
International Center for Transitional Justice (ICTJ), 245–246
International Committee for the Red Cross (ICRC) 32–33
international law, 64, 93, 237, 239, 241–242, 254
international legal protection, 149
intimidation, 55, 88, 121

jails, 74, 256
Jalisco, 48, 204, 243
journalists, 43, 58–59, 116–120, 138–139, 150, 155, 158, 204, 206
judicial decision-making site (JDMS), 251, 253, 256–258, 260, 263–271
judicial progress, 251–255, 259–260
judicial protection, 50, 239
judicialization (of social rights), 229, 232, 234–236, 249
justice (access to), 67, 87, 95, 98, 103, 201, 234–235
Justicia para Nuestras Hijas, 77, 264

kidnappings, 72, 85, 109–122, 129, 142, 179–180, 182, 215, 254. *See also* abduction; disappearances

Lagarde, Marcela, 69, 84
Laguna, Norma, 77
Las Americas Immigrant Advocacy Center, 153
law enforcement, 2, 17, 40, 136, 147–148, 159, 161–162, 164, 175, 222, 234, 244–245, 247
Law on National Security, 112
legal formalism, 159–160, 164

lethal force, 12, 24–26, 30, 33, 36, 38–42
lethal violence, 20, 146, 250–255, 260, 268, 270
lethality index, 11–12, 24–27, 32–38, 42
Ledezma, Norma, 77, 264–265
local advocacy, 271
López, Irma, 92
lower courts (Mexican), 233–235, 240, 246, 250, 252

machismo, 141
macho culture, 147, 151, 159, 161
mafia, 161
Manual on the Use of Force to Be Applied to the Three Armed Forces, 40–41, 274
March of National Dignity, 80
marginalization, 46
masculinity, 160
mass violence, 146
Massey, Crystal, 164
massive migration, 15
Mastrogiovanni, Federico, 111, 116, 120
Maternal mortality, 13, 87, 94–99
Mazatlán, 49
McNulty, Sheila (Judge), 165
Mechanism for the Protection of Human Rights Defenders and Journalists, 58–59
medical malpractice, 94
Medina-Mora, Eduardo, 198
Méndez, Juan, 8, 93, 203
Mesoamerican Migrant Movement, 110
Mexican Commission for the Defense and Promotion of Human Rights (CMD-PDH), 43, 49, 54, 58–59, 84, 214
Mexican Institute of Social Security (IMSS), 49
Mexico Evalua, 214–215, 219, 250
Mexico's National Autonomous University (UNAM), 199
Michoacán, 1, 15, 38, 46, 48, 61, 80, 84, 95, 124, 130–134, 139–141, 144, 204, 216, 224
migrants, 14, 15, 55, 57, 73, 107–123, 125–129, 133–135, 140–146, 160, 168–169, 277–278; economic, 57; illegal, 73; undocumented, 14, 107–111, 114–115, 119, 122, 163
migration flows, 46, 119
militarization, 10, 222, 267
military (Mexican), 1, 8, 28–29, 39, 45–46, 67, 109, 117, 136, 154–155, 179–180, 182, 203–204, 222, 254, 283
militia groups, 145

Millennium Development Goals, 95
Ministry of National Defense (SEDENA), 23, 26–31, 34, 38–40
Ministry of the Interior (SEGOB), 24, 56, 58, 70–71, 81–83, 98
Ministry of the Navy (SEMAR), 31
misogyny, 161
mobilization resources, 65, 85
money laundering, 136, 279
Movement for Peace with Justice and Dignity (MPJD), 250, 262–263, 265, 267–268

narco-dictatorship, 76
narcodólares, 135
narcos, 135–141
National Action Party (PAN), 187
National Citizen Observatory for Femicide, 83
National Code of Penal Procedures, 102
National Council for the Evaluation of Social Development (CONEVAL), 188, 194–196
National Fund for Workers' Housing Institute (INFONAVIT), 49, 61
National Health Program, 89
National Human Rights Commission (CNDH), 9, 23, 74–75, 82, 90–98, 110–111, 115, 117–119, 120, 122, 203, 218–219, 222, 277
National Human Rights Program, 236, 238
National Institute for Women (INMU-JERES), 70–71, 81
National Institute of Migration (INM), 15, 109, 113, 118–120
National Institute of Statistics and Geography (INEGI), 47–48, 54–55, 91, 131–132, 151, 201, 203, 212, 214
National Population Council (CONAPO), 54, 131
National Program for the Prevention, Sanction, and Eradication of Crimes, 82
National Program for the Social Prevention of Violence and Crime, 51
National Registry of Victims of Crime (RENAVI), 53, 59–60
National Search Brigade for Disappeared People, 79
National Strategy to Reduce Adolescent Pregnancy, 99
National System for the Assistance of Victims of Crime, 51

Navy (Mexican), 2, 11–12, 24, 26–28, 31–38, 202, 274
Navy (Ministry of the, SEMAR), 31
Nayarit, 44
necessity (principle of), 42
neoliberalism, 193
Nochixtlan, 24
NOM 046, 89, 102
nondiscrimination, 95–96, 103
non-refoulement, 16, 151, 169, 172
Nuevo León, 7, 20, 46, 48, 77, 80, 151, 216, 243, 252, 254, 258–268

Oaxaca, 44–45, 48–50, 87, 92–93, 95, 118–119, 199
Observatory on Disappearances and Impunity, 7
obstetric violence, 13, 87, 90–94, 99
Office of the Chief Immigration Judge (OCIJ), 162
Office of the UN High Commissioner for Human Rights, 197
omissions, 68, 89–91, 95, 152, 234
opportuneness (principle of), 40–41, 274
Oretskin, Nancy, 154
Organization for Economic Cooperation and Development (OECD), 99, 213
Organization of American States (OAS), 45, 51–52, 57, 60–62, 64
organized crime, 2, 7–8, 10–17, 27, 29, 39, 63–75, 78–79, 81–82, 115–122, 137, 144–146, 160, 197, 216–223, 274
organized criminal groups, 13, 41. See also carteles; drug cartels
Ortiz, Marisela, 77

Palacios, Cristina, 76–77
paramilitay, 45, 55, 125
particular social group, 152–157, 165, 168–172, 260
peacebuilding, 64, 66, 76, 85
PEMEX, 143
Peña Nieto, Enrique, 11, 24, 28–29, 32–37, 46, 48, 52, 122, 198, 218, 222–224, 236, 277–278, 281
Permanent Council of the OAS, 51–52, 60–62
Permanent People's Tribunal (TPP), 188, 200
persecution, 16, 148, 150–158, 163, 165, 169–171, 279

personal security, 50
police forces, 8, 10, 15, 17–18, 26, 38, 117, 136, 145, 215–219, 222, 226
political asylum, 16, 152, 170–173, 176–177, 179–180, 183
political liberalization, 232, 235
political opinion (persecution for), 16–17, 152, 154–155, 158–159, 165, 168–172
politics, 16, 20, 192, 194, 197, 229, 253, 255, 260, 271; accountability, 256; information, 256; leverage, 256, 257; symbolic, 253, 256
pornography, 13, 69; sadistic, 71, 73
Posner, Richard (Judge), 180–183
poverty, 17, 47, 49, 52, 125, 129, 134, 188, 194–196, 212
preemptive measures, 51, 62
pro-person (principle), 231, 241
property rights, 50
proportionality (principle of), 39–42
Prospera (government program), 50, 275
prostitution, 13, 69, 72, 111, 116
Protocol to the United Nations Convention against Transnational Organized Crime, 72
psychological violence, 74, 88 91

racial prejudice, 112, 278
racism, 164
Radilla Pacheco v. Mexico (Inter-American Court of Human Rights), 19, 233, 235, 238–240, 243
rape, 74–75, 87, 99–103, 107, 110–111, 150, 161, 174
ratification (of human rights treaties), 237–238
recommendations (by international human rights organs), 44, 51, 58–61, 67, 89–90, 96, 154, 245, 276
recommendations (by the CNDH), 23, 74–75, 90, 92–94, 98, 203, 219
refugee, 51, 61, 149, 153, 158, 163, 168–172
Refugee Act of 1980, 151
Refugee Convention and Protocol, 158, 169
rehabilitation, 56, 59, 60, 90
relationship politics, 20, 255, 271
religious intolerance, 44–45, 48, 54–55
remittances, 126–128, 130, 132, 134, 141–142, 145
reparations, 52–53, 59, 87, 89–90, 98, 103, 190, 200, 245; claims of, 52
reproductive health, 86, 88, 90

reproductive rights, 13–14, 86–90, 103
resettlement, 61
Resolution 1325 of the UN, 65–67
right to health, 100, 102
right to information, 91, 97
right to life, 5, 39, 42, 83, 96–97, 103, 250, 255
right to privacy, 91
Rivas, María Hortencia, 77, 79
Rivera Hurtado, Angélica, 198
Roepke, Thomas C. (Judge), 164
Ruelas, María Luisa, 146
Ruhle, Stephen M. (Judge), 164
rule of law, 42, 148, 189, 213–215, 220, 225, 280

safe houses, 110, 117–118, 160
Salcedo, Aracely, 77–78
Santibañez Margarito, Elvira, 1, 8
Sarre, Miguel, 198
Secretariat of Public Offices (*Secretaría de la Función Pública*) (Mexico), 198
securitization, 14, 18, 108–119, 122, 208, 212, 220, 224–225, 278
Security Council, 65–66
security crisis, 13
security forces, 11–13, 23–32, 35–36, 39–42, 48, 50, 55, 58, 70, 73–74, 84, 109, 114–119, 202, 204, 218, 221, 281
self-defense groups, 130, 216
self-defense forces, 43, 216
sex slavery, 63
sexual abuse, 49, 99, 150
sexual violence, 13–14, 65, 67, 73–75, 81–82, 87, 99–100, 111, 151, 279
Sicilia, Javier, 262, 267
Sinaloa, 46–50, 53, 55, 57–58, 60, 71, 76, 84, 95, 151
social visibility, 155
socialization process, 18, 207–209, 212, 224
Sonora, 48–49, 54–55, 120
Southwest Asylum and Migration Institute (SAMI), 154, 163
Special Prosecutor for Crimes Against Migrants in Chiapas, 107
Special Prosecutor's Office for Political and Social Movements from the Past (FEMO-SPP), 236, 245–246, 248
Special Rapporteur on Extrajudicial Executions, 39

Special Weapons and Tactics Team, 79
Specialized Assistant Attorney General for the Investigation of Organized Crime, 73
State Attorney General, 258, 262–263, 265
State of Mexico, 1, 23, 25, 37, 46, 48, 84, 101–103, 151, 204
statehood, 18, 208, 210, 212–216, 224–226
sterilization (forced), 92
Supreme Court (SCJN), 19, 198, 233–235, 237, 239–240, 242, 246–247, 250, 282

Tamaulipas, 25–26, 37–38, 46, 48, 60, 71, 151, 224,
Tanhuato, 1, 24, 42, 130, 204
Tapia-Madrigal, Victor Hugo, 179–180
Tlatlaya, 23–25, 30, 37, 42, 204
Tlaxcala, 56, 73, 95
torture, 1–3, 8–9, 13–17, 43, 45, 71–75, 81, 86, 88, 91, 93, 109–110, 114, 118, 130, 149–154, 163, 169–182, 188, 190, 197, 202–204, 219, 224, 266, 281
trafficking. *See* drug trafficking; human trafficking
trafficking in persons, 13, 67, 72. *See also* human trafficking
transmigrants, 108–116, 119–122
transnational advocacy networks (TANs), 20, 75, 209, 211, 251–252, 255–257, 260, 263, 268
transnational human rights advocates, 11, 261
transnational mobility, 43
transparency, 25, 38–39, 199, 201, 277
Transparency International, 199, 201
Treatment of Punishment, 169

UN Committee on Enforced Disappear-ances, 7–8, 188, 197, 203, 244
UN Convention Relating to the Status of Refugees, 151–152
UN High Commissioner for Human Rights (UNHCHR), 45, 174, 197, 236, 261
UN Human Rights Council, 1, 7–8, 39, 74, 88, 93–96, 188, 203
UN Refugees Convention, 155
UN Special Rapporteur on Enforced Disap-pearances, 261
UN Women, 70–71, 87
United Nationsq, 39, 45, 51, 56, 64, 99, 108, 123, 152, 158, 166, 203, 207

United Nations High Commissioner for
    Refugees, 61, 66
United Nations Special Rapporteur on
    Torture, 8, 88, 93, 188
United States, 14–15, 17, 39, 44, 73, 107–
    108, 110, 112–116, 122, 126, 130, 134,
    142, 146–152, 160, 164–178, 180–183,
    212, 221, 239, 263, 279, 281
U.S. Board of Immigration Appeals (BIA),
    152, 155–156, 163, 172–173, 176–182
U.S. Circuit of Appeals, 16, 157, 164, 176,
    178–179, 233
U.S. Citizenship and Immigration Services
    (USCIS), 162, 171
U.S. Department of Justice, 162, 165,
    173–174, 176
U.S. Department of State, 73, 169, 179,
    181–182
U.S. Drug Enforcement Administration,
    180
U.S. federal courts, 162, 170, 172, 174, 27
use of force, 12, 25, 30, 37–38, 40–42, 72,
    211, 216, 274

Vargas González, Yolanda, 77, 79
Veracruz, 37, 46, 48–50, 54–55, 60, 77–80,
    92, 219, 279

victimization, 15, 43, 44, 46–47, 52, 55, 160,
    253
Videgaray, Luis, 198
Villa Purificación (Jalisco), 204
Vinikoor, Robert D. (Judge), 165
vulnerability, 12, 49, 72, 86, 119, 188,
    194–196, 210–211, 218

war crime, 32, 65
"war on drugs," 2, 4, 9, 11, 24, 27, 41–42,
    109, 111, 115–116, 118, 122, 134, 145,
    148, 155, 158, 220, 222–223, 262
Weberian rationality, 159
willingness, 12, 18–19, 53, 59, 152–154, 210,
    219, 225–226
women (empowerment of), 67, 76
women's rights, 13, 67, 87, 91, 95, 101, 150,
    158, 160; human, 13, 64, 67, 73, 75, 83,
    85–86, 94–95; reproductive, 13, 86–89
World Health Organization (WHO), 93–94,
    96, 99

Zacatecas, 12, 24, 37–38, 151
Zapatista, 45, 55
Zapatista National Liberation Army, 55, 236
Zeid Ra'ad Al Hussein, 45, 169, 174
Zetas, 73, 109, 115–120, 179–180, 279

ACKNOWLEDGMENTS

Our vision was to bring together the voices of scholars on Mexico into a single English-language publication that provides a broad view of the human rights challenges gripping the country. We are deeply grateful to every author in this volume, whose diligent scholarship and generosity of spirit have made that vision a reality.

In addition to the written contributors, we want to thank the many Mexican human rights defenders who assisted us with their insights, including Jorge Santiago Aguirre Espinosa, Michael Chamberlin, Sister Consuelo Morales Elizondo, Humberto Guerrero Rosales, José Antonio Guevara, Maria Luisa Aguilar, Rocio Maldonado, Perseo Quiroz, Ana Cristina Ruelas, and Liz Sanchez Reyna.

Thank you to the Center for Research and Teaching in Economics (CIDE), the Open Society Foundations, and the Ohanessian Endowment Fund for Justice and Peace Studies of the Minneapolis Foundation for funding support. Additionally, we acknowledge the financial support for Alejandro's year as a visiting Fulbright Scholar at the University of Minnesota's Human Rights Program, from the Fulbright–García Robles scholarship and Mexico's Council on Science and Technology (CONACYT).

Thank you to James Ron and Leigh Payne, who contributed to the scope and shape of this book project, and to other colleagues who brought their ideas to our attention, including David Crow, Oscar Chacon, and Sandra Serrano Garcia. We are grateful for Amy Hill Cosimini's translations of several chapters. Thanks, also, to Rochelle Hammer for managing the Human Rights Program during Barbara's work on the book, and to our student assistants, Sara Halimah, Paula Cuellar, and Irlanda Argaz, for their invaluable help. We appreciate Peter Agree and Bert Lockwood for their support of our project and the Penn Press editorial staff for their fine work.

Finally, we would like to thank our spouses, Howard and Mariana, for their constant support and encouragement of our work.